SINGING ALEXANDRIA

MNEMOSYNE

BIBLIOTHECA CLASSICA BATAVA

COLLEGERUNT

H. PINKSTER · H. S. VERSNEL

I.J.F. DE JONG · P. H. SCHRIJVERS

BIBLIOTHECAE FASCICULOS EDENDOS CURAVIT

H. PINKSTER, KLASSIEK SEMINARIUM, SPUISTRAAT 134, AMSTERDAM

SUPPLEMENTUM DUCENTESIMUM SEPTUAGESIMUM QUARTUM

L. PRAUSCELLO

SINGING ALEXANDRIA

SINGING ALEXANDRIA

MUSIC BETWEEN PRACTICE
AND TEXTUAL TRANSMISSION

BY

L. PRAUSCELLO

BRILL
LEIDEN · BOSTON
2006

ML
93
P73
2006
/

This book is printed on acid-free paper.

Library of Congress Cataloging-in-Publication Data

A C.I.P. record for this book is available from the Library of Congress.

ISSN   0169-8958
ISBN   90 04 14985 6

PRINTED IN THE NETHERLANDS

To my parents

CONTENTS

List of Abbreviations ix

Preface xiii

List of Plates xv

Introduction 1

Chapter 1

I. Alexandrian editing technique and texts with
   musical notation: looking for ancient evidence 7

   I.1   Verbal metrics and musical rhythm: some
   observations on Dion. Hal. *De comp. verb.*
   11. 22–3 Auj.-Leb. 10

   I.2   Apollonius εἰδογράφος 28

   I.3   Visualizing the music: functional analogy or
   graphical plagiarism? Aristophanes' lesson
   according to Pseudo-Arcadius (with a minor
   appendix on the Pindaric scholia to *Ol.* 2. 48c
   and f [= 1. 73 Drachm.]) 33

   I.4   Sending a song: what texts cannot convey. Some
   observations on the scholium to Pind. *Pyth.* 2. 6b
   (= 2. 33 Drachm.) 40

   I.5   Contextualizing a misunderstanding: some
   historical considerations on the scholium to
   Dion. Thr. *Ars gramm.* 2 = Bekker, *AG* II,
   751 ll. 30–2 51

   I.6   Cic. *Orator*, 183–4: the disguises of songs 59

   I.7   Metrical colon and instrumental cola in Arist.
   Quint. pp. 31. 18–32. 4 W-I: making sense of a
   difference 63

   I.8   The Lycurgan *Staatsexemplar*: real and mental
   paths from Athens to Alexandria 68

   I.9   Looking for an alternative. A first synthesis 78

      I.9.1   What alternative? The 'paths' of songs
   between persistence and innovation 83

      I.9.2   What alternative? The 'paths' of texts 116

Chapter 2
 II. Papyrus evidence: musical practice and textual
      transmission   123
      II.1 P.Vind. G 2315: the material evidence   125
            II.1.1 P.Vind. G 2315: the visual formatting.
                    Something to do with Alexandrian
                    colometry?   127
            II.1.2 P.Vind. G 2315: reading signs.
                    Looking for a performative explanation
                    of ⌐ and ⌐⌐⌐   138
            II.1.3 P.Vind. G 2315 ll. 5–6 and the
                    scholium to Eur. *Or.* 340   143
            II.1.4 P.Vind. G 2315. Textual and/or
                    performative variants: some
                    considerations   154
      II.2 P.Leid. inv. 510: the limits of the tradition   160
            II.2.1 P.Leid. inv. 510: the material
                    evidence   161
            II.2.2 P.Leid. inv. 510: layout and variants.
                    Which tradition?   166
            II.2.3 P.Leid. inv. 510: which kind of
                    performance?   178
      II.3 Some concluding remarks   182

Chapter 3
 III. The 'other' paths of the song: musical mimicry
      'without music' in Theocritus' *Idyll* 29   185
      III.1 The Lesbian models of *Idylls* 28–30   188
             III.1.1 The Lesbian models: series of gl^{2d}
                     and gl^{2c} and strophic structure   189
             III.1.2 The Lesbian models: syntactic structure
                     and distichic articulation in odes
                     composed of series of gl^{2d} and gl^{2c}   196
      III.2 Aeolic pentameters and greater asclepiads:
             looking for a tradition   202
      III.3 Theocritus' *Idyll* 29 between past and
             present: letting words sound their 'music'   206

Bibliography   215
Index of ancient passages cited   231
General index   240

LIST OF ABBREVIATIONS

Barker, *GMW* A. Barker, *Greek Musical Writings*, 2 vols. (Cambridge, 1984–9)

Bekker, *AG* I. Bekker, *Anecdota Graeca*, 3 vols. (Berlin, 1814–21)

CA *Collectanea Alexandrina*, ed. J.U. Powell (Oxford, 1925)

DAGR C. Daremberg and E. Saglio, *Dictionnaire des antiquités grecques et romaines d'après les textes et les monuments* (Paris, 1877–1919)

Dale, *LMGD*² A.M. Dale, *The Lyric Metres of Greek Drama* (Cambridge, 1968²)

Dale, *MATC* ead., *Metrical Analyses of Tragic Choruses*, BICS Suppl. 21. I (*Dactylo-Epitrite*), 1971; 21. II (*Aeolo-Choriambic*), 1981; 21. III (*Dochmiac-Iambic*), 1983

Diggle, *OCT* *Euripidis fabulae*, 3 vols., ed. J. Diggle (Oxford, 1984–94)

FD *Fouilles de Delphes* (Paris, 1902–)

FGrH *Die Fragmente der griechischen Historiker*, ed. F. Jacoby (Leiden, 1923–58)

GG *Grammatici Graeci*, 4 vols. Vol. 1 ed. G. Uhlig and A. Hilgard (Leipzig, 1883–1901); vol. 2 ed. R. Schneider and G. Uhlig (Leipzig, 1878–1910); vol. 3 ed. A. Lentz (Leipzig, 1867–70); vol. 4 ed. A. Hilgard (Leipzig, 1889–94)

GL *Grammatici Latini*, ed. H. Keil, 8 vols. (Leipzig, 1855–80)

*GP*² J.D. Denniston, *Greek Particles*² (Oxford, 1954)

IDidyma *Didyma. II. Die Inschriften*, ed. A. Rhem (Berlin, 1958)

IG II–III² *Inscriptiones Atticae Euclidis Anno Posteriores*², ed. J. Kirchner (Berlin, 1913–35)

IKourion *The Inscriptions of Kourion*, Memoirs of the American Philosophical Society vol. 83, ed. T.B. Mitford (Philadelphia, 1971)

IMagn *Die Inschriften von Magnesia am Maeander*, ed. O. Kern (Berlin, 1900)

ITeos *Teos Inscriptions*. Texts and Lists, ed. D.F. McCabe and M.A. Plunkett (Princeton, 1985)

K-A	*Poetae Comici Graeci*, ed. R. Kassel and C. Austin (Berlin and New York, 1983–)
LSJ	H.G. Liddell, R. Scott, H.S. Jones, *A Greek-English Lexicon, with a revised Supplement*⁹ (Oxford, 1996)
Michel	Ch. Michel, *Recueil d'inscriptions grecques* (Brussels, 1900)
GPL	G.W.H. Lampe, *A Greek Patristic Lexicon* (Oxford, 1961)
PMG	*Poetae Melici Graeci*, ed. D.L. Page (Oxford, 1962)
PMGF	*Poetarum Melicorum Graecorum Fragmenta*, vol. 1, ed. M. Davies (Oxford, 1991)
Pöhlmann-West, *DAGM*	E. Pöhlmann and M.L. West, *Documents of Ancient Greek Music* (Oxford, 2001)
RE	A. Pauly and G. Wissowa, *Real-Encyclopädie der classischen Altertumswissenschaft*, ed. by W. Kranz *et al.* (Stuttgart and Munich, 1894–1980)
SEG	*Supplementum Epigraphicum Graecum* (Leiden, 1923–)
SH	*Supplementum Hellenisticum*, ed. H. Lloyd-Jones and P.J. Parsons (Oxford, 1983)
*SIG*³	*Sylloge Inscriptionum Graecarum*³, ed. G. Dittenberger and F. Hiller von Gärtringen, 4 vols. (Leipzig, 1915–24)
TrGF	*Tragicorum Graecorum Fragmenta*, ed. B. Snell, R. Kannicht and S. Radt, 5 vols. (Göttingen, 1971–2004)
Turner, *GMAW*²	E.G. Turner, *Greek Manuscripts of the Ancient World*² (London, 1987)
West, *AGM*	M.L. West, *Ancient Greek Music* (Oxford, 1992)

Other abbreviations generally follow the conventions of *L'Année philologique*. Metrical symbols and *sigla* used in Greek texts coincide mostly with those of West 1982. The following symbols may need elucidation: I have used the dovetail symbol, i.e. ∫, to mean runover of any number of syllables from one metrical unit to the next, rather than restricting it to one syllable (cf. West 1982, xi). For Dim cho B I mean the sequence x x x x - ⌣ ⌣ - (see Martinelli 1997², 234).

Ancient sources have usually been quoted according to LSJ. Translations of passages, when not otherwise specified, are my own. Longer quotations from modern languages other than English, especially when embedded in the main text, have generally been translated into English for the sake of clarity.

PREFACE

This book originated as a Ph.D. dissertation at the Scuola Normale Superiore, Pisa, where it was examined in July 2003. The work was then virtually complete by the summer of 2004 in Pisa while I was benefiting from a Junior Research Fellowship at the Scuola Normale Superiore and finally revised and proofread in London in the summer of 2005 during the first year of my tenure of the Momigliano Fellowship in the Arts at University College London, Department of Greek and Latin. The final version has been delivered to the Press at the end of August 2005. I have generally taken account of bibliography which appeared during 2004: only in a few instances was I able to take account of works that appeared later.

Earlier versions of selected parts of chapters 2 and 3 appeared originally as articles in *ZPE* 141 (2002), 144 (2003) and *MD* 46 (2001) (co-authored with M. Fassino): they have been thoroughly revised and updated for the present publication. Thanks are due to the Österreichische Nationalbibliothek in Vienna and the Papyrologisch Instituut of the Rijksuniversiteit at Leiden for permission to publish new photographs of P.Vind. G 2315 and P.Leid. inv. 510 respectively.

It is a pleasure and an honour to be able to acknowledge here the huge debt of gratitude I have contracted over the years to a number of friends and scholars who read the whole manuscript or part of it at some stage: L. Battezzato, A.C. Cassio, G.B. D'Alessio, M. Fassino, F. Ferrari, M.S. Funghi, M.C. Martinelli, G.W. Most and especially M. Telò. Their generous criticism and acumen have prevented me from many mistakes and have made Pisa an outstandingly inspiring, stimulating place in which to study. I am also indebted to the Department of Greek and Latin of University College London for the excellent conditions of research I am enjoying here. Thanks for proofreading are due to R. Rawles.

Finally, a major, endless debt of gratitude is owed to D.J. Mastronarde: no one could have been more undeservedly fortunate than I in being able to benefit from his invaluable corrections, criticism and suggestions through all the different stages of the preparation of the manuscript. This book simply could not have been written without his unstinting encouragement and tireless patience,

and anything valuable in this book may be attributed largely to his
exceptional generosity and acuity. Every responsibility for any remaining error of fact or judgment is of course entirely my own.

London,   L.P.
August 2005

LIST OF PLATES

1. P.Vind. G 2315 (Eur. *Or.* 338–44), by permission of the Österreichische Nationalbibliothek, Papyrussammlung, Vienna

2. P.Leid. inv. 510 (Eur. *IA* 1500?–09, 784–93), by permission of
   the Papyrologisch Instituut of the Rijksuniversiteit at Leiden

.

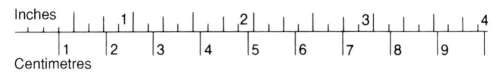

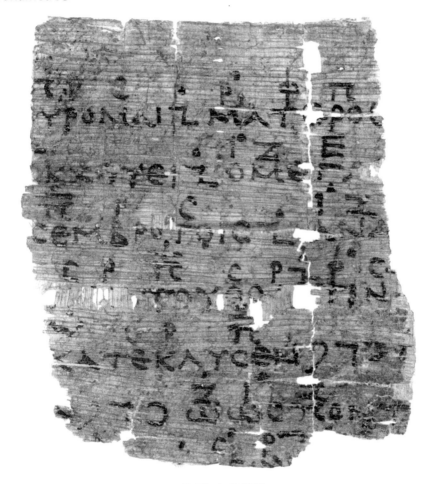

P. Vind. G 2315

P. Leid. inv. 510

INTRODUCTION

Written texts are always amazing conveyers of cultural dissemination. Together with their ideas and descriptions of the world they unavoidably carry from author (whether a single individual precisely framed in space and time, an anonymous writer lost to us, or a whole strand of collective tradition) to both present and would-be readers scattered pieces of information on their broader cultural context and on the meandering routes and byways by which their potentially protean identity has repeatedly been negotiated, at least from a recipient-oriented perspective. The fluid processes of transmission and reception, the tensions triggered by what we could call the inherent 'insularity' of a literary text and, at the same time, its being an item within broader communicative economies are all elements which help to construct, with varying degrees of flexibility, the identity of the text itself. A constant self-conscious awareness of the modes of survival and contextual adaptability is thus an indispensable aspect of a textual history which aims at sketching also the cultural outlines of such an identity.

The present study aims to investigate a particular aspect of this broader process of self-definition involved in the *Textgeschichte* of any literary product, focusing primarily on that very peculiar case of precarious identity represented by texts set to music, that is, texts conceived from the outset for musical performance. The link between music and text, sound and word, is a leading feature of ancient Greek culture, both classical and Hellenistic, which perceived and structured itself in terms of institutionalized practices of public and private musical performances. The starting premise of this inquiry is that in ancient Greece musical performance always rests upon and reflects a broader set of underlying cultural practices. In this sense, every attempt at reconstructing, by means of philological tools, the different stages through which such a precarious identity shapes itself has to be, at the same time, an effort to understand and contextualize these perceived changes within a wider cultural horizon. It is within this frame of reference that I have tried to examine some selected aspects of the processes of transmission and reception in Hellenistic times of lyric texts (tragic and non-tragic as well: in both cases texts originally composed for a precise musical performance), while attempting to reconstruct the different typological dynamics which seem to have oriented the re-use and actualization of the past poetic tradition in the renewed space of Hellenistic performance, both public and private.

As will be apparent, the inner organization of the material does not follow a thoroughly consistent diachronic order and more than once the complexity of the historical layers involved has necessitated some jumps backwards and forwards. Priority has thus been given to setting out from the very beginning the main areas of concern, which have then been explored in subsequent chapters from slightly varying perspectives, all designed to test, on different levels and by means of different tools, the constantly fluctuating (and unfortunately not always recoverable to us) interplay between textual and musical tradition. The relationship between text and music, or, to put it better, the dynamics triggered by their interlacing and nevertheless diverging modes of survival and persistence in contexts even radically different from the original ones, have received increasing interest among scholars of Classics in recent years and have been shown to be far more complex than can be adequately described using the clear-cut dichotomy between *Lesebücher* and *Bühnenexemplare*. Both the work of E. Csapo – W.J. Slater 1994 and the collected volumes edited by P. Easterling – E. Hall 2002 and P. Murray – P. Wilson 2004 have recently provided a wide-ranging, indispensable set of concepts for further investigation of the different aspects (socio-historical setting, performativity, cultural reception) conveyed by the notion of musical performance in the ancient world. This book originated, then, as an attempt to contribute, from a yet unexplored angle, to this challenge of rescuing from the darkness of a broader documentary shipwreck some further insights into the modes of transmission and reception of ancient Greek music. If compared with the wide-ranging theoretical commitment of the works quoted above, my own approach has been far more minutely philological and text-based, and the very nature of the issues discussed has sometimes necessarily required technical treatment. Yet my main concern has always been to use these technicalities as a critical tool to open a window on more general issues and to contextualize the microscopic into its broader cultural frame of reference: it is my hope that I have not abused too much my readers' generosity.

Several major questions spontaneously arise from the following pages. Does a musical score assure *a priori* a more faithful textual reliability than a written support devoid of musical notation? Is a score to be conceived of as a completely stable conveyer of textual and musical information? To what extent can a text carrying musical notation be read simply as an inert recipient of an unchanging past? That is, at once to put the question at its strongest (and perhaps in quite an inadequate and rough way), is an ancient score to be normatively interpreted as a tool to write down and fix once and for all an entire strand of the tradition, which is otherwise at risk of being lost, or, just because this preceding tradition is deeply absorbed and encoded in the contemporary cultural practice, may a score, under given conditions, record not the norm but the exception, that is, minor variations ascribable to the 'here and now' of that isolated performance? Can a closer inspection of the physical and typological features displayed by the musical scores at our disposal allow us to grasp some further insights into these processes of transmission and reception? How does such an analysis affect our way of looking at the modes of preserving or altering the identity of a text? There are of course no easy and standardized solutions for these tantalizing questions, and every attempt at providing an all-encompassing answer must be regarded with suspicion. Yet, even if certainty is far from being reached and sometimes perhaps even wished for, these basic questions are worth asking, and I have tried to suggest to the reader *some* possible guidelines among others, paying every time detailed attention to the specific context of the evidence investigated.

In the first section the starting point (and, in a sense, the privileged subject) of this enquiry has been the attempt at challenging an increasingly shared tenet within the field of Classics, that is, the belief, strongly argued by T. Fleming and Ch. Kopff, in a close relationship between Alexandrian editorial technique (colization) and texts provided with musical notation. At the core of the most engaging and thought-provoking literary archaeology outlined by Fleming-Kopff (that is, the alleged existence of an uninterrupted osmosis between textual and musical tradition from the fifth century BC till the Ptolemaic period) lies the otherwise largely welcome decision to thoroughly re-think and update Wilamowitz's well-known and long-accepted view of a complete separation, from the fourth century BC

onwards, of the textual tradition and colization from any musical
tradition. Fleming-Kopff perceived a need to tackle again, from its
very premises, Wilamowitz's authoritative stricture on the issue and
to point out its historically conditioned bias, and their project is still
more compelling inasmuch as in recent years Pöhlmann, taking up
Wilamowitz's negative judgment, has repeatedly reaffirmed the validity of a textual history that one-sidedly emphasizes a rigidly normative separation of a merely textual tradition (the Alexandrian
editions) from the scenic one (that is, Bühnenexemplare carrying
musical notation). Fleming-Kopff's agenda thus pinpoints a real gap
to be filled in, yet their critical approach, although moving from
largely shareable premises, entails a more general reconstruction of
the modes of production, transmission and reception of poetic texts
that turns out ultimately to misrepresent the nature of a process
whose very hallmark seems to have been an ongoing interplay of
multiple channels preserving continuity through diversity.

The appealing hypothesis of envisaging musical papyri as the long-
desired, institutionalized missing link between Alexandrian colization
and theatrical tradition has raised and continues to raise a heated
debate, splitting current scholarship on the issue between supporters
of this view (mostly among Italian classicists: see especially Gentili,
Lomiento, Marino) and more skeptical critics (Johnson, Parker,
Pöhlmann-West). The wide-ranging spectrum of consequences entailed
by Fleming-Kopff's claim, particularly in terms of conceptualizing a
whole cultural heritage, has so far prevented most scholars from
approaching this topic in an unbiased perspective. Different answers
to this question have often been given on the basis of deeply rooted
ideological premises without direct interrogation of the evidence at
our disposal. The aim of Chapter One is therefore to go back, once
again, to ancient sources and subject them to a careful, systematic
re-examination in order to check the inner validity of Fleming-Kopff's
working hypothesis, wondering at the same time whether the different
degrees of musical re-setting, rhythmic and/or textual adaptations
which we can otherwise detect through a crosscheck of epigraphic
and literary evidence for the Hellenistic and late Hellenistic period
may suggest a less straightforward picture of the tradition. Moving
from this beginning, the first chapter thus explores what degrees of
flexibility (and what boundaries) are inherent in the fluid identity
conveyed by a lyric text originally composed to be sung. Looking
for the remaining vestiges of this shifting identity from early times

onwards, I have tried to outline a less monolithic and more diversified scenario, a pluralistic horizon of possibilities where the 'true' form of survival and persistence of a text through different periods seems to have been its inner capability of being adapted to changed performance practices without losing its own identity.

Chapter Two examines in detail two examples of this fluid literary identity, that is, the direct evidence provided by P.Vind. G 2315 (= Eur. *Or.* 338–44) and P.Leid. inv. 510 (= Eur. *IA* 1500?–09, 784–93), the only surviving Euripidean papyri carrying musical notation. Occasionally in the past, scholars have claimed that these papyri preserve a coherent colization that might have been transmitted directly, so that some even suggest that the music too might go back to Euripides himself. Such claims are tested here. Moreover, the papyrological data, usually examined just as a bare skeleton of minor technicalities to be confined to specialists, have been investigated according to a new perspective, one that encompasses the generally macroscopic (typology of performances: what do these papyri tell us about the cultural scenario underlying such musical re-settings?) as well as the minutely philological (for both papyri a new edition based on re-examination by autopsy has been provided). Since among the musical papyri at our disposal the Vienna and Leiden papyri are the only ones which are susceptible to a comparison with medieval tradition, the main point of this section has been an attempt to go beyond a strictly 'Maasian' approach and to verify to what extent we can discover in these scores some traces of those processes of textual and rhythmic re-adaptation usually examined in their macroscopic aspect as cultural phenomena, sketching at the same time the outline of the multifaceted Hellenistic entertainment industry in its fluctuating balance between recovery of the past and actualization of the present.

Finally, Chapter Three is devoted to investigating the other (apparently contrasting) side of the coin, a phenomenon which becomes fully understandable within the process of re-appropriation of the past literary tradition enacted by Hellenistic poets, that is, the (intentional) absence of music. Theocritus' *Idyll* 29 has been interpreted as a paradigmatic example of musical mimicry 'without music' as re-shaped and exploited by Hellenistic poetry. Shifting the focus from the seeming surplus of evidence (texts carrying musical notation) to the forced lack of evidence, the burden of proof has been, in a sense, slightly shifted too. That is, given the absence of music, I have tried to ask myself what we should need to add to or subtract from a text, if compared with its originally 'musical' model, to re-create vicariously a merely verbal 'music'. Previous scholars have altogether denied the possibility of an underlying strophic frame in *Idyll* 29 (Leo) or, on the contrary, they have variously argued for the presence in it of an irregular strophic structuring (Hunter 1996). My own attempt has been to show that, according to the two-line strophic frame of its Lesbian models, *Idyll* 29 displays a clearly distichic structure which can be properly detected by checking the correspondence between sense-break at the end of a syntactic segment and metrical pause at period-end by means of Stintonian criteria. The major question underlying this chapter has thus been to see whether and how the musical dimension inherent in the model (in this case Lesbian poetry: that is, both the instrumental accompaniment and vocal melody), even if it has actually vanished, still somehow affects the authorial memory and inner structure of a poetic text which has been conceived for mere reading. If it is true that, at least from the point of view of a reader-oriented literary history, the meaning of a text stems also from its later accretions and that it is every time reconstructed and re-thought at the point of reception, Theocritus' sophisticated appropriative strategy displayed in *Idyll* 29 programmatically mirrors a rather paradoxical literary gesture of faithfulness to and, at the same time, betrayal of the past poetic tradition (Lesbian lyric).

Although each chapter of this book may be read as a relatively self-contained essay, all three sections have originally been intended to be complementary and, in a sense, cumulative, each of them trying to cast some new light on a particular aspect of Hellenistic performance culture, reflecting more generally on the different modes of transmission, reception and re-vitalization to which tragic and lyric texts of the past have been subject in that ongoing process of adaptation and self-definition that turns out to be the underground history of a text. Objective limits of time and, far more, objective limits of personal competence have unavoidably led me to favor some case-studies rather than others, determining more or less conspicuous absences and gaps. Many questions have necessarily been left open and, perhaps even worse, some of them, escaping my attention, have remained unasked: if a thorough comprehensiveness may be lacking, I hope that the instances selected can however be of some avail for further debate.

CHAPTER 1

ALEXANDRIAN SCHOLARSHIP AND TEXTS WITH MUSICAL NOTATION

I. *Alexandrian editing technique and texts with musical notation:*
looking for ancient evidence

"The editing of the lyric poetry that has survived from the Fifth Century BC is in a state of crisis or, to be more precise, in a state of schizophrenia." This is the challenging conclusion drawn by Thomas Fleming and Christian Kopff [hereafter, Fleming-Kopff] about the much-debated issue among modern scholars of the true value to be assigned to manuscript colometry of ancient Greek lyric and tragic texts.[1] Generally speaking, Fleming-Kopff's claim of the importance, for both dramatic and lyric texts, of the medieval colometry[2] falls within a broader and well-grounded trend of current criticism,[3] one engaged in showing the reliability and inherent consistency of the manuscript colization, although Wilamowitz's authoritative strictures still find many supporters.[4] Beside the extensive surveys focusing on

---

[1] Fleming-Kopff 1992, 758. For a critical survey of the long-standing history of the question, from Wilamowitz's well-known rhetorical interpretation of the colon onwards (Wilamowitz 1889, 142–3 and id. 1900, 42), see Fleming-Kopff 1992, 758–61 and Fleming 1999, 18–20. As to the textual tradition of Pindar and Bacchylides cf. recently Nagy 2000, 9–14 on previous scholars' undervaluation of the colon as a "working principle in metrics," as a result of Maas' discoveries, which promoted the view of the period as the only "viable unit of rhythmic replication."

[2] Fleming-Kopff 1992 (esp. 764).

[3] For the Euripidean tradition see e.g. Barrett 1964, 84–90, Zuntz 1965, 31–5 (counterbalanced by Mastronarde-Bremer 1982, 151–64, who cautiously warn against an overconfident appreciation of the substantial agreement exhibited by the medieval tradition understood as a true copy of "one and the same arrangement of the text [i.e. that of Aristophanes]"). As to Aeschylus, see Fleming 1975 (supplemented by the sound criticism expressed by Tessier 2001, 52, 54–5 against the blind belief in an absolute continuity between Hellenistic and medieval colometry) and Zuntz 1984, 50–8. More recently, among Italian scholarship, cf. the collected volume edited by Gentili-Perusino 1999 and also Gentili-Lomiento 2003, 7–12.

[4] See Wilamowitz 1921, 83 "Es hat lange Zeit gebraucht, bis die Wahrheit durch-drang, dass die Handschriften mit ihrer Versabteilung unverbindlich sind." Wilamowitz's negative judgment, although resting on different bases, has been partially taken up

the Euripidean manuscript tradition,[5] there have recently been valuable, although circumscribed, contributions to the textual tradition of the other tragedians as well.[6]

Equally welcome is Fleming-Kopff's attempt to reassess and update Wilamowitz's judgment that there was a total divorce, in terms of transmission and reception, between music and lyric poetry from the fourth century BC onwards,[7] creating a Dark Age which would not allow us to credit Alexandrian scholars with any musical skill at all.[8]

Starting from the legitimate premises quoted above, Fleming-Kopff have provokingly argued for the positive existence of a close relationship between Alexandrian editorial technique (colon-division) and texts with musical notation, suggesting a direct interplay between both traditions in terms of transmission and reception. In other words, Alexandrian γραμματικοί would have systematically resorted to scores

---

by Parker 2001, 51–2, who regards the Alexandrian colon-division as a device only "approximately metrical," aimed at helping the reader "to identify interpolations and other types of corruption." Yet Parker's approach turns out ultimately to be an updated version of Irigoin's hypothesis (Irigoin 1958, 33–4 "elle [i.e. the colometry] répondait d'abord à un but pratique: permettre une mise en page uniforme, contrôlée par la stichométrie"), provided with the partial corrective of shifting the focus from the writer (the producer of the text) to the reader (the user of the text produced). In both cases we are dealing with a merely outward appreciation of colometry leading towards the denial of an "existence métrique réelle" of the colon (cf. Irigoin 1952, 47). Nagy's recent attempt (Nagy 2000) to map in a single coherent frame both the material data displayed by the layout ("the visual formatting of colon" for easier reading) and their functional value in metrical terms (the colon as "functional building-block of the period" by means of hyphenation), seems indeed to be more appealing, although some of Nagy's inferences need more detailed investigation. See recently Willett's observations (id. 2002) on 'working memory' and its constraints on "colon-counting Hellenistic colometry as a guide to performance," which are to be supplemented by the balanced criticism of Gentili 2002.

[5] See e.g. Daitz 1990[2], xiii–xxvii and 85–102, Mastronarde-Bremer 1982, 151–64, Diggle 1991, 131–51.

[6] See especially Pardini 1999, whose colometrical analysis of Soph. *Aj.* 879–90~925–36 makes a strong case for the possibility, as far as *Ajax* is concerned, of identifying in the codex Zp (= Marc. gr. 617) a strand of sound tradition virtually independent from L.

[7] Wilamowitz 1889, 142 and id. 1900, 41–3.

[8] Exceedingly restrictive from this point of view are also Parker's remarks on the issue (ead. 2001, 31, 35–6, 38), which are still influenced by Wilamowitz. A reasonably moderate approach to the topic, successfully negotiating between Fleming-Kopff's assertive statements (a specific musical connoisseurship to be ascribed to the γραμματικοί) and Parker's radical skepticism (the denial of any kind of musical interests shared by Alexandrian scholars) has been adopted by Fantuzzi in Fantuzzi-Hunter 2002, 52–3 n. 101 (= iid. 2004, 27–8 n. 101).

provided with musical notation in order to divide lyric and tragic texts into metrical cola.[9] This hypothesis, if accepted, entails serious consequences encompassing the modes of production as well as the subsequent processes of transmission and reception of poetic texts, both lyric and dramatic. A close derivation of Alexandrian editing technique (applied to lyric texts: colometry) from scores with musical notation would mean believing in the existence of an early and uninterrupted continuum between textual and musical tradition, a long-standing synergy that we should suppose to be substantially unchanged in its own dynamics from the fifth century BC till at least the Ptolemaic period.[10]

The starting point of the present study is therefore a preliminary attempt at fathoming the inner consistency and boundaries of this particular aspect of the literary archaeology outlined by Fleming-Kopff's working hypothesis. Ancient direct and indirect evidence will be investigated as we look for the possible paths, in terms of traditional channels, followed by texts originally conceived for performance. All this involves a systematic review of the ancient sources supposed to refer to the existence (or not) of a close osmosis between musical and textual tradition as a standard feature in the processes of transmission and reception of lyric texts. Such an inquiry means therefore thoroughly rethinking the premises, range and limits underlying the major critical trends currently prominent among scholars of this topic, while negotiating at the same time the possibility of a third more comprehensive approach.

As we shall see, current scholarship is split into two main streams: on the one hand we find Fleming-Kopff arguing for an early symbiosis, in terms of textual transmission, between *Lesetexte* and *Bühnenexemplare*, and on the other hand we see Pöhlmann's definitive splitting of the two traditions, the merely textual and the scenic, into two distinct media.[11] In fact both reconstructions outlined above, although

---

[9] According to this hypothesis a colometrical layout has recently been argued for P.Vind. G 2315 (= Eur. *Or.* 338–44): cf. Marino 1999a and independently Landels 1999, 250–2. For the unlikelihood of such a reconstruction see II.1.1.

[10] A necessary complement to such a view is the belief that the Lycurgan *Staatsexemplar* was already furnished with musical notation, preserving thus the original music of the three great Attic tragedians: cf. Fleming-Kopff 1992, 763. This opinion is shared also by Tessier 1995, 21–2 and Marino 1999b, 17 n. 16. Cf. also Wilson 2005, 192.

[11] Pöhlmann 1960, 1976, 1986, 1988, 1991 and 1997. Paradoxically, Pöhlmann's

arising from antithetical premises, turn out to share the same defect: the inherent degree of systematicity and consistency they improbably suppose to operate within the dynamics of textual tradition. Fleming-Kopff's belief in the Lycurgan copy already provided with the *original* score as the lost necessary link between music and text for the Alexandrian editing practice of colizing lyric texts and Pöhlmann's clear separation of the Alexandrian tradition from the theatrical one both aim at filling in the gaps of our evidence by suggesting a consistency of the processes of transmission that escapes more detailed analysis. The high degree of uniformity posited by both approaches runs the risk of oversimplifying the processes of textual transmission by forcing into a straightforward frame a reality that seems to have been, fortunately or not, far more unsettled and 'contaminated'.[12]

The aim of the following pages is thus to cast new light on some aspects of this broader question, exploring what degrees of flexibility (and what boundaries) are inherent in the precarious identity conveyed by a lyric text originally composed to be sung. Let us now turn directly to ancient sources.

I.1 *Verbal metrics and musical rhythm: some observations on Dion. Hal. De comp. verb. 11. 22–3 Auj.-Leb.*

One of the major arguments alleged by Fleming-Kopff to support a close relationship between Alexandrian editorial technique (colometry) and texts provided with musical notation rests on the assump-

---

idiosyncratic view of the *Textgeschichte* (one-sidedly emphasizing the discontinuity between the two traditions) seems to be ultimately as static and conservative as Fleming-Kopff's.

[12] For a more realistic view of these dynamics cf. already Dihle 1981, 37–8, who while recognizing the idiosyncratic features of the different paths of transmission (*Lesetexte* and *Bühnenexemplare*), at the same time escapes the difficulty engendered by a rigid and institutionalized separation of both traditions, which are not to be regarded as mutually exclusive but as interplaying at least till a certain date. In the same direction cf. also Falkner 2002 (especially at 346, 348), reconstructing on the basis of the information conveyed by tragic scholia the common guidelines "about the cultural dynamics in which both scholars and actors participated" (ibid. 344). This relatively fluid situation is mirrored by the parodos of *Orestes* as transmitted by Dion. Hal. *De comp. verb.* 11. 19 Auj.-Leb. (i.e. with ll. 140–1 assigned to Electra), although Pöhlmann 1960, 12 still considered the passage quoted by Dion. Hal. as a testimony "von der alexandrinischen Textredaktion unabhängig" (for a detailed discussion of the passage see I.9.2).

tion that a shared principle of the Greek lyric seems to have been a general trend to make the tempo of the musical phrase (vocal as well as instrumental) correspond with the rhythm indicated by verbal metrics.[13]

Granted that this inner correspondence between verbal metrics and musical rhythm can be detected in some of the surviving musical scores we actually know,[14] to infer from that isolated issue a broader systematic consistency to be applied, on a general basis, to the whole corpus of Greek lyric without any diachronic and generic distinctions seems to go too far.[15] A thorough consistency between metrics as reconstructed by the textual frame (the binary opposition of short and long syllables) and musical tempo inferred from scores provided with rhythmical signs is therefore just one performative possibility among several others, and that within a musical universe widely diversified (and not only from a diachronic point of view).[16]

---

[13] Fleming-Kopff 1992, 762 "Since the basic task was the conversion of musical rhythm into a layout that preserved the rhythmic phrases, the easiest method would be to utilize musical texts" and further "a musically literate scholar could simply translate the rhythmic notation into a set of cola that represented, as clear as possible, the musical phrases composed by the poet" (the same generalizing approach can be found also in their subsequent treatment of the rhythmic signs, cf. ibid. 762 with n. 25). The hypothesis of a direct and systematic equivalence between musical and metrical rhythm had been previously suggested also by Koster 1941, 1–43 (especially 13–4: "singula cola notis rhythmicis et musicis additis facile distingui potuisse verisimile est"), who decided neverthless that the Alexandrian scholars did not use musical scores to help them to colize lyric and tragic texts. More recently the attempt of Georgiades (1958) and Zaminer (1989, 123–4) to argue for a close identity between metrics and rhythmics in ancient Greek lyric as a sign of a long-standing continuity surviving in neo-Hellenic popular songs has been strongly confuted in its historical and theoretical premises by Pöhlmann 1995a and 1998.

[14] See e.g. Pöhlmann-West's observations on the Delphic paeans of Athenaios and Limenios (iid. *DAGM*, 72).

[15] Among the most notable examples that disregard this automatism in converting musical rhythm into rhythmical phrases we can quote e.g. P.Osl. inv. 1413 ll. 1–15 (cf. especially the musical delivery of the proper nouns Ἰξίων, Δηιδάμεια and Τάνταλος at ll. 4, 5, 7 together with the anomalous scansion of ὑπὸ τροχόν at l. 6; on these 'distorted scansions' cf. Pöhlmann-West *DAGM*, 130). Also worth mentioning is Mesom. *Hymn.* 27–28 Pöhlmann-West, where the λεῖμμα is placed between the penultimate and last syllable of enopliac sequences (x ‒ ⏑ ⏑ ‒ ⏑ ⏑ ‒ x: *Hymn.* 27 ll. 8, 9, 21; *Hymn.* 28 ll. 3, 10, 13) and thus prolongs the length of the previous long syllable to the extent of a μακρὰ τρίσημος, and ultimately assimilates these sequences with metrical patterns like ^gl^d(‒‒ ‒ ⏑ ⏑ ‒ ‒ ⏑ ⏑ ‒ ‒; Comotti 1991², 109 prefers to speak of three anapaests followed by an iambic foot).

[16] Cf. West *AGM*, 132–3.

Moreover, even if the papyrological and epigraphic evidence on the issue pre-eminently belongs to the common era and at present we have no data prior to the third century BC, the possibility of identifying, already in the classical age, distinctly isolated traces of metrical frames re-shaped according to the musical rhythm has been enhanced by Gentili's treatment of the much-discussed phenomenon of free response in choral and dramatic lyric.[17] Gentili's approach allows us to deal with this epiphenomenon (which should have had an actual counterpart during the performance) by overcoming the abstract determinism still prominent in Maas' view of the issue and at the same time by pointing out the importance of the performative aspects.[18]

The same generalizing approach has been adopted by Fleming-Kopff also as regards the function and meaning of rhythmical signs, especially the λεῖμμα, to which these scholars seem to assign the somewhat too restrictive function of marking the "location of pauses (and therefore period end)."[19] The use of the *leimma* as a marker of rhythmic pause is of course well attested in late technical treatises on the topic: cf. e.g. Arist. Quint. p. 38. 28 ff. W-I κενὸϲ μὲν οὖν ἐϲτι χρόνοϲ ἄνευ φθόγγου πρὸϲ ἀναπλήρωϲιν τοῦ ῥυθμοῦ, λεῖμμα δὲ ἐν ῥυθμῶι χρόνοϲ ἐλάχιϲτοϲ κτλ.[20] and *Anon. Bell.* 102 Najock (χρόνοϲ) κενὸϲ βραχύϲ. Yet the concrete surviving examples of *leimma* trans-

---

[17] Gentili 1988, 11–2: "[. . .] dobbiamo presumere che già nel V sec. a.C. l'esecuzione vocale e strumentale di un testo poteva normalizzare le 'aporie'—per così dire—del metro secondo quella stessa prassi esecutiva etc." In this direction, although at a more embryonic stage, see also Wilamowitz's final observations in id. 1895, 31–2. More recently Gentili 1998, 146–9 has further developed his reflections on free responsion.

[18] Gentili's remarks, however correct in themselves, need anyway to be circumscribed. The statistically low incidence of free responsion in Greek lyric as a whole limits significantly the extent to which this phenomenon could be measured by the audience during the performance. Another example of the various degrees of flexibility and interplay between verbal metrics and musical rhythm in the fifth century BC might be the debated cases of *brevis in longo* in the so-called 'light dactyls' like Eur. *Phoen.* 796, 1498, 1557, cf. West 1982, 131, Dale *MATC* III, 300 and Mastronarde 1994a, *ad loc.* Also in these cases it is, however, worth noticing the rarity of this phenomenon.

[19] Fleming-Kopff 1992, 762 with n. 25.

[20] The relevance of an interval (διάϲταϲιϲ) between strong and weak beats in the actual phonic implementation of the verbal material has been emphasized in its rhythmic and stylistic implications by Rossi 1963, 65 ff. (cf. especially 74 n. 165 on [Long.] *Subl.* 40. 4 as regards the reception and re-appropriation of this phenomenon within the rhetorical tradition).

mitted by musical papyri testify to a broader range of application. Beside indicating pause at the end of a rhythmic phrase and/or syntactic period,[21] the *leimma* seems also to be used to increase the time value of the previous syllable within (and not just at the end of) a metrical series, whether it happens to be the end of the colon and/or period or not.[22] Finally, an especially interesting case is that of P.Mich. inv. 2958, where both functions of the *leimma* (pause occasionally coinciding with period end and overlengthening of the syllable above which it is placed) seem to be present in the same score without any consistency.[23] Therefore Fleming-Kopff's conclusive statement that "the interpretation of individual [i.e. rhythmical] signs is often doubtful, but the extent of information they provide is not" must be regarded as overconfident, and every single case still has to be judged on its own.[24]

Furthermore, the lack of a systematically predictable correspondence between the metrical frame outlined by the text and the musical rhythm of the actual performance is clearly supported by indirect tradition.[25] Together with Aristoxenus,[26] Longinus[27] and Marius Victorinus,[28] one of the most valuable sources on the issue is the well-known and much-debated passage of Dion. Hal. *De comp. verb.* 11. 22–3 Auj.-Leb.:

---

[21] Cf. e.g. P.Osl. inv. 1413, ll. 1, 8, 9, 10 and 14: in all these cases the *leimma* indicates catalexis in series of non-lyric anapaestic tetrameters. As to *leimma* denoting catalectic verse-ends in P.Berol. inv. 6870 ll. 1–12, cf. Pöhlmann-West *DAGM*, 168.

[22] Cf. e.g. Mesom. *Hymn.* 27–8 Pöhlmann-West.

[23] See Pöhlmann-West *DAGM*, 144.

[24] Cf. Comotti 1988, 18 ff. and id. 1991², 110.

[25] As to the development, from the fourth century BC onwards and above all under the influence of Aristoxenus of Tarentum, of rhythmics as an independent branch of learning kept distinct from metrical speculations, see Gentili 1988, 13–4 and id. 1990, 20.

[26] Aristox. *El. rhythm.* 2. 19 (= 12, ll. 13 ff. Pearson) νοητέον δὲ χωρὶϲ τά τε τὴν τοῦ ποδὸϲ δύναμιν φυλάϲϲοντα ϲημεῖα καὶ τὰϲ ὑπὸ τῆϲ ῥυθμοποιίαϲ γινομέναϲ διαιρέϲειϲ. καὶ προϲθετέον δὲ τοῖϲ εἰρημένοιϲ, ὅτι τὰ μὲν ἑκάϲτου ποδὸϲ ϲημεῖα διαμένει ἴϲα ὄντα καὶ τῶι ἀριθμῶι καὶ τῶι μεγέθει, αἱ δ' ὑπὸ τῆϲ ῥυθμοποιίαϲ γινόμεναι διαιρέϲειϲ πολλὴν λαμβάνουϲι ποικιλίαν.

[27] Longin. *Proleg. in Heph.* 83. 14–6 Consbr. ὁ δὲ ῥυθμὸϲ ὡϲ βούλεται ἕλκει τοὺϲ χρόνουϲ. πολλάκιϲ γοῦν καὶ τὸν βραχὺν χρόνον ποιεῖ μακρόν.

[28] Mar. Vict. *GL* VI, 41. 28 ff. Keil *differt autem rhythmus a metro [. . .] et quod metrum certo numero syllabarum vel pedum finitum sit, rhythmus autem numquam numero circumscribatur. nam ut volet, protrahit tempora, ita ut breve tempus plerumque longum efficiat, longum contrahat.*

τὸ δ᾽ αὐτὸ γίνεται καὶ περὶ τοὺς ῥυθμούς. ἡ μὲν γὰρ πεζὴ λέξις οὐδενὸς
οὔτε ὀνόματος οὔτε ῥήματος βιάζεται τοὺς χρόνους οὐδὲ μετατίθησιν, ἀλλ᾽
οἵας παρείληφεν τῆι φύσει τὰς συλλαβὰς τάς τε μακρὰς καὶ τὰς βραχείας,
τοιαύτας φυλάττει. ἡ δὲ ῥυθμικὴ καὶ μουσικὴ μεταβάλλουσιν αὐτὰς μειοῦσαι
καὶ αὔξουσαι, ὥστε πολλάκις εἰς τἀναντία μεταχωρεῖν· οὐ γὰρ ταῖς συλλαβαῖς
ἀπευθύνουσι τοὺς χρόνους, ἀλλὰ τοῖς χρόνοις τὰς συλλαβάς.

The same thing happens also with regard to rhythm. Prose diction
does not infringe or change the quantities of a noun or a verb but
preserves the syllables, the long as well as the short ones, just as it
found them to be by nature. On the contrary *the rhythmike and the mousike*
change the time value of the syllables by shortening or lengthening
them so that they are often converted into their opposites: in fact *the
rhythmike and the mousike* do not adapt the time values to the quantity
of the syllables but the quantity of the syllables to the time values.

The main difficulty raised by this passage lies in its correct contextualization. A first substantial *discrimen* has been drawn by Devine-
Stephens, who have reasonably claimed that here "Dionysius means
moraic (phonological) shifts rather than submoraic (phonetic) adaptation."[29] Devine-Stephens' detailed analysis has convincingly shown
that in Greek poetry, in spite of previous belief on the issue, neither the syllable onset nor the intrinsic and contextual segmental
duration of vowels and consonants turns out to be metrically relevant.[30] In other words, in antiquity there was a widespread awareness of the fact that during the actual process of delivery not all the
long and short syllables, distinctly uttered, had one and the same
time value.[31] Nevertheless, this rhythmic awareness did not invali-
date the conventional metrical rules where the duration of a short
syllable is half that of a long one.[32] It is therefore not overconfident
to conclude that in this passage Dionysius is not dealing with phonetic phenomena related to submoraic durational distinctions, but
with real phonological shifts in the quantity of the syllables.

Once these premises are established, the next step is to specify
the most likely frame of reference assumed by Dionysius in discussing

---

[29] Devine-Stephens 1994, 120.
[30] Devine-Stephens 1994, 84. See also Dobrov 1995 and Fortson 1995 on the
issue.
[31] Cf. Dion. Hal. *De comp. verb.* 15. 1–10 Auj.-Leb. and Choerob. in Hephaest.
180. 4 Consbr. quoted by Devine-Stephens 1994, 50–1.
[32] Cf. Gentili 1990, 12.

the opposition between spoken language (prose) and song (lyric poetry). What is at stake here is in fact the precise meaning of the single expression ἡ δὲ ῥυθμικὴ καὶ μουϲική and the corresponding sense conveyed by the whole sentence μεταβάλλουϲιν αὐτὰϲ (that is, ϲυλλαβάϲ) μειοῦϲαι καὶ αὔξουϲαι. Are we to understand these words within a merely metrical perspective, that is, in terms of the relation between the quantities of syllables as implementation of metrical elements? Or are we instead dealing with a more circumscribed reference to a further rhythmical level, the musical one, closely connected to the aural experience of the text in its performative dimension? Is Dionysius referring here only to prosodic features inherent in the purely quantitative aspect of verbal metrics (e.g. Attic *correptio*, synizesis, shortening in hiatus)[33] or is he alluding to possible alterations of these prosodic relations underlying the original metrical frame by means of the overlapping melodic tune?[34] Or, finally, are we to suppose some kind of overlap between the two levels (metrical and rhythmical)? Any attempt to answer such questions must start from a broader contextualization of the passage within the mental map sketched by Dionysius. Therefore let us cast a glance at the whole argumentative structure displayed by Chapter 11 of *De comp. verb.*

In this chapter Dionysius is explaining the guidelines of his own phonostylistic analysis by outlining the range of application and related boundaries of what has been successfully defined by Gentili as the 'real aesthetics of reception'.[35] The argumentative thread developed

---

[33] See Usher 1985, 82 n. 1, according to whom "Dionysius is here referring especially to the metrical devices of correption, synizesis, and perhaps syncopation." For the irrelevance of the phenomenon of synizesis and syncopation to the Dionysius passage see recently Parker 2001, 37 n. 24. Apparently in this direction, although dubiously, see also West *AGM*, 132–3 n. 12, according to whom Dionysius could have in mind the metrical device of epic correption. Yet, granted that here Dionysius is more generally speaking of lyric poetry as a whole and not just of Euripidean lyric (the parodos of the *Orestes* has been mentioned just because it was one of the most famous lyric passages known to his readers), a strong objection against this approach is the episodic and isolated occurrence in lyric poetry, at least from a statistical point of view, of the shortening of a long vowel or diphthong at the end of a word when the following word begins with another vowel. It is clear enough that Dionysius' statement makes sense only if loosely referring to a generalized trend (for the rarity of epic correption in dramatic lyric see e.g. Barrett 1964, ad *Hipp.* 170, Bond 1981, ad *HF* 116 and Mastronarde 1994a, ad *Phoen.* 1718).

[34] See Pöhlmann 1960, 39, Rossi 1963, 26–8, Gentili 1988, 12–3, id. 1990, 19 and Parker 2001, 37 with n. 24.

[35] Gentili 1990, 9, following the insights of Rossi (1963) on the topic.

by Dionysius is then the following. To begin with (11. 1–5 Auj.-
Leb.), he lists the four main ingredients necessary to achieve a style
which is to be at the same time attractive and beautiful (ἡ λέξις
ἡδεῖα καὶ καλή): melody (μέλος), rhythm (ῥυθμός), variety (μεταβολή)
and appropriateness (πρέπον). That a pleasant arrangement (ἁρμογή)
of these four elements must be, according to Dionysius, a quality
generally shared by every serious literary composition, that is, a hallmark prior to (and independent of) any genre distinction between
prose and poetry, is clearly expressed in 11. 3 Auj.-Leb.: ὧν μὲν οὖν
στοχάζονται πάντες οἱ σπουδῆι γράφοντες μέτρον ἢ μέλος[36] ἢ τὴν
λεγομένην πεζὴν λέξιν, ταῦτ᾽ ἐστί κτλ. So far Dionysius is thus speaking of phonostylistics as a broad-ranging spectrum to be applied
indifferently to every literary work that is to be enjoyed in its aural
dimension. Hence the priority to be assigned to the faculty of hearing (ἀκοή) as a major criterion by which to judge the pleasantness
of a melody (11. 6–10 Auj.-Leb.). We are actually told that even in
a theatre crowded with a heterogeneous and uncultured mob (παν-
τοδαπὸς καὶ ἄμουσος ὄχλος) there exists a sort of natural agreement
on what is to be perceived as a tuneful, harmonious melody (φυσική
τίς ἐστιν ἁπάντων ἡμῶν οἰκειότης πρὸς ἐμμέλειάν τε καὶ εὐρυθμίαν),
as shown by several examples drawn from theatrical performances
(citharistic as well as auletic).[37] Such an innate sensitivity must be
extended to rhythm as well (11. 10 τὸ δ᾽ αὐτὸ καὶ ἐπὶ τῶν ῥυθμῶν
γινόμενον ἐθεασάμην), and even in this case it is the experience, once
again, that testifies to the general validity of this principle.[38]

After stating this universal truth, Dionysius' interest focuses on a
more restricted and less speculative subject (11. 12 Auj.-Leb.): the
down-to-earth examples actually offered by instrumental and vocal
music (τῆς ὀργανικῆς μούσης καὶ τῆς ἐν ὠιδαῖς γοητείας) as well as
by dance (τῆς ἐν ὀρχήσει χάριτος). It is just at this point (11. 13–14

---

[36] For the traditional distinction between μέτρον (poetry to be delivered: hexameters, iambics and, generally speaking, τὰ ὁμοειδῆ μέτρα) and μέλος (poetry to
be sung) cf. De comp. verb. 26. 3–5 Auj.-Leb., and iid. 91 n. 3.

[37] Dionysius explicitly refers to his own experience, cf. 11. 8 Auj.-Leb. ἤδη ἔγωγε
καὶ ἐν τοῖς πολυανθρωποτάτοις θεάτροις [...] ἔδοξα καταμαθεῖν ὡς κτλ.

[38] Aujac-Lebel 1981, 207 n. 1 correctly refer the sentence ὅτε τις ἢ κροῦσιν ἢ
κίνησιν ἢ φωνὴν ἐν ἀσυμμέτροις ποιήσαιτο χρόνοις καὶ τοὺς ῥυθμοὺς ἀφανίσειεν to
"acteurs qui à la fois chantent et dansent, par exemple les choreutes et le coryphée
dans le chœurs tragiques, ou encore les exécutants de la lyrique corale."

Auj.-Leb.) that we find the comparison mentioned above between civil oratory (ἡ τῶν πολιτικῶν λόγων ἐπιστήμη), that is, prose, and instrumental and vocal music (τῆς ἐν ᾠδαῖς καὶ ὀργάνοις [i.e. μουσικῆς]), that is, lyric poetry. Dionysius resorts again to those criteria (melody, rhythm, variety and appropriateness) previously established as standard guidelines for judging any literary composition (11. 1–5 Auj.-Leb.). In fact, the treatment of the similarities and differences existing between διάλεκτος and μέλος sticks strictly to the general scheme previously drawn, by reproducing in this minor sub-section the very same ordering by the four major critical categories that have previously been introduced. The first label to be discussed is again μέλος (11. 15–21 Auj.-Leb.), followed by ῥυθμός (11. 22–23 Auj.-Leb.), then by a concise summary on the main melodic and rhythmic differences between prose and lyric poetry, and finally by a brief glimpse of the subsequent treatment reserved for μεταβολή and πρέπον (11. 24–26 Auj.-Leb.[39]). Therefore it is within this broader frame that the comparison drawn by Dionysius between prose and poetry has to be properly understood.

The first 'label' to be filled in according to Dionysius' mental map is thus μέλος. As regards this heading, the major distinction between spoken language (διάλεκτος) and melic poetry (ἡ δὲ ὀργανική τε καὶ ᾠδικὴ μοῦσα) is simply one of degree (11. 15–18 Auj.-Leb.). Whereas the pitch-range of spoken language, if referring to a single word not yet embedded in the connected speech,[40] is an interval of a fifth, whether we regard the rising of the voice towards the acute or its falling towards the grave,[41] that of the song employs a broader spectrum of intervals (the octave, fifth, fourth, third, the tone, semitone

[39] For a full treatment of these topics see further 12. 1–4, 5–13 Auj.-Leb. As to the identity of καιρός and πρέπον as aesthetic categories within the discourse of Dionysius cf. Gentili 1990, 10–11.

[40] Cf. 11. 15 Auj.-Leb. ἅπασα γ᾽ ἡ λέξις ἡ καθ᾽ ἓν μόριον λόγου τατττομένη. The limits of Dionysius' analysis, restricted "to the domain of word, and not to the domain of the utterance" have been clearly demonstrated by Devine-Stephens 1991, 243.

[41] For the much debated passage οὔτ᾽ ἀνίεται τοῦ χωρίου τούτου πλέον ἐπὶ τὸ βαρύ (11. 15 Auj.-Leb.) see Devine-Stephens 1991, 230–2, 243 and Usher 1985, 78–9 n. 1. Both scholars cogently object to 'the midline hypothesis' previously advocated by Carson 1969, 34–7 (i.e. a range of a fifth on either side of a not better specified 'mean pitch or midline', a hypothesis which would entail a range of an octave even for spoken language).

and quarter-tone).[42] Now, it is also as a result of this broader pitch-range inherent in song that Dionysius utters the well-known statement that words should be subordinate to melody and not the opposite, quoting as an example the first lines of the parodos of the *Orestes* (11. 19–21 Auj.-Leb.):[43]

τάϲ τε λέξειϲ τοῖϲ μέλεϲιν ὑποτάττειν ἀξιοῖ καὶ οὐ τὰ μέλη ταῖϲ λέξεϲιν, ὡϲ ἐξ ἄλλων τε πολλῶν δῆλον καὶ μάλιϲτα τῶν Εὐριπίδου μελῶν ἃ πεποίηκεν τὴν Ἠλέκτραν λέγουϲαν[44] ἐν Ὀρέϲτηι πρὸϲ τὸν χορόν κτλ.

[instrumental and vocal music] require that words must be subordinate to melody, and not melody to words, as is exemplified by many other songs and especially by what Euripides makes Electra address to the chorus in the *Orestes*.

It is just at this point, that is, after having provided the reader with a concrete example of words being subordinated to μέλοϲ as regards the tonal accent and pitch, that we arrive at the sentence that was

---

[42] This difference rests on the Aristoxenean distinction between κίνηϲιϲ ϲυνεχήϲ (proper to spoken language) and κίνηϲιϲ διαϲτηματική (proper to song), see Aristox. *El. harm.* 1. 8 = 13 ll. 14 ff. Da Rios) and later Arist. Quint. *De mus.* p. 6. 4 ff. W-I. Cf. Devine-Stephens 1991, 230–1, id. 1994, 164 and Hall 1999, 104–5.

[43] For the absence of any conscious diachronic perspective in Dionysius' words (he seems to believe in the invariability of performance or, to put it better, the possibility of changes in musical taste does not affect his discourse at this point) see Dale *LMGD*² 204–6 and more recently Parker 2001, 37–8 (especially nn. 22–3 and 25). That is to say, Dionysius seems just to be referring to his own experience (cf. πολυανθρωπότατα θέατρα in 11. 8 Auj.-Leb.), without taking care to put the data in their historical perspective (Devine-Stephens 1994, 169 argue for a Hellenistic setting). Therefore, in a sense Koller's analysis of this passage (Koller 1956, 25–7) turns out ultimately to share the same limits as Dionysius': Koller's main interest lies in drawing a clear distinction between "die ältere Stufe griechischer Musik" and the late and post-Euripidean developments labelled *tout court* as a homogeneous phenomenon not to be further distinguished (the same limit can be found also in Wahlström 1970, 7–8 and Gentili 1988, 12–3, id. 1990, 20–1). For a different interpretation of this much contended issue (authenticity of the Euripidean music referred to by Dionysius), cf. Dihle 1981, 31, Bélis 1991, 49 (cf. also ead. 2001, 37) and more recently Chandezon 1998, 56, Mathiesen 1999, 120–2, Pöhlmann-West *DAGM*, 11 and Hall 2002, 10 n. 26. Suffice it here to note that Chandezon's statement that "Denys d'Halicarnasse connaissait encore la musique qu'Euripide avait composée pour son *Oreste* puisque c'est sur elle qu'est bâti tout un raisonnement de son traité [. . .] visant à montrer que chez Euripide, c'est le mètre qui, de façon alors tout-à-fait nouvelle, se soumet à la musique et non plus l'inverse" is a strongly circular argument.

[44] As to λέγουϲαν [. . .] πρόϲ conveying here a mere notion of address while providing "keine Auskunft über seine phonetische Aktualisierung im Sprechvorgang" (and thus not contrasting with the following μελωιδεῖται), cf. Koller 1956, 25 n. 1.

our starting point (11. 22–3 Auj.-Leb.): τὸ δ᾽ αὐτὸ γίνεται καὶ περὶ τοὺς ῥυθμούς κτλ. The use of the prepositive καί suggests that the phenomenon we are told about belongs still to the domain of ἡ δὲ ὀργανική τε καὶ ὠιδικὴ μοῦϲα of 11. 18 Auj.-Leb. To the lack of identity to be found in lyric poetry between the pitch of words and their musical setting corresponds a similar lack of consistency (τὸ δ᾽ αὐτό) as regards the level of the 'applied rhythmics'. The comparison with the πεζὴ λέξιϲ is drawn precisely in order to enhance what goes on being the main subject of this subsection: the poetry to be sung.[45] Once again emphasis is put on the performative aspect encompassing the actual delivery and aural perception of verbal data. The frame of reference assumed here by Dionysius as a guideline is thus not metrics *stricto sensu* but more likely rhythmics applied to song.[46]

To draw such a distinction does not mean of course to doubt, on a larger scale, the necessary interplay between metrics and rhythmics, an overlap Dionysius himself is certainly aware of,[47] but to try to contextualize in a more precise way the testimony of 11. 21–22 Auj.-Leb. In the context examined above, where, to let Kroll's words speak for themselves, the critical categories "are taken up from the music,"[48] Dionysius' attention is focused prominently on performative aspects. This is evidently not tantamount to saying that Dionysius is here making a contrast between metrics and rhythmics (which would be wrong), but that in the present passage he is devoting greater attention simply to one of these two poles. There is therefore no contradiction between the approach adopted by Devine-Stephens (metrics as a subdivision of rhythmics in its broader sense)[49] and what we are told by Dionysius. What Devine-Stephens call "the surface phonetic rhythmics that are generated in the performance of

---

[45] Cf. 11. 24 Auj.-Leb. δεδειγμένης δὴ τῆς διαφορᾶς ἧι διαφέρει μουϲικὴ λογικῆς.

[46] A useful term of comparison in order to grasp the logic underlying Dionysius' argumentation may be the very beginning of 11. 10 Auj.-Leb.: τὸ δ᾽ αὐτὸ καὶ ἐπὶ τῶν ῥυθμῶν γινόμενον ἐθεαϲάμην (see above). In this case too there is a shifting of the focus from the melodic to the rhythmic aspect, but again within the domain of instrumental and vocal music.

[47] See e.g. *De comp. verb.* 17. 1 Auj.-Leb.; cf. also Gentili 1990, 19–20.

[48] Kroll 1907, 94 and *passim* 95–6. See also Koller 1954, 207–9.

[49] Devine-Stephens 1994, 100: metrics is regarded as a central level within a hierarchic system where above metrics lies "the highly abstract rhythmics that is the ontogenetic basis of metre" and below it there is "the surface phonetic rhythmics that are generated in the performance of verse."

verse" turns out ultimately to coincide with the rhythmic ἀγωγή, acutely defined by Rossi as "la realizzazione concreta nel suono del materiale verbale,"[50] once the verbal material has been already metrically determined.

Let us now go back and pay more detailed attention to a passage briefly mentioned above, that is, 11. 19–21 Auj.-Leb., where Dionysius exemplifies the subordination of λέξιϲ to μέλοϲ by quoting the beginning of the parodos of *Orestes* (ll. 140–2). This is the segment of the text we are presently concerned with as edited by Auj.-Leb.:

ϲῖγα ϲῖγα, λευκὸν ἴχνοϲ ἀρβύληϲ
τίθετε, μὴ κτυπεῖτ᾽·
ἀποπρόβατ᾽ ἐκεῖϲ᾽, ἀποπρό μοι κοίταϲ.

ἐν γὰρ δὴ τούτοιϲ τὸ ϲῖγα ϲῖγα λευκὸν ἐφ᾽ ἑνὸϲ φθόγγου μελωιδεῖται, καίτοι τῶν τριῶν λέξεων ἑκάϲτη βαρείαϲ τε τάϲειϲ ἔχει καὶ ὀξείαϲ. καὶ τὸ ἀρβύληϲ ἐπὶ μέϲηι ϲυλλαβῆι τὴν τρίτην ὁμότονον ἔχει, ἀμηχάνου ὄντοϲ ἓν ὄνομα δύο λαβεῖν ὀξείαϲ. καὶ τοῦ τίθετε βαρυτέρα μὲν ἡ πρώτη γίνεται, δύο δ᾽ αἱ μετ᾽ αὐτὴν ὀξύτονοί τε καὶ ὁμόφωνοι. τοῦ τε κτυπεῖτ᾽ ὁ περιϲπαϲμὸϲ ἠφάνιϲται· μιᾶι γὰρ αἱ δύο ϲυλλαβαὶ λέγονται τάϲει. καὶ τὸ ἀποπρόβατε οὐ λαμβάνει τὴν τῆϲ μέϲηϲ ϲυλλαβῆϲ προϲωιδίαν ὀξεῖαν, ἀλλ᾽ ἐπὶ τὴν τετάρτην ϲυλλαβὴν καταβέβηκεν ἡ τάϲιϲ τῆϲ τρίτηϲ.

Be silent, be silent! Put down the white tread of your
sandal, do not make noise.
Depart from here, withdraw from this bed.

In these lines the words ϲῖγα ϲῖγα λευκὸν are sung on one note, although each of the three words has both low and high pitch. And the word ἀρβύληϲ has its third syllable sung at the same pitch as its middle one, although it is impossible for a single word to carry two acute accents. And the first syllable of τίθετε is sung in a lower pitch, whereas both the following syllables are sung on the same high note. The circumflex accent on κτυπεῖτε has vanished: the two syllables are actually uttered at the same pitch. And the word ἀποπρόβατε does not carry the acute accent on the middle syllable but the pitch of the third syllable has been transferred to the fourth one.

Are we allowed to believe on the basis of this passage that Dionysius, while quoting the examples of speech-song tonal mismatches from the first lines of the *Orestes* parodos, has at hand a score provided

[50] Rossi 1963, 60–3.

with musical notation? And, if so, does this score reproduce the original Euripidean music or not? Unfortunately, the documentary evidence we possess is too scanty to allow us to draw definitive conclusions on the issue, but some useful observations can still be made.

Granted that the general economy of *De compositione verborum* enables us to credit Dionysius with a certain degree of musical skill,[51] this does not mean, at least not necessarily, that Dionysius is resorting here to a musical score. Another alternative has to be constantly kept in mind: Dionysius' iterated references to his personal experience as an assiduous theatregoer.[52] Furthermore it is worth noticing that the melody of Eur. *Or.* 140–2 (= 11. 19–21 Auj.-Leb.) is described by Dionysius only in its general trend (its ups and downs, we would say):[53] the tonal relationships between syllables are always expressed in terms of relative pitch (acute or grave), without any reference to precise intervals.[54]

---

[51] See Rossi 1963, 5 n. 5.

[52] See e.g. 11. 8 ff. Auj.-Leb. ἤδη ἔγωγε καὶ ἐν τοῖς πολυανθρωποτάτοις θεάτροις [. . .] ἔδοξα καταμαθεῖν ὡς κτλ.; cf. Parker 2001, 37, West *AGM*, 272 and most recently Pöhlmann-West *DAGM*, 11. M.T. Luzzatto brought to my attention a third possibility (not incompatible with what we have suggested above). According to her, Dionysius could be resorting to his own practice of musical performance as a teacher of those disciplines commonly labelled under the heading of ἐγκύκλιος παιδεία (for Dionysius' career as a teacher of the sons of the Roman leisured class see Gabba 1991, 3–4). Granted that the didactic aim of the work is an important feature (cf. 1. 1–3 Auj.-Leb.: the addressee of the *De comp. verb.* is actually Rufus Metilius, the son of an old friend who has just come εἰς ἀνδρὸς ἡλικίαν), Luzzatto's hypothesis that the main source of Dionysius musical competence is to be sought in his own didactic experience seems to me to neglect two aspects. First, this would involve playing down the broader narrative frame within which the excursus of 11. 19–21 Auj.-Leb. is to be contextualized. All the concrete examples offered by Dionysius come in fact from professional performances that take place in the πολυανθρωπότατα θέατρα (the only explicit point of reference for Dionysius as to ἡ δὲ ὀργανική τε καὶ ᾠδικὴ μοῦσα: we are not told about school exercises held in an ἀκροατήριον). Secondly, we have to keep in mind, as already pointed out by Morgan 1998, 12, that in the Hellenistic period, differing in this regard from the classical one, we are facing a "virtual exclusion of the 'musical' element in *mousike* (in the modern sense of playing and singing) from the Hellenistic literate education," with a perceptible shift of focus towards "the theoretical side of the music at the expense of the practical" (Morgan 1998, 35 with n. 119).

[53] The boundary of the melodic trend outlined by Dionysius is once again the single word not yet embedded in the pitch-sandhi.

[54] The same can be said of 11. 15–17 Auj.-Leb. (cf. especially ταῖς δὲ πολυσυλλάβοις, ἡλίκαι ποτ᾽ ἂν ὦσιν, ἡ τὸν ὀξὺν τόνον ἔχουσα μία ἐν πολλαῖς βαρείαις ἔνεστιν): Dionysius does not distinctly specify the different tonal nuances existing ἐν πολλαῖς βαρείαις, as we would expect if he were actually quoting from a score. For this passage cf. also Devine-Stephens 1991, 243–4.

Equally telling, moreover, is the fact that Dionysius' analysis of
the speech-song tonal mismatches is always circumscribed to the
domain of the single word not yet embedded in the chain of the
pitch-sandhi.[55] What Dionysius is saying here rests indeed on a mental process of double abstraction. The terms of comparison he adopts
are respectively (1) the cχῆμα εὔρυθμον of the single word as it should
be prior to and apart from its phonetic contextual implementation
(that is, at the level of the *parole*) and (2) its musical delivery, always
conceived within such an atomized perspective, that is, decontextu-
alized from its broader frame (the musical phrase as a whole). In
other words, Dionysius' analysis does not take into account the possibility of a third, intermediate stage which could hierarchically medi-
ate between both the levels examined above: that is, the level of the
word actually uttered by a concrete speaker, and therefore subjected
to those segmental and suprasegmental oscillations usually recorded
in connected speech.

Dionysius' apparently negative conclusions about a possible agreement, in terms of pitch accent, between speech and song turn out
in fact to be ultimately the true result of his dismissing the possibility, if not the very existence at all, of this third level. If we keep
in mind this bias inherent in Dionysius' investigation and try to apply
to ll. 19–21 Auj.-Leb., with a certain degree of flexibility due to
the differing verifiability of the matter examined,[56] those rules of correspondence between linguistic pitch accent and musical setting tested
by Devine-Stephens on the Delphic hymns,[57] the results of the com-

---

[55] On a more general level see Albano Leoni 2001, 58: "un segmento intona-
tivo di prosodia ritagliato dal suo contesto è in sé totalmente privo di significato e
di funzione, perché i valori che determinano la prosodia, e dunque anche l'intona-
zione, sono sempre e tutti radicalmente relativi, valutabili e interpretabili solo in
rapporto a ciò che segue e a ciò che precede all'interno dell'intera unità proso-
dica considerata."

[56] Unfortunately, Devine-Stephens' remark (id. 1991, 245) that "in general, it is
much more important for song melody to preserve the direction of pitch movement than it is for it to maintain the true pitch of an utterance or to replicate the
pitch intervals precisely" cannot be tested for ll. 19–21 Auj.-Leb., as already argued
above (Dionysius' analysis is limited to the domain of the word, not of the whole
utterance). Furthermore, Dionysius' report is affected by selective omissions: we
might suppose that words like ἴχνοc, ἐκεῖc(ε), ἀποπρό μοι κοίταc, which are not
commented on by Dionysius, do not entail speech-song tonal mismatches (cf.
Pöhlmann-West *DAGM*, 11), yet no certainty can be gained with regard to this.

[57] Devine-Stephens 1991, 245–6. Whenever possible, full relevance must be
assigned to the phenomenon of downtrend, cf. iid. 235–40.

parison between spoken language and song seem to suggest a less drastic conclusion than what we could expect. By adopting the criteria singled out by Devine-Stephens, examples of true tonal mismatches are to be found only when an unaccented syllable is set higher than (and not just at the same pitch as) the accented syllable of the same word. Isotonic relations between accented and unaccented syllables, once set to music, do not represent true violations of the rules governing the surface phonetic patterns of pitch in Greek speech.[58] Therefore, the only real cases of violated correspondence between linguistic pitch accent and musical setting in Dionysius' report are τίθετε[59] and ἀποπρόβατ(ε),[60] after all a smaller and less puzzling proportion than is usually assumed,[61] and this is so whether Dionysius is referring to a strophic performance of the *Orestes* parodos or to an astrophic one.

More to the point, West confidently remarks that Dionysius "omits to mention that the song is strophic."[62] Now, granted that Dionysius does not specify anywhere in the text the astrophic or antistrophic nature of the lyric song he is quoting, I do not believe that his silence is tantamount here to saying that Dionysius does necessarily suppose a strophic performance. We have always to keep in mind the possibility of a musical resetting: an all-inclusive label that in the

---

[58] Very instructive is the comparison drawn by Devine-Stephens 1991, 245 with the Hausa, a language typologically akin to ancient Greek in this respect: "in the Hausa tonal sequence High Low High, the Low tone can sometimes be realized by the same musical note as the preceding High; this is not a mismatch but reflects a feature of phrase intonation in fluent speech." We can therefore confidently assess that "the tonal relations reflected in the music are those of the surface phonetic output, after the lexical tones have been adjusted by factors like sandhi and intonation."

[59] Porson's necessary emendation (*praeeunte* Hermann: cf. Diggle 1994, 140) of the Euripidean text: Dionysius' codices are split between τίθεται (P) and τιθεῖτε (FE), erroneous readings shared by the Euripidean manuscript tradition too. In any case, Dionysius' comment (βαρυτέρα μὲν ἡ πρώτη γίνεται, δύο δ' αἱ μετ' αὐτὴν ὀξύτονοί τε καὶ ὁμόφωνοι) testifies to the necessity of a proparoxyton reading, cf. Dale *LMGD*², 205 n. 1.

[60] Once again it is Dionysius' linguistic comment (οὐ λαμβάνει τὴν τῆc μέcηc cυλλαβῆc προcῳιδίαν ὀξεῖαν, ἀλλ' ἐπὶ τὴν τετάρτην cυλλαβὴν καταβέβηκεν ἡ τάcιc τῆc τρίτηc) that allows us to choose the right reading (ἄπο προβατ' PM: ἄπο πρόβατ' FE: ἀποπρόβατ' V), cf. Dale *LMGD*², 205.

[61] Cf. e.g. West *AGM*, 198–9, Bélis 1992, 31–2, Ruijgh 2001, 310.

[62] West, *AGM*, 199 n. 16.

Hellenistic entertainment industry might well entail an astrophic performance of tragic songs originally conceived as strophic.[63]

Given these premises (that is, the insolubility of this problem on a merely textual basis), what is perhaps more interesting is precisely Dionysius' substantial indifference to the issue (strophic or astrophic performance of the *Orestes'* parodos), at least at this point of his argument.[64]

Granted that the evidence we possess does not enable us to draw any inference on the strophic or astrophic nature of the performance of *Or.* 140–2 as referred to by Dionysius, the corresponding lines in the antistrophe, according to Euripidean tradition, are *Or.* 153–5. The fact that P.Köln VI 252 (= once P.Köln III 131: first/second century BC) does provide a text philologically and editorially accurate (*verso* unwritten, careful literary bookhand, colization of the lyric parts distinguished from the trimeters by means of *eisthesis*, *ekthesis* probably indicating change of speaker within a dochmiac section at l. 8 = *Or.* 142) and that omits the sequence μηδ' ἔςτω κτύποc at l. 141, as does the manuscript tradition of Dionysius (see Gronewald 1987, 129), make less likely the possibility that this textual omission is a mere accident of transmission. Especially significant in this respect is also the papyrus' reading ψοφο[c for l. 137 *vs.* κτύποc of the extant manuscript tradition (as to ll. 136–9, a likely ancient interpolated section cf. Di Benedetto 1961, 311 and more recently Medda 2001, 102). Of course, on the basis of these data (the direct evidence of P.Köln and the indirect evidence offered by Dionysius' quotation) we cannot entirely exclude the possibility of a textual arrangement of the first lines of the *Orestes* parodos other than that preserved by the remaining manuscript tradition (at least from the second century BC onwards). Nevertheless, if we want to compare, tentatively, the direction of pitch movement in strophe (140–2) and antistrophe (153–5), it would be appropriate, at least in my opinion, to adopt as the text to be tested ll. 153–5 as edited by Diggle *OCT* III (thus accepting the athetesis, already advanced by Schenkl, of the second dochmiac τίνα δὲ cυμφοράν; at l. 154: the following hiatus between 154–5 would be, however, a minor difficulty if compared with the syntactic harshness resulting from the deletion of the first dochmiac τίνα τύχαν εἴπω as argued by Biehl *et alii*. See Di Benedetto 1961, 311–2).

---

[63] Cf. e.g. P.Stras.W.G. 306ʳ col. II = Eur. *Med.* 841–65, 976–82 and col. III = Eur. *Med.* 1251–92.

[64] The polarity orienting Dionysius' survey at this point is the comparison between spoken language (διάλεκτοc) and lyric poetry as a whole (ἡ δὲ ὀργανική τε καὶ ᾠδικὴ μοῦcα), without any further distinction between strophic or astrophic compositions, even supposing that at Dionysius' time such a normative distinction still entailed a perceivable, standardized difference in terms of musical performance.

Turning back to the major question, we may consider another passage of Dionysius repeatedly quoted by scholars as a further piece
of evidence supporting the lack of correspondence between linguistic pitch accent and musical setting: 19. 4–8 Auj.-Leb.[65]

In this section Dionysius' attention is focused on variety (μεταβολή)
as the third main ingredient of an attractive and beautiful style (λέξις
ἡδεῖα καὶ καλή), singling out as the hallmark of prose (πεζὴ λέξις)
a greater freedom than poetry to adopt variations of structure and
rhythm.[66] As concerns poetry, Dionysius introduces then a further
discrimen between compositions to be delivered (τὰ μέτρα)[67] and those
to be sung (τὰ μέλη) and within this latter subsection sketches a
roughly diachronic outline of the lyric poetry from οἱ ἀρχαῖοι μελοποιοί
(monodic and choral lyric) up to the New Dithyramb.[68] 19. 7 Auj.-
Leb. has to be regarded in fact as a self-contained parenthetic clause:[69]

οἱ μὲν οὖν ἀρχαῖοι μελοποιοί, λέγω δὲ Ἀλκαῖόν τε καὶ Σαπφώ, μικρὰς
ἐποιοῦντο ϲτροφάϲ, ὥϲτ' ἐν ὀλίγοιϲ τοῖϲ κώλοιϲ οὐ πολλὰϲ εἰϲῆγον τὰϲ
μεταβολάϲ, ἐπῳδοῖϲ τε πάνυ ἐχρῶντο ὀλίγοιϲ. οἱ δὲ περὶ Στηϲίχορόν τε
καὶ Πίνδαρον μείζουϲ ἐργαϲάμενοι τὰϲ περιόδουϲ εἰϲ πολλὰ μέτρα καὶ
κῶλα διένειμαν αὐτὰϲ οὐκ ἄλλου τινὸϲ ἢ τῆϲ μεταβολῆϲ ἔρωτι.

Thus the ancient lyric poets, I mean Alcaeus and Sappho, made their
strophes short and consequently they could not introduce many variations

---

[65] See Pöhlmann 1960, 23 and Gentili 1990, 20–1 with n. 51, who ascribes the
speech-song tonal mismatches to the "necessità di conservare nella responsione
strofica la stessa melodia, come è espressamente detto da Dionigi nell'enunciato che
ai poeti melici non è possibile alterare nell'antistrofe la melodia della strofe, ma
debbono mantenere la medesima linea melodica nell'intero componimento." Cf.
also Ruijgh 2001, 303–4, 313–5.

[66] Cf. 19. 9 Auj.-Leb. ἡ δὲ πεζὴ λέξις ἅπασαν ἐλευθερίαν ἔχει καὶ ἄδειαν
ποικίλλειν ταῖϲ μεταβολαῖϲ τὴν ϲύνθεϲιν ὅπωϲ βούλεται.

[67] For τὰ μέτρα loosely referring to the meters of recitative poetry (hexameter,
iambic series and all those compositions consisting of stichic repetitions of measures
metrically ὁμοειδῆ) cf. 26. 3–5 Auj.-Leb. In our particular case (19. 3 Auj.-Leb.) it
is the hexameter that is assumed as the concrete example of poetry to be delivered.

[68] Also the New Dithyramb is intrinsically regarded as a diachronic development,
cf. 19. 8 Auj.-Leb. [...] οἵ γε κατὰ Φιλόξενον καὶ Τιμόθεον καὶ Τελεϲτήν, ἐπεὶ
παρά γε τοῖϲ ἀρχαίοιϲ τεταγμένος ἦν καὶ ὁ διθύραμβοϲ.

[69] The syntactic and narrative autonomy of this digression (cf. οἱ μὲν οὖν ἀρχαῖοι
μελοποιοί [...] οἱ δὲ περὶ Στηϲίχορόν τε καὶ Πίνδαρον) is especially evident if compared with the beginning of the following section 19. 8 Auj.-Leb.: οἱ δέ γε διθυραμβοποιοὶ καὶ τοὺς τρόπους μετέβαλλον Δωρίουϲ τε καὶ Φρυγίουϲ καὶ Λυδίουϲ ἐν
τῶι αὐτῶι ᾄϲματι ποιοῦντεϲ κτλ. For δέ γε strongly adversative in continuous speech
see Denniston *GP²*, 155.

in their cola, which are not numerous, and employed very few epodes.
Stesichorus and Pindar,[70] making their periods longer, divided them
into many metres and cola just because they loved variation.

The comparison drawn by Dionysius between monodic and choral
poetry is a secondary one which is subsumed within a broader
cύγκριcιc: that is, it does not regard the qualitative nature of the
variations involved (preservation or not of the musical γένοc adopted
from the outset of the composition) but only the different extent of
their exploitation (a greater length of strophes, a greater variety of
metres and cola in choral lyrics). The main opposition to which
Dionysius turns his attention is not, as already stressed by D'Alfonso,
the distinction "between the brief strophe of the old lyric poets [. . .]
and the more ample articulation of the Stesichorean and Pindaric
strophe, since both types, despite their obvious differences, respect
in a uniform manner the melodic modes and pre-established rhythms,"[71]
but that between the archaic lyric *tout court* and the innovative trend
inaugurated by the New Dithyramb.[72]

Therefore it is precisely within this broader argumentative frame
(repetition, for recitative poetry, of the same metres and rhythms *vs.*
variety of lyric poetry and its partial licence of changing τό τε μέλοc
καὶ τὸν ῥυθμόν as concerns the epodes of traditional triadic compositions and the astrophic dithyrambs of New Music) that the much-
discussed passage 19. 4 Auj.-Leb. has to be contextualized:

> τοῖc δὲ τὰ μέλη γράφουcιν τὸ μὲν τῶν cτροφῶν τε καὶ ἀντιcτρόφων οὐχ
> οἷόν τε ἀλλάξαι μέλοc, ἀλλ᾽ ἐάν τ᾽ ἐναρμονίουc ἐάν τε χρωματικὰc ἐάν
> τε διατόνουc ὑποθῶνται μελωιδίαc, ἐν πάcαιc δεῖ ταῖc cτροφαῖc καὶ
> ἀντιcτρόφοιc τὰc αὐτὰc ἀγωγὰc φυλάττειν.

---

[70] The previous mention of the proper names Alcaeus and Sappho seems to suggest that we are possibly dealing here with an instance of the so-called 'periphrastic'
use of οἱ περί + acc. *nominis proprii*, cf. LSJ s.v. περί C I. 2. Differently Usher 1985,
151 ("Stesichorus and Pindar and their followers"), who inclines here for an 'inclu-
sive' use of οἱ περί + acc. of a proper name: more generally on the issue see
Gorman 2001, followed recently by Ceccarelli 2004, 110.

[71] D'Alfonso 1994, 68: "fra la breve strofa degli ἀρχαῖοι μελοποιοί [. . .] e la più
ampia articolazione della strofe stesicorea e pindarica, poiché entrambe, pur nelle
evidenti differenze, rispettarono i modi melodici e i ritmi prefissati in modo unitario."

[72] An analogous distinction, however less explicitly stated, with Stesichorus regarded
again as the representative of οἱ ἀρχαῖοι μελοποιοί, can be found also in Heracl.
Pont. fr. 157 Wehrli = [Plut.] *De mus.* 1132b 10–c 3; cf. Gottschalk 1980, 134.

the writers of lyric poetry cannot vary the melos[73] of strophes and anti-strophes but whether they set them to enharmonic, chromatic or diatonic melodies, they have to maintain in all the strophes and antistrophes the same melodic harmonic sequence.

Saying that the logical thread of the comment about the *Orestes* parodos (11. 19–21 Auj.-Leb.) is the same as that of the passage just quoted is to blur together two different levels of thought. Τὰς αὐτὰς ἀγωγὰς[74] φυλάττειν does not actually mean 'to preserve the melody unchanged in its tonal relations between spoken language and song', but 'to observe, through the whole length of the composition, the same musical γένος (enharmonic, chromatic or diatonic) chosen at the very beginning', a bare datum which does not allow us to infer any correspondence, either positive or negative, between the pitch accent of the words and their musical setting.[75] The expression οὐχ οἷόν τε ἀλλάξαι μέλος refers thus to the prohibition of mingling different musical γένη[76] within the same composition (at least among οἱ ἀρχαῖοι μελοποιοί), as is confirmed by the following reference to the New Dithyramb.[77]

But let us turn back to the starting point of our enquiry (the question whether Dionysius resorted, or not, to a musical score while quoting the *Orestes* parodos, that is 11. 19–21 Auj.-Leb.). Much more interesting than this aporetic question is indeed the fact that previous scholars have usually (and almost unconsciously) linked the answer,

---

[73] For the precise meaning of μέλος in this context see below.

[74] For ἀγωγή bearing here the technical meaning of harmonic (and not rhythmic) sequence, see Rossi 1963, 56 n. 129 and 64 n. 148.

[75] Ruijgh 2001, 303–4 with n. 75 understands correctly the meaning of 19. 4 Auj.-Leb. even if his misleading conception of "chant traditionnel" (encompassing true traditional songs like the Delphic hymns as well as a documentary *hapax* like Sikilos' epitaph) leads him to reaffirm the necessity of a link between observance of the melodic genos and observance of the 'melodic contour' of the spoken language (id. 2001, 313).

[76] This is the meaning we have to assign to μέλος at 19. 5 Auj.-Leb. περὶ δὲ τὰς καλουμένας ἐπωιδοὺς ἀμφότερα κινεῖν ταῦτα ἔξεστι τό τε μέλος καὶ ῥυθμόν.

[77] 19. 8 Auj.-Leb. οἱ δέ γε διθυραμβοποιοὶ καὶ τοὺς τρόπους μετέβαλλον Δωρίους τε καὶ Φρυγίους καὶ Λυδίους ἐν τῶι αὐτῶι ἄιϲματι ποιοῦντες, καὶ τὰς μελωιδίας ἐξήλλαττον τότε μὲν ἐναρμονίους ποιοῦντες, τότε δὲ χρωματικάς, τότε δὲ διατόνους, καὶ τοῖς ῥυθμοῖς κατὰ πολλὴν ἄδειαν ἐνεξουσιάζοντες διετέλουν, οἵ γε κατὰ Φιλόξενον καὶ Τιμόθεον καὶ Τελεστήν κτλ. For a broader contextualization of the present passage in the much-contended debate on tradition and innovation within the musical discourse at the end of the fifth/beginning of the fourth century BC see the brilliant survey of Csapo 2004a.

whether affirmative or negative, to this question to the solution of
another vexed question, certainly akin to it but to be sharply distinguished from it, at least in terms of modes of transmission and
reception. In other words, an affirmative answer to the first question (Dionysius actually had some musical score to hand)[78] has been
automatically regarded as indirect evidence for a systematic exploitation of texts with musical notation by Alexandrian philologists.[79]
These two elements need instead to be distinguished. An alleged use
of a musical score by Dionysius does not necessarily entail such a
generalizing inference about an early osmosis between Alexandrian
editorial technique and musical tradition. Dionysius himself, from 11.
6 ff. Auj.-Leb. onwards, lets us suppose a far more fluid and less
one-sided dimension as regards the material sources of his musical
excursus: his main test-bed seems indeed to be the theatrical space
of the ἐπιδείξεις and ἀκροάσεις.[80]

Summing up, in such a fluid and variable scenario as that sketched
by the direct and indirect evidence we have, if Alexandrian scholars did occasionally resort to texts carrying musical notation, this
practice may have aimed sporadically at understanding the metrical
frame of the text itself. Yet, even apart from the several, serious
problems of transmission, reception and survival that such an early
and uninterrupted osmosis between textual and musical tradition
entails, the sources examined here cannot be assumed to provide
positive evidence supporting a widespread and normative use of this
device in order to colize lyric texts.

I.2 *Apollonius εἰδογράφος*

Another major tenet on which Fleming-Kopff's hypothesis rests is
the high degree of musical skill, almost professional, that they are

---

[78] Cf. Wessely 1892, 269, followed by Bataille 1961, 20 n. 1, Wahlström 1970,
8, Pöhlmann 1960, 12, id. 1995b, 1637 and 1997, 288 (differently Pöhlmann-West
DAGM, 11 where this hypothesis is now rejected) and more recently Bélis 2001,
31, 36–7, 47, Willink 2001, 130 and Hall 2002, 10 n. 26.
[79] See especially Wessely, Bataille and also Fleming-Kopff 1992, 763 and Fleming
1999, 25–6 (the last less unequivocal: while asserting that "Dionysius [. . .] possessed
a copy with musical notation which he knew how to interpret," he also recognizes,
together with Gentili 1990, that Dionysius' critical essay "is based on observation,
and Dionysius clearly refers to his own musical experiences in crowded theaters").
[80] See e.g. 11. 8 ff. Auj.-Leb.

somehow necessarily forced to ascribe to Alexandrian scholars in order to enable them to employ successfully texts provided with musical notation.[81] It is thus within this perspective that Fleming-Kopff consider the much disputed entry of the *Etym. gen.* AB s.v. εἰδογράφος = *Et. M.* 295. 52 ff. Gaisford:

εἰδογράφος· Ἀπολλών⟨ιος⟩ εἰδογράφος (alterum εἰδογράφος om. B), ἐπειδὴ εὐφυὴς ὢν ἐν τῆι βιβλιοθήκηι τὰ εἴδη τοῖς εἴδεσιν ἐπένειμεν. τὰς γὰρ δοκούσας τῶν ὠιδῶν (coniecit fort. Sylburg: εἰδῶν codd.) Δώριον μέλος ἔχειν ἐπὶ τὸ αὐτὸ συνῆγε, καὶ Φρυγίας καὶ Λυδίας, μιξολυδιστὶ καὶ ἰαστί.

Classifier: Apollonius <called> the Classifier, because, being naturally talented, he distinguished in the Library the different genres [of literary compositions] according to their musical mode: in fact, among the various odes, he put together those which were supposed to be performed to a Dorian mode, and he did the same for those performed to a Phrygian, Lydian, Mixolydian and Ionic mode too.

The problematic evidence that Apollonius εἰδογράφος had classified the odes (most likely the Pindaric ones, cf. Σ to *Pyth.* 2 inscr. = 2. 31 Drachm.) according to their harmony[82] cannot of course be neglected.[83] Yet the assumption that "Apollonios was able to classify the odes according to the mode because he was in possession of musical texts,"[84] and that he was himself thus able to read a musical

---

[81] Fleming-Kopff 1992, 762, Fleming 1999, 25: Wilamowitz's previous strictures on the issue certainly needed to be updated and in this regard Fleming-Kopff's claim is a most welcome one, yet we shall see that they seem to push it too far.

[82] Even granted that Apollonius was Aristophanes' predecessor at the direction of the Library, such an editorial criterion, apparently not followed in the edition of any lyric poet, does not seem to have influenced at all Aristophanes' authoritative edition of Pindar: cf. D'Alessio 1997, 53 with n. 178.

[83] Pöhlmann's repeated attempts (id. 1960, 12, id. 1991, 3 n. 15 and 1994, 34–5; in the same direction cf. already C.-E. Ruelle's note in Wessely 1892, 269 n. 1) to argue against a 'musical' classification of the Pindaric odes arranged by Apollonius on the basis of the scholium to Pind. *Pyth.* 2 inscr. (2. 31 Drachm.) are unconvincing: see Fleming's detailed objections in id. 1999, 25 (the misleading interpretation of εἴδη as "Klassen" and not as "Tonarten" had already been pointed out by Boeckh: cf. Pfeiffer 1968, 184 n. 6). For a critical survey on Apollonius' work on Pindar's odes see D'Alessio 1997, 53–5 and most recently Negri 2004, 211–12.

[84] Fleming 1999, 25; cf. recently Lomiento 2001, 308, Gentili-Lomiento 2001, 10 and iid. 2003, 10. Nagy 2000, 21 n. 40 more cautiously speaks of a generic "access to a melodic tradition when he was working on the accents of Bacchylides." Fleming's position on the issue had already been advocated in the past by Wessely 1892, 269 with n. 1, Martin 1953, 15 and Bataille 1961, 19; differently Pfeiffer 1968, 184 n. 6, who gave a negative answer to this question.

score, is just one possibility among many others (possibilities, of course, which are not necessarily to be regarded as mutually exclusive).

First of all, if we look at the inner argumentative frame underlying the entry of the *Etym.* quoted above, due attention is to be paid to the meaning and function conveyed by such an expression as "being naturally talented" (εὐφυὴς ὤν).[85] Given the context, the emphasis on Apollonius' own natural skill seems indeed to suggest something different from routine work, something which requires an intuitive mind and not simply the bare observance of pre-existent rules, however complicated they may be (as for instance reading musical scores). In other words, the expression εὐφυὴς ὤν is probably present here to explain why Apollonius was able to perform this unusual classification. It is thus worth wondering whether the entry would have specified that (that is, Apollonius' natural talent) if the Alexandrian scholar had simply read texts carrying musical notation rather that used his own talents to conjecture the proper labels.[86]

Secondly, already Aristotle had told us that, in order to competently enjoy the various melodies, we are not required to have any technical skill, theoretical or practical (a necessary qualification instead for professional musicians).[87] In the same direction, although on a more theoretical level, points also Aristox. *El. harm.* 2. 39 (= 49, ll. 9 ff. Da Rios), sharply disputing with those who regard the παρασημαντικὴ τέχνη[88] as the ultimate aim of harmonic science. Since it is not necessary that whoever is able to write down the scheme of the iambic metre should at the same time be able to know what the iambus actually means, similarly "this is also true in the case of

---

[85] Negri's translation of εὐφυὴς ὤν as "essendo in posizione di rilievo" (ead. 2004, 211–2 n. 3) is misleading: εὐφυὴς ὤν is not to be linked to the following ἐν τῆι βιβλιοθήκηι.

[86] I owe this suggestion to D.J. Mastronarde.

[87] Aristot. *Pol.* 1339b 8–10, 1341 a 9–17. For Aristotle's strictures on professional musicians see Anderson 1966, 124 n. 30, 130–2, Wallace 2003, 90 and above all the illuminating socio-cultural analysis of both Martin 2003, 155–7 and Ford 2004, 312 ff. Being able to write and read musical notation entailed a high degree of professionalism, see Bélis 1999, 159 and 163–4, according to whom the "notateur" was a person other than the poet.

[88] On the much-debated nature of the notation alluded to at this early date (likely a diagram of intervals) see Herington 1985, 235 n. 7, Bélis 1986, 105 and 114 n. 105, Barker *GMW* II, 155 n. 38. Differently Pöhlmann, who identifies the παρασημαντική of Aristoxenus *tout court* with the Alypian notational system, cf. id. 1991, 4, id. 1995b, 1657 and id. 1997, 285–6.

lyric passages: for it is not necessary for the one who has written down the Phrygian harmony also to understand fully what the Phrygian harmony is" (= 49, ll. 12–14 Da Rios οὕτως ἔχει καὶ ἐπὶ τῶν μελωιδουμένων — οὐ γὰρ ἀναγκαῖόν ἐcτι τὸν γραψάμενον τὸ Φρύγιον μέλοc καὶ ἄριcτά γε εἰδέναι τί ἐcτι τὸ Φρύγιον μέλοc).[89] Furthermore, in the preceding lines (= 49, ll. 1 ff. Da Rios) Aristoxenus has explicitly claimed, even more radically, that the *parasemantiké*, far from being the aim (πέραc) of harmonic science, is not even a part (μέροc) of it. In other words, being able to grasp and recognize the different musical modes does not seem necessarily to entail the ability to write down and then consequently decipher musical diagrams.

Yet the data collected by both Aristotle and Aristoxenus rest on the possibility of hearing a live musical performance.[90] This assumption is indeed difficult to accept if referred to the Pindaric odes in Apollonius' time,[91] especially if we take into account that already Eupolis, the Athenian comedian of the second half of the fifth century BC, could say that Pindar's odes were completely reduced to silence (κατᾳcεcιγαcμένα) because of the increasingly perverted taste of the contemporary audience in the matter of songs.[92] What then

---

[89] For a good defence of this textual section, previously athetized by Marquard and Laloy as an interpolated gloss, see Da Rios 1954, 60 n. 2. Barker *GMW* II, 156 also regards this passage as substantially sound.

[90] Cf. Aristox. *El. harm.* 2. 38 (= 48, ll. 11 ff. Da Rios), especially the statement that ἐκ δύο γὰρ δὴ τούτων ἡ τῆc μουcικῆc ξύνεcίc ἐcτιν, αἰcθήcεώc τε καὶ μνήμηc· αἰcθάνεcθαι μὲν γὰρ δεῖ τὸ γινόμενον, μνημονεύειν δὲ τὸ γεγονόc. For the main role played by sense perception (αἴcθηcιc) within Aristoxenus' reflection see Rossi 1963, 29 n. 7 and 32 n. 76.

[91] As to the increasing disaffection displayed by the Athenian audience towards the choral lyric in general and Pindar in particular, at least from the last quarter of the fifth century BC onwards, see Irigoin 1952, 12–21 (especially 19–21). Cameron 1995, 46 suggests that "Pindar must still have been performed musically from time to time (presumably by professionals)," admitting however eventually that "Callimachus and his peers will normally have read him as we do—and were well enough informed to understand the difference." Most recently Hubbard has challengingly argued for "iterative re-performances" of Pindar's epinicians at the very site of the athletic victory on the occasion of the following festival's convocation (Hubbard 2004, 75). Yet even this hypothetical scenario does not allow one to draw an uninterrupted line of 'performative' continuity down to the Hellenistic age. Besides, and more to the point, even in the case of some sporadic re-performance of Pindar's odes in the Hellenistic period, what is worth asking is what kind of re-performances we are dealing with (citharodic? choral?). On Pindaric solo re-performances at symposia see Kurke 1991, 5 with n. 17. The possibility of musical re-setting cannot thus be entirely ruled out.

[92] Eup. 398 K-A (= Athen. 1. 2d–3a): Larensis' encyclopaedic erudition encompasses

was the evidence to which Apollonius is likely to have resorted in classifying Pindar's odes according to their musical modes? Are we compelled to suppose, as the only practicable way, the possession of musical scores by Apollonius? And if this is the case, what kind of scores are we to imagine? Did they reproduce the Pindaric original performance or were they rearranged according to the different occasions, private as well as public, to which they were adapted? What authoritative value could such a re-adapted score have had for classifying Pindar's odes? Finally, is there some other alternative to account for Apollonius' classification?

Sound skepticism about the somewhat romantic idea of Apollonius compulsively inspecting musical manuscripts had been already expressed by Irigoin, who more reasonably argued instead for an internal, autoschediastic explanation. According to Irigoin, Apollonius could well have resorted to the several references to musical tones and modes scattered throughout Pindar's odes by the poet himself.[93] Furthermore, it is worth asking, especially in view of what seems to have been a quite close and somehow standard, consistent link between musical modes and metrical types in Pindar's odes, whether the metrical frame itself of a lyric composition, together with the inner stage directions we have mentioned, could have aided Apollonius in labelling the harmony originally conceived for the ode's performance.[94]

Summing up, as to Apollonius εἰδογράφος we cannot confidently rule out the possibility of explaining his classification according to criteria other than the actual possession of musical scores. Secondly, and perhaps more to the point, there is still another consideration that strongly invalidates Fleming-Kopff's challenging hypothesis. Even

---

also a proper juridical competence drawn ἐκ παλαιῶν ψηφιςμάτων καὶ δογμάτων τηρήςεως, ἔτι δὲ νόμων ϲυναγωγῆς οὓς <οὐκ>έτι (suppl. Kaibel) διδάϲκουϲιν, ὡϲ τὰ Πινδάρου <ὁ add. cod. B> κωμωιδοποιὸϲ Εὔπολίϲ φηϲιν, ἤδη καταϲεϲιγαϲμένων ὑπὸ τῆϲ τῶν πολλῶν ἀφιλοκαλίαϲ. For the defence of the transmitted reading καταϲεϲιγαϲμένων against Schweighäuser's emendation καταϲεϲιγαϲμένα see Srebrny's remarks on the issue quoted by K-A in their apparatus.

[93] Irigoin1952, 50. An analogous internal explanation can be found also in Fraser 1972, II, 666 n. 126, who supposes that "Apollonius may have prepared a hand-list of the musical elements of lyric odes."

[94] Cf. Most 1985, 100 n. 26. We know that different harmoniai had distinct styles and/or tempos of performance; for the correlation between harmoniai and lyric genres in the classical period see Rutherford 2001, 80.

if we were forced to suppose an exploitation of texts with musical notation by Apollonius (and we have seen that we are not), the problem would remain of explaining why this editorial criterion καθ' ἁρμονίαν cannot be found elsewhere, that is, not only in Pindar's authoritative edition arranged by Aristophanes but also in other editions of lyric poets. If it was simply a documentary *hapax*, it must not have worked very well.

Finally, there is a further aspect we have to take into account: the difference, in terms of tradition and transmission, between dramatic texts and those originally conceived for a lyric performance (either monodic or choral) *stricto sensu*.[95] If, as regards dramatic texts, it is easier (although not without problems) to posit some sort of survival for the musical transmission through a multiplicity of channels till the Hellenistic age,[96] the performance of choral and monodic lyric was originally closely linked to a very specific occasion (the monodic in a lower degree), and this linkage seems to suggest a more rapid disappearance of such a musical tradition.[97]

I.3 *Visualizing the music: functional analogy or graphical plagiarism?*
Aristophanes' lesson according to Pseudo-Arcadius (with a minor appendix on the Pindaric scholia to Ol. *2. 48c and f [= 1. 73 Drachm.])*

The next text to be discussed has also been quoted by Fleming-Kopff as a further piece of evidence supporting a close familiarity of Alexandrian scholars with the technicalities entailed by the musical notation.[98] Chapter 20 of the epitome of Herodianus' handbook ascribed to Pseudo-Arcadius is a section revealing a clearly spurious origin and generally known under the title περὶ τῆς τῶν τόνων εὑρέσεως καὶ τῶν ϲχημάτων αὐτῶν καὶ περὶ χρόνων καὶ πνευμάτων.[99] In particular, the fact that Aristophanes of Byzantium is credited here with

---

[95] See Wilamowitz 1889, 121–3, Irigoin 1952, 21–2 and Pöhlmann 1991, 2–3.
[96] Cf. Pickard-Cambridge 1968², 72 ff., 286–7 as regards the re-performance of παλαιὰ δράματα in the Hellenistic period. The problem of possible rearrangements still remain: see Bélis 1999, 174–7.
[97] Cf. Wilamowitz's skepticism on the issue: id. 1889, 122.
[98] Fleming-Kopff 1992, 762 and in a more detailed way Fleming 1999, 26, who, however, admits that the probatory value of the present evidence is "less direct and less conclusive."
[99] This heading is transmitted only by the codex Par. gr. 2102, a manuscript written by the sixteenth-century falsifier Jacobus Diassorinus: see Pfeiffer 1968, 179

having been "guided by musical analogies in his work on the accentuation system" would confirm, according to Fleming-Kopff, the high
degree of musical skill displayed by Aristophanes himself. Once
granted that assumption, the step towards assuming a systematic
practice by Aristophanes of resorting to musical scores in order to
colize lyric texts is evidently short. The passage Fleming-Kopff are
concerned with is the following:[100]

> οἱ χρόνοι καὶ οἱ τόνοι καὶ τὰ πνεύματα Ἀριϲτοφάνουϲ ἐκτυπώϲαντοϲ γέγονε
> πρόϲ τε διάκριϲιν[a] τῆϲ ἀμφιβόλου λέξεωϲ καὶ πρὸϲ τὸ μέλοϲ[b] τῆϲ φωνῆϲ
> ϲυμπάϲηϲ καὶ τὴν ἁρμονίαν, ὡϲ ἐὰν ἐπάιδοιμεν φθεγγόμενοι. ϲκέψαι δ᾽
> ὡϲ ἕκαϲτον αὐτῶν φυϲικῶϲ ἅμα καὶ οἰκείωϲ καθάπερ τὰ ὄργανα ἐϲχημάτιϲται
> καὶ ὠνόμαϲται· ἐπειδὴ καὶ ταῦτα ἔμελλε τῶι λόγωι ὥϲπερ ὄργανα ἔϲεϲθαι.
> ἑώρακε γὰρ καὶ τὴν μουϲικὴν οὕτω τὸ μέλοϲ καὶ τοὺϲ ῥυθμοὺϲ[c]
> ϲημαινομένην[d] καὶ πῆ μὲν ἀνιεῖϲαν, πῆ δ᾽ ἐπιτείνουϲαν, καὶ τὸ μὲν βαρύ,
> τὸ δ᾽ ὀξὺ ὀνομάζουϲαν. εἰ δέ ποτε ἐπάιδοιμεν, ἢ τέλεον ἐπιτείνοντεϲ ἢ
> πάλιν ἀνιέντεϲ, τοῦτο ϲκληρὸν καὶ μαλακὸν ἐκάλει. οὕτω[e] καὶ ὁ
> Ἀριϲτοφάνηϲ ϲημεῖα ἔθετο τῶι λόγωι πρῶτα ταῦτα, ἵν᾽ ἅμα ϲυλλαβῆϲ καὶ
> λέξεωϲ γενομένηϲ κανών τιϲ ἕποιτο καὶ ϲημεῖον ὀρθότητοϲ.

> [a]διάκριϲιν A: διαϲτολὴν B [b]μέλοϲ Villoison: μέλλον AB [c]ῥυθμοὺϲ vulgo:
> ἀριθμοὺϲ AB [d]ϲημαινομένην B: ϲημαινομένων A: ϲημαίνουϲαν susp. Nauck
> [e]οὕτω A: κατὰ τοῦτο B

> Aristophanes shaped time-value, accents and breathing marks in order
> to distinguish ambiguous expressions and observe the melodic outline
> of the voice, as if we were singing while speaking. Do examine now
> how naturally and properly each sign has been shaped and named,
> just like instruments, for they too should be like the instruments for

---

with n. 1 and more recently Nagy 2000, 15–6 n. 21 as regards the necessity to
"reassess Pfeiffer's notion of forgery." Suffice it here to say that the Par. gr. 2102
consists of an array of heterogeneous material variously drawn from Theodosius'
grammar (Par. gr. 2603) and scholia on Dionysius Thrax. In this codex Aristophanes
of Byzantium is erroneously depicted as πρῶτοϲ εὑρετήϲ of both the graphic systems of interpunction and accentuation (the exceedingly optimistic conclusions formulated by Laum 1928, 108–9 on Aristophanes' role in 'inventing' the punctuation
system have been reassessed by Pfeiffer 1968, 179–81 [esp. 181 with n. 1], now to
be supplemented with Dettori 2000, 166–7 n. 511; see also D'Alessio 2000, 239
n. 26). Slater 1986 does not include Chapter 20 of the Pseudo-Arcadius in his edition of Aristophanes' fragments.

[100] The standard edition of the Pseudo-Arcadius is still that of Nauck 1848, 12–8
(for the passage above quoted see id. 1848, 12 [186] ll. 4–19); cf. also Schmidt
1860, 211 ff. I have recorded in apparatus only the main variants. Lameere's edition (Lameere 1960, 91–2), providing the reader with a syncrisis of the two different
versions transmitted by Par. gr. 2102 (B) and Par. gr. 2603 (A), includes only the
section dealing with punctuation.

speech. [He] has seen in fact that the music too indicates [the trend of] melody and rhythm now by relaxing its tune now by tightening it and that music calls respectively the first tune 'low/grave' and the second one 'high/acute'. Whenever we sing either by tightening completely our voice or by relaxing it, [he] called that 'rough' and 'soft'. In the same way Aristophanes too first shaped these signs for speech in order to provide a normative rule and mark of correctness for syllables and words.

According to Pseudo-Arcadius, Aristophanes has invented the accentuation system for two reasons: first, that of distinguishing expressions otherwise ambiguous (πρὸς τὴν διάκρισιν τῆς ἀμφιβόλου λέξεως); secondly, that of observing the melodic outline of the word once embedded in the prosodic sandhi (πρὸς τὸ μέλος τῆς φωνῆς συμπάσης καὶ τὴν ἀρμονίαν).[101] It is just within this context (different tonal pitch of syllables within the same word) that the following reference to music must be understood. Music too points out (σημαινομένην) the melodic and rhythmic trend of the song (its ups and downs) now by tightening/increasing the tune now by loosening/diminishing it.

Up to here it is clear enough that the σημεῖα explicitly mentioned as Aristophanes' devices some lines below do refer to a precise physical (we could say 'graphic') entity: they are indeed the accentuation marks actually put above letters in the very act of writing. But is it proper to ascribe *a priori* also to the previous participle σημαινομένην such a concrete meaning (that is, a circumscribed allusion to the notational musical system)?[102]

In the case of an affirmative answer to this question, the natural consequence would be that in elaborating his accentuation system Aristophanes has not only been guided by a generic analogy with musical 'grammar' (by pointing out the ups and downs of the phonetic surface of words) but also drawn the very shape of his phonetic and

---

[101] For the documentary evidence provided by papyri as regards the matter of accentuation see Moore-Blunt 1978, arguing against Laum's skepticism on Alexandrian grammarians' consciousness of *Satzphonetik* (Laum 1928, 152, 159 and 161); cf. also Nagy 2000, 18. As to the scanty evidence testifying to a specific prosodic interest of Aristophanes see frr. 382, 400 Slater and Σ in O 606b and η 317 (quoted respectively at p. 187 and 198 of Slater's appendix).

[102] Cf. Pöhlmann 1960, 25 "Ihre Entstehung (i.e. that of the phonetic signs) wurde zwar durch die griechische Notenschrift angeregt" (in his later contributions on the issue Pöhlmann seems to be inclined to a more prudent evaluation of the present passage, see id. 1976, 1988 and 1991). In the same direction, at least apparently, see also Laum 1928, 120 with n. 1.

prosodic signs directly from the musical notation. Yet I believe that
the correct interpretation of the passage of Pseudo-Arcadius is another
and simpler one.

First of all, that the verb ἑώρακε does not necessarily convey a
literal reference to the domain of sight and, consequently, to the act
of reading a written text,[103] but that it loosely means the acknowledgment of a more generic intellectual awareness (note the use of
the perfect tense), is confirmed by the only other occurrence of ὁράω
in this chapter. Here again the verb conveys the bare notion of
recording mentally an empiric datum perceived by the auditory-
faculty.[104]

Secondly, the first οὕτω, that is, the one within the comparison
with μουϲική, has to be regarded as proleptic of the four following
cola πῆ μὲν ἀνιεῖϲαν, πῆ δ᾽ ἐπιτείνουϲαν, καὶ τὸ μὲν βαρύ, τὸ δ᾽ ὀξὺ
ὀνομάζουϲαν. In other words, what is meant here is that music makes
evident, and thus recognizable, its melodic and rhythmic outline now
by increasing the tune now by diminishing it. Both ἐπίταϲιϲ and
ἄνεϲιϲ are empiric data which can well be perceived by the mere
faculty of hearing without resorting to the aid of a musical score.
The fact that, on the basis of this mental diagram (the increasing
and diminishing tunes being analogically compared respectively with
a rising and falling line), Aristophanes has shaped by a process of
association the acute accent with a rising stroke and the grave accent
with a falling one, is a completely different matter which has to be
held carefully separate. Given these premises, I believe that this passage of Pseudo-Arcadius does not attest anything but Aristophanes'
generic use of musical analogies without any specific reference to the
music notational system.[105]

---

[103] The very act of seeing (and thus of reading in this case), together with an
attitude of reflection, is in contrast present in ϲκέψαι δ᾽ ὡϲ ἕκαϲτον αὐτῶν φυϲικῶϲ
ἅμα καὶ οἰκείωϲ καθάπερ τὰ ὄργανα ἐϲχημάτιϲται καὶ ὠνόμαϲται. Here the reference is actually not to musical symbols but to those critical ϲημεῖα (accents and
breathings) devised according to our source by Aristophanes. These signs will later
be described and graphically reproduced by Pseudo-Arcadius.

[104] Nauck 1848, 13 [187] ll. 14 ff. ἐπεὶ δὲ ἑώρα τὴν ἔξω τοῦ μέλουϲ λέξιν οὐ
κατὰ τὸ βαρὺ μόνον οὐδ᾽ ἐν τῶι ὀξεῖ καταμένουϲαν, ἀλλὰ καὶ τρίτου τινὸϲ δεομένην
τόνου, τούτου δὴ τοῦ περιϲπωμένου, πρότερον αὐτῆϲ τῆϲ φωνῆϲ τὴν δύναμιν ἐϲκοπεῖτο.

[105] This aspect does not, however, escape Fleming's attention: see his remark that
"in using the analogy of musical instruments, Aristophanes saw that music signified
both tune (*melos*) and rhythms (*rhythmoi*) and referred to that which was relaxed as
'low' and to that which was stretched tight as 'high'" (Fleming 1999, 26).

A further element supporting this conclusion is the fact that the other semantic overlaps we can detect in Pseudo-Arcadius between the sphere of music and that of prosody/accentuation put themselves on a level which does not go beyond that of a barely functional analogy.[106] Especially telling from this perspective is the comparison drawn between the mechanical device invented for opening and closing the ever increasing numbers of holes of the aulos, a mechanism consisting of a hook-shaped projection from the surface of the band (κέρατα or βόμβυκες),[107] and the rounded graphic shape (ὥσπερ κέρατα: like hooks) assigned to the breathing marks by Aristophanes. The text as edited by Nauck is the following:[108]

ἀλλ᾽ ἑκάστωι πνεύματι οὐκ ἀτέχνως οὐδ᾽ ἀμούσως τὰ σημεῖα ὅλα ἐπέθετο· καθάπερ οἱ τοῖς αὐλοῖς τὰ τρήματα εὑράμενοι ἐπιφράττειν αὐτὰ καὶ ὑπανοίγειν ὁπότε βούλοιντο, κέρασί τισιν ἢ βόμβυξιν ὑφολμίοις (Nauck: ὑφόρκιος B: ὑφολκίοις A) ἐπετεχνάσαντο, ἄνω τε καὶ κάτω καὶ ἔνδον τε καὶ ἔξω στρέφοντες ταῦτα, οὑτωσὶ κἀκεῖνος ὥσπερ κέρατα τὰ σημεῖα ἐποιήσατο τῶι πνεύματι, ἕν τι σχῆμα ἑκατέρωι σημηνάμενος, τοῦτο δὴ τὸ ἓν ὥσπερ αὐλῶι ἐοικός, ὅπερ ἔνδον καὶ ἔξω στρέφων ἐπιφράττειν τε καὶ ὑπανοίγειν τὸ πνεῦμα ἐδίδαξεν.

But [Aristophanes] ascribed a sign to each breathing and did it competently and properly. Just as those who, having discovered the holes on the auloi, devised a way to close and open the holes whenever they wish by means of some kerata or bombykes applied on the surface of the band by turning them up and down, inwards and outwards, in the same way [Aristophanes] too shaped the signs for breathing like kerata, by assigning one and only shape to each of them. This one indeed seemed like the aulos: by turning it inwards or outwards he instructed [the reader] to stop or open the breath.

---

[106] Cf. Nauck 1848, 13 [187] ll. 2–3 and [188] ll. 12–22 (see below).

[107] For the extant archaeological and literary evidence on this sophisticated kind of aulos provided with rotating collars see West *AGM*, 87, Landels 1999, 36–7 and Mathiesen 1999, 191–2. I add here only two minor observations. West's suggestion that the bombykes mentioned by Plut. *Mor.* 713a may refer to this technical device (id. *AGM*, 87 n. 30) seems to be supported by the hendiadys βόμβυξι καὶ πολυχορδίαις. In this context πολυχορδίαι refers to the wide harmonic range of the instrument (cf. Frazier-Sirinelli 1996, 225 n. 206 and Landels 1999, 38) and we know that one of the effects produced by this technical innovation ascribed to Pronomos, at least according to Paus. 9. 12. 5 and Athen. 14. 631e, consisted precisely of the aulos' increased tonal range. Finally, I do not believe that τὰ κέρατα of [Arist.] *De audib.* 801b 9–10, quoted by Reinach 1919, 307 n. 11, is to be referred to the same mechanism mentioned by Pseudo-Arcadius. Flashar 1972, 244 has rightly pointed out that in the pseudo-Aristotelian passage we are most likely dealing with some kind of resonance box (cf. also Barker *GMW* II, 102 and 104 n. 23).

[108] Nauck 1848, 13 [188] ll. 12–22.

Also in this passage it is evident that this μετατύπωϲιϲ, supposing that
it really happened in this way, plays here a merely descriptive role.

It is worth taking into account here also another piece of evidence
concerning Aristophanes' activity, this time no longer his pioneering
role in the matter of accentuation but his work as κωλιϲτήϲ. I refer
to the well-known scholia to Pind. *Ol.* 2. 48c and f (= 1. 73 Drachm.),[109]
both of which have occasionally been quoted by scholars in order
to support the Alexandrian philologists' use of musical scores and
consequently the high degree of professional musical skill that such
an activity would have entailed.[110] This is the text:

> Σ to Pind. *Ol.* 2. 48c: φιλέοντι δὲ Μοῖϲαι]: τὸ κῶλον τοῦτο ἀθετεῖ
> Ἀριϲτοφάνηϲ· περιττεύειν γὰρ αὐτό φηϲι πρὸ <τὰϲ> ἀντιϲτρόφουϲ.[111]

Aristophanes athetizes this colon, for he says that it is redundant in
comparison to the antistrophes.

> Σ to Pind. *Ol.* 2. 48f: φιλέοντι δὲ Μοῖϲαι]: περιϲϲόν ἐϲτι κῶλον ὡϲ πρὸϲ
> τὴν ἀντίϲτροφον· ὅθεν καὶ ὀβελίϲκοϲ αὐτῶι παράκειται. πᾶϲαι γάρ εἰϲι
> δεκατεϲϲάρων [ὁμοῦ] κώλων, αὕτη δὲ μόνη δεκαπέντε εὑρίϲκεται ἔχουϲα.

This colon is redundant in comparison to the antistrophe: hence an
obeliskos has been put beside it. All the strophes consist of fourteen
cola, whereas this strophe turns out to be the only one consisting of
fifteen cola.

According to these scholia, Aristophanes is credited with having
athetized by means of putting an ὄβελοϲ beside the colon of *Ol.* 2.
27a φιλέοντι δὲ Μοῖϲαι inasmuch as it does not observe proper responsion to the other strophes of the second Olympian ode.[112] Quite
apart from the vexed question of the exact role played by Aristophanes
in the 'invention'[113] of colometry, inferring from both these passages

---

[109] Both passages are joined by Slater 1986 under the fragment 380 A.
[110] See Lasserre 1959, 346–7 and more recently Tessier 1995, 24–5 with n. 39.
[111] Slater's textual arrangement of these passages (Slater 1986, 145) differs slightly
from that of Drachmann: as regards the first scholium Slater omits the transmitted
αὐτό and does not accept Schroeder's supplement <τὰϲ>.
[112] See Pfeiffer 1968, 187 with n. 3 on the issue. The authoritative value of
Aristophanes' remark (i.e. the interpolated nature of φιλέοντι δὲ Μοῖϲαι) seems to
be supported by the fact that the metrical scholia omit this colon, see Slater 1986,
145 and Marino 1999b, *ad loc.*
[113] For a balanced judgment of the ancient sources on the issue see D'Alessio
1997, 55–6: "the evidence does not necessarily imply that Aristophanes was the *first*

that Aristophanes positively resorted to texts provided with musical notation seems to go a step too far. If we keep in mind that already in the fourth century BC Pindar's odes were usually no longer performed, at least chorally, but were instead read,[114] the empirical remark of the anonymous scholiast (πᾶcαι γάρ εἰcι δεκατεccάρων [ὁμοῦ] κώλων, αὕτη δὲ μόνη δεκαπέντε εὑρίcκεται ἔχουcα), although likely autoschediastic, is none the less true. The recognition of the interpolated nature of the colon 27a φιλέοντι δὲ Μοῖcαι (which was probably aided by the coincidence of colon end with word end) may well have been derived from listing the cola of the other strophes.

Lasserre's claim that "qu'il (that is, Aristophanes) ait décelé en *Ol.* II. 48a un κῶλον interpolé prouve simplement qu'il estimait inviolables les règles de la *responsio* strophique, et non qu'il aurait eu sous les yeux un texte écrit comme de la prose et sans notation mélodique"[115] must be correctly contextualized. Whereas Lasserre's provocative dismissal of Irigoin's faith in Aristophanes as "vraiment l'inventeur, le πρῶτοc εὑρετήc" of colometry[116] is now shared by an increasing number of scholars,[117] the last part of his statement ("et sans notation mélodique") should not be equally accepted. In fact Lasserre quotes

---

one to elaborate a colometric division for the lyric poets, but suggests that his work was particularly influential. Since all our papyri and later manuscripts seem to derive from a standard colometry, [. . .], they must reflect the colometry of a single authoritative edition. It is reasonable to think that it was the one by Aristophanes." Most convincing is especially D'Alessio's criticism (id. 1997, 52 n. 172 and 55 n. 188) of the exceeding skepticism displayed by Slater 1986, 145–6, according to whom Aristophanes' work would have been limited to a mere "cataloguing."

[114] See Irigoin 1952, 19–21 and id. 1958, 18.

[115] Lasserre 1959, 347.

[116] Irigoin 1958, 18.

[117] Cf. above n. 113 and Tessier 1995, 15–6, especially as regards the evidence provided by P.Lille 76 (Stesichorus) and P.Mil.Vogl. 17 (third/second century BC: fragments of the aeolic lyric already divided into cola, with paragraphos marking strophe's end and coronis at the end of the whole composition). The parallelism, in terms of colometric layout, drawn by Malnati 1992, 322–3 between P.Mil.Vogl. 17 and PSI XIII 1300 (third/second century BC: Sapph. 2 V), accepted also by Tessier, is incorrect. In the case of the Florentine ostrakon we have to keep in mind that the writer was most likely a schoolchild, writing thus from dictation (cf. Nicosia 1976, 98–9 n. 58). The unwritten space at the end of each Sapphic strophe has not therefore to be intended as an editorial criterion but as the pupil's effective recording of the performative pause of the teacher reading aloud. Thus the idiosyncratic nature of the school exercise displayed by PSI XIII 1300 does not allow us to establish a close resemblance, at least in terms of editorial technique, between that and P.Mil.Vogl.17.

as a decisive example the alleged colometric layout of P.Vind. G 2315 (= Eur. *Or.* 338–44), a layout which we can now confidently assess to be wrong.[118]

All in all, neither Pseudo-Arcadius not the scholia to Pind. *Ol.* 2. 48c and f (= 1. 73 Drachm.) can be assumed to be positive evidence for a systematic use by Alexandrian philologists of scores with musical notation.

I.4 *Sending a song: what texts cannot convey. Some observations on the scholium to Pind.* Pyth. *2. 6b (= 2. 33 Drachm.)*

As we have already seen, Fleming-Kopff's argument relies on the assumption of the existence of a close osmosis between textual and musical tradition in terms of transmission and reception, an osmosis of course to be carried back already to an early stage. In other words, the alleged familiarity with lyric texts carrying musical notation displayed by Alexandrian philologists and the closely related possibility that the Lycurgan *Staatsexemplar* might preserve the original music of fifth-century Attic tragedy[119] would argue for a long-standing and well-rooted practice of committing to writing not only the poetic text but also the musical phrases accompanying the lyrics.[120]

---

[118] For a detailed discussion of the layout of P.Vind. G 2315 see II.1.1.

[119] Fleming-Kopff 1992, 763 (followed by Tessier 1995, 21 with n. 30) and Fleming 1999, 23–5; *contra* Parker 2001, 36–7. A slightly different version of these dynamics had already been advanced by Wartelle 1971, 154–5, who nevertheless argued for a clear divergence of both traditions (that is, the performative one and the scholarly tradition represented by mere *Lesetexte*) in a post-Lycurgan period.

[120] It is not my purpose to treat here exhaustively the much-contested issue of the development and diffusion of the musical notational system. Modern scholars broadly disagree on this topic, the two alternative dates oscillating between the second half and the end of the fifth century BC (respectively for the instrumental and vocal notation) and the late fourth century BC, cf. e.g. West *AGM*, 269–73 and Comotti 1991², 9. For Pöhlmann's reiterated attempts (id. 1960, 10–11 and 1976, 61–9) to identify with scores the book-rolls depicted in some fifth-century vase-paintings portraying musical performances (most likely mere *libretti*), see *contra* Bélis 1988, 34–5, West *AGM*, 263–4 n. 23 and Parker 2001, 36 n. 19 (a collection of the main iconographic material on reading and singing scenes can be found in Catenacci 1999, 60–1 [appendix II]). As to the existence, already in the fifth century BC, of a rough solfège system allegedly recorded on an early fifth-century BC clay *epinetron* as advocated by Bélis 1984 and 1988, see now Pöhlmann-West *DAGM*, 8. This, of course, is not to deny that some kind of broadly 'musical' inscriptions did exist at quite an early date (see Veleni 2002): see Yatromanolakis' right observation on the Munich *kalathos-psykter* (inv. 2416) portraying the 'vowels' "o o o o o" coming out from Alcaeus' mouth, vowels which presumably are intended to represent "a melodic

It is within this general picture that Fleming[121] quotes the scholium to Pind. *Pyth*. 2. 6b (= 2. 33 Drachm.) as evidence testifying to the diffusion and circulation of musical scores already in the seventies of the fifth century BC.[122] The text of the scholium as edited by Drachmann is the following:

φέρων μέλος ἔρχομαι· οὐκ αὐτὸς ὁ Πίνδαρος ἥκων εἰς τὰς Cυρακούcας ταῦτά φηcιν· οὐ γὰρ ἀφῖκται πρὸς τὸν Ἱέρωνα, ἀλλ' ἡ ᾠδὴ ἀποcτολική· ἤτοι οὖν ἐκ τοῦ διακομίcαντος τὴν ᾠδὴν πρὸς τὸν τύραννόν ἐcτιν ὁ λόγος ἢ ἐκ τοῦ χοροῦ· διὰ γὰρ χοροῦ ἔπεμπε τοὺς ἐπινίκους.

I come bearing this song: we are not to suppose that these words are delivered by Pindar coming himself to Syracuse: in fact he did not reach Hieron but the ode had been sent. Therefore these words are spoken either by the person who carried the ode to the tyrant or by the chorus: it is in fact by means of a chorus that Pindar used to send epinicians.

The several references to the poet's absence[123] and to the 'shipping' of the ode that we can find scattered in the second Pythian ode[124] lead the anonymous scholiast to advance a double hypothesis on the

---

line of his song, however minimalist or *vocalise*-like this string of sounds may now appear" (Yatromanolakis 2005, 21). More generally, on the "visual performability of poetry" on vases see Yatromanolakis 2001, 165–6.

[121] Fleming 1999, 20–1.

[122] In the same direction see already Wilamowitz 1900, 48, Irigoin 1952, 5–8 and Neubecker 1977, 118. Irigoin in particular suggests that Pindar would have given to the chorodidaskalos a copy of the ode provided with musical notation of just the first triad, but eventually he himself is forced to admit that "aucun texte antique ne fait allusion à ces exemplaires" (ibid. 8 n. 1). More recently Loscalzo 2003, 98 has tentatively suggested that also the copy of the ode provided for the family members of the addressee must have included musical notation. The irrelevance of the Pindaric scholium to *Pyth*. 2. 6b as positive evidence for such an early spreading of the notational system has been argued by Herington 1985, 43–5 with nn. 5 and 10, 190, Anderson 1994, 96 n. 20 and Parker 2001, 36–7; Dearden 1999, 227 with n. 20 leaves the question open. For the most likely dating of the second Pythian ode to 470 BC (probably Hieron's first chariot victory at Delphi), see Cingano 1998², 43–7.

[123] Recently Hubbard 2004, 89–90 has argued for Pindar being indeed aboard the ship along with "his cargo of praise." Against the risks of such a literal interpretation see already Ferrari 2000, 233.

[124] The logical time of sending and receiving appears in a reversed order within the narrative textual frame of the ode: see 3–4 ὕμμιν τόδε τᾶν λιπαρᾶν ἀπὸ Θηβᾶν φέρων| μέλος ἔρχομαι ἀγγελίαν τετραορίας ἐλελίχθονος and 67–8 χαῖρε· τόδε μὲν κατὰ Φοίνιccαν ἐμπολάν| μέλος ὑπὲρ πολιᾶς ἁλὸς πέμπεται. For the overlap of different temporal levels in Pindar's second Pythian ode see Ferrari 2000, 232–7.

conveyance of the ᾠδὴ ἀποϲτολική: either the song has been carried to Syracuse by the chorus[125] or we have to suppose the presence of a personal emissary[126] entrusted by Pindar (3 τᾶν λιπαρᾶν ἀπὸ Θηβᾶν) with performing monodically the ode at Hieron's court, like Nicasippus in *Isthm.* 2. 47–8.[127] In both cases we have still to face the same problem: which mode of transmission, which inner dynamics in terms of *Textgeschichte* are entailed by an expression like ᾠδὴ ἀποϲτολική? Are we entitled to suppose some kind of written evidence, and if so which kind of writing? Or should we see in the emphasis put on the 'shipping' and 'receiving' of the song just a loose reference to the immediacy of the oral performance, which has taken place at Syracuse rather than at Delphi? Scanty as the evidence we possess may be, and even if our discussion must necessarily remain hypothetical, it may nevertheless be useful to try to distinguish the different degrees of likelihood that such hypotheses entail.

To begin with, it is worth noticing the insistent process of reification which the song itself is repeatedly undergoing throughout the whole ode: 3–4 ὕμμιν τόδε τᾶν λιπαρᾶν ἀπὸ Θηβᾶν φέρων| μέλος ἔρχομαι ἀγγελίαν τετραορίας ἐλελίχθονος, 67–8 τόδε μὲν κατὰ Φοίνιϲϲαν ἐμπολάν| μέλος ὑπὲρ πολιᾶς ἁλὸς πέμπεται, 70 ἄθρηϲον (referring to a second 'shipped' song, probably to be performed after the present epinician and strictly related to it, that is, the Καϲτόρειον).[128] The progressive

---

[125] This hypothesis would nevertheless leave unexplained the unusual absence of any reference to the place of victory: see Ferrari 2000, 232 n. 59.

[126] The likely autoschediastic origin of the guess formulated by the scholiast (cf. 4 ἀγγελίαν) does not compromise its potential validity.

[127] Pind. *Isthm.* 2. 47–8 ταῦτα, Νικάϲιππ', ἀπόνειμον, ὅταν| ξεῖνον ἐμὸν ἠθαῖον ἔλθηιϲ. For a monodic performance of the second Pythian and Isthmian odes see Gentili 1998², liv–lv and Ferrari 2000, 232 with n. 60. The third occurrence of a go-between emissary of the poet within the Pindaric odes is to be found in the χοροδιδάϲκαλος Aineas in *Ol.* 6. 87–91 (in this case the ode is performed chorally). For a balanced assessment of the much-discussed issue of the performance of Pindaric epinicians see D'Alessio 1994, 117 n. 2. As to the most recent (and excitingly thought-provoking) installments in this debate see Hubbard 2004 (esp. 88 ff.) and Currie 2004.

[128] See Cingano 1998², 391–2. The participles θέλων (69) and ἀντόμενος (71) confirm the pre-eminently metaphorical value conveyed in this passage by the verb ἀθρέω, aiming at raising a well-disposed attitude in the addressee towards the poet's musical gift, cf. in this sense also Bacch. *Ep.* 5. 8 δεῦρ' <ἄγ'> ἄθρηϲον νόωι. Of course this is not tantamount to saying that the primary sense of ἄθρηϲον, that is, its reference to the physical domain of the sight, has to be entirely effaced: the idea of seeing a written text as a tangible and exchangeable value may certainly be present here.

objectification of the song has not escaped the scholiast's attention: the use of the participle διακομίϲαντοϲ makes the ode, one more time, a material object to be carried and performed. Therefore, the gift referred to by the authorial voice does not seem to be only the very performance of the song at Hieron's court (a performance strictly circumscribed in space and time) but does suppose some kind of written evidence. Yet what has been committed to writing? The song's words, the underlying music, or both of them?[129] If we rely only on the information provided within the ode, it is difficult to arrive at an unambiguous answer to this question. Nevertheless, on

---

[129] Bélis has repeatedly argued for the shipping of the musical score together with the text, see Bélis 1988, 30, 38 n. 7 and ead. 1999, 158–9. Bélis 1999, 274 n. 3 quotes also *Nem.* 5. 1–3 (οὐκ ἀνδριαντοποιόϲ εἰμ', ὥϲτ' ἐλινύϲοντα ἐργάζεϲθαι ἀγάλματ' ἐπ' αὐτᾶϲ βαθμίδοϲ| ἑϲταότ'· ἀλλ' ἐπὶ πάϲαϲ ὁλκάδοϲ ἔν τ' ἀκάτωι, γλυκεῖ' ἀοιδά,| ϲτεῖχ' ἀπ' Αἰγίναϲ διαγγέλλοιϲ', ὅτι κτλ.) as positive evidence for the circulation of musical scores in the 80s of the fifth century BC. Yet, also in this case the risk of an overliteral interpretation has to be avoided. Pfeijffer 1999, 101–2 has correctly pointed out that "Pindar does not specify exactly how he imagines his song to circulate" inasmuch as what prevails in the rhetoric of praise is the general will of emphasizing the song's faculty of going beyond the territorial boundaries and spreading the winner's fame, whose range amounts to that of the Aeginetan fleet (see also *Ol.* 9. 21–6, where we again find the image of the ship's speed as a metaphor for the immediate spreading of the song over countries). Furthermore, as already suggested by Pfeijffer 1999, 102, in the fifth Nemean ode we find the hyperbolic formulation ἐπὶ πάϲαϲ ὁλκάδοϲ, which implies "a much less regulated scenario." What is at stake here is likely some kind of an "unregulated oral transmission," conveyed by the image of the song as remembered and mentally recorded by foreign spectators; see in this direction also Gerber's observation (id. 2005, 16) on the risks of Loscalzo's too literal interpretation of *Nem.* 6. 32 ἴδια ναυϲτολέοντεϲ ἐπικώμια (Loscalzo 2003, 108–9: the Bassidai, being rich tradesmen and sea-traffickers, would have materially "transported" Pindar's ode along with other cargo). Finally, Bélis 1988, 30 adduces as evidence for the diffusion of musical scores, although at a later stage, the fact that "durante una campagna Alessandro Magno si fece inviare le ultime 'novità' musicali" (Bélis does not quote the precise source of the passage). This claim would not be a problem in terms of chronological development, yet if the passage referred to by Bélis is Plut. *Alex.* 8. 3 (the only one to my knowledge which is compatible with Bélis' statement cited above), I do not believe that this text does tell us anything about the circulation of musical scores. The episode told by Plutarch is the following: Alexander the Great, by nature fond of literature and reading (φιλόλογοϲ καὶ φιλαναγνώϲτηϲ) to the point of sleeping with a copy of the *Iliad* under his pillow (the so-called copy ἐκ τοῦ νάρθηκοϲ, revised by Aristotle), while in the wild inner regions of Asia where he could not find books to read (τῶν δ' ἄλλων βιβλίων οὐκ εὐπορῶν), ordered Harpalus to send him τάϲ τε Φιλίϲτου βίβλουϲ καὶ τῶν Εὐριπίδου καὶ Σοφοκλέουϲ καὶ Αἰϲχύλου τραγωιδιῶν ϲυχνάϲ, καὶ Τελέϲτου καὶ Φιλοξένου διθυράμβουϲ. The emphasis put on Alexander's fondness for reading and the subsequent mention of the *Iliad*, of Philistus' historical work and of Euripides and Sophocles' tragedies strongly suggest that we are dealing with mere *Lesetexte* also in the case of Telestes and Philoxenus' dithyrambic poetry.

the basis of some literary and iconographic parallels, we can at least sketch some possible alternative scenario to that outlined by Fleming.

First, the presence at l. 69 of inner musical stage directions referring to a very precise kind of melody (τὸ Καστόρειον) and harmony (ἐν Αἰολίδεσσι χορδαῖς)[130] to be exploited in the performance of the 'other' ᾠδὴ ἀποστολική inserted within the second Pythian ode does not necessarily entail that ἄθρησον has to be understood as alluding to the actual reading of a score. On the contrary, this very mention of a certain musical mode and harmony could represent for the would-be performer a more than adequate instruction on which to graft "something more like improvisation within a set of rules."[131] In this case, what needed to be learned by heart would be just the textual frame, that is, the words of the song. A telling parallel is provided by the closing lines of *Isthm*. 2. 47–8.[132] Here the verb ἀπόνειμον, as glossed by the scholium to *Isthm*. 2. 68 (= 3. 222 Drachm.), refers metaphorically to the domain of reading[133] (and thus to that of learning by heart and 'sharing' the song[134]) and the object (ταῦτα) of such a performative utterance is again just the textual content of the ode itself that has already been performed. Another clue pointing towards the same direction (that is, rejection of the musical score as the only interpretative hypothesis to be accepted) is the likely monodic performance of the second Pythian ode itself.[135] In the case of a solo performance, the person to be directly instructed by the poet is just one singer (and no longer the sophisticated *ensemble* of the chorus),

---

[130] Given the emphasis put on the performative aspect of the song (70–1 ἑπτακτύπου] φόρμιγγος), it seems more reasonable to see in Αἰολίδεσσι χορδαῖς a reference to the Aeolic mode rather than to a specific metrical frame, see also *Ol*. 1. 102 and *Nem*. 3. 79. Cf. Most 1985, 100 n. 26, Barker *GMW* I, 55 n. 3, West *AGM*, 183 n. 90, 347 nn. 86–7 and Anderson 1994, 96–7.

[131] Parker 2001, 36.

[132] See n. 127.

[133] For ἀπονέμω meaning "to read," also on the basis of the transmitted text of Soph. 144. 2 Radt, see Catenacci 1999, 49–61. Following Radt, Svenbro 1991, 540 accepts Madvig's deletion of the transmitted ἀπόνειμον (Madvig 1846, 671) and replaces it with Bergk's emendation νέμ(ε). Yet an up-to-date, balanced defence of the transmitted reading ἀπόνειμον in the Sophoclean fragment, focusing above all on the link with the Pindaric text as established by the scholium to *Isthm*. 2. 68, can be now found in Ferrari 2000, 232 n. 60.

[134] See Svenbro's remark (id. 1991, 540) according to which "le sens fondamental de νέμειν est 'distribuer'. La lecture est donc envisagée comme une 'distribution orale', dont le lecteur est l'instrument."

[135] See n. 127.

and there is no reason to suppose that this teaching took place in any way other than orally, the performer being taught directly by Pindar himself without the need to resort to some written musical score.[136] From this perspective the evidence offered by Plut. *Mor.* 46b is even more telling:

Εὐριπίδης μὲν οὖν ὁ ποιητής, ὡς ὑπολέγοντος αὐτοῦ τοῖς χορευταῖς ᾠδήν τινα πεποιημένην ἐφ᾽ ἁρμονίας εἷς ἐγέλαςεν, "εἰ μή τις ἦς ἀναίςθητος" εἶπε "καὶ ἀμαθής, οὐκ ἂν ἐγέλας ἐμοῦ μιξολυδιςτὶ ᾄδοντος".

When Euripides the poet was himself suggesting to the choreuts how to perform a song composed in the enharmonic scale, since one of them happened to laugh, Euripides said "if you were not such a stupid and ignorant man, you would have not laughed while I was singing in the Mixolydian tune."

Although the correct meaning of the expression ὑπολέγοντος [. . .] ᾠδήν τινα πεποιημένην ἐφ᾽ ἁρμονίας and the very reason it provoked the laugh of the choreut go on being a matter of debate,[137] what

---

[136] The same oral process of learning can be easily supposed also for the chorodidaskalos Aineas in the sixth Olympian ode.

[137] See Hillyard 1981, 218–20: the choreut's ἀμαθία is likely to consist of his misunderstanding the true threnodic nature of the Mixolydian tone (cf. e.g. Plat. *Resp.* 398e, Arist. *Pol.* 1340b 1) and not of his deliberately "snickering at Euripides' singing in a mode associated with the New Music," as most recently argued by Marshall 2004, 27. I do not agree, however, with Hillyard in separating ἐφ᾽ ἁρμονίας from ᾠδὴν [. . .] πεποιημένην and linking it consequently to the remote ὑπολέγοντος. Pointing out that the song was 'composed in the enharmonic scale' (cf. the similar expression ἐφ᾽ ἁρμονίας ᾄδειν in P.Hibeh 13, col. II l. 21, already quoted by Crönert 1909, 508; more recently also Lapini 2003, 176 translates ἐφ᾽ ἁρμονίας ᾄδειν as "cantare nell'enarmonico") might perhaps sound pleonastic, if not preposterous, to a fifth-century BC listener, the enharmonic scale being then the established one, but not to a second-century AD reader, Plutarch's obvious addressee. As to the difficulty of referring ὑπολέγοντος to singing (Hillyard 1981, 219: "the compound cannot itself mean 'sing', and yet Euripides was singing [46b 3]"), it may be worth remembering Koller's remark warning against a strictly literal interpretation of Dion. Hal. *De comp. verb.* 11. 19 Auj.-Leb. ὡς ἐξ ἄλλων τε πολλῶν δῆλον καὶ μάλιςτα τῶν Εὐριπίδου μελῶν ἃ πεποίηκεν τὴν Ἠλέκτραν λέγουςαν ἐν Ὀρέςτηι πρὸς τὸν χορόν κτλ. (Koller 1956, 25 n. 1). The participle λέγουςαν does not mean that in the *Orestes'* parodos Electra is speaking and not actually singing, inasmuch as λέγουςαν conveys here just "eine inhaltliche Bestimmung," without any further information "über seine phonetische Aktualisierung im Sprechvorgang." Similarly, in the Plutarchan passage ὑπολέγω seems to be referring to Euripides' prompter-like role (i.e. suggesting the words of the song) as well as to his function of musical teacher (i.e. accompanist). For the verbal prefix ὑπο- meaning musical accompaniment when attached to verbs related to musical performances, see e.g. Alcm. 37b *PMGF* ἁμὶν δ᾽ ὑπαυληςεῖ μέλος, Luc. *De salt.* 30 ἄλλους αὐτοῖς ὑπᾴδειν,

rests nevertheless on solid ground is the fact that in the second half of the fifth century BC a tragic chorus was still orally instructed by the poet-composer without resorting to a musical score (Euripides himself is portrayed as singing in front of the chorus members who had to imitate him, cf. ἐμοῦ μιξολυδιϲτὶ ἄιδοντοϲ).[138]

Furthermore, vase-paintings portraying school-scenes to be dated to the end of the sixth and the beginning of the fifth century BC[139] clearly show that the practice of teaching singing and playing, from the amateur level up to a professional one, was aural and mimetic:[140] pupils had to imitate their teacher's gestures and technique as faithfully as possible. To the iconographic evidence one should add also later literary texts apparently testifying to the relative continuity and stability of the ancient educational system in its various degrees of specialization.[141] From this perspective, one of the most telling passages about the actual practice underlying elementary music teaching (cf. the mention of the γραμματοδιδάϲκαλοϲ[142]) is Plut. *Mor.* 790e 7– f 2:

Ar. *Ra.* 366 κυκλίοιϲι χοροῖϲιν ὑπάιδων (cf. Van Leeuwen 1968², 67 "succinens, modo dans" and Dover 1993, 242) and the expression ὑπὸ τὴν ὠιδήν in [Plut.] *De mus.* 1141b (see West *AGM*, 206 n. 41). Cf. also Phot. *Lex.* s.v. ὑποδιδάϲκαλοϲ, glossed as ὁ τῶι χορῶι καταλέγων (cf. Sifakis 1967, 119) and the term ὑποτραγωιδεῖν in a third century AD inscription from Dura Europos, cf. M. Bonaria in *RE* Suppl. X (1965) 949 no. 16 (i) and Bosnakis 2004, 103.

[138] See West *AGM*, 270: "Poet-composers taught choruses by singing to them. By the fifth century it may be that *copies of the words* were provided to assist the learning process, but as for the melodies, much the easiest way to pick them up was aurally and few would have been helped by note-symbols" (my italics). West's words perfectly pinpoint the problem: what is at stake here is not whether professional musicians of the early fifth century BC could have resorted to musical notation, but the distinction between professional practice and broader transmission; cf. also Herington 1985, 24–5 and Wilson 2002, 64 n. 79, id. 2005, 191.

[139] Cf. e.g. Phinthias' *hydria*, ca. 500 BC: lesson in lyre-playing (München, Staatliche Antikensammlung, no. inv. 2421); Attic red-figure *skyphos* of Pistoxenos, 470 BC: Iphicles being taught to play the lyre by Linus (Schwerin, Landesmuseum, no. inv. 708); Attic red-figure *skyphos* of Douris, ca. 480 BC: lesson of playing the aulos and the lyre (Berlin, Staatliche Museen, no. inv. F 2285).

[140] Cf. Marrou 1965⁶, 207–8 and Herington 1985, 43–5. See partially in this direction also Bélis 1988, 34.

[141] Marrou 1965⁶, 553 n. 7 argues for a predominantly oral tradition of teaching music also in post-classical times. For the debate on the terms ῥυθμογραφία and μελογραφία found in late-Hellenistic school inscriptions (*ITeos* 82 [= Michel no. 913] and *IMagn* 107 [= *SIG*³ 960]) see West *AGM*, 271–2 with n. 49.

[142] For the functions and role of the γραμματοδιδάϲκαλοϲ within the Hellenistic educational system see Cribiore 1996, 13 ff.

ὡς γὰρ οἱ γράμματα καὶ μουςικὴν διδάςκοντες αὐτοὶ προανακρούονται
καὶ προαναγινώςκουςιν ὑφηγούμενοι τοῖς μανθάνουςιν, οὕτως ὁ πολιτικὸς
οὐ λέγων μόνον οὐδ᾽ ὑπαγορεύων ἔξωθεν, ἀλλὰ πράττων τὰ κοινὰ καὶ
διοικῶν ἐπευθύνει τὸν νέον, ἔργοις ἅμα καὶ λόγοις πλαττόμενον ἐμψύχως
καὶ καταςχηματιζόμενον.

For just as those who teach writing and music themselves first play
the music or read, leading the way for their pupils, so the politician,
not only by speaking or offering suggestions from outside, but by taking part actively in the administration of public affairs, guides the
young man who is vividly formed and modelled by his words and
actions.

In this passage Plutarch, by drawing a precise parallel between the
school-teacher (διδάςκαλος) and the politician (πολιτικός), underlines
in both cases the didactic, maieutic relevance of a practical example to be followed. The task of the γραμματοδιδάςκαλος (who taught
the very beginning of education, that is, reading and writing) as well
as that of the teacher of instrumental music (κρουματοποιός) consists
in orienting the pupil by himself showing first what the pupil should
then reproduce in his turn.[143]

Summing up, an interlocking analysis of the different documentary evidence that we have at our disposal, scanty as it may be, does
not allow us to trace back already to the beginning of the fifth century BC any positive evidence supporting a well-rooted symbiosis
between textual and musical tradition in terms of channels of transmission and reception.[144] Restricted circles of professional musicians

---

[143] See e.g. also Ael. *V.H.* 3. 32 where the cithara teacher himself points out to
Alexander the Great which string of the kithara he should pluck. For professional
teaching see Plut. *Demetr.* 1. 6 (the teachers this time being the Theban Ismenias
and Antigenidas, the acclaimed *virtuosi* of the auletiké in the fifth/fourth century
BC).

[144] Bélis 1999, 163 suggests that we are dealing with the "vol sordide ou l'usurpa-
tion pure et simple d'une partition" also in the case of the story about Diagoras
of Melos reported by Suda s.v. Διαγόρας (δ 523), the only source that specifies the
nature of the injury against Diagoras (a case of literary plagiarism), which apparently turned out to be the cause of his atheism. The date of the episode remains
uncertain but the mischief is probably to be dated prior to 423 BC, granted that
Diagoras' activity is to be placed between 484–1 or 468/7 and 415/4 BC, cf. Janko
1997, 87 with n. 228. Yet, according to the words of Suda's entry, all that can be
said with any confidence about this anecdote is that we are told about a literary
theft (cf. παιᾶνα ἀφελόμενος [. . .] ἐξωμόςατο μὴ κεκλοφέναι τοῦτον), without being
able to specify whether a musical score was involved or not (the thief could have
stolen just the written text containing the words of the paean).

could well have occasionally resorted to musical scores by that time, but this is quite different from positing a whole strand of musical transmission closely associated with the textual one.

Similarly, looking for positive evidence to support this alleged traditional osmosis in later epigraphic documentation turns out to be equally unproductive. As Bélis has already shown,[145] the strongly standardized features underlying the language of the inscriptions do not allow us to assign to γράφειν and similar verbal formations, when referring to musicians and lyric poets, anything more than the loose, generic meaning of composing; we cannot infer from the use of this verb any reference to writing down musical phrases and so on.[146]

From this perspective, the only ambiguous evidence among the passages quoted by Bélis might be the Suda entry s.v. Ἀντιγενίδης (α 2657), according to which Antigenidas, the famous Theban auletes active from about 400 to about 370 BC, composed some unspecified 'airs' (μέλη). This is the text of the entry:

Ἀντιγενίδης Cατύρου Θηβαῖος, μουϲικὸς, αὐλωιδὸς Φιλοξένου. οὗτος ὑποδήμαϲι Μιληϲίοιϲ πρῶτος ἐχρήϲατο καὶ κροκωτὸν ἐν τῶι Κωμαϲτῆι περιεβάλλετο ἱμάτιον. ἔγραψε μέλη.

---

[145] Bélis 1999, 163–4 and ead. 1994, 49–50. The inscriptions analyzed by Bélis are the following ones: *SIG*³ 450 (= R 72 in Rutherford 2001, 464; ca. 230–220 BC), *SIG*³ 662 (165/4 BC) and *SEG* 26 (1976/1977) no. 1288 (beginning of the second century AD). Among these, especially interesting in terms of genre identity is *SIG*³ 450, where the Athenian Kleochares, ποιητὴς μελῶν, is honoured by the Delphians for having written a processional song, a paean and a hymn for the local Theoxenia (ll. 3–4 γέγραφε τῶι θεῶι ποθόδιόν τε καὶ παιᾶνα καὶ ὕμνον, ὅπως ἄιδωντι οἱ παῖδες τᾶι θυϲίαι τῶν Θεοξενίων): Rutherford 1997, 17 n. 53 and D'Alessio 1997, 29–30 have convincingly argued that we are most likely dealing with three different generic compositions and not with a hendiadys referring to one and the same poem, that is, a hybrid label such a παιὰν προϲοδιακόϲ. Rutherford 2003, 722 n. 32 interestingly suggests that the order prosodion/paean/hymn as attested by *SIG*³ 450 "might perhaps correspond to three stages in sacrificial ritual," that is, that they might reflect the actual sequence of performances within the time of the feast. On the lyric category of the poem performed by Amphicles in *SIG*³ 662 ll. 8–12 καὶ προϲόδιον γράψαϲ [...] καὶ τὸν δῆμον τῶν Ἀθηναίων ὕμνηϲεν see Chaniotis 1988, 350 (E 72b).

[146] The second part of Bélis' statement (ead. 1999, 164) that "ce qu' 'écrivaient' ces musiciens, c'état donc à tout le moins leurs textes poétiques (ce qui suffit à justifier l'emploi du verbe *graphein*), *laissant au notateur le soin d'y associer ultérieurement les signes de notation musicale sur la partition achevée*" (my italics) is a mere hypothesis which cannot be verified; cf. also Bélis 1994, 49–50.

Antigenidas of Thebes, son of Satyros, musician, aulode [sic][147] of
Philoxenus. He was the first to wear Milesian shoes and a yellow cloak
in the *Reveller*.[148] He wrote airs.

First of all, some textual observations. Although the manuscript tradition is unanimous, it may be legitimate to question the textual
soundness of such an indeterminate and brachylogic expression as
ἔγραψε μέλη. If compared with the other occurrences of this syntagm in the Suda, the absence of connective particles and of any
further specification about the nature of these μέλη induces one to
ask whether after μέλη we should suppose a lacuna or some kind of
textual corruption, e.g. μελῶν η΄ (i.e. βιβλία) > μέλη η΄ > μέλη or,
more likely, μέλη η΄ > μέλη.[149] Actually, among the other instances
of (cυγ)γράφειν + μέλη attested in the Suda,[150] all but one are provided with further specification on the nature of the songs, these
supplements usually consisting of adjectives or hendiadys.[151] Even the
instance of Suda's entry s.v. Ἀλκμάν (α 1289) [. . .] ἔγραψε βιβλία
ἓξ μέλη καὶ Κολυμβώcαc,[152] although apparently more akin to our
case, cannot be regarded as perfectly comparable with the bare
ἔγραψε μέλη quoted above. In fact in this entry it is difficult to avoid
understanding μέλη as an apposition to the previous βιβλία ἓξ.[153]

---

[147] Most probably a mistake for 'auletes', see West *AGM*, 367.

[148] On the "mimetic role" of the costume worn by Antigenidas in Philoxenus'
Komast see Csapo 2004a, 214 with n. 29.

[149] I owe this point to D.J. Mastronarde.

[150] Suda s.v. Ἀλκμάν (α 1289), Ἀνακρέων (α 1916), Μεcομήδηc (μ 668), Μουcαῖοc
(μ 1295), Cαπφώ (c 107), Τυρταῖοc (τ 1205).

[151] Cf. respectively Suda s.v. Ἀνακρέων (α 1916) [. . .] καὶ cυνέγραψε παροίνιά
τε μέλη καὶ ἰάμβουc καὶ τὰ καλούμενα Ἀνακρεόντεια, s.v. Μεcομήδηc (μ 668) [. . .]
γράφει οὖν εἰc Ἀντίνοον ἔπαινον, ὃc ἦν Ἀδριανοῦ παιδικά· καὶ ἄλλα διάφορα
μέλη, s.v. Μουcαῖοc (μ 1295) [. . .] ἔγραψε μέλη καὶ ᾄcματα, s.v. Cαπφώ (c 107)
[...] ἔγραψε δὲ μελῶν λυρικῶν βιβλία θ΄, s.v. Τυρταῖοc (τ 1205) [. . .] ἔγραψε
πολιτείαν Λακεδαιμονίοιc, καὶ ὑποθήκαc δι᾽ ἐλεγείαc, καὶ μέλη πολεμιcτήρια,
βιβλία ε΄.

[152] Adler punctuates after βιβλία ἓξ, i.e. ἔγραψε βιβλία ἓξ, μέλη καὶ Κολυμβώcαc.
This passage has a much-debated exegetical tradition, depending on the inclusion
or not of the Κολυμβῶcαι in the six-book Alexandrian edition of Alcman, see Calame
1977 II, 171–4, id. 1983, xxii–iv and Haslam 1977, 2–3 with n. 1. For the only
other reference to the Κολυμβῶcαι and its likely attribution to Alcman see 158
PMGF = Ptolem. Heph. *Nov. hist.* apud Phot. *Bibl.* 151 a 7 ff. (Ἀλκμάνουc codd.:
Ἀλκμᾶνοc corr. Casaubon).

[153] Putting aside other considerations, we can say that the bare word order would
allow two possible alternatives: (1) regarding *tout court* μέλη καὶ Κολυμβώcαc as an

Furthermore, the missing, more detailed specification of the nature of these songs can easily be supplied from the context, since in the previous sentence we are told that Alcman, being by nature ἐρωτικὸς πάνυ, himself was the first to write erotic songs (εὑρετὴς γέγονε τῶν ἐρωτικῶν μελῶν).

Once we have established these premises as regards the textual soundness of ἔγραψε μέλη in Suda s.v. Ἀντιγενίδης (α 2657), and granted that even here, as usually, the verb ἔγραψε refers loosely to the act of composing poems and not to actually writing down the musical score, the next problem lies in identifying the possible nature of these μέλη: vocal airs (that is, lyric texts to be sung)[154] or bare instrumental melodies?[155] In this latter case, the issue of a potential score would arise again. Bélis has already argued that the fact that all the other sources we have about Antigenidas depict him as an αὐλητής (thus a mere instrumental musician),[156] and not as an αὐλῳδός, does not represent a difficulty for understanding μέλη in the usual meaning of lyric airs to be sung. Indeed, cases of instrumental musi-

---

apposition to βιβλία ἕξ; (2) considering μέλη as well as Κολυμβῶσας as different supplements to the six-book Alexandrian edition. Yet both interpretations lend themselves to criticism. All in all, (2) seems to be the less likely hypothesis: granted that we are just told about the erotic nature of Alcman's poetry (εὑρετὴς γέγονε τῶν ἐρωτικῶν μελῶν), such a distinction of some μέλη not otherwise specified from the previous ones belonging to the Alexandrian edition (i.e. the ἐρωτικὰ μέλη) seems highly improbable. As to (1), the problem still remains of explaining the presence of such heterogeneous compositions within the Alexandrian edition of Alcman's poetry, an edition that the sources represent as apparently homogeneous in its content. Yet, if we have somehow to explain the transmitted text, it seems to me not entirely implausible to limit the appositive function to μέλη, i.e. an epexegetic gloss of the previous βιβλία ἕξ (although we could expect a reversed order, cf. Suda s.v. Τυρταῖος [τ 1205]), and to regard καὶ Κολυμβῶσας as a poem not included in the six-book edition. Otherwise, if we have to emend the text, Haslam's solution, that is, ἔγραψε βιβλία ϛ´ μελ<ῶν>, καὶ Κολυμβῶσας (id. 1977, 2) seems to be the most likely.
[154] See Bélis 1999, 164–5 translating μέλη "compositions lyriques," "œuvres chantées."
[155] Apparently more inclined to this hypothesis, although their formulations are somewhat ambiguous, Jan, RE I. 2 (1894) s.v. Antigenidas (3) col. 2400 "Aulet, auch Komponist" and Weil-Reinach 1900, 84 n. 198 "auteur de melodie."
[156] Theophr. De hist. plant. 4. 11. 4, Plut. Mor. 193f 11–12, Demetr. 1.6, [Plut.] De mus. 1138b, Aul. Gell. N.A. 15. 17. 1. As to the αὐλῳδός of Suda's entry s.v. Ἀντιγενίδας, see supra n. 147. The normative distinction between κρουματοποιός and μελοποιός is well singled out in Et. M. 367. 21 Gaisford s.v. ἐπὶ Χαριξένης· αὐλητρὶς ἡ Χαριξένη ἀρχαία, καὶ ποιήτρια κρουμάτων· οἱ δὲ μελοποιούν.

cians who also composed lyric texts to be sung by a vocalist and not merely κρούματα are not an outstanding novelty in the multi-faceted cosmos of Greek music.[157] Furthermore, while the word μέλος can actually be used also to denote mere instrumental music devoid of vocal accompaniment,[158] it is worth noticing that in such cases μέλος is almost never used absolutely, that is, without any reference to the relative instruments producing the sound.

Summing up, as regards Antigenidas, we are most likely facing another example of a principally instrumental musician who also wrote lyric texts for vocalists.

I.5 *Contextualizing a misunderstanding: some historical considerations on the scholium to Dion. Thr. Ars gramm. 2 = Bekker, AG II, 751 ll. 30–2*

Fleming-Kopff are not the only ones who have looked for an intrinsic, long-standing link between Alexandrian philological tradition and texts provided with musical notation as a necessarily fixed point of reference on which to base our knowledge of the lyric texts' colometry as transmitted by medieval manuscript tradition. By downdating the birth of the Greek instrumental notational system to the end of the fourth and beginning of the third century BC on the basis of a purely paleographic analysis of the σήματα preserved in Alypius' tables,[159] Bataille came to an even more radical conclusion about the alleged relationship between Alexandrian editorial technique and musical scores. "La pensée claire, cartésienne" underlying the Greek

---

[157] See Bélis 1994, 47–8, ead. 1999, 164–5 and more recently Wilson 2002, 55 n. 49.

[158] Cf. Thgn. 761 φόρμιγξ δ' αὖ φθέγγοιθ' ἱερὸν μέλος ἠδὲ καὶ αὐλός (see also Van Groeningen 1966, 294), Pind. *Pyth.* 12. 19 παρθένος αὐλῶν τεῦχε πάμφωνον μέλος νόμος, id. fr. 75. 18 S-M ἀχεῖ τ' ὀμφαὶ μελέων ςὺν αὐλοῖς (see Lavecchia 2000, 271), id. fr. 140b 15–17 S-M ἁλίου δελφῖνος ὑπόκρισιν| τὸν μὲν ἀκύμονος ἐν πόντου πελάγει| αὐλῶν ἐκίνης' ἐρατὸν μέλος, Soph. 241 Radt (*Thamyris*) ὤιχωκε γὰρ κροτητὰ πηκτίδων μέλη, *PMG* 947b μή μοι καταπαύετ' ἐπεί περ ἤρξατο| τερπνότατων μελέων ὁ καλλιβόας πολύχορδος αὐλός, Paus. 9. 12. 5–6 (Pronomus) πρῶτος δὲ διάφορα ἐς τοςοῦτο μέλη ἐπ' αὐλοῖς ηὔληςε τοῖς αὐτοῖς (referring to the various modes: Doric, Phrygian and Lydian), Nonn. *Dion.* 20. 305 αὐλοῦ μελπομένοιο μέλος Βερεκύντιδος ἠχοῦς.

[159] Bataille 1961, 19–20, with a clear preference for the later date because of "certaines influences des graphies cursives." This chronological *terminus* has been accepted also by Chailley 1967, 214–5 and id. 1979, 124–5, who, however, argues for the priority of the instrumental notation, at least at its earliest stage, against the vocal one.

notational system induced him to regard the notation itself as an "effort de systématisation" which could only be the product of the Alexandrian rationalistic fondness for taxonomy and classification.[160]

The weakness of such a chronological picture has already been shown by previous scholars on paleographic and historical grounds,[161] and does not deserve further consideration here. It may, however, be useful, since the issue has never been discussed again after Bataille, to pay more detailed attention to a scholiastic source adduced by Bataille as positive evidence for the view that Alexandrian colization depended on texts carrying musical notation. This is the scholium to Dion. Thr. *Ars gramm.* 2 = Bekker, *AG* II, 751 ll. 30–2, already quoted by Wessely.[162]

Before focusing on the scholium, let us dwell for a while upon the second chapter (περὶ ἀναγνώϲεωϲ) of Dionysius Thrax's *Ars grammatica* (= *GG* I. 1, 6 ll. 5–14 Uhlig):

ἀνάγνωϲίϲ ἐϲτι ποιημάτων ἢ ϲυγγραμμάτων ἀδιάπτωτοϲ προφορά. ἀναγνωϲτέον δὲ καθ᾽ ὑπόκριϲιν, κατὰ προϲῳδίαν, κατὰ διαϲτολήν. ἐκ μὲν γὰρ τῆϲ ὑποκρίϲεωϲ τὴν ἀρετήν, ἐκ δὲ τῆϲ προϲῳδίαϲ τὴν τέχνην, ἐκ δὲ τῆϲ διαϲτολῆϲ τὸν περιεχόμενον νοῦν ὁρῶμεν· ἵνα τὴν μὲν τραγῳδίαν ἡρωϊκῶϲ ἀναγνῶμεν, τὴν δὲ κωμῳδίαν βιωτικῶϲ, τὰ δὲ ἐλεγεῖα λιγυρῶϲ, τὸ δὲ ἔποϲ εὐτόνωϲ, τὴν δὲ λυρικὴν ποίηϲιν ἐμμελῶϲ, τοὺϲ δὲ οἴκτουϲ ὑφειμένωϲ καὶ γοερῶϲ. τὰ γὰρ μὴ παρὰ τὴν τούτων γινόμενα παρατήρηϲιν καὶ τὰϲ τῶν ποιητῶν ἀρετὰϲ καταρριπτεῖ καὶ τὰϲ ἕξειϲ τῶν ἀναγινωϲκόντων καταγελάϲτουϲ παρίϲτηϲιν.

Reading consists of a faultless delivery of poetry or prose works. A text must be read according to the gestures required by its genre,

---

[160] See Bataille 1961, 19: "un effort de systématisation, de mise en parallèle [. . .] qui sent l'arrangement, la pensée claire, cartésienne, dirais-je presque, des périodes où l'on établit des bilans et qui succèdent à d'autres, [. . .]; une tendance à vouloir scientifiquement tout symboliser [. . .]: donc de la mise en ordre, de l'érudition, de l'humanisme. Tout cela nous suggère un nome: celui d'Alexandrie." More cautiously Chailley 1967, 214, while asserting the validity of the chronological outline sketched by Bataille (a Hellenistic date for the musical notation), does not speak of a precise Alexandrian origin, arguing loosely that "la nomenclature topique des aspects d'octave" is to be traced back to the third century BC, without mentioning explicitly the editorial technique of the philologists of the Library.

[161] See e.g. the objections raised by Jourdan-Hemmerdinger 1981b (some of them of uneven value: cf. Bélis 1992, 37 n. 60) as regards the vocal notation, and more authoritatively West *AGM*, 261.

[162] See Wessely 1892, 269–70 (= id. 1892a 67), followed by Crusius 1894, 182 and Bataille 1961, 20 n. 1 (who still quotes the scholium according to Bekker's misleading edition).

according to its prosody, and according to its punctuation. For from the first of these devices we can realize the true value of the text itself, from the second the reader's ability, and from the third the underlying meaning. All that in order to be able to read tragedy solemnly, comedy according to the average behavior usually displayed in everyday life, elegy melodiously, epic with a stentorian voice, lyric poetry harmoniously and tunefully, threnodic poems in a low and mournful voice. Not observing these rules does not do justice to the poet's qualities and makes ridiculous the readers' ability.

After listing the three ways in which a text, whether poetry or prose, should be read, and their respective functions (καθ᾽ ὑπόκρισιν: with an *actio* suited to the ethos required by the literary genre in order to bring out the qualities of the text itself;[163] κατὰ προσωιδίαν: by observing the prosodic sandhi [accents, quantities, breathings and so on] in order to reveal the reader's technical ability;[164] κατὰ διαστολήν: according to a correct punctuation in order to avoid semantic ambiguities), Dionysius focuses first on the domain of ὑπόκρισις,[165] detailing the different manners of reading required by the different genres (tragedy, comedy, elegy, epic, lyric and threnodic poetry). It is therefore within this frame that we have to contextualize the expression τὴν δὲ λυρικὴν ποίησιν ἐμμελῶς[166] glossed by the scholium we are presently concerned with: lyric poetry has to be read with a harmonious and tuneful delivery.

The text of the scholium quoted by Wessely and taken up by Bataille is the following (= Bekker, *AG* II, 751 ll. 30–2):

---

[163] Cf. Σᵈ in *GG* I. 3, 16 ll. 19–21 Hilgard τίνος δὲ τὴν ἀρετὴν ὁρῶμεν; τῶν ἀναγινωσκομένων· ἐκ τῆς μιμήσεως γὰρ ἐνάρετα γίνεται καὶ δείκνυται τὰ ἀναγινωσκόμενα. See also Lallot 1989, 84.

[164] Cf. Σᵈ in *GG* I. 3, 16 ll. 27–8 Hilgard τίνος δὲ τέχνην ὁρῶμεν; δῆλον ὅτι τοῦ ἀναγινώσκοντος.

[165] That the section beginning at ἵνα τὴν μὲν τραγωιδίαν ἡρωϊκῶς ἀναγνῶμεν κτλ. does actually belong to the domain of the *actio* is assured also by Σᵈ in *GG* I. 3, 17 ll. 14–5 Hilgard: εἰπὼν τὰ τρία τὰ διδάσκοντα ἡμᾶς καλῶς ἀναγινώσκειν, ὑπόκρισιν, τέχνην, στιγμήν, διαλαμβάνει πρῶτον περὶ τῆς διαφορᾶς τῆς ὑποκρίσεως κτλ.

[166] ἐμμελῶς is the reading of most of the codd., εὐμελῶς being instead transmitted only by G and Bvᵖᶜ. For the distinction between a σχῆμα ἐμμελές, belonging to μουσική (that is, poetry to be sung and accompanied by instruments) and a σχῆμα εὐμελές, belonging to λογική (that is, prose), see Dion. Hal. *De comp. verb.* 11. 24 Auj.-Leb. That the adverb εὐτόνως referring to epic poetry is not to be understood literally but that we are dealing with a rhetorical *abusio* or κατάχρησις is confirmed by Σᵈ in *GG* I. 3, 21 ll. 9–11 Hilgard.

ἔϲτιν τινὰ ποιήματα, ἃ οὐ μόνον ἐμμέτρωϲ γέγραπται, ἀλλὰ καὶ μετὰ
μέλουϲ· διὸ οὐδ᾽ ὁ ϲτίχοϲ κεῖται ἐν τῆι ϲτοιχήϲει τέλειοϲ, ἀλλὰ μέχρι τοῦ
ἀπηχήματοϲ τῆϲ λύραϲ ϲτίζει τὴν ὁρμήν, ὡϲ ὁρᾶιϲ τὰ τοῦ Πινδάρου
ϲυγκεκομμένωϲ ἐκφερόμενα.[167]

There are some poems that are composed not only according to a
metrical frame but even μετὰ μέλουϲ [that is, to musical accompani-
ment]: therefore the verse is not written down in the lineation in its
complete length but only until it marks the pause of the lyre, as you
can see from Pindar's poems that are edited cut into small pieces.

According to Wessely, this scholium would attest "que, dans quelques
manuscrits, on écrivait les vers non seulement suivant leur disposition métrique, mai aussi *avec la mélodie*."[168] Before we analyze the
textual evidence on which Wessely's interpretation relies, some
considerations about the *Textgeschichte* of this scholium are necessary.
First, the text as quoted by Wessely, that is, according to Bekker's
edition, is the result of a conflation of two distinct grammatical
sources that have been put together arbitrarily.[169] Actually, the textual segment διὸ οὐδ᾽ ὁ ϲτίχοϲ κεῖται—ἐκφερόμενα is not transmitted
by the cod. Vat. gr. 14 (= C), which preserves various commentaries
going back to late antiquity (among which we can find also that of
Melampus, to which the very beginning of the quotation does indeed
belong, that is, the segment ἔϲτιν τινὰ ποιήματα—μέλουϲ).[170] This
segment can be found only in the codd. Par. gr. 2553 (A) and Par.
gr. 2555 (B), both of them being collecting basins of ancient grammatical knowledge of blurred origin (the so called Σθ) which were
erroneously assigned by Goettling to Theodosius of Alexandria.[171]

Let us then consider these two textual segments conflated by Bekker
as they operate back in their own original context.

Melampus' scholium to Dionysius' lemma τὴν δὲ λυρικὴν ποίηϲιν
ἐμμελῶϲ, considered in its full length without being misleadingly muti-
lated, is as follows:[172]

[167] The final segment ὡϲ ὁρᾶιϲ—ἐκφερόμενα is already omitted in Wessely's quotation (on the contrary, Crusius 1894, 182 cites the whole text).
[168] Wessely 1892, 269 (italics of the author); see also id. 1892a, 67 "gewisse
Gedichte wurden nicht nur im Metrum, sondern auch mit der Melodie geschrieben").
Wessely's interpretation has been followed also by Martin 1953, 15–6.
[169] See Goettling 1822, 223 "Ex Theodosio in marginem commentarii apud
Bekkerum Anecd. p. 751 haec notatio migravit" (see *infra*) and *GG* I. 3, xliii ff.
Hilgard.
[170] For the Vatican scholia see *GG* I. 3, x and xix ff. Hilgard.
[171] See *GG* I. 3, xxxvi–vii and cxxvii–xxix Hilgard.
[172] Σd in *GG* I. 3, 21 ll. 12–21 Hilgard.

ἔϲτιν τινὰ ποιήματα ἃ οὐ μόνον ἐμμέτρωϲ γέγραπται, ἀλλὰ καὶ μετὰ
μέλουϲ ἔϲκεπται, ἃ καὶ διπλαϲίονα κάματον παρεῖχε τοῖϲ ϲκεπτομένοιϲ,
τό τε μέτρον ϲπουδάζουϲι διαϲῴζειν καὶ τῶν μελῶν ἐπινοεῖν τὴν εὕρεϲιν.
Ταῦτα οὖν τὰ ποιήματα καλεῖται λυρικά, ὡϲ ὑπὸ λύραν ἐϲκεμμένα καὶ
μετὰ λύραϲ ἐπιδεικνύμενα. Γεγόναϲι δὲ λυρικοὶ οἱ καὶ πραττόμενοι ἐννέα,
ὧν τὰ ὀνόματά ἐϲτι ταῦτα, Ἀνακρέων, Ἀλκμάν, Ἀλκαῖοϲ, Βακχυλίδηϲ,
Ἴβυκοϲ, Πίνδαροϲ, Ϲτηϲίχοροϲ, Ϲιμωνίδηϲ, Ϲαπφώ, καὶ δεκάτη Κόριννα.
Ταύτην οὖν τὴν λυρικὴν ποίηϲιν δεῖ μετὰ μέλουϲ ἀναγινώϲκειν, εἰ καὶ
μὴ παρελάβομεν μηδὲ ἀπομεμνήμεθα τὰ ἐκείνων μέλη.

There are some poems that have not only been written according to
a metrical frame but that have also been composed with a musical
accompaniment, and this entailed a double effort for the composers,
for they have to observe the metre and at the same time to invent
and create the songs. These poetic works are called lyric inasmuch as
they are composed to the lyre as well as performed to the lyre. Nine
are the canonized lyric poets, whose names are the following: Anacreon,
Alcman, Alcaeus, Bacchylides, Ibycus, Pindar, Stesichorus, Simonides,
Sappho and tenth Corinna. Lyric poetry must thus be read musically
even if we have not inherited the music by those poets nor do we
remember it any more.

First, it is immediately obvious that the expression τινὰ ποιήματα
does not refer to 'some manuscripts', that is, to the concrete dimension of possible antigraphs, but that it simply means 'poetic works'
in the broadest sense, as is explicitly clarified by the following clause
ταῦτα οὖν τὰ ποιήματα καλεῖται λυρικά. Therefore the verb γέγραπται too does not strictly refer to the very precise act of writing down
the text on some material support but as we have already seen in
other instances previously analyzed, it loosely alludes to the creative
process of poetic composition. The contiguous καὶ μετὰ μέλουϲ ἔϲκεπται also points in the same direction. That the verb ϲκέπτομαι, usually conveying the notion of 'providing, preparing, elaborating', does
actually here mean 'to compose' lyric poetry, referring to the creative process itself,[173] is confirmed both by the following τοῖϲ ϲκεπτομένοιϲ (here used absolutely in the middle form to refer to the
poets as composers, cf. τῶν μελῶν ἐπινοεῖν τὴν εὕρεϲιν),[174] and by

---

[173] See LSJ s.v. ϲκέπτομαι II. 3 (esp. Xen. *Hell.* 3. 3. 8 and Dem. 24. 158).
[174] The equivalence οἱ ϲκεπτόμενοι = οἱ ποιηταί is assured also by Σᵈ in *GG* I.
3, 22 ll. 5–6 Hilgard: Dionysius' words τὰϲ τῶν ποιητῶν ἀρετὰϲ καταρριπτεῖ (*GG*
I. 1, 6 l. 12 Uhlig) are paraphrased by καὶ τῶν ϲκεψαμένων ἀνδρῶν τὸν ἐνάρετον
κάματον καταβάλλει εἰϲ ἔδαφοϲ.

the subsequent detailed distinction of the two main constituents of
the ancient poetic practice, that is, the creative, compositional process
(ὑπὸ λύραν ἐϲκεμμένα) and the strictly related performative element
(καὶ μετὰ λύραϲ ἐπιδεικνύμενα).[175] Up to this point, we are not entitled to draw from Melampus' scholium any reference to a definite
use of musical scores by ancient grammarians.

Furthermore, the very conclusion of the scholium seems to display a clear awareness of the impossibility of recovering the ancient
original music: ταύτην οὖν τὴν λυρικὴν ποίηϲιν δεῖ μετὰ μέλουϲ ἀναγινώϲκειν, εἰ καὶ μὴ παρελάβομεν μηδὲ ἀπομεμνήμεθα τὰ ἐκείνων μέλη.
And this is not an isolated drop in the ocean of ancient scholiastic
knowledge. A similar skepticism is explicitly stated also in Heliodorus'
scholia (= Σ[h] in GG I. 3, 476 l. 29 ff. Hilgard) glossing Dionysius'
very same lemma (τὴν δὲ λυρικὴν ποίηϲιν ἐμμελῶϲ):[176]

> "ἐμμελῶϲ" δὲ εἶπεν, ὅτι δεῖ μετὰ μέλουϲ τοῦ προϲήκοντοϲ ἄιδειν τὰ
> λυρικά· ὅπερ νῦν ἡμῖν ἀδύνατον· εἰ μὲν γάρ τιϲ ἐθελήϲει κατὰ τὴν
> ἀρχαίαν μουϲικήν, καθ' ἣν καὶ ἐγέγραπτο, ἀδύνατον, ἑτέρα γάρ ἡ ἀρχαία
> πρὸϲ τὴν νῦν· [. . .] πῶϲ ἄν οὖν τιϲ δύναιτο κατὰ τὴν ἀρχαϊκὴν ἁρμονίαν
> γεγραμμένα μέλη κατὰ τὴν νῦν μελωιδίαν ἄιδειν; ὥϲτε ἀδύνατον τὸ τοιοῦ-
> τον ἐν γραμματικῆι διὰ τὸ γεγενῆϲθαι μεταβολὴν τῆϲ ἁρμονικῆϲ κτλ.

> Dionysius said *emmelôs* because lyric poetry has to be sung with the
> appropriate music, which is actually impossible for us nowadays: if
> someone wanted to sing it according to the ancient music to which
> the lyric compositions had been set, he would not be able to, ancient
> music being different from the modern one [. . .] How, then, would
> someone be able to sing to the present music poems composed accord-
> ing to the ancient harmony? So that the same thing is impossible in
> grammatical studies because of the musical transformations that have
> meanwhile occurred.

Let us now turn to the second part of the scholium quoted by
Wessely, a textual segment that, as we have seen, does not actually
belong to Σ[d] but is transmitted only by Σ[θ]. This is the text as edited
by Goettling:[177]

---

[175] For ἐπιδείκνυμι as a common term referring to the performance itself see e.g.
Ael. *V.H.* 36. 1. It would actually not make sense, at least to me, to understand
ὑπὸ λύραν ἐϲκεμμένα καὶ μετὰ λύραϲ ἐπιδεικνύμενα as a hendiadys: the resulting
tautology would however leave unexplained the previous use of ἔϲκεπται and τοῖϲ
ϲκεπτομένοιϲ.

[176] See Pecorella 1962, 88–9, Pöhlmann 1965, 137–8 and Lallot 1989, 85.

[177] Goettling 1822, 59 ll. 24–8.

τί ἔςτι ποίηςιc λυρική; ἥτιc οὐ μόνον ἐμμέτρωc γέγραπται ἀλλὰ καὶ μετὰ
μέλουc· διὸ οὐδ' ὁ cτίχοc κεῖται ἐν τῆι cτοιχήcει τέλειοc ἀλλὰ μέχρι τοῦ
ἀπηχήματοc τῆc λύραc cτίζει τὴν ὁρμήν, ὡc ὁρᾶιc τὰ τοῦ Πινδάρου
cυγκεκομμένωc ἐκφερόμενα.

What is lyric poetry? It is a kind of poetry that has not only been
written according to a metrical scheme but also to music; therefore
the verse is not written down in the lineation in its complete length
but only until it marks the pause of the lyre, as you can see from
Pindar's poems that are edited cut into small pieces.

Once again, I do not believe that the anonymous scholiast's words
allow us to infer that we are dealing with copies of lyric poetry provided with musical notation. It seems to me much more likely that
the reference here is to the visual formatting in which Pindar's odes
are transmitted in the medieval manuscript tradition: lyric verses are
not disposed in a single continuous lineation[178] but they are 'edited
cut into small pieces' (τὰ τοῦ Πινδάρου cυγκεκομμένωc ἐκφερόμενα),
that is, they are disposed according to a colometric layout.[179] As to
the fact that the scholium links this practice with the musical performance (μετὰ μέλουc) underlying lyric poetry, this certainly does
betray a surprising historical awareness, but nevertheless does not
imply that the anonymous scholiast is here referring to texts provided with musical notations.

Wessely's interpretation of the scholium as edited by Bekker, *AG*
II, 751, however substantially wrong, does actually exhibit a certain
degree of inner consistency if we consider the historical context in

---

[178] The term cτοίχηcιc, as already pointed out by Ruelle in Wessely 1892, 270
n. 1, is a *hapax*. The only modern translation, to my knowledge, of this passage,
the one provided by Martin 1953, 66 n. 12 following Chantraine's suggestion ("donc,
le vers n'est pas achevé par le simple alignement des pieds etc."), avoids translating this term.

[179] LSJ s.v. cυγκεκομμένωc by quoting the scholium as edited by Bekker, *AG* II,
751 translates the adverb cυγκεκομμένωc "concisely." Yet I do not believe that the
scholium is referring here to the grammatical and syntactic phenomenon of the
cυγκοπή (cf. e.g. [Long.] *De subl.* 41. 3 τὰ λίαν cυγκείμενα καὶ εἰc μικρὰ καὶ
βραχυcύλλαβα cυγκεκομμένα). Goettling's remark (id. 1822, 223–4) that according
to the grammarian Theodosius "in Pindari poëmatis non cum linea (cτοιχήcει) finiri
versus (cτίχουc), sed dividi (cυγκεκομμένωc ἐκφέρεcθαι) propterea, quod linea cre-
bro sint longiores: id quod nuper a Boeckhio demonstratum est. cυγκεκομμένωc non
est *divisis propter metrorum vocabulis* sed propter chartarum brevitatem" (author's italics), is only partially correct. That writing lyric verses cυγκεκομμένωc may be just
a mere editorial device engendered by practical reasons is a modern inference
(cf. recently Parker 2001, 50–2).

which he operated. Wessely's misunderstanding of the scholium was
strongly influenced by the contemporary discovery of the Vienna
musical papyrus (P.Vind. G 2315 = Eur. *Or.* 338–44) and its erroneous dating to the first century AD.[180] Driven by the enthusiasm
for the alleged contemporary date of the Vienna papyrus and the
testimony of Dion. Hal. *De comp. verb.* 11. 18–21 Auj.-Leb. on the
Orestes parodos, Wessely was persuaded that the Vienna papyrus was
actually part of the very same score which he supposed that Dion.
Hal. had resorted to in quoting Electra's words. Hence it followed,
and quite understandably, that Wessely was very inclined to believe
that there was a close relationship between the philological activity
of the Alexandrian Library and the preservation of texts provided
with musical notation.[181]

If therefore Wessely's distorted interpretation of the scholium may
have an inner justification in its very genealogy, this cannot be said
as regards Bataille. From 1956 onwards the Vienna papyrus had
correctly been backdated by Turner to the third century BC, consequently calling into question the necessity of supposing a direct
link between P.Vind. G 3215 and the passage of Dion. Hal. quoted
above.[182] Furthermore, Bataille's hypothesis of the Alexandrian origin of the system of musical notation entails extremely unlikely consequences also as regards the addressee of the musical scores. According
to Bataille, "bien peu de gens avaient besoin des textes notés. En
dehors des compositeurs et des chefs de chœurs ou d'ensembles
instrumentaux, la chose n'intéressait que des érudits. Exécutants amateurs ou même professionels appreniaent leurs parties en les serinant,
comme souvent encore de nos jours."[183] Granted the very practical
reasons underlying the writing of these musical scores, that is, the
performance itself, Bataille's lumping together of professional musicians and the Library's scholars turns out to be very questionable.

---

[180] See Wessely 1892, 268.
[181] Cf. Wessely 1892, 269 "il est manifeste que Denys d'Halicarnasse a eu sous
les yeux cette même partition de l'*Oreste* [. . .] L'écriture est fort ancienne et nous
ne risquons rien à la placer au siècle d'Auguste, dans le temps même où Denys
d'Halicarnasse écrivait l'important passage relatif à la musique de l'*Oreste*, vers 140
et suivants. Il y avait d'ailleurs, dans les bibliothèques, même antérieurement, des
manuscrits contenant les partitions musicales des anciens poètes." The same perspective is still operating also in Martin 1953, 15–6.
[182] Cf. Turner 1956, 95–6; a brief history of the question can now be found in
Pöhlmann-West *DAGM*, 14.
[183] Bataille 1961, 19–20.

I.6   *Cic.* Orator, *183–4: the disguises of songs*

Recently Gentili-Lomiento, carrying on the interpretative frame already outlined by Fleming-Kopff, have argued that Cic. *Orator* 183–4 ll. 5–13 can also be taken as indirect evidence supporting the existence of a close link between the Alexandrian editorial practice of colizing lyric texts and musical scores.[184] This is the Ciceronian passage as edited by Westman 1980:

> *sed in versibus res est apertior, quamquam etiam a modis quibusdam cantu remoto soluta esse videatur oratio, maximeque id in optimo quoque eorum poetarum qui* λυρικοί *a Graecis nominantur; quos cum cantu spoliaveris, nuda paene remanet oratio. quorum similia sunt quaedam etiam apud nostros, velut illa in Thyeste* [Enn. fr. 348 Vahlen² = fr. CLI, l. 300 Jocelyn]:
> > '*quemnam te esse dicam qui tarda in senectute*'[185]
> *et quae secuntur; quae, nisi cum tibicen accessit, orationis sunt solutae simillima.*

but in poetry the presence of rhythm is more obvious, although there are certain metres which, once devoid of musical accompaniment, seem to be bare prose; this is particulary evident in the best among the poets the Greeks call 'lyric'. Once they are deprived of musical accompaniment, there remains nothing but bare prose. Also some lines of our poets look like these, as for instance in the *Thyestes*:
> "quemnam te esse dicam qui tarda in senectute"

and what follows, which, if not accompanied by the pipe-player, is exactly like prose.

I believe that a more detailed contextualization of this passage can confidently lead to a different conclusion by tracing the Ciceronian evidence back to a much less eccentric and more likely scenario for the experience supposed to be shared by the average Roman reader of the mid first century BC.[186]

---

[184] Gentili-Lomiento 2001, 10–11: "Una ripartizione [that is, καθ' ἁρμονίαν] che egli [Apollonius the Classifier] poté realizzare soltanto disponendo di copie con notazione musicale. Del resto, senza l'ausilio della musica sarebbe stato molto difficile ricostruire l'assetto colometrico dei canti se, come Cicerone osserva nell'*Orator* 55, 183 etc." The same Ciceronian passage has been taken up also by Gentili-Lomiento 2003, 10 but in a somewhat more cautious and neutral way.

[185] We are dealing with a series of bacchic measures, a rhythm labelled by Dion. Hal. *De comp. verb.* 17. 14 Auj.-Leb. as ἀνδρῶδες δὴ πάνυ τοῦτο τὸ cχῆμα καὶ εἰc cεμνότητα ἐπιτήδειον. The transmitted reading *senectute* is rightly defended by Westman vs. Bothe's emendation *senecta*. The hypermetrical effect produced by *senectute* could well be only an apparent one if the first syllable of the following verse began with a vowel, see Vahlen², 185, Ribbeck³, 65 and Jocelyn's remark on the unnecessary assumption of a stichic articulation for Ennius' bacchei (id. 1967, 422–3).

[186] Cicero's *Orator* dates back to 46 BC.

First of all, the immediately surrounding context. In the previous paragraphs Cicero has focused on the very nature of rhythm, regarded as a property independent of (and prior to) the poetic or prosaic nature of the text (179–180), and then has turned to a more detailed treatment of rhythmic prose, that is, *oratio numerosa* (181–2). Still within this subsection, Cicero adduces as a self-evident proof of the presence of rhythm even in a prose text the fact that rhythm itself is the direct result of our natural faculty of hearing, the so-called *sensus* or αἴϲθηϲιϲ (183 ll. 1–5).[187] It is just at this point that Cicero establishes a more direct comparison between prose and poetry. We are told that rhythm is usually more easily detected (*apertior*) in poetry, yet there may be some exceptions, as is the case for some Greek lyric verses[188] that can look like mere prose (ψιλὴ λέξιϲ) once devoid of the musical accompaniment they were originally conceived for (probably the instrumental one: *cantu remoto*).[189] Cicero then quotes as an analogous instance in Latin poetry a verse drawn from Ennius' *Thyestes* which evidently should belong to a *canticum*, as the protasis *nisi cum tibicen accessit* (184 l. 12) clearly assures us.[190] Gentili-Lomiento's quotation of the Ciceronian text stops precisely at this point, yet the following lines (184 ll. 13–5) may turn out to be useful for a proper understanding of the argumentative line here sketched:

> *at comicorum senarii propter similitudinem sermonis sic saepe sunt abiecti ut nonnumquam vix in eis numerus et versus intellegi possit. quo est ad inveniendum difficilior in oratione numerus quam in versibus.*

> but comic senarii because of their resemblance to common conversation are often so low and plain that sometimes it is hardly possible to recognize rhythm and metre in them. Hence it is more difficult to discover rhythm in prose than in poetry.

---

[187] Cic. *Or.* 183 ll. 1–5 *esse ergo in oratione numerum quendam non est difficile cognoscere. iudicat enim sensus; in quo est iniquum quod accidit non agnoscere, si cur id accidat reperire nequeamus. neque enim ipse versus ratione est cognitus, sed natura atque sensu, quem dimensa ratio docuit quid acciderit. ita notatio naturae et animadversio peperit artem.* For the common equivalence *sensus~aures* see also § 162, 173 and 198; cf. Kroll 1958, 160 and Wille 1967, 464 with n. 557.

[188] The most likely reference here is to the Greek choral lyric, first of all the Pindaric one, cf. Kroll 1958, 160–1 mentioning also Simonides, Stesichorus together with "die Vertreter des jüngeren Dithyrambus" on the basis of *De orat.* 3. 185, and D'Arbela 1958, 233 *ad loc.*

[189] Cf. also *nisi cum tibicen accessit.* For *cantus/cantare* referring to mere instrumental music see Peruzzi 1998, 139 n. 1, 144.

[190] Cf. Sandys 1885, 203.

The adversative link (*at*)[191] opposing the comic senarii of the *diverbia* to the *cantica* of dramatic texts makes clear that the former, although performed by delivering a speech and not by singing a song (and therefore without musical accompaniment), are not to be regarded as less metrical than lyric cola. What distinguishes them from the latter is only a different degree of recognizability (*quo est ad inveniendum difficilior in oratione numerus quam in versibus*).[192]

Since the leading criterion informing this comparison of kinds and degrees of rhythmic quality turns out ultimately to be the natural faculty of hearing (*natura atque sensus*), it is obvious that music itself is the normative element that enables us to recognize immediately the underlying rhythm because of its regularly recurrent melodic pattern. What Cicero is saying here cannot be used thus as a theoretical buttress supporting, even only indirectly, Fleming-Kopff's challenging hypothesis. Granted that it seems quite unlikely that in the first century BC Cicero could have been acquainted with the great Greek lyric poetry of the past by any means other than reading, his knowledge of this poetic tradition being thus eminently bookish,[193] it is not an accident that the concrete instances he then quotes are drawn from contemporary Roman theatrical praxis (tragedy as well as comedy), a reality that he could still experience himself at that time. Actually, although we do not have other information about theatrical reperformance of Ennius' *Thyestes* (169 BC) in the late republican period except for this Ciceronian passage,[194] there is plenty of evidence testifying to the widespread use in the first century BC of revived παλαιὰ δράματα on the Roman stage (especially Ennius,

---

[191] The adversative meaning conveyed by *at* has been correctly underlined by Sandys 1885, 203, Kroll 1958, 161 and Yon 1964, 151 n. 5.

[192] Westman, like all other modern editors of the *Orator*, rightly defends the textual soundness of this sentence, which had previously been questioned by Stangl because it is omitted by the Florentine codex m (= Florentinus Magliabechianus VI 185).

[193] Differently Wille 1967, 237 (followed more recently by Bohnenkamp 1972, 321–33), arguing that the Ciceronian passage quoted above would show that "der Gebrauch der Musik in der lyrischen Gattung damals lebendig war." Yet regarding the odes of Horace *tout court* as actual *Gesanglyrik* is doubtful: see especially the balanced objections *ad hoc* raised by Rossi 1998 (esp. 171–4, 177–9) and Fantuzzi in Fantuzzi-Hunter 2002, 55 n. 126 (= iid. 2004, 32 n. 124).

[194] I cannot agree with Wright's analysis of *In Pis.* 43 and *Verr.* 2. 1. 81, cf. id. 1931, 50–1.

Naevius, Pacuvius and Accius for tragedy; Plautus for comedy), according to a theatrical practice broadly attested in the Greek world from the first quarter of the fourth century BC onwards.[195]

In this sense the most significant passages referring to reperformance of old Roman tragedies are: Cic. *De off.* 1. 113–4 (we are told about contemporary theatrical performances of Ennius [*Melanippa, Ajax*], Pacuvius [*Antiopa*] and Accius [*Clytaemestra, Epigoni, Medus*]); *Ad fam.* 7. 1. 2 (during the *ludi* organized by Pompey in order to celebrate the first stone theater and the temple of *Venus Victrix*, i.e. 55 BC, had been performed Accius' *Clytaemestra* and an *Equus Troianus*, perhaps by Livius Andronicus or Naevius, cf. Shackleton Bailey 1977, 326); *Pro Sest.* 120–2 (the well-known tragic actor Aesopus performs Accius' *Eurysaces*, cf. Questa-Raffaelli 1990, 168 n. 52); *De orat.* 2. 193 (Antonius claims that he has attended a dramatic performance of Pacuvius' *Teucer*. The fictional time of *De oratore* is 91 BC: in any case forty years after Pacuvius' death); *De off.* 1. 97 *at Atreo dicente plausus excitantur* (a reference to Accius' *Atreus*: the word *plausus* seems to point to a theatrical audience, as is confirmed also by *De orat.* 217, 219 and *Tusc.* 4. 55); *Tusc.* 1. 106 (a quotation from Pacuvius' *Iliona*: the reference here is to the musical accompaniment *pressus et flebilis* which induces tears in the audience); *Ad Att.* 16. 2. 3, 16. 5. 1 (a performance of Accius' *Tereus*, 44 BC). The case of *Ad Att.* 4. 15. 6 seems to me to rest on less certain ground. Cicero's judgment on the histrionic ability displayed by Antiphon on the occasion of the *ludi Apollinares* of 44 BC (*in Andromacha tamen maior fuit quam Astyanax*), especially in the light of the following reference to mimic performances, seems indeed to suggest that we are dealing here with playing single distinct roles rather than with whole tragedies (cf. Shackleton Bailey 1965, 210). The possible roles played in this case are numerous and equally speculative: we can think e.g. of Ennius' *Hermiona* or *Hecuba*, of Naevius' *Andromacha* or *Hector*, of Accius' *Troades* and so on. For these reasons I cannot completely agree with Jocelyn 1967, 47 with n. 6 asserting that *Ad Att.* 4. 15. 6 does represent positive evidence for "the last public performance of a play by Ennius". Performances of excerpted tragic 'airs' (*tragoedia cantata*) are well attested in the second half of the first century BC, see e.g. Suet. *Iul.* 84. 2: *inter ludos cantata sunt quaedam ad miserationem et invidiam caedis eius accommodata, ex Pacuvi Armorum iudicio [. . .] et ex Electra Atili* (Roth: *Atilii* codd. recc.: *Acilii* codd. ant.; cf. Butler-Cary 1927, 152) *ad similem sententiam*; cf. Beare 1964[3], 234 and esp. Kelly 1979, 27–37. As to the revival of old comedies see e.g. *Pro Rosc. com.* 20 (Plautus' *Pseudolus*).

[195] That is, respectively 386 BC for tragedy and 339 BC for comedy, see Pickard-Cambridge 1968[2], 72, 99; for a detailed synthesis of Roman *Bühnenpraxis* in the late republican period see Questa-Raffaelli 1990, 163 ff. and Beacham 1991, 154–98 (as to the sporadic survival of such performances till the imperial period see Jory 1986, 149–50 n. 2).

It can be reasonably argued thus that the music (*cantus*) referred to by Cicero in *Or.* 183–4 is not the theoretical and soundless one of the musical notation committed to the written page but the concrete and tuneful one experienced in contemporary theatrical performances. The higher or lower rhythmic recognizability discussed in the Ciceronian passage is thus analyzed from the perspective of the listener, not from that of the writer of the text or of a would-be editor of bare *Lesetexte*.[196]

I.7 *Metrical colon and instrumental cola in Arist. Quint. pp. 31. 18–32. 4 W-I: making sense of a difference*

As a further theoretical buttress supporting Fleming-Kopff's working hypothesis, Marino has recently adduced also the evidence of Arist. Quint. p. 31. 24 ff. W-I.[197] This is the text as quoted by Marino:[198]

μέλος μὲν γὰρ νοεῖται καθ᾽ αὑτὸ μὲν <ἐν> (suppl. Jahn) τοῖς διαγράμμασι καὶ ἀτάκτοις μελωιδίαις, μετὰ δὲ ῥυθμοῦ μόνου, ὡς ἐπὶ τῶν κρουμάτων καὶ κώλων [. . .] ῥυθμὸς δὲ καθ᾽ αὑτὸν μὲν ἐπὶ ψιλῆς ὀρχήσεως, μετὰ δὲ μέλους ἐν κώλοις.

As clearly shown by the translation provided by the scholar herself,[199] Marino assigns here to the word κῶλον the common meaning of 'minor metrical unit' widely attested in metrical treatises and handbooks, ancient as well as modern.[200] According to Marino, the κῶλα Aristides Quintilianus is talking about are therefore the metrical units as "understood by metricians" and therefore to be distinguished

---

[196] Of course, this is not the same as denying to Roman drama the co-existence, from times certainly prior to the first century BC onwards, of a double path of transmission and reception, that is, its circulation through *Lesebücher* and at the same time as real theatrical performances: cf. Questa-Raffaelli 1990 (esp. 144–5, 156, 174). What I should like to emphasize here is the possibility, broadly attested, that Cicero drew his knowledge of Ennius' tragedies not only from reading books but also from attending contemporary theatrical performances.

[197] Marino 1999b, 23.

[198] Marino 1999b, *ibid.*, citing according to Winnington-Ingram's edition. As we shall see, what is puzzling is Marino's idiosyncratic and selective misreading of Winnington-Ingram's text.

[199] Marino 1999b, 23: "il melos viene percepito di per se stesso nei diagrammi e nelle melodie irregolari; con il ritmo soltanto, come nel caso delle *note strumentali e dei cola* [. . .] il ritmo di per se stesso è percepito nel caso della pura danza; con il melos nei *cola*" (italics are mine).

[200] See LSJ s.v. κῶλον II. 4 and West 1982, 5.

from rhetorical κῶλα (in this regard especially telling is Marino's reference to the activity of Aristophanes of Byzantium).[201] This first linguistic interpretation, together with the bias that Aristides is dealing here with "the link between colon and rhythmic-musical frame," leads Marino towards a second semantic shift, which seems to me to obscure the whole sense of the clause. After assuming that the meaning of κῶλον in this passage is the metrical one, Marino considers that the word κρούματα too, which is strictly connected to κῶλα at least on a syntactic level (cf. ἐπὶ τῶν κρουμάτων καὶ κώλων), must necessarily convey the technical meaning of "instrumental notes," that is signs written down on a diagram referring to precise notes, and not the more common and well documented one of "instrumental compositions" *tout court*.[202] The result of such a reading of the Aristides passage is easily predictable: Aristides' alleged reference to metrical cola and musical notation would turn out to be the much desired proof testifying to ancient theoreticians' awareness of the close relationship existing between Alexandrian colometry and musical scores.

But is this the correct interpretation of Aristides' words? Is Aristides really speaking of metrical units and musical notation? Once again, a more detailed analysis of the original context leads to a different conclusion.

The whole thirteenth chapter of Aristides' *On Music* is devoted to rhythm according to a well structured frame skilfully alternating macroscopic survey and minute analysis, with expansions and contractions of the argumentative focus. First (p. 31. 3–6 W-I) we meet the definition of rhythm regarded in its pure theoretical abstractness as a property which can be predicated of three different objects (ῥυθμὸς τοίνυν καλεῖται τριχῶς): motionless bodies (ἐπί τε τῶν ἀκινημάτων ϲωμάτων), things which move by themselves (κἀπὶ πάντων τῶν κινουμένων), and finally, and in quite a particular sense, sound (καὶ ἰδίωϲ ἐπὶ φωνῆϲ), which is also the main topic of the following argumentation (p. 31. 6–7 W-I περὶ οὗ νῦν πρόκειται λέγειν). Still within this third category (p. 31. 8–17 W-I) Aristides next considers rhythm

[201] Cf. Marino's precise quotation of Dion. Hal. *De comp. verb.* 22. 17 Auj.-Leb. and Arist. *Rhet.* 1409b 8 (where a clear distinction is drawn between syntactic and metrical κῶλα): ead. 1999b, 23 n. 34.
[202] See LSJ s.v. κροῦμα 2.

as a system of chronoi disposed according to a certain order (cύcτημα ἐκ χρόνων κατά τινα τάξιν cυγκειμένων), chronoi which we respectively call arsis and thesis within a binary system. At this point (p. 31. 18–20 W-I) Aristides' argumentative perspective begins expanding again, going back to rhythm as an abstract entity no longer to be limited to the domain of sound. There are three faculties of sense by which rhythm can be perceived (πᾶc μὲν οὖν ῥυθμὸc τρισὶ τούτοιc αἰcθητηρίοιc νοεῖται): (1) sight (ὄψιc), as in the case of dance (ὡc ἐν ὀρχήcει), (2) hearing (ἀκοή), as in the case of melody (ὡc ἐν μέλει),[203] and (3) touch (ἀφή) as in the case of the pulse beats of the arteries (ὡc οἱ τῶν ἀρτηριῶν cφυγμοί). It is at this point of the argumentative frame that Aristides focuses attention on a special kind of rhythm, that is the musical one (p. 31. 20–24 W-I):

ὁ δὲ [i.e. ῥυθμόc] κατὰ μουcικὴν ὑπὸ δυεῖν, ὄψεώc τε καὶ ἀκοῆc. ῥυθμίζεται δὲ ἐν μουcικῆι κίνηcιc cωμάτων, μελωιδία, λέξιc. τούτων δὲ ἕκαcτον καὶ καθ᾽ αὑτὸ θεωρεῖται καὶ μετὰ τῶν λοιπῶν, ἰδίαι τε ἑκατέρου καὶ ἀμφοῖν ἅμα.

but rhythm in music is perceived only by two faculties: sight and hearing. In music motion of body, melody and diction are rhythmically structured. Each of these elements is regarded in itself and together with the others, that is with each by itself and with both put together.

We are told that in music rhythm can be perceived only by sight and hearing and that its main constituents are three,[204] that is, the motion of body (κίνηcιc cωμάτων), the melodic line (μελωιδία), and the words (λέξιc), each of them being able to manifest itself alone (καθ᾽ αὑτό) or joined together with the other elements (μετὰ τῶν λοιπῶν: only one of the two or both).

It is precisely here that Marino's quotation from Aristides must be inserted in its entire length (pp. 31. 24–32. 4 W-I):

μέλοc μὲν γὰρ νοεῖται καθ᾽ αὑτὸ μὲν <ἐν> (suppl. Jahn) τοῖc διαγράμμαcι καὶ ἀτάκτοιc μελωιδίαιc, μετὰ δὲ ῥυθμοῦ μόνου, ὡc ἐπὶ τῶν κρουμάτων καὶ κώλων, μετὰ δὲ λέξεωc μόνηc ἐπὶ τῶν καλουμένων κεχυμένων αἰcμάτων·

---

[203] For the meaning of μέλοc in this passage see Mathiesen 1983, 16–7 n. 111 ("a technical term that refers to the complete musical complex: words, melody, rhythm, the production of all these and their perception").

[204] The tripartite distinction is of course already Aristoxenean cf. Aristox. *El. rhythm.* 2. 9 = 6. 15–8 Pearson διαιρεῖται δὲ ὁ χρόνοc ὑπὸ τῶν ῥυθμιζομένων τοῖc ἑκάcτου αὐτῶν μέρεcιν. ἔcτι δὲ τὰ ῥυθμιζόμενα τρία· λέξιc, μέλοc, κίνηcιc cωματική.

ῥυθμὸϲ δὲ καθ᾽ αὑτὸν μὲν ἐπὶ ψιλῆϲ ὀρχήϲεωϲ, μετὰ δὲ μέλουϲ ἐν κώλοιϲ,
μετὰ δὲ λέξεωϲ μόνηϲ ἐπὶ τῶν ποιημάτων μετὰ πεπλαϲμένηϲ ὑποκρίϲεωϲ,
οἷον τῶν Cωτάδου καί τινων τοιούτων· λέξιϲ δ᾽ ὅπωϲ μεθ᾽ ἑκατέρου
θεωρεῖται, προείπομεν. ταῦτα ϲύμπαντα μιγνύμενα τὴν ᾠδὴν ποιεῖ.

For melos is perceived in itself in the diagrams and irregular melodies,
while it (is perceived) with rhythm alone as in the case of instrumental interludes and pieces, and with the words alone as in the case of
the so-called 'loose' melodies'. Rhythm is perceived in itself in the bare
dance, with the melos in instrumental pieces and with the words alone
in poems with a contrived delivery, like those of Sotades and similar
poems. We have already said how the words are regarded with each
of the other two. All these elements mixed together make the song.

The close syntactic link (cf. μέλοϲ μὲν γὰρ νοεῖται) established between
this textual section and the preceding lines makes it immediately
clear that the passage quoted by Marino has to be understood as
an explicative digression,[205] that is, a concrete instance of the broader
assumption mentioned above. What we have here is detailed treatment of the elements (first regarded each by itself and then put
together with the other two) which are organized in music according to some kind of rhythmical structure (a close equivalent of the
Aristoxenian τὰ ῥυθμιζόμενα). We are told that the melodic line
(μέλοϲ) shows itself in its intact purity in the diagrams[206] and in the
so-called ἄτακτα songs,[207] whereas it manifests itself together with the
rhythm alone ἐπὶ τῶν κρουμάτων καὶ κώλων, that is, in instrumental interludes and pieces, and finally with the words alone in the so-
called κεχυμένα ᾄϲματα.[208]

In other words, the apparently hendiadys-like expression ἐπὶ τῶν
κρουμάτων καὶ κώλων strongly suggests that we should assign to the

---

[205] The explanatory nature of this passage (Arist. Quint. pp. 31. 24–32. 3 W-I)
had wrongly induced J. Caesar to question its textual soundness and to suggest that
we are dealing with a possible gloss.

[206] Most likely the tables representing 'tonal scales', see Barker *GMW* II, 434–5
n. 159. Differently Duysinx 1999, 77 n. 2.

[207] As to the irregular nature of these melodies, probably "sequences in scores
written without rhythmic symbols," see Barker *GMW* II, 435 n. 161. Slightly
differently Duysinx 1999, 77 n. 3, who supposes a reference either to some kind
of musical improvisation "sans essayer de 'composer' une mélodie véritable, sans
marquer un rythme précis" or, less likely, to some vocal exercise involving "poser
la voix sur tel ou tel son sans qu'un rhythme soit perçu."

[208] Probably "something rather like recitative," see Barker *GMW* II, 435 n. 161.

second member of the syntagm (i.e. κῶλων) the meaning (well-attested in musical literature) of 'instrumental piece'[209] as opposed to 'vocal piece' (ᾠδή)[210] rather than that of 'minor metrical unit' as proposed by Marino.

Especially telling with regard to this is the evidence of *Anon. Bell.* 68 (= p. 22. 1–11 Najock). The anonymous author of the treatise here says that the notational system entails two different sets of signs, the first being employed for outlining the vocal melody (ἐπὶ λέξεωϲ) while the second is used to write down the instrumental music (ἐπὶ κρούϲεωϲ). What follows then is an explanation of the reason underlying this double *Notenschrift* (p. 22. 2–4 Najock): ὅτι ἐν τοῖϲ ᾄιϲμαϲί ποτε μεϲολαβεῖ καὶ κῶλα καὶ διαφόρωι χαρακτῆρι (i.e. τῶν φθόγγων) τότ᾽ ἀνάγκη χρήϲαϲθαι. We are clearly dealing with an opposition between vocal melody (ᾄιϲματα) and instrumental pieces (κῶλα), that is, what requires a double notational system is the presence of instrumental interludes (the so-called μεϲαυλικά or μεϲαύλια:[211] cf. μεϲολαβεῖ καὶ κῶλα) embedded in airs to be sung (ἐν τοῖϲ ᾄιϲμαϲι). The same distinction (vocal vs. instrumental melody) emerges again at p. 22. 7–9 Najock: the instrumental note put over the words (ἡ ϲτίξιϲ) either is a prolongation of the vocal line (ἢ παρελκυϲμὸϲ μέλουϲ κατὰ τὰϲ τοῦ ῥητοῦ ϲυλλαβάϲ) or marks a transition towards an instrumental interlude or closure (ἢ μεταβολὴ ἐπὶ κῶλον μεϲολαβοῦν ἢ ἐπαγόμενον).[212]

It seems therefore reasonable to conclude that in Arist. Quint. p. 31. 24 ss. W-I we are dealing with instrumental interludes and not with Aristophanes' metrical cola. Similarly, the word κρούματα does not imply any reference to the actual writing down of the signs employed

---

[209] This is also the interpretation provided by Barker *GMW* II, 435 (see esp. n. 160 as to the interchangeability in ancient sources of κροῦμα/κῶλον to designate an instrumental phrase), Mathiesen 1983, 94, Duysinx 1999, 77 with n. 4 and Rocconi 2003, 37 n. 195.

[210] The same distinction can be found also in Arist. Quint. p. 21. 19 W-I οὕτωϲ οὖν καὶ τὰϲ ᾠιδὰϲ ἢ τὰ κῶλα τοῖϲ τρόποιϲ ϲυϲτηϲόμεθα and p. 77. 30 ff. W-I τῆϲ δὲ μελωιδίαϲ ἔν τε ταῖϲ ᾠιδαῖϲ κἀν τοῖϲ κώλοιϲ ἐκ τῆϲ ὁμοιότητοϲ τῆϲ πρὸϲ τοὺϲ ὀργανικοὺϲ ἤχουϲ λαμβανομένηϲ κτλ.

[211] Cf. Pickard-Cambridge 1968², 262 nn. 2–3 (it is perhaps worth noticing that in Eustath. ad *Il.* Λ 547, 862 ll. 19–20 van der Valk, a passage quoted by the author in note 3, μεταξὺ τῆϲ ᾠιδῆϲ is Schneider's emendation of the transmitted reading μεταξὺ τῆϲ αὐλῆϲ) and West *AGM*, 205 n. 36. Najock 1972, 119 correctly translates κῶλα as "instrumentale Abschnitte."

[212] For an analogous formulation see also Arist. Quint. p. 23. 18 ff. W-I.

for outlining the instrumental melody[213] but simply refers to sounds produced by musical instruments, that is instrumental pieces.[214]

Summing up, Aristides' passage does not allow one to draw any inference about the close relationship allegedly existing between Alexandrian editorial technique (colization of lyric texts) and scores provided with musical notation.

I.8   *The Lycurgan* Staatsexemplar: *real and mental paths from Athens to Alexandria*

As we have already mentioned to briefly elsewhere,[215] among the necessary corollaries of Fleming-Kopff's literary archaeology there are two assumptions that deserve, I believe, more detailed attention. The first (1) is that the Lycurgan copy of Attic drama was already provided with musical notation, and indeed the very original one (that is, going back to Aeschylus,' Sophocles' and Euripides' own music).[216] The second (2) is the consequent belief that Alexandrian editions of poetic texts do actually derive their authority and relia- bility *recta via* from the Lycurgan copy as regards colometric articu- lation (supposed to be guaranteed, of course, by the concomitant preservation of the original score).

In other terms, according to Fleming-Kopff, about 330 BC there must have been close authorial control not only over the tragedians' texts (a conceptually non-problematic issue, whatever the means of such a control and the sources employed in order to safeguard it may have been)[217] but also over the original musical phrases, which

---

[213] Marino 1999b, 23.
[214] In this direction see Barker *GMW* II, 435, Mathiesen 1983, 94 and Duysinx 1999, 77.
[215] See I., 9 n. 10 and I. 4, 40 and n. 119.
[216] Fleming-Kopff 1992, 763, Fleming 1999, 23–4, followed by Tessier 1995, 21–2, Marino 1999b, 17 n. 16, 21 and Wilson 2005, 192. More generally, for the rele- vance of the theatre reform accomplished by Lycurgus within his political program see Faraguna 1992, 259–60, Engels 1992, 5–18 and 26–8 and Wilson 2000, 266–7.
[217] Putting aside the extreme and opposite conclusions drawn by Wilamowitz 1889, 131 ("Lykurgos brauchte dazu nur die Dramen aus dem Buchladen zu kaufen") and Blum 1977, coll. 90–1 (emphasizing the contribution of Aristotle and the Peripatos to "this first critical edition," but cf. the remarks of Ziegler 1937, coll. 2068–9), the most balanced position is still that of Pfeiffer 1968, 82, suggesting that we not overestimate the Lycurgan copy's critical value. Partially in the same direc- tion see also Erbse 1961, 217–8 (who nevertheless speaks of "eine hervorragende Rezension" at 224). Differently Tessier, 1995, 20, arguing for the Lycurgan copy as a true "ἔκδοσις provvista di notazione musicale."

we should suppose in this case to have been unchanged through all that time. This cultural continuity would thus have been preserved substantially unaltered down to the Ptolemaic period, when the philologists of the Library produced their editions of tragic texts. Hence it is clear enough that Fleming-Kopff's hypothesis strongly relies on two main points of transition (that is, the Lycurgan copy in 330s Athens and the textual criticism practised in Ptolemaic Alexandria) whose guiding principle is not a historically conditioned and thus pragmatically flexible persistence of a given cultural heritage, but a somehow inherent and atemporal unalterability.[218]

Let us thus start with (1). The only explicit evidence of a restrictive measure imposed by Lycurgus in order to avoid actors' interpolations being embedded in the original tragic text is the pseudo-Plutarchean passage of *Dec. or. vit.* 841f:[219]

εἰσήνεγκε δὲ καὶ νόμους, τὸν μὲν περὶ κωμωιδῶν, ἀγῶνα τοῖς Χύτροις ἐπιτελεῖν ἐφάμιλλον ἐν τῶι θεάτρωι καὶ τὸν νικήσαντα εἰς ἄστυ καταλέγεσθαι, πρότερον οὐκ ἐξόν, ἀναλαμβάνων τὸν ἀγῶνα ἐκλελοιπότα· τὸν δέ, ὡς χαλκᾶς εἰκόνας ἀναθεῖναι τῶν ποιητῶν Αἰσχύλου, Σοφοκλέους, Εὐριπίδου, καὶ τὰς τραγωιδίας αὐτῶν ἐν κοινῶι γραψαμένους φυλάττειν καὶ τὸν τῆς πόλεως γραμματέα παραναγινώσκειν τοῖς ὑποκρινομένοις· οὐκ ἐξεῖναι γὰρ <παρ'>[a] αὐτὰς ὑποκρίνεσθαι.

[a] <παρ'> e con. Wyttenbach add. Westermann in ed. pr.: γὰρ αὐτὰς <ἄλλως> ὑποκρίνεσθαι Grysarius: τοῖς <δ'> ὑποκριμένοις οὐκ ἐξεῖναι παρ' αὐτὰς ὑποκρίνεσθαι Bernhardy

[Lycurgus] introduced also new laws, the first concerning comic actors and according to which at the Χύτροι a performative contest should take place in the theatre and the winner should be enlisted as eligible for acting at the City Dionysia, which was not allowed before, and in doing this he restored a contest that had fallen into abeyance;[220] the second that bronze statues of the poets Aeschylus, Sophocles and Euripides should be erected and that their tragedies be written out and conserved in a public depository, and that the secretary of the

---

[218] The same limitation underlies also Chandezon's interpretation of *SIG*³ 648B (id. 1998). See I.9.1.

[219] This is the text according to Cuvigny's edition (Cuvigny 1981, 65; cf. also Lowe 1924, 100).

[220] On this measure see Pickard-Cambridge 1968², 15–6. The goal seems to have been that of increasing the number of potentially eligible comic actors for the City Dionysia.

State read them to actors in order to compare [i.e. the different versions], for it was illegal to act them by departing from the authorized text.

We are here told that Lycurgus' legislative measures entailed, among other tasks to be accomplished, that of writing out and keeping in some kind of public depository (ἐν κοινῶι)[221] the official copy of the three great Attic tragedians' texts, and directed the State secretary in particular to perform the task of παραναγινώϲκειν this copy to actors in order to prevent the performance of any possible alterations of the authorized text (οὐκ ἐξεῖναι γὰρ <παρ'> αὐτὰϲ ὑποκρίνεϲθαι).

Before inquiring whether the Lycurgan copy did actually preserve the tragedians' original music,[222] it may be useful to try to define in a more detailed way the task the γραμματεὺϲ τῆϲ πόλεωϲ has been charged with. What kind of control underlies an expression such as παραναγινώϲκειν τοῖϲ ὑποκρινομένοιϲ?[223] How have we to regard

---

[221] Although the general sense of this expression seems to be clear enough (that is, a reference to some kind of public place officially guarded), the more common formula ἐν τῶι δημοϲίωι would here be expected, see Boegehold 1972, 27 and Sickinger 1999, 110–2, 134–5. In any case Cuvigny 1981, 65 translates ἐν κοινῶι as "in a public depository" and "aux archives," cf. also Pfeiffer 1968, 82. Reynolds-Wilson 1974², 5 seem indeed to be inclined to trace this practice of conserving dramatic copies "in the public record office" back to a pre-Lycurgan period (cf. also Erbse 1961, 218), but see the balanced objections raised by Blum 1977, col. 89 n. 175.

[222] Fleming's argument that "since no one has made the unlikely suggestion that either papyrus [i.e. P.Vind. G 2315 as to Euripides' *Or.* and P.Leid. inv. 510 as to *IA*] was a Euripidean autograph, one has to conclude that at least some musical manuscripts were in circulation at the time of Lycurgus' decree" relies on a vicious circle inasmuch as it assumes *a priori* that the music transmitted by both papyri (one of which is of certain anthological origin, that is, P.Leid.) is originally Euripidean. As to the revival of παλαιὰ δράματα, assuming that it necessarily required the existence of an 'original' musical score (Fleming-Kopff 1992, 763, Fleming 1999, 24, followed by Tessier 1995, 20–2 and Lomiento 2001, 318) seems to take no account whatsoever of the possibility of any musical re-setting. See *contra* Parker 2001, 36 arguing for "something more like improvisation within a set of rules," and against believing that "fourth-century and later performers passed down 'Euripides music' note for note, or, as time went on, even approximately."

[223] A long-standing vexed passage, see Korn 1863, 2–7. Korn's suggestion (id. 1863, 6 n.2) of emending παραναγινώϲκειν τοῖϲ τῶν ὑποκριτῶν ἀντιγράφοιϲ is unconvincing: as already observed by Battezzato 2003, 11 n. 18, Korn does not take into account the possibility that the verb παραναγινώϲκειν might refer to a pre-eminently oral comparison (that is, actors simply declaiming the texts learned by heart and the State secretary reading aloud; see below).

the parenthetic explicative clause οὐκ ἐξεῖναι γὰρ <παρ'> αὐτὰς ὑποκρίνεςθαι?[224]

According to Fleming-Kopff, "since the point of the decree was to curb improvisation in performances, this copy should have been a performance text, complete with music."[225] Yet, granted that the Lycurgan measure was certainly meant to protect a supposed ortho-doxy of the theatrical *Bühnenpraxis*, Fleming-Kopff's inference about a distinct policy of control covering also the domain of the music is not necessarily to be drawn from the pseudo-Plutarchean passage.

Before focusing narrowly on the function and role likely accom-plished by the 'secretary of the State' in our passage, let us briefly cast a glance at another γραμματεύς, that is, the one we often meet in reading Attic forensic oratory.[226] In this context, the verb παρανα-γινώςκειν seems indeed to refer to a well-attested practice accom-plished by the γραμματεύς fulfilling his own juridical tasks, that is, that of "reading aloud by comparing" (cf. the prefix παρα-)[227] the original copy of the documents adduced by legal contenders (ψηφίςματα, νόμοι, ἐπιςτολαί, ἐπιγράμματα and so on) in order to allow the ἀντίδικος to verify the correctness of the words quoted.[228]

Among the most telling instances of such a meaning conveyed by παραναγιγνώςκειν, see Aeschin. *In Ctes.* 188 παρανάγνωθι δὴ καὶ ὃ γέγραφε Κτηςιφῶν Δημοςθένει τῶι τῶν μεγίςτων αἰτίωι κακῶν (Aeschines referring to the decree περὶ δωρεᾶς τοῖς ἀπὸ Φύλης previously mentioned at 187); Aeschin. *De falsa leg.* 61 παρανάγνωθι δή μοι καὶ τὸ Δημοςθένους ψήφιςμα κτλ.; Dem. *De cor.* 267 φέρε δὴ καὶ τὰς λῃτουργιῶν μαρτυρίας ὧν λελῃτούργηκα ὑμῖν ἀναγνῶ. παρ' ἃς παρανάγνωθι καὶ ςύ μοι τὰς ῥήςεις ἃς ἐλυμαίνου (what fol-lows is the quotation of the first line from Euripides' *Hecuba* and from another Euripidean tragedy unknown to us. Demosthenes mocks Aeschines by playing down his acting ability and by comparing him to a γραμματεύς). More generally, still within the juridical sphere, see esp. Plat. *Theaet.* 172e

---

[224] Kovacs 1994, 116–7 n. 1 accepts the text as edited by Nachstädt (deletion of γάρ), and corrects the transmitted οὐκ in οὐδ', but see Mastronarde's syntactic objec-tion against this textual arrangement in id. 1994b, 328.

[225] Fleming-Kopff 1992,763, quoted also by Tessier 1995, 21 n. 30 and Marino 1999b, 17 n. 16.

[226] The link as concerns the role of the γραμματεύς between forensic oratory and the pseudo-Plutarchan passage has been pointed out already by Dué 2001, 368–70. See now also Battezzato 2003, 12 ff.

[227] See LSJ s.v. παραναγιγνώςκω I.

[228] On that practice see the valuable survey by Battezzato 2003, 14–9.

ἀλλ᾽ ἀνάγκην ἔχων ὁ ἀντίδικος ἐφέϲτηκεν καὶ ὑπογραφὴν παραναγιγνωϲκομένην
ὧν ἐκτὸϲ οὐ ῥητέον (orators are always short of time at trials: the adver-
saries urge them by reading the accusation line by line); Dem. *In Tim.* 38
καὶ νόμον εἰϲήνεγκεν (i.e. Timocrates) ἅπαϲιν ἐναντίον ὡϲ ἔποϲ εἰπεῖν τοῖϲ
οὖϲιν, οὐ παραγνούϲ, οὐ λύϲαϲ οὐ δοὺϲ αἵρεϲιν κτλ.; Aeschin. *In Ctes.* 201
ὑπομνήϲατ᾽ αὐτὸν [. . .] τοὺϲ νόμουϲ τῶι ψηφίϲματι παραναγνῶναι. This juridical use of παραναγιγνώϲκειν is well attested also by the epigraphic and papyrological evidence, cf. e.g. P.Ryl. II 234. 15 (second century AD), PSI VII
768. 14 (465 AD). Thus, on the basis of these data it is reasonable to
believe that the qualification for the office of γραμματεύϲ must probably
have been the relatively non-specialized knowledge of a well-educated individual. This means that the γραμματεύϲ should certainly have been skilled
at reading and writing, but he was not necessarily expected to possess the
ability to read musical notation. On the contrary, Fleming-Kopff have to
assume that such an ability was widespread among ordinary educated
Athenians.[229]

The verb παραναγιγνώϲκω seems therefore to refer to a form of control applicable above all to the text regarded in its literal meaning
and correctness: a guarantee of preserving the authenticity of the
verbatim text. An interesting example, in terms of textual criticism, is
the passage of Porph. *Vita Plot.* 19, "although I do possess an apparently complete collection of texts and the ones that have now been
sent by you, I possess them only halfway. For these texts were in
no small degree corrupt [. . .] And I would really wish that accu-
rately copied texts should come to me from you, in order that I
may simply read them alongside for collation, and then send them
back to you" (καὶ κέκτημαι μὲν ὅϲα δοκεῖν πάντα καὶ τὰ νῦν ὑπὸ ϲοῦ
πεμφθέντα, κέκτημαι δὲ ἡμιτελῶϲ· οὐ γὰρ μετρίωϲ ἦν διημαρτημένα
[. . .] καὶ πάνυ βουλοίμην ἄν ἐλθεῖν μοι παρὰ ϲοῦ τὰ μετ᾽ ἀκριβείαϲ
γεγραμμένα τοῦ παραναγνῶναι μόνον, εἶτα ἀποπέμψαι πάλιν). Longinus'
passionate longing to possess accurate copies of Plotinus' works (τὰ
μετ᾽ ἀκριβείαϲ γεγραμμένα) aims at using them in collation (τοῦ
παραναγνῶναι) to improve the inferior texts he already has.

    On the basis of the data collected here, it thus seems quite rea-
sonable to posit an analogous role also for the State secretary of the
pseudo-Plutarchan passage about the Lycurgan laws. Most likely the
γραμματεὺϲ τῆϲ πόλεωϲ is to read aloud to the actors the tragedians'
authorized text for comparison with other possibly different versions

---

[229] I owe this observation to D.J. Mastronarde.

(not only written copies but also, for example, oral versions learned by heart by performers),[230] in order to avoid above all *textual* divergences engendered by histrionic interpolations, misrememberings and the like.[231] Of course, textual divergences ascribable to actors' interpolations may coincide with actual modifications in performing the dramatic action as compared with the hypothetical performance based on authorial stage-directions.[232] In this sense, the control exercised by the State secretary over the textual correctness turns out ultimately to have also very precise connections with the actual *mise en scène* of the performance as well. From this limited perspective, Fleming-Kopff's claim that the Lycurgan *Staatsexemplar* "should have been a performance text" is certainly a correct and valuable one. What is, however, debatable, is their more or less automatic conclusion that a performance text should necessarily be provided with musical notation, and indeed the original one. To challenge such a conclusion is not of course tantamount to saying that the musical aspect was completely neglected during revivals[233] but simply to

---

[230] Irigoin 1997, 241 takes into account only the possibility of comparing written texts: the Lycurgan law would have instructed the γραμματεὺϲ τῆϲ πόλεωϲ to "confronter avec cette copie (i.e. the official one) l'exemplaire des acteurs," but see Battezzato's criticism of this perspective (id. 2003, 9).

[231] A control of the mere textual data by means of comparison is argued also by Fowler 1960, 401 and Erbse 1961, 218. Cuvigny's translation "lire" (id. 1981, 65) reduces the compound παραναγινώϲκειν to a mere synonym of the simpler ἀναγιγνώϲκειν.

[232] Suffice it here to mention the way Helen entered the stage in Eur. *Or.* 71 ff. as recorded by the Σ^MTAB to *Or.* 57: νύκτα μή τιϲ εἰϲιδών· οὐκ ὀρθῶϲ νῦν ποιοῦϲί τινεϲ τῶν ὑποκριτῶν πρὼι εἰϲπορευομένην τὴν Ἑλένην καὶ τὰ λάφυρα. ῥητῶϲ γὰρ αὐτὴν νυκτὸϲ ἀπεϲτάλθαι φηϲί, τὰ δὲ κατὰ τὸ δρᾶμα ἡμέραι ϲυντελεῖται. This means that in Hellenistic or late Hellenistic times (νῦν) a *mise en scène* aiming at increasing the visual effect of Helen's entry was preferred, with the actor playing Helen entering the stage not from the skene (here representing the Argive palace), but entering spectacularly from one of the εἴϲοδοι followed by Menelaus' war spoils and servants (τὰ λάφυρα). As pointed out by Medda 2001, 89–90 with nn. 19–20, this different directorial choice relies on a quite cunning manipulation of the fictional time that, unless we suppose a patent contradiction with ll. 56–7, must have entailed also some textual rearrangements no longer recorded by medieval manuscript tradition.

[233] The most balanced hypothesis seems to me that advanced by Parker 2001, 36, according to which we have to suppose that the chorodidaskalos of the revival employed "a combination of memory from earlier performers and performances and his own traditional skills to recreate the music on the basis of the rhythm supplied by the words, while introducing such modernization as current fashion and his own taste might suggest." See also Willink 2001, 130 n. 12 on the issue.

recognizing that the text of [Plut.] *Dec. or. vit.* 841f does not allow us to draw any positive inference about some kind of institutionalized control of the music.

Given these premises, Fleming-Kopff's second keystone (2), that is, the belief that Alexandrian editions of poetic texts derive directly from the Lycurgan copy their authority and reliability as concerns colometric articulation, seems to assume a somewhat too linear and one-sided picture of the dynamics of transmission. Actually, the only ancient evidence on which Fleming-Kopff's argument relies is Galen's commentary to Hipp. *Epid.* III = XVII. 1, 607. 4–14 Kühn:

> ὅτι δ' οὕτως ἐςπούδαζε περὶ τὴν τῶν παλαιῶν βιβλίων κτῆςιν ὁ Πτολεμαῖος ἐκεῖνος οὐ μικρὸν εἶναι μαρτύριόν φαςιν ὃ πρὸς Ἀθηναίους ἔπραξε. δοὺς γὰρ αὐτοῖς ἐνέχυρα πεντεκαίδεκα τάλαντα ἀργυρίου καὶ λαβὼν τὰ Cοφοκλέους καὶ Εὐριπίδου καὶ Αἰςχύλου βιβλία χάριν γράψαι μόνον ἐξ αὐτῶν, εἶτ' εὐθέως ἀποδοῦναι ςῶα, καταςκευάςας πολυτελῶς ἐν χάρταις καλλίςτοις, ἃ μὲν ἔλαβε παρὰ Ἀθηναίων κατέςχεν, ἃ δ' αὐτὸς κατεςκεύαςεν ἔπεμψεν αὐτοῖς παρακαλῶν ἔχειν τε τὰ πεντεκαίδεκα τάλαντα καὶ λαβεῖν ἄνθ' ὧν ἔδοςαν βιβλίων παλαιῶν τὰ καινά.

> That Ptolemy [i.e. probably Ptolemy III Euergetes][234] longed to acquire ancient books, is clearly shown by what he is said to have done to the Athenians. For he gave them fifteen silver talents as security and got the texts of Sophocles, Euripides and Aeschylus just in order to copy and then return them safely. But he had luxurious copies of them prepared on marvellous papyrus rolls, kept the books the Athenians gave him, sent them the copies he had himself had prepared and invited the Athenians to keep the fifteen silver talents he left as guarantee and to accept the new copies instead of the ancient ones.

Some preliminary remarks may be useful to contextualize this passage. The Athenian episode, that is, Ptolemy's appropriation of the Athenian texts of Aeschylus, Sophocles and Euripides by giving a deposit of about fifteen silver talents[235] and sending them back new luxurious copies, does indeed represent a marginal digression within

---

[234] For ὁ Πτολεμαῖος ἐκεῖνος referring most likely to Ptolemy III Euergetes (247–21 BC) and not to Ptolemy II Philadelphus (285–46 BC; in this direction, however dubiously, Ziegler 1937, col. 2068) or Ptolemy VII (146–17 BC; see Fraser 1972 II, 1112, *addendum* to 480–1 n. 147), cf. Blum 1977, col. 90 n. 175, Tessier 1995, 19 n. 23 and Battezzato 2003, 20 n. 5.

[235] As regards the possible reasons for such a large amount of money see again Blum 1977, col. 90 n. 175.

a broader account of Ptolemy III Euergetes' passionate bibliophily.[236] We are first told about his burning passion some lines before (XVII. 1, 606 Kühn) as regards the so-called 'copies from the ships', that is, αἱ (i.e. βίβλοι) ἐκ πλοίων, which were catalogued under such a heading in the Library because Ptolemy had collected them from sailors docking at Alexandria at that time. This excursus on 'the copies from the ships' is, in its turn, only a small part of Galen's broader, detailed critical reflection aiming at explaining, almost philologically, the origin of the so-called χαρακτῆρες inserted in the antigraphs of the third book of Hippocrates' *Epidemics*.[237] Through this whole section Galen dwells (rather unusually) for quite a long time[238] and in a very detailed way on the different aetiologies reported by second-century BC medical literature about these χαρακτῆρες, quoting explicitly each time the sources he relies on and expressing his own critical opinion about them.[239] Here, at a glance, is a brief summary of the information collected by Galen on the issue.

According to Zenon, a follower of Herophilus and representative of a minority wing, the characters should be traced back to Hippocrates himself (XVII. 1, 603. 7–8 Kühn ἀλλ᾽ ἐὰν ἀναγνῶι τις τὰ τῶν ἀντειπόντων τῶι Ζήνωνι βιβλία, μηθ᾽ Ἱπποκράτους εἶναι λεγόντων τοὺς χαρακτῆρας κτλ.; as to dating Zenon's activity to the first half of the second century BC, see F. Kudlien, *RE* s.v. Zenon (12) coll. 144–6). Differently Zeuxis, one of the more authoritative among the παλαίτατοι ἐμπειρικοί (see F. Kudlien, *RE* s.v. Zeuxis (7) coll. 386–7), in the first book of his commentary on the book concerned (XVII. 1, 605. 13–4 Kühn: ἐν τῶι πρώτωι τῶν εἰς τὸ προκείμενον βιβλίον ὑπομνημάτων) mentions two different versions, which Galen quotes at length because of the rarity of the text he is citing (ἐπειδὴ τὰ τοῦ Ζεύξιδος ὑπομνήματα

---

[236] The parenthetical nature of the Athenian anecdote is clearly pointed out by the very beginning of the following textual segment, i.e. ὁ δ᾽ οὖν Μνήμων κτλ. (= XVII. 1, 608 Kühn). For the resumptive use of οὖν see Denniston, *GP*[2] 428–9.

[237] The so-called χαρακτῆρες are indeed a kind of tachygraphical writing summing up by means of codified initials the clinical picture outlined in the previous lines. The very precise *casus belli* for the long digression of Galen we are presently concerned with are the letters ΠΔΕΕΘ added at the end of the case history describing a woman suffering from angina (that is, ἡ κυναγχική of Hipp. *Epid.* III = Littré III, 52–4: the seventh patient of the first section).

[238] Namely from XVII. 1, 594 to XVII. 1, 613 Kühn, leaving aside pages 595–8 (explanation of the symptom πνεῦμα μετέωρον recorded by Hippocrates for the patient suffering from angina) and 608–10 (Galen turning back to the cause of the patient's death: ἐπάνειμι τοίνυν ἐπὶ τὸ χρήσιμον, οὗπερ ἕνεκα καὶ τὴν τῶν ἀρρώστων τούτων ἱστορίαν ἀναλεγόμεθα κτλ.).

[239] A survey of the different positions can be found in Littré III, 28–32 n. 14.

μηκέτι ϲπουδαζόμενα ϲπανίζει). According to Zeuxis' first version the characters would be late interpolations inserted for the sake of personal gain
by Mnemon in a copy of the third book of Hippocrates' *Epidemics* conserved in the Library (a hypothesis Galen seems to agree with, cf. XVII.
1, 608. 3 ff. Kühn). The second version claims instead that among the endless books ἐκ πλοίων 'landed' at Alexandria there would have been also a
Pamphylian copy of this book already provided with these characters and
bearing the heading κατὰ διορθωτὴν Μνήμονα ϲιδίτην. Finally, others claim
that Mnemon is not the name of the διορθωτήϲ but that of the owner of
the book itself (XVII. 1, 606. 16 ff. Kühn).

We are dealing thus with a minutely detailed text-critical digression
in which Galen does not avoid displaying precise bio-bibliographi-
cal information,[240] by quoting and comparing critically the different
and sometimes contrasting sources he has used. All the more striking, therefore, are the summary nature of the 'Athenian episode' as
narrated by Galen and the lack of precise references to the sources
consulted. The object itself of this bibliophilic theft is loosely referred
to by Galen as τὰ ϲοφοκλέουϲ καὶ Εὐριπίδου καὶ Αἰϲχύλου βιβλία,
without any explicit mention of the Lycurgan copy at all. Of course,
the mention of the Athenians *tout court* as Ptolemy's interlocutors
seems indeed to suggest that the expression τὰ ϲοφοκλέουϲ καὶ
Εὐριπίδου καὶ Αἰϲχύλου βιβλία does refer to some official copy of
the tragedies, a copy probably subject to some form of public care.

Nor can we entirely rule out the possibility that the scantiness of
information on the issue provided by Galen has to be ascribed to
the alleged notoriety of such an episode to his potential readers.
Even so, the lack of an explicit reference to the Lycurgan *Staatsexemplar*
in a context otherwise highly philologically accurate does suggest
caution.[241] And caution has to be especially urged if we are trying,

---

[240] Cf. e.g. ἐν τῶι πρώτωι τῶν εἰϲ τὸ προκείμενον βιβλίον ὑπομνημάτων as regards
Zeuxis, and the constant attention paid to the traditional dynamics of textual transmission (see esp. XVII. 1, 594 Kühn: a detailed survey of the textual variants of
the Hippocratic text, together with a full enumeration of the sources and discussion of the possible origin of textual corruptions).

[241] If compared with the zeal previously displayed by Galen in specifying the origin and classification of the new books acquired by Alexandrian philologists (see in
particular the report on αἱ βίβλοι ἐκ πλοίων in XVII. 1, 606. 12–13 Kühn: εἰϲ δὲ
τὰϲ βιβλιοθήκαϲ ἀποτίθεϲθαι τὰ κομιϲθέντα καὶ εἶναι τὰϲ ἐπιγραφὰϲ αὐτοῖϲ τῶν ἐκ
πλοίων), the lack of any such detail for the potential Lycurgan *Staatsexemplar*, provided that the Lycurgan copy is really meant here, is somehow puzzling.

as Fleming-Kopff actually do, to draw straight genealogical lines regarding traditional processes of transmission.[242] In this sense it may still be useful to remember Wilamowitz's sound warning against the understandably enticing step of establishing *a priori* a direct connection between the Lycurgan *Staatsexemplar* and Alexandrian editions: one should resist the all too modern temptation to see in the Lycurgan measure an early instance of a critical edition,[243] and one should stress the confluence into the Alexandrian Library of copies (*Lesebücher* as well as *Schauspielerexemplare*) coming from a broad range of geographical sources.[244]

In fact we are told by Athen. 1. 3a-b that Ptolemaic sovereigns' bibliophily went so far as to purchase books from the whole Mediterranean basin and not just from Athens. In order to praise the extent of Larensis' learning, Athenaeus' epitomator tells us that he owned so many books that he surpassed all who had previously been admired for their huge library (ὡς ὑπερβάλλειν πάντας τοὺς ἐπὶ ϲυναγωγῆι τεθαυμαϲμένουϲ). Among the names listed in this long enumeration of famous book collectors (that is, Polycrates of Samos, Peisistratus the Athenian tyrant, Eucleides of Athens, Nicocrates of Cyprus, the kings of Pergamum, Euripides, Aristotle, Theophrastus [supplemented by Wilamowitz], Neleus of Scepsis), we can find also that of Ptolemy II Philadelphus. More to the point, the Ptolemaic king is said to have purchased from Neleus all the books owned by Aristotle and Theophrastus and to have transferred them to Alexandria together with those that he had procured at Athens and Rhodes (καὶ τὸν τὰ τούτων διατηρήϲαντα βιβλία Νηλέα· παρ' οὗ πάντα, φηϲί, πριάμενος ὁ ἡμεδαπὸϲ βαϲιλεὺϲ Πτολεμαῖοϲ, Φιλάδελφοϲ δὲ ἐπίκλην, μετὰ τῶν Ἀθήνηθεν καὶ τῶν ἀπὸ Ῥόδου εἰϲ τὴν καλὴν Ἀλεξάνδρειαν μετήγαγε). This passage is certainly a well-known and difficult one inasmuch as it is closely related to the extremely problematic issue of the fate of Aristotle's books, for which we

---

[242] Cf. e.g. Knox 1985, 15, Tessier 1995, 20–1, Perrin 1997, 213–4 with n. 67 and Lomiento 2001, 302.

[243] Wilamowitz 1889, 132 "vollends in diesem Staatsexemplar ein Werk diplomatischer Kritik zu sehen und es gar zu einer Art Archetypus für unsere Handschriften zu machen, ist ein recht unhistorischer Einfall der Modernen." See also Pfeiffer 1968, 82. Erbse 1961, 224 argues for "eine verbindliche Grundlage, [. . .] eine hervorragende Rezension." Of course the Athenian copy should be somehow authoritative, yet [Plut.] *Dec. or. vit.* 841f does not allow us to see behind Lycurgus' measure a real "Rezension" critically understood.

[244] Wilamowitz 1889, 132–3 "das freilich war ganz natürlich, dass auch Schauspielerexemplare in die Bibliotheken kamen und die antiken Philologen auch solche einsahen [. . .]. Auch das ist sicher, dass sie sich über die Verwilderung des Textes durch die Schauspieler keinerlei Illusionen gemacht und mit der Möglichkeit gerechnet haben, dass der Text unter deren Einwirkung gelitten hätte."

seem to have at least two distinct traditions.[245] The evidence of Strab. 13. 1. 51 and Plut. *Sull.* 26 leads to a Roman path, whereas Athen. 1. 3a–b, as we have seen, points to Alexandria, although later at 5. 214d–e, we are told that Apellicon of Teos bought Aristotle's books, providing thus a link, as clumsy as it may be, with the 'other' Roman version.[246] What is, however, relevant to us is that Ptolemy II Philadelphus purchased books not only from Athens but also from Rhodes, another well-known main centre of the ancient book-trade in the Ptolemaic period (see Fraser 1972 I, 325 and II, 481 n. 148).

This of course does not amount to denying that the Athenian copies of the tragedians, Lycurgan or not, probably had a higher prestige and authority among Alexandrian philologists than that of copies coming from other parts of the Hellenized world. Still, we have to keep in mind that along with this privileged link 'Athens-Alexandria' we must not ignore the co-existence of diversified and sometimes overlapping traditional channels. This multifaceted scenario, even if potentially a threat to our attempts at reconstructing a rigorously unitary and consistent picture of the processes of transmission, seems indeed the only one positively attested by the sources we possess.

Summing up, somehow Athenian 'official' copies of the three tragedians' works, perhaps the very Lycurgan copy itself, reached Alexandria and most likely became an important point of reference for the forthcoming editions of tragic texts. But that these Athenian copies were provided with musical notation, and the original one, is an additional conclusion that ancient sources do not seem to authorize.

I.9 *Looking for an alternative. A first synthesis*

As we have already seen, a more detailed analysis of the ancient sources lets us catch a glimpse of a much less coherent and normative picture of the processes of transmission and reception concerning lyric texts than that suggestively outlined by Fleming-Kopff. Granted that the evidence at our disposal is both scanty and selec-

---

[245] There is also a third version of Aristotle's *fata libellorum*: according to al-Farabi (Theophr. T 41 Fortenbaugh) Augustus, after defeating Cleopatra at Actium, found Aristotle and Theophrastus' books at Alexandria. It is difficult to escape the impression that we are dealing here with a sort of compromise between the pro-Egyptian and Roman versions above mentioned.

[246] See Blum 1977, coll. 109–123 and Battezzato 2003, 22–5.

tive, Fleming-Kopff's approach seems to rest ultimately on a basic misunderstanding. Instead of asserting the documentary value of ancient colometry (Alexandrian as well as medieval) in itself as a valuable piece of historical information and interpretation, Fleming-Kopff have tried to trace its value back to external elements that are deeply non-homogeneous both quantitatively and qualitatively (that is, the musical papyri), thereby establishing automatic links of transmission which, however tempting as fillers of gaps in our knowledge, cannot be subjected to more precise verification.[247]

Of course, this is not tantamount to saying that before Aristophanes of Byzantium the Greeks did not have a clear awareness of structures κατὰ μέτρον.[248] Among the most recently acquired new evidence leading to the opposite conclusion we can just mention, as regards tragic texts, the case of P.Berol. inv. 21257, a third-century BC papyrus scrap preserving lines from Euripides' *Medea* that on the basis of its material features and *mise en page*[249] has rightly been called by Luppe "die für uns mit Abstand älteste 'Medeia-Edition.'"[250]

---

[247] The same argumentative weakness (that is, the lack of distinction between two substantially independent traditions only occasionally overlapping) has been embraced also by those scholars who have otherwise contributed a good deal towards a better-based re-evaluation of the importance of manuscript colometry. See e.g. Gentili 1998, 145–6: "Ora, è possibile immaginare che i grammatici alessandrini abbiano restituito il sistema colometrico prescindendo totalmente dalla struttura ritmico-musicale? Se questa ipotesi è corretta—come sembrano credere anche T. Fleming e E.C. Kopff—*essa non può che avvalorare ancor più* l'attendibilità della colometria antica, che fornisce un contributo non secondario alla ricostruzione dello stemma codicum" (italics are mine; the same argument can be found now in Gentili-Lomiento 2003, 8). What is telling in Gentili's statement is the presence of a symptomatic shifting of focus. The fact that Alexandrian philologists do not seem to have resorted systematically to musical scores as a supporting aid for colizing lyric texts does not imply by any means that they operated quite apart from the rhythmical structure of these texts.

[248] Cf. Gentili 1998, 144. Gentili is deeply conscious of that, yet the automatism operating in Fleming-Kopff's hypothesis (that is, a straightforward link between musical scores and learned scholarship) still operates in his argumentation.

[249] Cf. especially the different colometry suggested for l. 1088 (and already attested by P.Lond. Pack² 407 = Π⁸ Diggle, fourth/fifth century AD), that is, the scansion of εὕροις ἄν ἴϲωϲ as an anapaestic monometer: for a defence of this colometry see Luppe 1995, 38 and id. 1997, 95. As regards the much-vexed l. 1087, the Berlin papyrus would seem to confirm the validity (already advocated by Schömann and Snell) of the syntactic sequence δέ τι δὴ *vs.* the manuscript tradition oscillating between δέ τι γένοϲ and δὲ δὴ γένοϲ (in P.Stras.W.G. 306ʳ col. III l. 1 we have most likely to read]δὴ γένοϲ, see Fassino 1999, 19). But see now Mastronarde's skepticism on the issue (id. 2002, 348).

[250] Luppe 1995, 39; cf. also id. 1997, 94. In P.Berol. inv. 21257 the chanted

What is, however, worth pondering is the possible heterogeneity of paths through which this rhythmical and metrical awareness has endured. Emphasizing univocally the evidence of musical papyri as privileged vehicles of such transmission entails assuming that they were prevalents across time and space in a way that the direct and indirect evidence does not seem to suggest. Furthermore, it runs the risk of significantly underestimating the sensitivity, in terms of *Satz*- and *Rhythmphonetik*, displayed by Alexandrian scholars and Hellenistic poets at large.[251] Quite paradoxically, invoking a normative use of texts carrying musical notation by Alexandrian grammarians turns out ultimately to fall back again, in a sense, into Wilamowitz's old-fashioned strictures on the Ptolemaic age as "a great cultural gap, a Dark Age for music and lyric poetry."[252]

The most attractive and productive result of Fleming-Kopff's inquiry lies instead in their attempt to revise and update Wilamowitz's negative judgment by framing it in an unbiased perspective. A perspective, that is, that envisions for the Hellenistic age, among the several and undeniable groundbreaking elements, also the underlying vestiges of a cultural continuity, although Fleming-Kopff turn out then to graft them onto modes of transmission that are not posi-

---

anapaests of *Med.* 1083–1089 are colized whereas in P.Stras.W.G. 306ʳ col. III ll. 1–10 (= *Med.* 1087–114) they are written in *scriptio continua*. Although anapaests have a partially autonomous status also in terms of writing practice, since they are measures subject both to a recitative delivery and to song, the case of P.Berol. is much more striking inasmuch as for the third century BC we possess also instances of *scriptio continua* for lyric anapaests (almost certainly P.Hib. I 24 fr. [a] = Eur. *IT* 174–91, cf. Grenfell-Hunt 1906, 111) as well as for non-lyric anapaests (P.Hib. I 25 = Eur. *Alc.* 1159–63 = *Andr.* 1284–8 = *Ba.* 1388–92 = *Hel.* 1688–92 ≈ *Med.* 1415–19): all these Euripidean instances are recorded by Fassino 1999, 4 n. 25. The philologically accurate nature of the Berlin papyrus seems to be confirmed by the presence of corrections, *variae lectiones* (see Fassino 2003, 51) and perhaps marginal glosses (cf. again Luppe 1995, 39 and id. 1997, 95 *ad loc.*). A recent valuable analysis of P.Berol. within the broader spectrum of the Euripidean Ptolemaic tradition can be found in Fassino 2003, 50–6. For another remarkable instance, as regards lyric poetry, see the two Köln papyri of Sappho (= P.Köln inv. 21351 + 21376, early third century BC) recently published by Gronewald-Daniel (iid. 2004a and 2004b): the two-line stanzas of greater parasclepiads are marked off by *paragraphos*.

[251] For the analysis of Theocr. *Id.* 29 (suggesting Theocritus' awareness of a structure κατὰ cύcτημα underlying aeolic pentameters of Lesbian poetry, a rhythmic effect which can be reproduced only by means of a sophisticated play of *métrique verbale*) see below chapter 3.

[252] Fleming-Kopff 1992, 764 with n. 34.

tively supportable. This effort may certainly prove to be productive if we look for such a continuity no longer in a forced and elusive unity of transmission, but in the multiple channels of transmission already operating, although with different dynamics, in classical times. We have therefore to look for a persistence rooted in the variety and adaptability (and thus mutability) of the different original contexts (performative as well as not-performative) for which poetic texts were conceived.[253] The line of development of such a cultural heritage is not to be sought therefore in an abstract fixity of uncontaminated forms and contents, but rather in the adaptability and flexibility that we can glimpse also in the classical period.[254] The εἴδωλον of being able to recover definitely the original Euripidean music by means of a mechanical and temporally unchangeable transmission has to face the documentary evidence testifying to a more diversified picture of ancient Greek musical practice.[255]

The main claim underlying Fleming-Kopff's somewhat idiosyncratic argumentation, that is, the relevance of manuscript colometry

[253] The most engaging insight of the thought-provoking synthesis drawn by Cameron 1995 (esp. 44–6 and 71–103) lies in fact in this synchronic heterogeneity of communicative media, in spite of the radicalism of certain of Cameron's assumptions (a systematic overvaluation of Hellenistic culture as a performative culture, cf. Bing 2000, Cozzoli 1998, 136–7 and Griffiths 1997, 340–1). A more critical and historically aware approach to this continuity within the diversity (a somewhat standardized and impoverished one) as regards the social occasions and pragmatic functions of the dialectic enacted by the comparison between classical and Hellenistic poetry is wisely adopted by Fantuzzi in Fantuzzi-Hunter 2002, 24–9, 40 (= iid. 2004, 22–6, 37).

[254] The dialectic between "(a) great heterogeneity of form" and "the continuity of subject matter" in the pluralistic and sophisticated entertainment industry of the Hellenistic age is stressed by Easterling 1997, 221. For the well-known presence of such ways of re-shaping and re-setting at symposia see Vetta 1983, xxxi–ii, id. 1992, 180, Rossi 1993, 238 ff. and Lai 1997. As to comic re-performances on stage and off stage in Hellenistic period see Handley 2002, esp. 166–73.

[255] In the same direction see Willink's balanced remark (id. 2001, 130 n. 12) on P.Vind. G 2315 that "we cannot exclude the possibility of an entirely new 3rd-century setting (no more 'authentic' than 18th-century settings of Shakespearian songs). At the same time there are various ways in which a *partial* memory of the original music might have been preserved: e.g. an associated note merely of the 'mode' of a stasimon, and/or memory merely of its hummable openings bar. Nor can we exclude the kinds of inaccuracy associable with *pirated* texts" (author's italics). Partial oral memory, musical re-setting and rhythmic-textual adaptations must have co-existed from a relatively early date. On the role of memory in shaping the perception and notion of the so-called 'original' music within Greek ancient culture see Giordano-Zecharya 2003.

for the *constitutio textus* of lyric and tragic texts, thus remains a critically valid and welcome warning. What is at stake here is instead
the attempt to distinguish the different levels of likelihood on which
this main assumption relies, by limiting the range of the inquiry to
the relationship, if there was one, between Alexandrian editing technique and papyri carrying musical notation. More to the point, as
regards the theoretical premises and cultural assumptions underlying
Fleming-Kopff's broader reconstruction of the processes of transmission, it is possible to single out, I believe, at least two critical points
that invite detailed criticism and that can be traced back to the basic
misunderstanding mentioned at the outset of the present section:

(1) Fleming-Kopff support the alleged close relationship between
Alexandrian editions and musical scores *only* on the basis of the
shared features represented by the colometrical articulation.[256] As we
shall see in more detail later, however, this datum is contradicted
by the physical layout of most of the musical papyri (which are usually written in *scriptio continua*),[257] and above all does not take into
account the possibility of musical and rhythmic resetting—a possibility that Hellenistic performances actually activated, as is widely
attested by epigraphic and literary evidence (we have to keep in
mind that musical papyri have primarily to be understood as scores
conceived for an actual performance to be placed in a precise space
and time).

(2) Fleming-Kopff's justified insistence on the need to revise and
reformulate on new bases Wilamowitz's well-known strictures has
somehow induced them to neglect some still valuable insights embedded in Wilamowitz's otherwise debatable major statement. In other
words, Fleming-Kopff have not only dismissed but almost entirely

---

[256] This is a selective approach which can perhaps be explained also by what
still turns out to be Fleming-Kopff's main polemical target, that is, Wilamowitz's
undervaluation of the colon as a metrical unit. The same shortcoming appears also
in Marino when she argues for a direct "musical origin of the colometrical *mise en
page* devised by Alexandrian philologists" and linking misleadingly this datum to the
bare physical layout of musical papyri (Marino 1999b, 19, 22). In this direction see
also Gentili-Lomiento 2001, 10–11.
[257] See Johnson 2000a, 67–8; as to P.Leid. inv. 510 see chapter II.2. The consequences of such an automatic connection are evident especially in Marino's misinterpretation of the instrumental ꙇ sign in P.Vind. G 2315 as fulfilling a "specific
function of colometrical division" (ead. 1999a, 150), see II.1.1.

effaced the possibility of regarding musical papyri as one potential source, among many others, of *textual* variants (and then, if so, colometrical variants) for authoritative Alexandrian ἐκδόϲειϲ.[258]

The next step to be taken is thus that of analyzing more closely the consequences entailed by these two major limits (cf. respectively the following paragraphs I.9.1 and I.9.2), by adopting a more comprehensive approach to the topic. An effort will be made to contextualize Fleming-Kopff's test bed (that is, the direct evidence provided by musical papyri) within the broader frame which the evidence at our disposal, however scanty, allows us to outline.

I.9.1 *What alternative? The 'paths' of songs between persistence and innovation*

One of the more conspicuous deficiencies of Fleming-Kopff's first assumption (1) is precisely that its own generality exposes it to the risk of not being able to motivate the sporadic but certainly attested presence of ancient colometrical variants in both papyrological and medieval traditions of tragic[259] and, to a smaller degree, lyric texts.[260]

---

[258] See Wilamowitz 1889, 132–3. Paradoxically, the same limitation is also the main shortcoming of Pöhlmann's alternative hypothesis (that is, the *Bühnenexemplare* provided with musical notation as clearly separated from and not interplaying with Alexandrian *Lesetexte*), which runs the risk of falling into the opposite extreme to Fleming-Kopff's view while curiously sharing the same underlying deterministic approach.

[259] Particularly instructive in this regard are Mastronarde-Bremer's remarks on the textual tradition of *Phoenissae* (iid. 1982, 151–2 and 164), arguing the possibility of the transliteration of more than one majuscule manuscript of Euripides' *Phoenissae*, against the opinion of Barrett 1964, 58–61.

[260] As to the Pindaric tradition, I do not agree with Tessier 1995, 49, according to whom the papyrological data would testify to such colometrical divergences that we are forced to suppose the existence of true "sistemazioni colometriche antagoniste" (*ibid.* 36). D'Alessio's systematic revision of the evidence alleged by Tessier 1995, 50 clearly shows "that we are dealing not with two *really different colometries*, but with *minor variations* of the *same* colometrical division" (D'Alessio 1997, 46–8; author's italics); see also Ferrari 1991, 759 n. 6. When Tessier infers on the basis of the single case of *Pae.* 6. 128–31 and 134–37, that "se per i Peani vi è traccia di più sistemazioni colometriche di epoca ellenistica, non vi sarà a questo punto motivo di negare tale possibilità per gli Epinici" (Tessier 1995, 54), his conclusion rests on an improper generalization. The heading Αἰγ[ινήτα]ιϲ [εἰ]ϲ Αἰα[κὸ]ν| προϲ[ό]δι[ο]ν preserved by P.Oxy. 841 in relation to the beginning of the third strophic system of *Pae.* 6 (Rutherford 1997, 3–6) and the scholiastic note to l. 124 ἐν τῶι ᾱ [τ]ῶν προϲοδί[ω]ν φέρεται (D'Alessio in Rutherford 1997, 7) clearly show that the third strophe of the sixth paean (123–183) was originally conceived as a distinct independent poem within both the book of paeans and the first book of

An attempt at solving this inner contradiction has recently been advanced by Marino, who invokes the potential obscurity and consequent misunderstanding of the musical signs as a possible intermediary link between Fleming-Kopff's assumption (an overall homogeneity of the transmitted colometry) and Tessier's picture of the Pindaric tradition (different competing colometries).[261] Let us quote Marino's very words on the issue:

> a shift from musical score to text devoid of musical notation and, consequently, from musical phrasing to metrical cola is not likely to have occurred without editorial compromises, misunderstandings or intentionally different interpretations on the part of various ancient scholars. To this we must add the difficulties entailed by the process of transmission [. . .]. All that would explain both the partial validity and obvious partial unreliability of the manuscript and scholiastic colometry.[262]

Yet Marino's tentative compromise is not convincing. The usefulness of texts provided with musical notation for the colization of lyric passages, at least as it is strongly advocated by Fleming-Kopff, turns out to be seriously jeopardized, and Marino's reformulation does not succeed in producing a complementary explanation of the different, non-mechanical articulations of the lyric texts such as are presupposed by the presence of competing colometries.

Once again, all these speculations and afterthoughts lead unavoidably towards assuming the theatrical performance to be substantially

---

the processional odes (cf. Rutherford 2001, 329–31). It can thus be reasonably argued that the colometrical divergences displayed by P.Oxy. 1792 frr. 15 and 16 as compared to the text of P.Oxy. 841 and PSI 147 do represent an unparalleled case within the Pindaric tradition (cf. D'Alessio 1997, 49). The very reason, then, for this documentary *hapax* has most probably to be sought in two distinct performative occasions, see D'Alessio 1997, 56–9 (differently Ferrari 2001, 156 with n. 25, arguing for traces of a pre-Alexandrian colometry).

[261] Tessier 1995, 35–54. The author, while largely agreeing with Fleming-Kopff's conclusions (cf. id. 1995, 16, 21, 33), does not seem to be aware of this potential inner *impasse*.

[262] Marino 1999b, 22: "una riduzione da testo musicale a testo privo di notazione, e dunque da fraseggio musicale a cola metrici, verosimilmente non può essere avvenuta senza compromessi editoriali, malintesi interpretativi, o interpretazioni volutamente differenti ad opera di più studiosi antichi. A ciò vanno aggiunte le difficili vicende della tradizione [. . .]. Tutto ciò renderebbe ragione sia della parziale validità, sia della parziale evidente inaffidabilità della colometria manoscritta e scoliastica." This possibility of misunderstanding engendered by the musical notation itself does not appear in Marino 1999a, who, on the other hand, regards the alleged colometrical function she assigned to ⌐ in P.Vind. G 2315 as a textual aid against "the dismembering of the tradition" (ead. 1999a, 151–2). See further II.1.4.

unchanged over time in its inner dynamics of transmission,[263] which is tantamount to playing down the possibility of re-setting and re-adaptations, although the latter are well attested for Hellenistic entertainment practice in its various forms, public as well as private, of diffusion and performance.[264] A comparative analysis of musical papyri and epigraphic evidence allows us in fact to reconstruct some of these dynamics: that is, for instance, conversion to song of metres originally conceived for spoken or recitative delivery,[265] astrophic and/or monodic re-performance of choral lyric,[266] rhythmic alterations of strophic as well as astrophic structures to produce heightened pathos and greater polymetry.[267]

For most of these practices we are dealing with later stages of a development for which it is possible to trace, side by side with the

---

[263] A similar conservative view of the Hellenistic *Bühnenpraxis* can be found also in Gentili-Lomiento 2001, 10–11 n. 11 and more recently iid. 2003, 10 n. 40 (see esp. the statement according to which "che ancora nel III sec. a.C. fossero eseguite *le musiche di testi di teatro* mostrano i papiri che contengono antologie di cantica con notazione musicale" [italics are mine]). Yet what may indeed be more productive is trying to go beyond the acknowledgment of the bare material datum and asking *what kind* of music and performance these papyri might mirror, and how this question is related to such idiosyncratic features as anthological origin and so on.

[264] For a synopsis, beside Sifakis 1967, 44–52 and Gentili 1977, 7–23, see more recently Xanthakis-Karamanos 1993, 120–2 and Hall 2002, 12–24.

[265] Suffice it here to quote the well-known example of P.Osl. inv. 1413 (first/second century AD): fragment (a) ll. 1–15 consists of an otherwise regular system of non-lyric anapaests (that is, originally conceived to be chanted) put to music, the non-lyric nature of which is linguistically assured by Attic forms like γῆς l. 6, τλήμων l. 7; cf. Eitrem-Amundsen in Eitrem-Amundsen-Winnington-Ingram 1955, 6. Even more interestingly, the fact that text, notation and musical corrections are in the same hand suggests that we are here dealing with an autograph. If this is the case, we are actually dealing with the result of the composer's improvised creativity; see Pöhlmann-West 2001, 128. The same process of melic reinterpretation is operating also in ll. 15–9 of the same fr. (a) and in P. Mich. 2958 ll. 1–18 (second century AD): in both cases we have iambic trimeters set to music.

[266] For tragic texts the most telling case is that attested by the so-called *Themison-Inschrift* recently revised by Bélis 1999, 174–7: for a detailed analysis of this inscription see below. If we cast a glance at lyric anthologies devoid of musical notation but almost certainly conceived for singing, a very instructive example of astrophic re-writing of strophic passages is provided by P.Stras.W.G. 306ʳ col. II (= Eur. *Med.* 841–65, 976–82) and col. III (= Eur. *Med.* 1251–92): see Fassino 2003, 47–50. In the realm of theoretical speculation, the most complete and conscious formulation of the guidelines orienting this process of reshaping can be found in [Arist.] *Probl.* 918b [= XIX. 15], cf. De Lucia 1997, 245 n. 1.

[267] An instance of increased pathos gained by emphasizing an almost certainly unauthentic rhythmical pattern is the case of δεινῶν πόνων (= Eur. *Or.* 342–3) in P.Vind. G 2315 ll. 5–6. See II.1.3.

innovative aspects, some kind of continuity with the fifth-century
entertainment scene, although of course with a lesser degree of virtuosity and professionalism in the earlier period and often with a
different social context in the later period.[268] This aspect is particularly evident if we limit our attention to the production of drama
and its reuses and adaptations. Modern scholars have recently stressed
that "the custom of singing songs and reciting iambic speeches from
tragedy at drinking parties, well known from the later period, seems
already to have come into fashion by the late 5th c. BC," thus
reassessing the right to full citizenship in classical Athens for entertainment practices attributed by previous scholars to later developments.[269] The Hellenistic practice of singing tragic passages, iambic
(and therefore originally conceived only for spoken delivery) as well
as lyric, before large theatre audiences[270] has its starting point already
in this first process of selection and contextual adaptation, that is,
performance in the symposium.

In this connection one of the most debated passages is a well-
known scene of Aristophanes' *Clouds* (Ar. *Nu.* 1353–72).[271] Here
Strepsiades tells the Chorus of Pheidippides' insolent refusal to sing
to the lyre after dinner a song of Simonides,[272] and reports how he

---

[268] The 'diversion' concerning the social space of Hellenistic performances (the
term of comparison being fifth-century Athens) has been emphasized by Fantuzzi
in Fantuzzi-Hunter 2002, 25–6 (= iid. 2004, 22–3). To this displacement (that is,
from the theatre as a physical place representative of social cohesion to the atomization of its spatial integrity, from private symposia to public ἐπίδειξιϲ) correspond
perceived changes of pragmatic functions: cf. also Hunter 2002.

[269] Csapo-Slater 1994, 2; in the same direction see also Vetta 1992, 216–7 and
Cameron 1995, 72. Dover's authoritative statement that "there are no grounds for
thinking that in Aristophanes' time recitation from tragedy was normal after dinner" (Dover 1968, 254) has influenced modern scholarship till recent times, see e.g.
among Italian scholars Corbato 1991, 48 (for his refusal to accept the oral circulation of tragic passages at symposia see the objections raised by Lai 1997, 143–4
n. 4).

[270] For the epigraphic evidence of *SIG*³ 648B (Satyros of Samos) see below.

[271] For the whole scene see esp. Nagy 1990, 106–10, Bowie 1997, 4–5, Fisher
2000, 369–71.

[272] Cf. 1354–6 (ἐπειδὴ γὰρ εἰϲτιώμεθ', ὥϲπερ ἴϲτε,| πρῶτον μὲν αὐτὸν τὴν λύραν
λαβόντ' ἐγὼ 'κέλευϲα| ᾆϲαι Cιμωνίδου μέλοϲ, τὸν Κριόν, ὡϲ ἐπέχθη. According to
the scholium 1356a the so-called 'song of the Ram' (= 507 *PMG*), named after a
famous Aeginetan wrestler, was actually an epinician ode. What Strepsiades is asking his son for is thus most likely a solo performance to the lyre of a choral song.
For Simonides as "a symbol of old-fashioned poetry" in fifth-century Athens and
his critical attitude towards the Athenian aulos revolution see Wallace 2003, 80.

eventually obtained from his debauched son (after an unsuccessful exhortation to recite something from the venerable old Aeschylus)[273] only the delivery of some sophisticated modern novelty (1369–70: cὺ δ' ἀλλὰ τούτωνl λέξον τι τῶν νεωτέρων, ἅττ' ἐcτὶ τὰ cοφὰ ταῦτα), that is, a rhesis drawn from Euripides' *Aiolos*. This is the text of Ar. *Nu.* 1371–2 as edited by Dover 1968:

ὁ δ' εὐθὺc ἦγ' Εὐριπίδου ῥῆcίν τιν', ὡc ἐκίνει
ἀδελφόc, ὦ' λεξίκακε, τὴν ὁμομητρίαν ἀδελφήν.

1371 ἦγ' Borthwick: ἦιc' R: ἦc' ἐξ Ε[pc]: ἦcεν VE[ac]KΘ: εἶπ' Römer (probante Austin): ἦκ' Sommerstein

And he [i.e. Pheidippides] right away tossed off some speech by Euripides about how a brother, god save me, was screwing his sister by the same mother! (Henderson 1998, 193)

Thus, from the last quarter of the fifth century BC onwards,[274] sympotic conduct allowed not only singing monodically samples of choral lyrics[275] but also reciting iambic speeches drawn from tragedy.[276]

The main difficulty raised by these lines consists of ascertaining, with a reasonable degree of confidence, what kind of concrete

---

[273] Cf. 1364–5 ἔπειτα δ' ἐκέλευc' αὐτὸν ἀλλὰ μυρρίνην λαβόνταl τῶν Αἰcχύλου λέξαι τί μοι.

[274] For dating the *Clouds'* second version to a year between 422 and 417 BC see Dover 1968, lxxx–lxxxi.

[275] Cf. e.g. Eup. 148 K–A τὰ Cτηcιχόρου τε καὶ 'Αλκμᾶνοc Cιμωνίδου τεl ἀρχαῖον ἀείδειν, ὁ δὲ Γνήcιπποc ἔcτ' ἀκούεινl κεῖνοc νυκτερίν' ηὗρε μοιχοῖc ἀείcματ' ἐκκαλεῖcθαιl γυναῖκαc ἔχονταc ἰαμβύκην τε καὶ τρίγωνον (for the recent debate on Gnesippus' literary pedigree see Prauscello forthcoming). Also Ar. 234 K–A καὶ τὴν 'Εκάβην ὀτοτύζουcαν καὶ καόμενον τὸν ἀχυρόν is probably to be traced back to a sympotic performance of a tragic lyric scene: see Cassio's objections (id. 1977, 77–8) against Wilamowitz's hypothesis of a lyric *Iliupersis* (Corbato 1991, 50 unconvincingly argues for isolating the second member of the line, i.e. καόμενον τὸν ἀχυρόν and referring it to a rhesis reporting a fire).

[276] Corbato 1991, 51, followed by Lai 1997, 147–8, quotes *à propos* also Ar. 161 K–A ἐν τοῖcι cυνδείπνοιc ἐπαινῶν Αἰcχύλον, ascribing to ἐπαινῶ the meaning of 'reciting, declaiming' recorded by LSJ entry s.v. ἐπαινέω IV (referring to rhapsodic poems, cf. Plat. *Ion* 536d, 541e). Although the sympotic context of this fragment is beyond any doubt (ἐν τοῖcι cυνδείπνοιc), it seems to me quite unsafe to infer from the bare ἐπαινῶν what kind of performance is meant here (that is, spoken rhesis or lyric song). The fragmentary nature of the text does not allow us to go beyond the reasonable statement that Aeschylus' tragedies (iambic or lyric parts), conveniently cut and anthologized, circulated at symposia, most likely warmly appreciated by the traditionalist bulwark. For the generic meaning of 'praising, appreciating' conveyed by ἐπαινέω cf. e.g. Ar. *Nu.* 1377 οὔκουν δικαίωc, ὅcτιc οὐκ Εὐριπίδην ἐπαινεῖc;

performance lies behind Pheidippides' delivery of the shocking Euripidean rhesis. Are we facing (1) an early and otherwise isolated instance of iambic trimeters already converted to song (1371: cf. ἦιϲ(ε) of manuscript tradition),[277] that is, a performative practice mainly if not exclusively attested for later periods (Hellenistic and imperial)? Or (2) should the text be emended[278] in order to assimilate Pheidippides' performance to the common delivery mode positively and consistently attested for late fifth-century/early fourth-century Athenian symposia (that is, reciting—and not singing—tragic passages in spoken or recitative metres)?[279] Or, finally, (3) is it possible to maintain the transmitted reading ἦιϲ(ε) by referring it to a chanted delivery (the so-called παρακαταλογή) and assuming some sort of equivalence and/or interchangeability between λέγειν and ἄιδειν in terms of actual performance?[280] And if this is the case, how should we under-

---

[277] In this case we should imagine a dynamics somehow akin to that attested by *SIG*³ 648B for Satyros of Samos in 194 BC: see Webster 1967, 159 n. 59, Kassel 1991, 385, Corbato 1991, 51 with n. 25. Also Renehan 1976, 90–1 first argues for a real singing performance ("this Εὐριπίδου ῥῆϲιϲ was lyrically sung here"), but also entertaining, as a secondary hypothesis, (*ibid.*, 91–2), that of a chanted delivery on the basis that "λέγειν and ἄιδειν are sometimes contrasted, sometimes used indifferently."

[278] Dover 1968, 255, Austin 1970, 21 (εἶπ᾽), Borthwick 1971, 318–20 (ἦγ᾽), followed by Vetta 1992, 216 n. 120, Cameron 1995, 321 n. 94, Guidorizzi 1996, 340–1, Henderson 1998, 192–3 and apparently Fantuzzi in Fantuzzi-Hunter 2002, 30 (iid. 2004, 26). Sommerstein's emendation ἦκ᾽ (id. 1982, 142 and 225 on the basis of *V.* 562 and *Ra.* 823) seems to underly Csapo-Slater's translation of this Aristophanic passage (iid. 1994, 7 "immediately he launched into a speech of Euripides." In any case, Csapo-Slater assume here that Pheidippides is reciting a tragic speech).

[279] See Xen. *Symp.* 6. 3 ἦ οὖν βούλεϲθε, ἔφη, ὥϲπερ Νικόϲτρατοϲ ὁ ὑποκριτὴϲ τετράμετρα πρὸϲ τὸν αὐλὸν κατέλεγεν, οὕτωϲ καὶ ὑπὸ τοῦ αὐλοῦ ὑμῖν διαλέγωμαι; (Hermogenes addressing Socrates and Callias; the fictional date of Xenophon's *Symposium* is about 422 BC). Here κατέλεγεν refers namely to "der melo-dramatische, wohl rezitativartige Stil der sog. παρακαταλογή" as noted by Huss 1999, 336. Pickard-Cambridge 1968² 156 n. 3 correctly argues for a sympotic recital of tragic passages rather than a proper theatrical performance onstage. Nikostratos' widespread fame as tragic actor allows us to infer that the tetrameters Hermogenes is speaking about, iambic, trochaic or anapaestic as may be (cf. Sicking 1993, 105 n. 3), are of tragic origin.

[280] See Reitzenstein 1893, 35 (but Ephipp. 16 K-A can hardly be adduced as a pertinent parallel as regards the mode of delivery), Renehan 1976, 91–92, followed by Mastromarco 1983, 90, Herington 1985, 224–5 n. 15, Nagy 1990, n. 150, Fabbro 1998, 60 n. 48, Kugelmeier 1996, 76 n. 130 and Hall 1999, 105 n. 48. Still different is the solution tentatively advanced by Tammaro as an alternative to Römer's emendation εἶπ(ε), see id. 1980–2,109. According to Tammaro ἦιϲ(ε) should

stand this interchangeability? Should we suppose that the bare λέγειν may convey the notion of singing (and *vice versa* that ἄιδειν may express spoken delivery), or should we suppose an intermediate meaning such as 'chanting' employed to convey a kind of performance in which a sharp distinction between spoken delivery and chant was somehow blurred?

Although we must avoid an over-rational and over-literal interpretation of this line, a critical re-examination of the proposals advanced by previous scholars, together with closer attention paid to the Aristophanic context, may perhaps still be useful to provide some rough benchmark to assess possible interpretations.

Let us start by taking up Renehan's remarks against Borthwick's emendation ἦγ' (1371), accepted, among other editors, by both Dover 1968 and Henderson 1998. Renehan's objections pinpoint a real difficulty which cannot be easily avoided after his argumentation.[281] Theophr. *Char.* 27. 2 ταύτας (that is, ῥήσεις) ἄγων παρὰ πότον (referring to the somewhat oddly maniacal behavior of the "late learning man," the ὀψιμαθής) cannot be regarded any longer as a certain parallel supporting the conjecture (and Borthwick himself conceded as much).[282] The reading ἄγων is in fact transmitted only by the cod. Vat. Palat. 149 (15th–16th century: codex β of Torraca's collation) against the unanimous λέγων of the tradition and it is more likely to be a graphic slip than a learned humanist's conjectural emendation.[283] Similarly, Renehan has convincingly shown that all the other passages quoted by Borthwick are unsatisfying inasmuch as he does

---

be perceived here as semantically equivalent to μάτην λέγειν, that is "chatting, saying idly the same things." Yet Tammaro's suggestion is quite unconvincing, even apart from the fact that it leaves open the question about the mode of delivery of the Euripidean rhesis. All the instances quoted by Tammaro do not represent proper parallels inasmuch as in those passages ἄιδω meaning "talking to no purpose" is used absolutely, cf. Ar. 101.1 K-A καὶ τὰς δίκας οὖν ἔλεγον ἄιδοντες τότε; 101. 3–5 K-A ἔτι γὰρ λέγουσ' οἱ πρεσβύτεροι καθήμενοι,Ι ὅταν κακῶς <τις> ἀπολογῆται τὴν δίκην·Ι ἄιδεις, Ar. *Av.* 41 ἐπὶ τῶν δικῶν ἄιδουσι πάντα τὸν βίον, Eup. 39 K-A ὅμοιον ἄιδειν· οὐ γὰρ ἔστ' ἄλλως ἔχον.

[281] Renehan 1976, 88–90.
[282] Borthwick 1971, 319.
[283] See Torraca 1994, 609 and 612. For a defence of the reading λέγων vs. ἄγων see now Diggle 2004, 478 with reference to *Char.* 15. 10 where a clear-cut distinction is drawn between 'singing' and 'reciting speeches' at symposia (the self-centred man does not want οὔτε ἆισαι οὔτε ῥῆσιν εἰπεῖν οὔτε ὀρχήσασθαι). As to Ar. *Nu.* 1371 Diggle 2004, 347 n. 80 apparently sides with Römer's εἶπ'.

not distinguish between ἄγω and its compounds (that is, ἀπάγω, ἀνάγω, εἰcάγω), and, even more to the point, in all the instances produced by Borthwick the direct object of the verb, whether simple or compound, refers to something entailing a musical performance (e.g. μέλοc in Prat. 708. 5 *PMG*, ὕμνοc in Las. 702. 2 *PMG* and so on).

Once it is accepted that Renehan's criticism is sound, the alternative of claiming that Pheidippides' snobbish refusal refers only to singing "an old-fashioned song" and not to the traditional practice itself of singing to the lyre at symposia,[284] seems, at least to me, rather misleading. Due attention has to be paid to the fact that according to Strepsiades' account of the discussion that took place indoors, his son, after being asked to sing a song of Simonides, explicitly ascribed the contemptuous label of "old-fashioned" (1357) *tout court* to the habit of singing to the kithara after dinner (1356–7 ὁ δ᾽ εὐθέωc ἀρχαῖον εἶν᾽ ἔφαcκε τὸ κιθαρίζεινǀ ᾄδειν τε πίνοντ᾽), and not just to certain kinds of songs, that is, the 'old' ones (implying that 'other' songs might be acceptable).[285]

Of course, this does not mean that the two explanations (that is, the general refusal of the whole practice of singing at symposia and the more limited objection to certain kinds of songs) must be regarded as antagonistic and mutually exclusive.[286] It is actually a matter of factors that co-exist and interplay, but the specific context seems to emphasize the first element (the mode of performance in itself) rather than the second one. In fact, once Strepsiades has sadly given up on hearing his son singing to the lyre and has asked him—as second-best choice—to recite something from Aeschylus (1365 τῶν Αἰcχύλου λέξαι τί μοι), this time the reason for denial adduced by Pheidippides focuses on the poor quality of Aeschylean poetry (1366–7 ἐγὼ γὰρ Αἰcχύλον νομίζω πρῶτον ἐν ποηταῖc—ǀ ψόφου πλέων, ἀξύcτατον, cτόμφακα, κρημνοποιόν). The datum of singing to the lyre does not appear again only because it is no longer implied by his father's second request. Strepasiades' second demand turns out actually to be a first defensive withdrawal: putting aside the manner of delivery

---

[284] Renehan 1976, 90.

[285] See Sommerstein 1982, 225, Guidorizzi 1996, 340–1 and Wilson 2004, 295. More generally, on the socially and politically charged role played by kithara-playing in the 'old' musical education in classical Athens see Pritchard 2003, 306–11, and Wilson 2004.

[286] Cf. indeed 1362 καὶ τὸν Cιμωνίδην ἔφαcκ᾽ εἶναι κακὸν ποητήν.

(the beloved old fashion of singing to the lyre), Strepsiades retreats and focuses on the content, asking for a mere spoken delivery, but at least an Aeschylean one, while holding a myrtle-branch (1364–5 ἔπειτα δ᾽ ἐκέλευς᾽ αὐτὸν ἀλλὰ μυρρίνην λαβόνται τῶν Αἰςχύλου λέξαι τί μοι).[287]

And even more to the point, the fact that Pheidippides' reluctance has in view primarily the traditional practice of singing to the lyre *tout court* is confirmed also by his first, sudden reply at 1360–1 (οὐ γὰρ τότ᾽ εὐθὺς χρῆν ς᾽ ἀράττεςθαί τε καὶ πατεῖςθαιl ἄιδειν κελεύονθ᾽, ὡςπερεὶ τέττιγας ἑςτιῶντα;). The very element disdainfully singled out by this insolent son is singing to the κιθάρα as proper sympotic conduct.

From this perspective the comparison drawn by Pheidippides with the cicadas (ὡςπερεὶ τέττιγας ἑςτιῶντα) is especially telling. Both in ancient Greek every-day experience and social imagery the cicada is canonized as the melodious insect *par excellence*: a well-attested and long-standing literary tradition[288] explicitly depicts it as the most tuneful and musical among the insects.[289] In other words, we are not entitled to see in this entomological comparison a reference to a shrill, irritating, unpleasant loud sound as our modern perception

---

[287] See Dover 1968, 254: "Strepsiades is compromising by not demanding a song to the lyre, but he preserves appearances by the myrtle-branch." In the same direction cf. also Sommerstein 1982, 225 "Pheidippides refuses to sing, but he is asked at least to hold the myrtle-branch during his recitation, as a concession to tradition."

[288] The cicada's literary pedigree begins already in ancient epic poetry, see Γ 150–2 ἀγορηταὶl ἐςθλοί, τεττίγεςςιν ἐοικότες, οἵ τε καθ᾽ ὕληνl δενδρέωι ἐφεζόμενοι ὄπα λειριόεςςαν ἱεῖςι (for the equivalence λειριόεις ~ εὐήκοος, if referred to the domain of sound, cf. West 1966, 171) and the famous lines of Hes. *Erg.* 583–4 καὶ ἠχέτα τέττιξl δενδρέωι ἐφεζόμενος λιγυρὴν καταχεύετ᾽ ἀοίδην taken up by Alc. 347. 3 V ἄχει δ᾽ ἐκ πετάλων ἄδεα τέττιξ. For a detailed treatment of the cicada's occurrence in Greek literature and its cultural and symbolic meaning see Davies-Kathirithamby 1986, 117–8; for the occurrence of this topos in Hellenistic literature see Asper 1997, 195 with n. 268. More recently, for Callimachus' reshaping of the traditional association poet/cicada by focusing on the insect's tirelessness as metaphorically equivalent to the literary πόνος see Lelli 2001, 247–8. For a cross-reference within the Aristophanic comedies see *Pax* 1159–60 ἡνίκ᾽ ἄν δ᾽ ἀχέταςl ἄιδηι τὸν ἡδὺν νόμον and *Av.* 1095–6 ἡνίκ᾽ ἄν ὁ θεςπέςιος ὀξὺ μέλος (Brunck: ὀξυμελὴς aB: ὀξυβελὴς RM) ἀχέταςl [. . .] βοᾶι.

[289] See e.g. Archias, *A.P.* 7. 213. 3–4, claiming that the cicada's song (μολπάν) is more pleasant to shepherds than that of the lyre (οἰονόμοις τερπνότερον χέλυος). Also interesting is the late Theophyl. *Ep.* 1, where there is an implicit comparison between τέττιξ and τραγωιδός (cf. Borthwick 1965, 256 n. 5; much more debatable is the treatment Borthwick gives to Suet. *Nero* 20. 2).

might at first glance suggest.[290] On the contrary, to an ancient Greek
audience, the comparison with cicadas stresses the bare datum of an
empty, frivolous, melodious pleasantness,[291] an opinion which, if put
in Pheidippides' mouth, turns out to be quite appropriate to the
well-known stricture of Socratic-sophistic origin on such a sympotic
practice.[292]

Thus, if Renehan is to be credited with successfully questioning
the documentary basis on which Borthwick's conjecture ἦγ' relies,
his attempt to argue for a truly sung delivery of the Euripidean rhesis performed by Pheidippides at *Nu.* 1371[293] is unfortunately not
convincing. In fact, Renehan's argumentation still depends strongly
on Webster's interpretation of the passage,[294] an interpretation which

---

[290] See Stanford's remark (id. 1969, 4) that "we must take into account the fact
that the Greeks seem to have liked shrillness in tone better than we do." More
diffusely, on the different perception and appreciation of the sound of the cicada
by modern northern Europeans, see Davies-Kathirithamby 1986, 116–7 and Dunbar
1995, 589. To the instances of this cultural misunderstanding quoted by Davies-
Kathirithamby 1986 we can add also *A.P.* 9. 264. 3–4: αὐτουργῶι μέλει‖ ἡδὺϲ (i.e.
τέττιξ) κατωργάνιζε τῆϲ ἐρημίαϲ. At l. 4 the manuscript tradition has unanimously
the reading ἡδύϲ, still glossed by Soury in Waltz-Soury 1957, 106 n. 1 as "bizarre"
and previously emended by Desrousseaux in ἤχουϲ (pl. acc.) governing the genitive
τῆϲ ἐρημίαϲ on the basis of Ar. *Av.* 224 κατεμελίτωϲε τὴν λόχμην. The latter is an
unnecessary correction: a parallel for the syntagm κατωργάνιζε τῆϲ ἐρημίαϲ can be
found in Theophr. fr. 726B Fortenbaugh (= Athen. 14. 624a 10–b 3) [. . .] ἰϲχιακοὺϲ
φάϲκων ἀνόϲουϲ διατελεῖν εἰ καταυλήϲοι τιϲ τοῦ τόπου τῆι Φρυγιϲτὶ ἁρμονίαι
(Theophrastus saying in his *On inspiration* that music can cure also sciatica if "someone played the aulos over the place in the Phrygian harmonia" as translated by
Fortenbaugh et alii 1992, II, 581; for the therapeutic power of the aulos in the
narrative of Theophrastus see recently Matelli 2004, 160ff.). For καταυλέω + *genit.
loci*, meaning literally 'playing the aulos over a place' and then 'making a place sound
with flute-playing' see LSJ s.v. καταυλέω I. 2 and Rocconi 2001, 285–6 with n. 48.
[291] Cf. Σ to *Nu.* 1360a πολύλαλον γὰρ τὸ ζῶιον RV and 1360b ὡϲπερεὶ τέττιγαϲ:
παρεποίηϲε τὸ ἄιδειν καί φηϲιν· ὅτι τὸ ἄιδειν φλυαρεῖν ὡϲ τέττιγαϲ καὶ οὐδὲν ἄλλο
ἢ ὡϲ γυναῖκαϲ ἄιδειν ἀλετρευούϲαϲ EΘ. For the traditional vacuity of the cicadas'
song see Capra 2000, 241–4. Of course, the mention of the cicada in the Aristophanic
passage entails also an underlying reference to the cicada's proverbial carelessness
about food, see Dover 1968, 254 *ad loc.* For the exploitation of this *topos* in comedy see the bibliographic references quoted by Lelli 2001, 248 n. 17.
[292] Cf. Σ to *Nu.* 1357b ἀρχαῖον εἶν' ἔφαϲκε: ἀντὶ τοῦ EΘM "μωρόν". EΘM[bis]Rs
παραιτοῦνται γὰρ οἱ φιλόϲοφοι κιθαρίζειν ἐν τῶι πίνειν EΘMNp. As to the Socratic
origin of Pheidippides' disdainful refusal see also Taillardat 1962, 459 n. 5 and
more generally Vetta 1992, 218.
[293] See Renehan 1976, 90: "to sing (rather than recite, as traditionally) a ῥῆϲιϲ
of his [i.e. Euripides] seems to me to have special point here as a glaring example of the corrupt new musical practices which Strepsiades deplores."
[294] Renehan 1976, 90 explicitly refers to the evidence alleged by Webster 1967,
158–9 as positive proof of "singing of even non-lyric parts of tragedy."

is liable to several objections. Webster's belief in a true conversion to song of an iambic rhesis from Euripides' *Aiolos* rests substantially on two elements strictly interconnected in his argumentative frame. The first one (1) is the parallel Webster establishes with Suet. *Nero* 21. 5, where we are told that Nero, in his unrestrained histrionic mood, among other themes (*inter cetera*), sang also 'Canace in labour', 'Orestes the matricide', 'Oedipus the blind' and 'Hercules the mad' (*inter cetera cantavit Canacem parturientem, Oresten matricidam, Oedipodem excaecatum, Herculem insanum*). The second element (2) is Webster's very peculiar assumption that in *Nu.* 1371 we are dealing with the first part of the prologue speech of *Aiolos* (in iambic trimeters, of course), which he identifies with the 'Canace in labour' performed by Nero.[295]

At least two basic objections can be raised against Webster's general reconstruction of the dramatic plot of *Aiolos* and, in a more detailed way, against the link he establishes between Suetonius' report of Nero's histrionic passion and the lines of the *Clouds* with which we are presently concerned.

Let us start with this second point. First of all, the comparison with Suetonius cannot be adduced as proper evidence for tracing the practice of singing iambic rheseis back to the late fifth-century Athens, for the chronological gap between the two episodes cannot be overcome by the identity of the subject performed. We have already seen that the practice of converting to song proper even non-lyric parts of tragedies does not represent a difficulty in itself if embedded in the diversified scenario of the Hellenistic and imperial entertainment industry, whereas such a mode of performance seems not to be attested as standard or even idiosyncratic practice in late fifth-century Athens.

For the very same reason also the evidence provided by Kassel as a parallel for our Aristophanic lines, that is, Luc. *De salt.* 27 is not cogent.[296] In fact, the conspicuous unseemliness both in speech

---

[295] See Webster 1967, 159 n. 59: "Strepsiades in the *Clouds* objects to his son 'singing' the earlier part of this speech" [that is, *Aiolos*' prologue speech that Webster supposes to be sung by Nero while performing 'Canaces in labour'].

[296] Kassel 1991, 385. It is worth noticing that Kugelmeier 1996, 76 n. 130 seems partially to misunderstand Kassel's argumentation. Kassel's defence of the transmitted ἦιϲ(ε) in *Nu.* 1371 does assume that Pheidippides actually sings the Euripidean rhesis (cf. *ibid.* "und eine euripideischen ῥῆϲιϲ wird auch schon von einem zeitgenössischen Früchtchen zum Ärger seines Vaters gesungen"). In this direction points

and gesture displayed by the τραγωιδός as depicted by Lykinus (ἔνδοθεν αὐτὸς κεκραγώς, ἑαυτὸν ἀνακλῶν καὶ κατακλῶν,[297] ἐνίοτε καὶ περιάιδων τὰ ἰαμβεῖα) implies, as is clearly shown by the previous description of a very sophisticated staging,[298] an explicit stricture on the increasing degeneration of contemporary theatrical performances (that is, of the second century AD), which were very often reduced to *Einzelszenen*.[299] Furthermore, neither Suetonius nor Lucian is referring to a sympotic context, but rather to true theatrical performances.[300]

---

also Kassel's correct re-evaluation of the reading ἐν μέλει (ΓΕ) *vs.* ἐν μέρει in a further passage of Lucian quoted by the scholar as an instance of a 'sung' rhesis, that is, Luc. *Hist. conscr.* 1. μάλιστα δὲ τὴν Εὐριπίδου Ἀνδρομέδαν ἐμονώιδουν καὶ τὴν τοῦ Περσέως ῥῆσιν ἐν μέλει διεξήιεσαν. The 'tragic' fever that had overwhelmed the people of Abdera went so far as to make them behave as if mad: they went around the streets in a ridiculous state of mind, mostly singing monodies from Euripides' *Andromeda* and "rendering Perseus' speech in song," see Kilburn 1959, 3 (Borthwick 1971, 319 n. 5 still argues for the reading ἐν μέρει). Unlike the case of the passage of the *Clouds*, this interpretation of Luc. *Hist. conscr.* 1 does not entail chronological problems: the episode refers to the reign of Lysimachus (Λυσιμάχου ἤδη βασιλεύοντος), and has thus to be dated between 323 and 281 BC (Bélis 1991, 32 n. 5 inclines to a late date, namely ca. 280 BC) and, more to the point, the context is a theatrical and not a sympotic one. A very similar anecdote (almost a variant), transposed to Nero's time, can be found in Eunap. fr. 54 *HGM* I, 246–8 Dindorf, see Easterling 1997, 222–3 with n. 39.

[297] I do not agree with Kokolakis 1960, 90–1, who argues that the participles ἀνακλῶν καὶ κατακλῶν refer to the "modulations of the voice as this occasionally rises to a pitch but soon sinks to deep and feeble notes." First, both ἀνακλάω and κατακλάω are used here reflexively (see ἑαυτόν) and thus do not refer "to vocal delivery" but to the unseemly, pathetic posture of this ὑποκριτής who oscillates by bending forward and backward during his performance. Kokolakis' objection that such a disorderly gesture would apply only to an ὀρχηστής and not to "a tragic actor's rather static posture" (id. 1960, 90) does not take into account that Lykinus is most likely speaking not of performances of whole tragedies but of the ἐπιδείξεις of *virtuosi*. Furthermore, all the other instances of ἀνακλάω/κατακλάω in Luc. always refer to a particular posture assumed by the person involved, see *De salt.* 5 (ἀνθρώπωι [. . .] κατακλωμένωι, about a mime's athletic skill), *Symp.* 18 (κατακλῶν ἑαυτὸν καὶ διαστρέφων said of a dancer), *Anach.* 7 (the right hand of a statue of Apollo is ὑπὲρ τῆς κεφαλῆς ἀνακεκλασμένη), 9 (ἀγχομένους πρὸς ἀλλήλων καὶ κατακλωμένους, referring to wrestlers). Finally, also Luc. *Demon.* 12 and Hipp. *Coac.* 246 (= V, 637 Littré) do not represent true parallels supporting Kokolakis' hypothesis of a kind of "vocal delivery." In the first passage τὸ ἐπικεκλασμένον refers to Favorinus' lax songs and in Hipp. *Coac.* 246 αἱ κατακλώμεναι φωναὶ μετὰ φαρμακείην allude to "la voix cassée après une purgation" (Littré, *ibid.*), cf. LSJ s.v. κατακλάω III.

[298] Cf. the mention of προστερνίδια καὶ προγαστρίδια to simulate a false sturdiness of limb or the huge mouth of the mask (καὶ στόμα κεχηνὸς πάμμεγα ὡς καταπιόμενος τοὺς θεατάς).

[299] Cf. Beta 1992, 121 n. 47.

[300] For Suetonius, see *Nero* 21. 3 *dubitavit etiam an privatis spectaculis operam inter*

Secondly, as regards the dramatic plot and structure of *Aiolos*, the close link drawn by Webster between Suet. *Nero* 21. 5 and *Nu.* 1371 is nothing but highly speculative. According to Webster's interpretation of Suetonius' account, "in the last two [that is, theatrical performances] what Nero 'sang' (whatever that means) about 'Oidipous blinded and Herakles mad' must have been a messenger-speech and we have *therefore* no right to suppose that Kanake sang a monody when she was on the point of giving birth. What Nero 'sang' may have been the prologue speech." The attached footnote adds that "Strepsiades in the Clouds (1371) objects to his son 'singing' the earlier part of *this* speech."[301]

Some obvious objections arise here. First, if expressions like *Canacem parturientem*, *Oresten matricidam*, *Oedipodem excaecatum* and *Herculem insanum* seem actually to point to a distinct, specific role performed onstage by Nero (an *Einzelszene*) rather than to whole tragedies,[302] Webster's inference that in the last two cases we are dealing with a messenger-speech (and thus with recitative metres converted to song)[303] is misleading, at least as regards *Hercules insanus*. If we look at the following lines (*Nero* 21. 6), we are told that on the occasion of the performance of Heracles becoming mad, a young recruit charged with guarding the stage entrances, when he saw Nero entering bound with chains according to the subject of the dramatic plot, rushed forward to help him: *in qua fabula* (i.e. *Hercules insanus*) *fama est tirunculum militem positum ad custodiam aditus, cum eum* (i.e. *Neronem*) *ornari ac vinciri catenis, sicut argumentum postulabat, videret, accurrisse ferendae opis gratia.*[304] The clumsy help provided by the recruit to Nero entering

---

scaenicos daret. As pointed out by Rolfe 1997, 112–3 n. (c), *privata spectacula* are those given by the magistrates, since in the imperial age everyone except the emperor himself was a *privatus*.

[301] Webster 1967, 159 with n. 59 (italics are mine).

[302] See Kierdorf 1992, 188. That Nero played also female parts has already been said at 21. 4 *tragoedias quoque cantavit personatus, heroum deorumque, item heroidum ac dearum, personis effectis ad similitudinem oris sui et feminae, prout quamque diligeret*. Nero's performing a 'Canace in labour' is recorded also by Cass. Dio 63. 10. 2.

[303] Nero's performances both as *citharoedus* (and thus to the accompaniment of the lyre, see *Nero* 21. 1 *ac sine mora nomen suum in albo profitentium citharoedorum iussit ascribi*) and as *tragoedus* required singing. For the difficulties of ascertaining the precise details of these two kinds of performances, which often overlapped, see Bartsch 1994, 224 n. 4.

[304] Cass. Dio reports the same episode at 63. 10. 2 οὐδὲ ἐτόλμησε οὐδεὶς αὐτῶν οὔτε ἐλεῆσαι τὸν κακοδαίμονα οὔτε μισῆσαι, ἀλλ᾽ εἷς μέν τις στρατιώτης ἰδὼν αὐτὸν

the stage 'bound with chains' does indeed suggest that the role performed by Nero was not that of the messenger but of Heracles. In
Euripides' *HF*[305] it is in fact Heracles that who enters the stage
'bound with chains' (*vinctus*), since immediately after having lost consciousness he is chained to a column by servants in order to prevent him from committing another impious slaughter.[306]

Thus Webster's hypothesis that Nero playing '*Hercules insanus*' is
actually performing a messenger-speech can reasonably be ruled out,
and the same can be argued for 'Canace in labour', 'Orestes the
matricide' and 'Oedipus the blind'. In other words, nothing prevents
us from imagining Nero performing a lyric monody instead of singing

δεδεμένον ἠγανάκτηϲε καὶ προϲδραμὼν ἔλυϲεν, ἕτεροϲ δὲ ἐρομένου τινὸϲ "τί ποιεῖ
ὁ αὐτοκράτωρ" ἀπεκρίνατο ὅτι "τίκτει"· καὶ γὰρ τὴν Κανάκην ὑπεκρίνετο. The
Verfremdungseffekt experienced by the young recruit is much more understandable if
we take into account that Nero, even if playing Heracles, was likely to bear a mask
reproducing his own physical outlines, see *Nero* 21. 4 *personis effectis ad similitudinem
oris sui*. Bartsch 1994, 49 acutely remarks that "Nero's mask of himself serves as a
catalyst of confusion, making it seemingly impossible for the spectator to apply either
'representation' or 'reality' as a consistent frame for viewing."

[305] The previous mention of 'Canace in labour' points strongly to Euripides'
homonymous tragedy: it thus seems reasonable to suppose that also the 'Heracles
the mad' performed by Nero is the Euripidean *HF*. Of course, the possibility of
some other authorship cannot be entirely ruled out, but it seems to me less likely,
the previous references to Orestes and Oedipus orienting apparently towards world-
known classical masterpieces, that is, those of Euripides and Sophocles. For Euripides'
Aiolos as the main source for Ovid's *Her.* 11, see Knox 1995, 257–8.

[306] Eur. *HF* 1032–8 ἴδεϲθε [. . .] περὶ δὲ δεϲμὰ καὶ πολύβροχ᾽ ἁμμάτωνl ἐρείϲμαθ᾽
Ἡράκλειονl ἀμφὶ δέμαϲ τάδε λαΐνοιϲl ἀνημμένα κίοϲιν οἴκων. The herald, in
Euripides' play, reports the chaining of Heracles, in which he himself, together with
other servants and Amphitryon, has taken part off-stage, cf. *HF* 1010–2 ἡμεῖϲ
[. . .]lϲὺν τῶι γέροντι δεϲμὰ ϲειραίων βρόχωνl ἀνήπτομεν πρὸϲ κίον᾽, ὡϲ λήξαϲ ὕπνουl
μηδὲν προϲεργάϲαιτο τοῖϲ δεδραμένοιϲ). Entering the stage *vinctus catenis* can refer
to nobody but Heracles himself. It is worth observing that in Seneca's homonymous tragedy chains are not mentioned any more, whereas there we find Amphitryon's
exhortation to move arms away from his son (1053 *removete, famuli, tela, ne repetat
furens*). This alteration of the Euripidean plot becomes dramatically useful in the
fifth act when Heracles asks for his own arms back (1229–36, 1242–5) in order to
commit suicide, see Billerbeck 1999, 536. Differently, Ailloud 1961, 167 with n. 1
believes that Suet. *Nero* 21. 6 refers to another episode of the Euripidean *HF*, that
is, Heracles' arrival at Thebes when the sacrifice of Megara and his sons is about
to be accomplished. The chain would be therefore those requested by the "usage
qui consistait à parer les victimes." Ailloud's interpretation can hardly be right: in
Euripides' *HF* the only feature denoting the sons' sacrificial status as victims are
wreaths with funerary bands on their heads (525–6 τέκν᾽ ὁρῶ πρὸ δωμάτωνl ϲτολμοῖϲι
νεκρῶν κρᾶταϲ ἐξεϲτεμμένα; cf. also 442–3 τούϲδε φθιμένωνl ἔνδυτ᾽ ἔχονταϲ), and
chains are mentioned only with regard to Heracles (1010–2, 1032–8), cf. Lesky
1966, 346–7.

an iambic speech. And what is even more important to us, the close link drawn by Webster between Nero's alleged prologue-speech portraying 'Canace in labour'[307] and Ar. *Nu.* 1371 turns out to be unfounded. Aristophanes' words at *Nu.* 1371–2[308] do not suppose a precise reference to a specific stage of the dramatic plot (prologue, first episode and so on) but designate the subject at large (that is, the incestuous love story between brother and sister) in order to enable the Athenian audience to grasp immediately that the Euripidean tragedy alluded to is *Aiolos*.

Finally, a second suggestion advanced by Renehan deserves further investigation. We have already mentioned that his alternative hypothesis is that of understanding the transmitted reading ἧιϲ' at *Nu.* 1371 as semantically equivalent to mere 'reciting', since "λέγειν and ἄιδειν are sometimes contrasted, sometimes used indifferently."[309] Such a general statement, to avoid being misleading, needs to be fleshed out with details and limitations:[310] as we shall see soon, most of the evidence produced by Renehan cannot be regarded as conclusive.[311] A close survey of this evidence for the equivalence λέγειν ~ ἄιδειν points, at the most, in one interpretative direction (and a problematic one). That is, it can be shown that the semantic range covered by ἄιδειν does not include a spoken delivery but only a chanted one (the so-called παρακαταλογή), and even in passages to which this interpretation may apply, alternative explanations cannot be ruled out.

---

[307] The hypothesis of *Aiolos* preserved by P.Oxy. 2457 ll. 25–7 (= *TrGF* V.1 [2] ΑΙΟΛΟϹ T ii) ἡ δ' ἔγκυοϲ γενη[θεῖϲα]‖ τὸν τόκον ἔκρυπτεν τῶι νοϲεῖν προ[ϲποιη]-|τῶϲ does not allow us to establish with any confidence at what stage of the dramatic development Canace's labour is to be assigned.

[308] ὁ δ' εὐθὺϲ ἦγ' Εὐριπίδου ῥῆϲίν τιν', ὡϲ ἐκίνει‖ ἀδελφόϲ, ὦ 'λεξίκακε, τὴν ὁμομητρίαν ἀδελφήν.

[309] Renehan 1976, 91–2.

[310] Renehan does not distinguish clearly between spoken and recitative delivery, extending indifferently the use of ἄιδειν to both kinds of performance, which is partially incorrect. This same shortcoming is present also in Mastromarco 1983, 90. Differently Herington 1985, 224–5 n. 15.

[311] Sommerstein 1982, 225 regards the possibility that ἄιδειν might be used for reciting a rhesis as a "very doubtful" one; nevertheless he does not re-examine Renehan's argumentation. Furthermore, Sommerstein observes that even once granted for *Nu.* 1371 a semantic equivalence between λέγειν and ἄιδειν the problem still remains that such an expression (ἧιϲ') "would be inappropriate here where singing and speaking have just been contrasted."

Let us then turn to the sources collected by Renehan. First, the participle λέγοντες in Theogn. 763 and 1047[312] is not to be considered as a proper instance of "λέγειν used for singing."[313] The meaning underlying both passages is that of carrying on "propos agréables,"[314] that is, pleasant conversation which is one of the normative values encompassed by sympotic *arete*.[315] Equally misleading is the parallel drawn with Philostr. *Vita Apoll.* 5. 16 ἐπιστρέψαι γὰρ ὑμᾶς διανοηθεὶς ἐς λόγους φυσικωτέρους τε καὶ ἀληθεστέρους ὧν οἱ πολλοὶ περὶ τῆς Αἴτνης ἄιδουσιν. The expression ἄιδειν λόγους is used here as equivalent to λέγειν μάτην, that is, 'chatting idly, telling fibs,'[316] as confirmed by the following words αὐτὸς ἐς ἔπαινον μύθων ἀπηνέχθην by which the narrator confesses to having let himself be drawn into praising *myths*.[317] Plat. *Tim.* 21b πολλῶν μὲν οὖν δὴ καὶ πολλὰ ἐλέχθη ποιητῶν ποιήματα, ἅτε δὲ νέα κατ' ἐκεῖνον τὸν χρόνον ὄντα τὰ Σόλωνος πολλοὶ τῶν παίδων ἤισαμεν, regarded by Renehan as "a very instructive passage,"[318] also provides insecure evidence. First, some preliminary notes on the Platonic context: the festive occasion is the rhapsodic contests (ἆθλα ῥαψωιδίας) to be celebrated on the third day of the Apaturia, when children born in the previous twelve months were formally presented to the φρατρίαι of their fathers. We are told that during these rhapsodic contests several poems of many poets were recited (ἐλέχθη) and that, on the other hand, Critias and many other boys performed by singing (ἤισαμεν) specifically Solon's compositions (τὰ Σόλωνος) because they were new at that time and therefore in fashion (ἅτε δὲ νέα κατ' ἐκεῖνον τὸν χρόνον ὄντα). Now, we know that Solon wrote didactic poems not only in recitative metres (iambi and trochaei) but also in elegiac couplets. Since the Platonic context does not allow one to infer which kind of poem is meant here, the 'elegiac' hypothesis (that is, singing proper with the aulos accompanying) has to be regarded at least as

[312] Respectively πίνωμεν χαρίεντα μετ' ἀλλήλοισι λέγοντες (763) and νῦν μὲν πίνοντες τερπώμεθα, καλὰ λέγοντες (1047).
[313] Renehan 1976, 91.
[314] Van Groeningen 1966, 294.
[315] Cf. Vetta 1992, 178.
[316] See Conybeare 1912, 499, Del Corno 1978, 231 and more recently Jones 2005, II, 29.
[317] That is, the aetiological stories explaining the volcanic origin of Mount Aetna.
[318] See also Mastromarco 1983, 90 *ad loc.*

equally likely as the iambic or trochaic alternative (a recitative performance by means of παρακαταλογή). If Solon's elegiac poems are intended, the verb ἤιcαμεν would not need here to be weakened to the point of equivalence with 'chanting' but would preserve its full semantic significance, that is, 'singing'.[319] In other words, the Platonic passage would turn out to be consistent with the other ancient sources about the manner of performing elegy: that is, singing to the aulos (and not reciting as for iambic poetry).[320] Be that as it may, given the possibility for Plat. *Tim.* 21b of an equally well-grounded alternative (elegy), this passage cannot be considered as a certain example of a proper equivalence λέγειν ~ ἄιδειν.

Quite interesting (and of course problematic) is the evidence provided by the scholium to Ar. *Nu.* 1264 preserved in the cod. Paris. 2821 (= *TrGF* I. 33 Xenocles F 2). Strepsiades' reply (1266 τί δαί cε Τληπόλεμόc ποτ' εἴργαcται κακόν;) to the tragic 'tirade' of his second creditor (1264–5: according to the scholia a parodic quotation drawn from the tragedy *Likymnios* or *Tlempolemos*[321] of Xenocles, Karkinos' son) is glossed by this scholium with the following words:

οἱ μὲν φαcὶν ὡc ὁ Τληπόλεμοc οὗτοc ποιητὴc ὢν πεποίηκε τὸν Φιλόξενον ταῦτα τὰ ἰαμβεῖα ἄιδειν ἀπὸ τοῦ 'ὦ cκληρὲ δαῖμον' μέχρι τοῦ 'ὥc μ' ἀπώλεcαc'. ἄλλοι δέ φαcιν ὡc Cοφοκλῆc ἐποίηcε τὸν Τληπόλεμον ταῦτα λέγοντα κτλ.

some claim that this Tlepolemos, a poet himself, made Philoxenos sing these iambi from 'alas, hard man' to 'how you killed me'. Others say that Sophocles was the one who made Tlepolemos say that.

In commenting on the scholium, Renehan focuses only on the parallelism τὸν Φιλόξενον ταῦτα τὰ ἰαμβεῖα ἄιδειν ~ τὸν Τληπόλεμον

---

[319] The same observation may be applied to Dem. *De fals. leg.* 252 ἐλεγεῖα ποιήcαc ἦιδε (referring again to Solon) quoted by Renehan 1976, 91.

[320] For the different manner of performing elegy (singing to the aulos) and iambic poetry (reciting to the aulos) since archaic times, see West 1974, 13–4, Vetta 1992, 188 with n. 37 and Gentili 1995³, 46–7 with nn. 29–31. Differently Campbell 1964 argues for a bare recitative delivery without the accompaniment of the aulos also for elegy. Yet, most of his argumentation is weak, especially his persisting in denying the presence of flute-accompaniment on the basis of a naive and subjective view of elegiac poetry (Campbell supposes an incompatibility of "poems with their own emotions" and "the admission of a second party to the performance," cf. *ibid.*, 63–4). For a balanced criticism of Campbell's arguments see Bowie 1986, 14 with n. 7.

[321] For the spelling Tlemp—advocated by Dover on the basis of epigraphic evidence, see Dover 1968, 243.

ταῦτα λέγοντα, adducing it as evidence of the interchangeability of
ἄιδειν and λέγειν.

The scholium follows an inner, consistent argumentative frame of
its own, which is not to be ignored in spite of a basic misunderstanding about the individuals named.[322] The reader is provided with
two alternative explanations (οἱ μέν/ἄλλοι δέ) as regards the original attribution of the tragic quotation parodied at *Nu.* 1264–5.[323]
According to the scholium these two iambic lines were delivered
either by Philoxenos (likely a tragic actor as suggested by the following parallelism with Tlempolemos) or by Tlepolemos himself.[324]
Since the scholiast's attention focuses exclusively on the problem of
authorship and identity of the actor, I do not believe that we are
entitled to assign to the participle λέγοντα a semantically pregnant
value as regards the manner of delivery, thus establishing a direct
equivalence between λέγοντα and τὰ ἰαμβεῖα ἄιδειν. More likely, the
point of the comment is merely that Sophocles assigned those lines
to Tlempolemos instead of Philoxenos, without any further intent to
imply a semantic identity between λέγοντα (that is, a spoken delivery of iambic trimeters) and τὰ ἰαμβεῖα ἄιδειν.[325] If it is granted that

---

[322] That is, the attribution of the authorship to Sophocles (and not to Xenocles)
and the erroneous identification of Tlempolemos with the tragic poet himself or,
as a second hypothesis, with the Sophoclean tragic actor and not with the hero of
the tragedy (cf. Σ to Ar. *Nu.* 1266 ἄλλοι δὲ τραγικὸν ὑποκριτὴν εἶναι τὸν Τληπόλεμον,
ϲυνεχῶϲ ὑποκρινόμενον Ϲοφοκλεῖ ENp). On the possible reason for this misunderstanding see E. Wüst, *RE* s.v. Tlepolemos (3), col. 1618 ll. 18–34.

[323] ὦ ϲκληρὲ δαῖμον· ὦ τύχαι θραυϲάντυγεϲl ἵππων ἐμῶν· ὦ Παλλάϲ, ὥϲ μ'
ἀπώλεϲαϲ.

[324] The likely autoschediastic nature of this misunderstanding does not matter
here: what is interesting, however, is that the scholium has its own argumentative
line that, if mistaken, nevertheless is self-consistent.

[325] The same argument can be applied also to Σ^MNAB to Eur. *Hipp.* 58 ἔπεϲθ'
ἄιδοντεϲ· τοῦτο ἔνιοι μὲν τὸν Ἱππόλυτον φαϲὶν ἄιδειν. ἄμεινον δὲ τοὺϲ ἑπομένουϲ
τῶι Ἱππολύτωι ἀπὸ τῶν κυνηγεϲίων ταῦτα λέγειν κτλ. Also in this case the alternation of ἄιδειν/λέγειν is not to be regarded as pregnantly meaningful as regards
the performative aspect: the scholiast's attention focuses only on the attribution of
lines 58–60 (lyric verses, that is in any case verses to be sung cf. Barrett 1964,
168–9), and not on their mode of performance. In other words, in the scholium
the word λέγειν loosely conveys the mere notion that at that point of the dramatic
development the speaking character is more likely to be the secondary Chorus of
Hippolytus' servants coming back from hunting (by 'speaking character' meaning
just the one to whom the lines are to be referred, and not implying a specific way
of delivery). Lesky 1972³, 40 traces back the scholiastic oscillation ἄιδειν/λέγειν to
a more generic stylistic carelessness: "es handelt sich ganz einfach um denselben
unscharfen Wortgebrauch, der bei Aristoteles in der Poetik [12. 1452b 22] vorliegt,

the expression τὰ ἰαμβεῖα ᾄδειν need not be regarded as equivalent to λέγειν and thus does not refer to a spoken delivery, the interesting problem still remains of making sense of ταῦτα τὰ ἰαμβεῖα ᾄδειν. What does it really mean? To what kind of performance, if any, does this expression refer to? Given the scanty information provided by the scholium itself, any hypothesis can only be highly speculative, yet it may still be of some use to try to distinguish the different degree of likelihood that various interpretations entail.

First of all, on the basis of the evidence here collected, it seems reasonable to rule out with a certain confidence the possibility that ᾄδειν must be perceived here as tantamount to λέγειν, that is, plain spoken delivery.[326] At this point two possible alternatives remain: (1) either we assign to ταῦτα τὰ ἰαμβεῖα ᾄδειν the full sense of 'singing iambi', meaning by that a real lyric performance of iambic trimeters; (2) or we understand the expression as referring to a kind of chanted delivery, that is the παρακαταλογή. The first hypothesis entails two further possibilities: (1a) we may imagine that originally in Xenocles' tragedy those lines that we now read parodied in the *Clouds* as spoken trimeters (1264–5) were an iambic series embedded into a broader lyric context, and thus actually sung;[327] (1b) or ταῦτα τὰ ἰαμβεῖα ᾄδειν may be an autoschediastic explanation inferred by the scholiast by analogy with contemporary theatrical practice (Hellenistic or late Hellenistic as it may be). In this latter case we

---

wenn er von der Parodos als ἡ πρώτη λέξις ὅλου χοροῦ [die erste Rede des Gesamtchores] spricht." Yet, the Aristotelian statement seems to me to point in the direction outlined above. Aristotle is not dealing here with the different manner of delivery involved in the various structural constituents of tragedy but with the formal structure of the tragedy itself. Thus, defining the parodos as Chorus' first 'spoken' words is not a slip but is actually perfectly consistent with Aristotle's broader framework.

[326] Eur. *Tro.* 472 πρῶτον μὲν οὖν μοι τἀγάθ' ἐξᾷσαι φίλον and *Ion* 757 τίς ἥδε μοῦσα χὠ φόβος τίνων πέρι; do not contrast with what is argued here. At *Tro.* 472 the verb ἐξᾴδειν likely conveys the meaning of 'singing one's last song', cf. Plat. *Phd.* 85a (referring to the last cry of a dying swan): see Lee 1976, 154–5 and Barlow 1986, 181. As to *Ion* 757, the line refers to the Chorus's song-like cries ἰὼ δαῖμον, ἰὼ τλᾶμον at 752, 754, cf. Lee 1997, 247.

[327] An instance of iambic trimeters sung by the Chorus can be found, e.g., in the kommos of *Medea*'s fifth stasimon, that is ll. 1284–5, 1288–9 (in responsion with 1271–2 and 1277–8, this time spoken iambi or, perhaps more likely, performed in παρακαταλογή by the children off stage). For lyric iambi in tragedy see Martinelli 1997², 195–7 and West 1982, 98–102.

would be facing again the problem of the absence of positive evidence for converting spoken metres to song as early as the second half of the fifth century BC.[328]

Alternative (1a), that is, iambi originally conceived to be sung, although theoretically possible, seems to me the less likely one, inasmuch as it would assume on the part of the scholiast a very detailed knowledge (both textual and metrical) of the original tragic context parodied by Aristophanes, which does not fit the following misunderstanding of Tlempolemos's identity. Once (1a) is ruled out, we are left with (1b), that is, alleged lyric performance of iambic trimeters as the result of projecting into the past later theatrical practice, and (2), that is, chanted delivery. Whichever possibility one may prefer, neither of them allows us to trace the practice of singing *tout court* spoken iambi back to fifth-century Athens.

An interesting case of projecting into the past contemporary performative practice[329] can perhaps be found also in the scholium to Aeschin. *In Tim.* 168 (a speech dated to 353/352 BC). Demosthenes is being charged by Aeschines with being boorish and uncultured (166 ἄμουϲοϲ καὶ ἀπαίδευτοϲ), since his innuendo is aimed at hitting not only Philippus but also his son Alexander. In particular we are told about Alexander's behaviour at a symposium: Alexander is said ἔν τωι πότωι [ἡμῶν] (del. Blass) κιθαρίζοι καὶ λέγοι ῥήϲειϲ τινὰϲ καὶ ἀντικρούϲειϲ[330] πρὸϲ ἕτερον παῖδα. Along with Theophr. *Char.* 15. 10 καὶ οὔτε ᾇϲαι οὔτε ῥῆϲιν εἰπεῖν οὔτε ὀρχήϲαϲθαι and Ephipp. 16. 3 K-A ῥήϲειϲ τε κατὰ δεῖπνον Θεόδωρόϲ μοι λέγοι (cf. Renehan 1976, 90, and Cameron 1995, 321 n. 94), this passage of Aeschines is one of the most commonly quoted pieces of evidence to exemplify the distinction between λέγειν and ᾄδειν. Thus, according to Aeschines' words (λέγοι ῥήϲειϲ τινὰϲ καὶ ἀντικρούϲειϲ πρὸϲ ἕτερον παῖδα), what we have here is Alexander reciting (and not singing) some speeches (most likely tragic ones: see also Athen. 12. 537d= Nikoboule 127 F2 *FGrH* ἐν τῶι τελευταίωι δείπνωι αὐτὸϲ ὁ Ἀλέξανδροϲ ἐπειϲόδιον τι <ἀπο>μνημονεύϲαϲ ἐκ τῆϲ Εὐριπίδου Ἀνδρομέδαϲ ἠγωνίϲατο, on which Cagnazzi 1997, 17–9) and making repartee with another

---

[328] Renehan's statement that "if this comment [i.e. ταῦτα τὰ ιαμβεῖα ᾄδειν] goes back to the high Hellenistic period, it is surely decisive. But even if of later date, the parallel cannot be comfortably disregarded" (Renehan 1976, 92) is misleading in this respect.

[329] For analogous misunderstandings as regards performance criticism to be found in tragic scholia see Falkner 2002, 348 ff.

[330] For ἀντίκρουϲιϲ meaning here 'repartee' see LSJ s.v. Cf. also Fisher 2001, 313. The only doubtful parallel for this sense is ἀντικρουϲτία (a somewhat obscure *hapax*) referring to a musical performative context in Phld. *Po.* 1677. 23.

boy. The scholium to Aeschin. *In Tim.* 168 glosses the lemma ἀντικρούϲειϲ πρὸϲ ἕτερον παῖδα with the following words: οἷον πρὸϲ[331] κῶλά τινα καὶ ἄϲματα (334, 50 ll. 954–5 Dilts). But what does πρόϲ κῶλά τινα mean? What kind of practice is here assumed? The only way to make sense of this expression seems to be to assign to κῶλα the attested meaning of 'instrumental pieces' (cf. I.7 above), as the following καὶ ἄϲματα strongly suggests. If this is the correct meaning of κῶλα, then the scholiast is likely to be imposing on what is told by Aeschines (that is, Alexander reciting rheseis and making sallies against another boy) a (later?) performative practice more familiar to him (lyric amoibaia).

Summing up, a bare indistinct equivalence between λέγειν and ἄιδειν without further qualification as argued by Renehan seems to be misleading. At *Nu.* 1371 we are not facing a lyric performance of a tragic rhesis, but at the most, and not without some problems, a chanted delivery of an iambic speech.[332] Therefore, whatever textual solution one is inclined to accept at *Nu.* 1371 (εῖπ᾽ Roemer; ἦκ᾽ Sommerstein;[333] or understanding the transmitted ἦιϲ᾽ as referring to a chanted delivery), one element rests on safer ground: Pheidippides' performance does not represent an early and isolated example of converting spoken iambic to song proper but is in keeping with the sympotic conduct otherwise attested in the second half of the fifth century BC. It is thus in fifth-century Athens that we can find the

---

[331] For πρόϲ + the sound produced by the relative instrument or voice rather than πρόϲ + the instrument itself (i.e. πρὸϲ λύραν, πρὸϲ αὐλόν and so on), see e.g. the scholium to Pind. *Pyth.* 1. 5a (= 2. 9 Drachm.) πρὸϲ δὲ τὰ κρούματα εὐρύθμωϲ αἱ Μοῦϲαι χορεύουϲι.

[332] The fact that the anonymous scholia recentiora (1371a) gloss the word ἦιϲεν (*sic*) at *Nu.* 1371 alternatively as ἔλεγεν (Cr), ἐμελώιδηϲεν (Cant. 2), εῖπεν (lb), ἔψαλεν (*sic* Chalc), ἔμελψεν (Ho) only increases our confusion. As to ἔψαλεν transmitted by Chalc. (that is, the codex Panagh. Kam. 156 of the sixteenth century, certainly to be traced back to a monastic environment, see Koster, *Scholia in Aristophanem* I. 3², lxxxiv), this is likely to be another interesting case of cultural interference. In classical Greek ψάλλω means 'playing a stringed instrument without the plectron' (see LSJ s.v. II. 1) and only at a later stage, that is, in the Christian era, it seems that its sense becomes that of "singing with musical accompaniment" (see Lampe, GPL s.v. ψάλλω 1). On the semantic development of ψάλλω in the Christian period and its shifting from the original sense of "suono che accompagna il canto" to that of "canto accompagnato tout court" see Rocconi 2003, 30–2 (esp. 32).

[333] Sommerstein's conjecture seems perhaps the more economical one. From a paleographic point of view the slip IC/K in capital writing is very common, and as regards the dramatic development, Pheidippides' launching passionately into a speech of the νεώτεροι would represent a properly ironic counterpart to his initial reluctance.

starting point of those more diversified and virtuosic entertainments that developed later, in the Hellenistic period.

Especially telling in this connection is some epigraphic evidence which allows us to project into a broader cultural scenario those isolated phenomena of rhythmic, performative and, to a minor degree, textual re-shaping and re-arrangements that we can occasionally single out in those papyri which can be compared with the medieval tradition (P.Vind. G 2315 and P.Leid. inv. 510). The importance of such evidence is that it allows us to glimpse, even if imperfectly and incompletely, the different degrees of re-elaboration and performative adaptation to which tragic and lyric texts of the fifth century BC are subject in the renewed context of Hellenistic performances. We shall try therefore to let this epigraphic evidence speak for itself as a 'macroscopic' counterpart to the practices attested by musical papyri, for the latter, if not contextualized in a broader frame, run the risk of being just minute technicalities.

An exhaustive survey of the epigraphic evidence is outside my intent and capacity: I shall focus here on only two inscriptions, *SIG*[3] 648B (Satyros of Samos) and *SEG* XI 52c (the so-called *Themisoninschrift*), both of which have recently been re-examined by current scholarship.[334] As we shall se, both inscriptions present in fact performative dynamics present also in P.Vind. and P.Leid.: selection of musical suites, monodic performance of choral or amoibaic lyric, musical re-setting.

---

[334] Respectively Chandezon 1998 for *SIG*[3] 648B and Bélis 1999, 174–7 for *SEG* XI 52c. In particular, Chandezon's interpretation of *SIG*[3] (id. 1998, 50 and 56) is clearly influenced by the classicistic bias that insists that Euripidean music, and not just the Euripidean text, would have been strictly controlled to preserve its authenticity. These alleged practices of musical censorship seem to be more the result of modern projections than a reflection of ancient Greek practice (cf. Giordano-Zecharya 2003, 88–9). A philological faith in the original score, as regards the performative aspect, seems to have been quite rare already in the archaic period, see e.g. [Plut.] *De mus.* 1132c κιθαρωιδικῶν ποιητὴν ὄντα νόμων, κατὰ νόμον ἕκαϲτον τοῖϲ ἔπεϲι τοῖϲ ἑαυτοῦ καὶ τοῖϲ Ὁμήρου μέλη περιτιθέντα ἄιδειν ἐν τοῖϲ ἀγῶϲιν (referring to Terpander setting Homeric hexameters to a music "appropriate to each nomos." For the much discussed meaning of the expression κατὰ νόμον ἕκαϲτον see Gostoli 1990, xxxiv–vii). In other words, one has the strong impression that writing down a score in Hellenistic time was not meant to ensure its spread and faithful re-performability by each potential user and/or performer (as happens today) but that it rather served the single performance precisely defined in space and time (for a different scenario reflecting the modern western European attitude to musical scores see the engaging remarks of Christensen 1999a and id. 1999b).

Let us start with *SIG*[3] 648B, a much-debated piece of evidence[335] which nevertheless allows us, if correctly understood, to observe already in the Ptolemaic period the virtuoso practice of performing monodically tragic texts originally conceived for spoken delivery.[336] This is the text of *SIG*[3] 648B:

Cάτυρος Εὐμένους Cάμιος.|
τούτωι πρώτωι cυμβέβηκεν μόνωι| ἄνευ ἀνταγωνιcτῶν αὐλῆcαι| τὸν ἀγῶνα,
καὶ ἀξιωθέντα ἐπιδοῦ|ναι τῶι θεῶι καὶ τοῖc Ἕλληcι μετὰ| τὸν γυμνικὸν
τῆι θυcίαι ἐν τῶι cτα|δίωι τῶι Πυθικῶι ἆιcμα μετὰ χοροῦ| Διόνυcον καὶ
κιθάριcμα ἐκ Βακχῶν| Εὐριπίδου.

Satyros, son of Eumenes, of Samos. He had the good fortune to be the first and only performer to win the pipe-players' contest without competition and to have been regarded worthy to offer a performance to the god [Apollo] and the Greeks after the athletic contest during the sacrifice in the Pythian stadium, a performance consisting of ἆιcμα μετὰ χοροῦ Διόνυcον καὶ κιθάριcμα ἐκ Βακχῶν Εὐριπίδου.

Satyros' outstanding success is first traced back to his musical versatility:[337] he has not only won the auletic contest 'without competitors'

---

[335] Cf. Sifakis 1967, 97 "Satyros seems to have conducted a musical performance, the details of which cannot be made out with certainty. Nevertheless the important thing is that an excerpt of tragedy could be executed separately as early as the beginning of the second century B.C." The relevance of the geographic factor (that is, remoteness from Athens as the center) for the early diffusion of this anthologizing practice according to which "die Aufführungen einzelner Partien eher die Regel als die Ausnahme bildeten" has been emphasized by Dihle 1981, 29–30, 37. A brief synthesis of the studies previously devoted to this inscription can be found in Gentili 1977, 17–8 n. 39 and Chandezon 1998, 50–1.

[336] The date traditionally accepted for the inscription is that advanced by Dittenberger, that is, ca. 194 BC, when the Pythian games seem to have been celebrated with particular magnificence, see Sifakis 1967, 96 and more cautiously Chandezon 1998, 40–1 n. 18. A certain *terminus ante quem* for Satyros' activity as auletes and kitharodos is provided by *SIG*[3] 648A (honours conferred by the δῆμος Δηλίων): the episode must necessarily be prior to 166 BC, when Delos fell again under Athenian control, see Dittenberger *SIG*[3], 210 n. 1. For an up-to-date survey of the prosopographic evidence referring to Satyros of Samos see Chandezon 1998, 40–5.

[337] The words πρώτωι [. . .] μόνωι are not to be understood literally: it is far more likely that such a formulation belongs to the rhetoric of encomiastic praise (cf. μόνον καὶ πρῶτον in *SEG* XI 52c ll. 7–8, where probably we have to take into account also reasons of epichoric pride, see Cameron 1995, 49). Instances of eclectic musicians (auletes performing also as kitharodoi and so on) are not so rare as one might expect, cf. the evidence on the issue collected by Bélis 1994, 47–8 and ead. 1999, 164–5. For Satyros' musical versatility see Gentili 1977, 18 n. 39. Cf. also Aneziri 2003, 222 n. 106, who rightly emphazises that *SIG*[3] 648B represents

(ἄνευ ἀνταγωνιϲτῶν), but at the sacrifice celebrated after the athletic
agon has performed in the Pythian stadium[338] an ἆιϲμα μετὰ χοροῦ
Διόνυϲον καὶ κιθάριϲμα ἐκ Βακχῶν Εὐριπίδου. The main difficulty is
the syntactic compression of these last lines. Does the kithara-solo
(κιθάριϲμα ἐκ Βακχῶν Εὐριπίδου) refer to a purely instrumental performance entirely separate from the previous song (ἆιϲμα)?[339] Or does
it refer to the instrumental accompaniment of this song that set to
music Dionysios' lines drawn from Euripides' *Bacchae*?[340] And more
to the point, what is really meant here by ἆιϲμα μετὰ χοροῦ? Should
we suppose a choral song *tout court* (not necessarily drawn from
Euripides' *Bacchae*) that Satyros accompanied on the aulos[341] or are
we dealing with a primarily monodic performance of some lines from
the Euripidean tragedy with an episodic participation of the chorus?

a significant instance of the co-existence of agonistic and non-agonistic performances.

[338] According to Chandezon 1998, 47 at this date (first quarter of the second
century BC) Apollo's sanctuary at Delphi did not yet have a permanent stone theatre: the space of Satyros' performance would have thus been a removable wooden
structure located "dans le stade pythique." More recently Mulliez 2000, 497 has
argued for the presence of a stone theatre already by Satyros' time.

[339] See Latte 1954, 126–7, Webster 1963, 540, Wilson 2000, 308–9, Bosnakis
2004, 103 and in a more detailed way Chandezon 1998, 35, 50–5 (partially followed by Bélis 2001, 32), who argue that κιθάριϲμα ἐκ Βακχῶν Εὐριπίδου here
means the bare instrumental music of one of the stasima of *Bacchae*. Chandezon's
statement that "l'inscription de Satyros fournit, à notre connaissance, la seule occurrence épigraphique de ce mot [i.e. κιθάριϲμα]" is incorrect. The word κιθάριϲμα
occurs also in an opisthographic lead tablet, that is, *tabula defixionis* Ziebarth nr. 22,
l. 7 τὸ κιθ{φε}άριϲ[μα] (= Audollent 1904, nr. 86), to be dated prior to the common era. For the interpretation of this curse tablet see Prauscello 2004. As for
IKourion 104 (an inscription assigned to 130/131 AD), the word κιθάριϲμα is almost
entirely the result of a conjectural supplement, cf. l. 5 χαρι]ϲθεὶϲ ? ὑπὸ αὐτ[οῦ] |
[τοῦτο τὸ κιθάρι]ϲμα ? ἀνέθηκεν.

[340] See Eitrem-Amundsen in Eitrem-Amundsen-Winnington Ingram 1955, 27,
Gentili 1977, 17–8, Dihle 1981, 31, Xanthakis-Karamanos 1993, 125–6, and Tedeschi
2003, 111–2.

[341] Cf. Webster 1963, 540 ("Dionysos is the title of the choral song to which
Satyrus played a flute accompaniment"). In the same direction, that is understanding
ἆιϲμα μετὰ χοροῦ Διόνυϲον as a song completely unrelated to and detached from
Euripides' *Bacchae*, see Csapo-Slater 1994, 45 ("a performance [...] of a song
'Dionysos' with chorus and a lyre solo from the *Bacchae* of Euripides"), Perrin 1997,
213 n. 64, Chandezon 1998, 51 (according to whom we would be dealing with
"soit de la composition même de Satyros, soit un hymne traditionnel à Delphes en
l'honneur d'Asclépios"), Wilson 2002, 63 ("Satyros' appearance at Delphi included
an 'extra' performance of a song—the 'Dionysus'—with choral accompaniment [...]
as well as a *kitharisma* from the *Bacchae* of Euripides") and Hall 2002, 13. Differently,
Holtzmann in Chandezon *ibid.*, 50 n. 45 suggests a reference to the parodos of
Bacchae (64–169).

The starting point for a proper understanding of Satyros' performance must rely on an adequate explanation of the syntactic structure of ᾆϲμα μετὰ χοροῦ Διόνυϲον καὶ κιθάριϲμα ἐκ Βακχῶν Εὐριπίδου. The most economical and reasonable explanation, and also the only one which is able to provide a consistent *mise en scène* of Satyros' actual performance,[342] still seems to me that first suggested by Winnington-Ingram and then taken up by Gentili and Dihle.[343] According to this explanation, Διόνυϲον καὶ κιθάριϲμα ἐκ Βακχῶν Εὐριπίδου works as an apposition detailing in a more circumscribed way the content of the previous generic ᾆϲμα μετὰ χοροῦ.[344] In other words, if we fill out the textual brachylogy of the inscription, Satyros is here performing a 'song with the ancillary involvement of a Chorus, that is, he is singing the parts of Dionysos and performing kithara-accompaniment from Euripides' *Bacchae*'.[345]

If this is the correct interpretation of the inscription, Satyros' performance should encompass at least those passages from *Bacchae* containing an exchange between Dionysos and the Chorus, that is, the

---

[342] It would indeed seem far-fetched to regard the words ᾆϲμα μετὰ χοροῦ Διόνυϲον as completely unrelated to the following final reference to Euripides' *Bacchae* (ἐκ Βακχῶν Εὐριπίδου). In fact amoibaia between Dionysos and the Chorus (ᾆϲμα μετὰ χοροῦ) are positively attested in Eur. *Ba.* 576–603 (lyric metres) and 604–41 (trochaic tetrameters). Gentili 1977, 19 does not rule out a possible reference also to lines 642–59 (iambic trimeters), which seems to me an unproven and unnecessary assumption: at 642–59 the dialogue is between Pentheus and Dionysos, not between the Chorus and Dionysos as we would actually expect.

[343] See above note 340. The expression ᾆϲμα μετὰ χοροῦ has partially been restored also in the third-century BC inscription honouring the Boeotian Xenotimos, see *FD* III.3 no. 86 l. 2 [ᾆϲμα ἐπέδωκεν τῶι θε]ῶι μετὰ χοροῦ. Guarducci 1929, 644 seems to incline for Xenotimos as "direttore d'orchestra" but the possibility of a solo song with the Chorus playing a secondary role cannot be ruled out.

[344] If we assign to Διόνυϲον καὶ κιθάριϲμα κτλ. an appositive function, we overcome Chandezon's syntactic objection that "il semble également que si ἐκ Βακχῶν Εὐριπίδου devait porter sur ᾆϲμα aussi bien que su κιθάριϲμα, on aurait employé une liaison du type τε . . . καί avec une formulation comme ᾆϲμα τε μετὰ χοροῦ Διόνυϲον καὶ κιθάριϲμα ἐκ Βακχῶν Εὐριπίδου" (Chandezon 1998, 51). A connective particle (τε) is needed only if we suppose that the expression Διόνυϲον καὶ κιθάριϲμα ἐκ Βακχῶν Εὐριπίδου must necessarily refer to two distinct performances. Furthermore Chandezon's equivalence ᾆϲμα = ὕμνοϲ, if theoretically possible (a hymn is an ᾆϲμα but not every ᾆϲμα must be a hymn), seems unlikely. The language of inscriptions seems actually to recognize the relevance of genre distinction in performative contexts, see e.g. *SIG*³ 450 ll. 3–4 (where ὕμνοϲ is clearly distinguished from παιάν and προϲόδιον).

[345] Holtzmann's device (id. in Chandezon 1998, 51, followed by Mulliez 2000, 497) according to which the auletes Satyros would have adapted for the aulos a score originally conceived for the κιθάρα is unnecessary.

scene following the second stasimon (576–641).[346] Satyros' song, then, should encompass not only passages already conceived to be sung (that is, the lyrics 576–603), but also, and covering more than half the passage, lines that were originally to be spoken or delivered in recitative (604–41: trochaic tetrameters).[347]

Furthermore, this interpretation of *SIG*[3] 648B (that is, the ancillary role of the chorus accompanying Satyros' otherwise primarily solo performance) has a precise counterpart in the theatrical and sympotic practice of performing tragic *Einzelszenen* in the late Hellenistic and Roman periods. A good example is the well-known episode of Plut. *Crass*. 33. 3–6[348] describing an enactment of the exodus of the *Bacchae*, namely Agave's famous dialogue with the Chorus (= Eur. *Ba*. 1168–215), just at the very moment when Crassus' head is exhibited by Silaces.[349] The social space of the performance is of course markedly different: no longer the Delphic stadium, that is, a highly institutionalized space, normatively devoted to tragic performances, but Horodes' magnificent private banquet celebrating the agreement

---

[346] Eitrem-Amundsen in Eitrem-Amundsen-Winnington Ingram 1955, 27 and Gentili 1977, 18–9 extend Satyros' process of lyric re-adaptation also to the other lines spoken by Dionysos in the *Bacchae* (all of them in iambic trimeters). This possibility of course deserves due consideration but the text does not allow us to infer it positively.

[347] Nilsson 1906, 16 ff., even more radically, believed in a thorough process of textual and metrical re-writing by Satyros of the trimeters delivered by Dionysos in Euripides' *Bacchae*, a hypothesis whose more cautious echoes can still be detected in Dihle 1981, 31 ("Satyros hat also entweder iambische Trimeter vertont [...] oder aber den Text umgedichtet bzw. erweitert"). Yet, as already shown by Eitrem-Amundsen in Eitrem-Amundsen-Winnington Ingram 1955, 27, this radical conclusion is not necessary (Chandezon's objections against Dihle, [id. 1998, 50] are thus not conclusive). For a brief account of the actual manner of performing by singing originally non-lyric pieces, see Hall 2002, 18.

[348] The analogy between *SIG*[3] 648B and the Plutarchan passage (already quoted by Dittenberger) in terms of performative practice has been stressed by Gentili 1977, 18 n. 39. Plutarch's episode has been taken up by Polyaen. *Strat*. 7. 41.

[349] A brilliant metatextual analysis of Plut. *Crass*. 33. 3–6 has recently been proposed by Braund 1993, who argues that the whole final chapter of *The Life of Crassus* is consciously shaped on the model of Euripides' *Bacchae*, thus staging an actual "re-enactment of the climax of that play" (id. 1993, 468) by a skilled manipulation of fictional time (Crassus' head makes its appearance at Horodes' banquet just at the same time as the actor Jason of Tralles was acting Agave entering the stage with Pentheus' head in her hand). The documentary value of the Plutarchan passage lies also in attesting the persistence of the sympotic practice of singing tragic *amoibaia* in geographically marginalized regions of Mediterranean culture in the middle of the first century BC.

achieved about the wedding of his own son Pacoros with Artavasdes' sister (33. 1 ἑcτιάcειc τε καὶ πότοι δι᾽ ἀλλήλων ἦcαν αὐτοῖc). Yet, granted these differences, the dynamics underlying Jason's performance role are very similar to those for Satyros'. In fact we are told that Horodes, in order to please Artavasdes' sympathy for Greek culture, brought in many Greek entertainments (33. 1 καὶ πολλὰ παρειcήγετο τῶν ἀπὸ τῆc Ἑλλάδοc ἀκουcμάτων), among which we find also the staging of famous tragic *Einzelszenen*. At the very same moment when Silaces is bringing Crassus' head to Horodes, the tragic actor Jason of Tralles is said to be singing from the final part of Euripides' *Bacchae* the dramatic dialogue between Agave and the Chorus (33. 3–6):

(3) τῆc δὲ κεφαλῆc τοῦ Κράccου κομιcθείcηc ἐπὶ θύραc, ἀπηρμέναι μὲν ἦcαν αἱ τράπεζαι, τραγωιδιῶν δ᾽ ὑποκριτὴc Ἰάcων ὄνομα Τραλλιανὸc ᾖδεν Εὐριπίδου Βακχῶν τὰ περὶ τὴν Ἀγαύην. [. . .] (4) ὁ δ᾽ Ἰάcων τὰ μὲν τοῦ Πενθέωc cκευοποιήματα παρέδωκέ τινι τῶν χορευτῶν, τῆc δὲ Κράccου κεφαλῆc λαβόμενοc καὶ ἀναβακχεύcαc ἐπέραινε ἐκεῖνα τὰ μέλη μετ᾽ ἐνθουcιαcμοῦ καὶ ᾠδῆc (5)

(*Ba.* 1169–71)   <Ἀγ.> φέρομεν ἐξ ὄρεοc
                  ἕλικα νεότομον ἐπὶ μέλαθρα,
                  μακάριον θήραμα.

(6) καὶ ταῦτα μὲν πάνταc ἔτερπεν. ᾀδομένων δὲ τῶν ἐφεξῆc ἀμοιβαίων πρὸc τὸν χορὸν

(*Ba.* 1178–9)   <Χο.> τίc ἐφόνευcεν;
                  <Ἀγ.> ἐμὸν τὸ γέραc
κτλ.

When Crassus' head was brought to the door, the tables had been removed and the tragic actor named Jason of Tralles was singing that part of Euripides' *Bacchae* concerning Agave [. . .]. Then Jason gave the mask of Pentheus to one of the choreuts, seized Crassus' head and inspired by bacchic frenzy sang those songs enthusiastically: "we are carrying from the mountains a recently cut tendril to the palace, a wonderful prey". And every one enjoyed those lines. But when the following dialogue with the Chorus was sung "Chorus: Who killed him? Agave: The honour is mine" etc.

As proposed for Satyros' inscription, this time too we are facing a case of a selection from a tragedy (*Ba.* 1168–1215) requiring the Chorus's ancillary accompaniment onstage. The further supposition that Jason's performance at Horodes' dinner party encompassed not only the lyric amoibaion between Agave and the Chorus (1168–99: that is, a part already to be sung in Euripides' tragedy), but also a section originally conceived to be spoken (1200–15: iambic trimeters), remains a mere hypothesis that Plutarch's text does not allow us to verify. Furthermore, as we shall see later, the secondary presence of a Chorus is a possibility, in terms of *Bühnenpraxis*, which deserves serious consideration also for P.Leid. inv. 510, at least as regards the first excerpt, that is, Eur. *IA* 1500?–09.[350] Although the fragmentary condition of the Leiden papyrus allows one to infer only hypothetical conclusions, it is hard to avoid the impression that the process of anthological selection has followed in this case a very precise guideline. In fact, of the long astrophic section represented by *IA* 1475–531 the Leiden papyrus selects exactly those lines (1500?-09)[351] which represent not only the most emotional point of the whole section, but also the only part where a lyric exchange between the Chorus and Iphigenia takes place.[352] Of course, the hypothesis of a solo performance also of 1500?-09 cannot be entirely ruled out;[353] nevertheless, the examples quoted above (Satyros of Samos, Jason of Tralles) suggest that we may regard the alternative of a lyric amoibaion as at least equally possible from a performative point of view.[354]

---

[350] Since the interlinear space we can reconstruct for P.Leid. ll. 1–6 (= Eur. *IA* 1500?-09) is roughly the same as what we can ascertain for ll. 7–10 (ca. 4/5 mm), it is likely that also above ll. 1–6 the copyist has left the space necessary for writing down, evidently at a later stage, the corresponding musical notation, see Mathiesen 1981, 24–5 and Pöhlmann-West *DAGM*, 20. Differently, for the second excerpt preserved by P.Leid. (that is, part of the epode of the second stasimon: *IA* 784–93) a solo performance of an already astrophic song (which does not require lyric amoibaia) seems to be the most reasonable hypothesis.

[351] Although the fragmentary state of P.Leid. does not allow us to verify at what precise point of the long astrophic section (1475–531) the first excerpt actually began, P.Leid. seems to have omitted a great part of Iphigenia's initial monody (1475–99: see II.2.2) and the Chorus's concluding lines (1510–31).

[352] This exchange between the Chorus and Iphigenia does not imply, from a dramatic point of view, an actual dialogical interaction, because Iphigenia is entirely absorbed in thoughts of her death and thus completely detached from the human presences surrounding her. This feature emphasizes the dramatic pathos of the situation.

[353] The evidence of Ar. *Th.* 101–29 (Agathon singing an astrophic lyric by reproducing mimetically the alternating voices of the female chorus-leader and chorus-members) seems to ensure that already at the end of the fifth century BC a skilful actor must have been able to perform successfully a 'duet' by exploiting vocal mimicry. For a more detailed analysis of the scenic implications underlying this Aristophanic passage see II.2.3.

[354] An analogous two-part performance of the astrophic duets from Eur. *Phoen.* 1530–81 and 1710–36 as preserved by P.Stras.W.G. 307ʳ has been convincingly

Due consideration has to be paid also to a second inscription, that is, *SEG* XI 52c (to be dated to the first half of the second century AD).[355] As for *SIG*[3] 648B, also in this case we are dealing with documentary evidence which allows us a glimpse of the processes of re-adaptation and re-appropriation which we can observe operating in Hellenistic and imperial performances. This is the text of the inscription as edited by Broneer:[356]

ἡ βουλὴ καὶ ὁ δῆμος
Μειληςίων Γ. Αἴλιον
Θεμίςωνα Θεοδότου ὑ(ιὸν)
νεικήςαντα Ἴςθμια
5   Νέμεα κοινὸν Ἀςίας ε̄
καὶ τοὺς λοιποὺς ἀγῶ-
νας Π̄Θ̄ μόνον καὶ
πρῶτον Εὐρειπίδην
Coφοκλέα καὶ Τιμόθεον
ἑαυτῶ(ι) μελοποιήςαντα
Ψ(ηφίςματι) Β(ουλῆς)

The Council and the demos of the Milesians [honour] Gaios Ailios Themison, Theodotos' son, who has won at both the Isthmian and Nemean competitions and at the *koinon* of Asia five times and at the remaining contests eighty-nine times. The first and only one, he set by himself to his own music Euripides, Sophocles and Timotheus. By decree of the Council.

The Milesian δῆμος is likely to be honouring a local luminary: to the much decorated Gaios[357] Ailios Themison is ascribed (and properly rewarded) the outstanding merit of having ἑαυτῶι μελοποιήςαντα Euripides, Sophocles and Timotheus (ll. 6–9).

---

argued by Fassino 2003, 49 n. 62 (see especially his treatment of *Phoen.* 1560–1 OI. ἔ. AN. τί τόδε καταςτένεις; OI. τέκνα: in this case the ἀντιλαβή actually points towards the presence of two actors).

[355] For the discovery of this honorary inscription (namely the base of a statue found in the Isthmian walls) and its dating, on letter style, to the first half of the second century AD see Broneer 1953, 192–3. Latte 1954, 125 has accepted this date too; more skeptical Robert 1954, 129, who however does not advance alternative dates.

[356] Broneer 1953, 192–3.

[357] Differently, Robert 1954, 215 regards the reading Γ. at l. 2 wrong: "on attend T(ίτον) ou Π(όπλιον) et le musicien devait tenir le droit de cité d'Hadrien ou d'Antonin le Pieux."

There are two main difficulties raised by these last lines: (1) grasping what kind of performance may be assumed behind such an expression as Εὐρειπίδην Cοφοκλέα καὶ Τιμόθεον ἑαυτῶι μελοποιήcαντα and (2) explaining what μόνον καὶ πρῶτον actually means in this context. In its turn, (1) raises two interconnected questions: the precise meaning of the rather peculiar syntagm ἑαυτῶι μελοποιήcαντα[358] and, consequently, the problem of how to explain such a practice, whatever it might be, when linked with a generic expression like Εὐρειπίδην Cοφοκλέα καὶ Τιμόθεον (thus tragic and lyric texts).[359]

As regards the most likely meaning of ἑαυτῶι μελοποιήcαντα, Latte's and Tabachovitz's contributions should be considered as conclusive. They have clearly shown that in imperial times the syntagm ἑαυτῶι ποιεῖν τι is actually equivalent to the classical expression ἀφ᾽ ἑαυτοῦ ποιεῖν τι usually conveying the meaning of "etwas von selber tun."[360] Themison's outstanding talent has to be sought, therefore, in 'having set to music by himself'[361] Εὐρειπίδην Cοφοκλέα καὶ Τιμόθεον. That is, we are entitled to suppose (according to the evidence previously examined) that in the second century AD the 'original' music

---

[358] See Broneer 1953, 193, according to whom "the verb μελοποιεῖν would seem to imply that he set the dramas of Sophocles, Euripides and Timotheos to music, but the exact force of ἑαυτῶι in that connection is obscure."

[359] A double presence that has to be kept in mind for a proper understanding of the last lines: see Latte 1954, 125 and Hordern 2002, 78; Broneer had erroneously dismissed the relevance of this double repertoire.

[360] See Latte 1954, 125–6. Among the instances quoted by Latte the most cogent are *Mart. Polycarpi* 13. 2 ἀποθέμενος ἑαυτῶι πάντα τὰ ἱμάτια and *Mart. Pionii* 4. 13 μήτε βιαcθέντεc ἑαυτοῖc ἦλθον ἐπὶ τὸ θύειν. Granted that Latte's interpretation of ἑαυτῶι ποιεῖν τι as "etwas von selber tun" is quite right, his explanation of ἑαυτῶι as *dativus commodi* is unsatisfactory. Tabachovitz 1946, 303 and id. 1955, 77–8 has convincingly shown that ἑαυτῶι has an instrumental/causal value and that supposes an underlying original expression such as (αὐτὸc) δι᾽ ἑαυτοῦ (cf. Lat. *per se*). The use of this "unklassische Dativ" in a period when the dative itself begins to disappear before an increasing use of other substitute prepositional syntagms, is likely to be regarded as a hypercorrection.

[361] See Latte 1954, 126 ("selbst in Musik setzen"), followed by Eitrem-Amundsen in Eitrem-Amundsen-Winnington Ingram 1955, 27–8, Xanthakis-Karamanos 1993, 125, Bélis 1999, 176 Hordern 2002, 78 and Bosnakis 2004, 103. Slightly differently, Robert 1954, 215 understands ἑαυτῶι as "pour lui, c'est-à-dire pour l'exécuter lui-même; c'était apparemment un citharède, et pas seulement un exécutant, mais un compositeur." Yet Robert's interpretation rests, I believe, on an unnecessary syntactic straining of the text. Already Tabachovitz's reconstruction (that is, ἑαυτῶι as instrumental dative) encompasses the possibility that Themison, besides being the composer himself of the music, is also the actual performer, as is also clearly suggested by his agonal career.

of the three great champions of the past poetic tradition (tragic as well as lyric) was already beyond recovery and that Euripides, Sophocles and Timotheus' texts "in erster Linie als Lektüre aufgenommen wurden."[362]

The next step to be taken is to grasp, if possible, what kind of dynamics underlies this process of re-shaping Εὐρειπίδην Cοφοκλέα καὶ Τιμόθεον. Are we to suppose that Themison set to music the whole work of Euripides, Sophocles (that is, tragedies) and Timotheus (that is, lyric compositions),[363] or is this too a case of a selection of *Einzelszenen*? And if there has been a selection, according to what criterion? Have parts been set to music that were originally conceived to be spoken or delivered in παρακαταλογή,[364] or does the musical resetting concern only lyric parts? Or should we accept both alternatives?

The text of the inscription does not allow us to gain any certainty about these questions, but again a comparative analysis with analogous instances previously examined might be of some aid in assessing

---

[362] Latte 1954, 126. Especially telling is also Latte's reference to Dio Chr. 19. 5: in the overcrowded theatres of the second century AD what had survived of the ancient tragedies was only the skeleton, that is, the iambic sections (τῆc δὲ τραγωιδίαc τὰ μέν ἰcχυρά, ὡc ἔοικε, μένει· λέγω δὲ τὰ ἰαμβεῖα καὶ τούτων μέρη διεξίαcιν ἐν τοῖc θεάτροιc), whereas the songs were lost once and for all (τὰ δὲ μαλακώτερα ἐξερρύηκε τὰ περὶ τὰ μέλη). Hall's assumption that "the context of the dialogue, which is comparing music to oratory and is inspired by the visit of a citharode to Cyzicus, suggests that these iambic parts are being *sung*, and sung, moreover, to music believed to be the work of the original poets" (ead. 2002, 18; Hall's italics) seems to me misleading. From the very beginning, the comparison drawn by Dio between music and oratory shifts almost immediately from the different ways of perfomance to matters of content and style: cf. 19. 4 ἥ τε λέξιc οὐκ αὐτοcχέδιοc, ὥcπερ ἡ τῶν ῥητόρων ἐξ ὑπογύου τὰ πολλὰ πειρομένων λέγειν, ἀλλὰ ποιητῶν ἐπιμελῶc καὶ κατὰ cχολὴν πεποιηκότων. καὶ τά γε πολλὰ αὐτῶν ἀρχαῖά ἐcτι καὶ πολὺ cοφωτέρων ἀνδρῶν ἢ τῶν νῦν. Thus Dio's penchant for kitharodoi and actors over orators rests on the fact that the former do not extemporize, the texts of ancient poets being already known and canonized. It is precisely at this point that we run into the sentences quoted above about the different fate of comedy and tragedy: all that we can elicit from this passage and its broader context is that the lyric parts of tragedy were not performed any longer in second century AD theatres, any specification about the original character of the music being lacking.

[363] See Bélis 1999, 176–7.

[364] Slightly different (and somewhat obscure, at least to me, in its final words) is the hypothesis advanced by Eitrem-Amundsen in Eitrem-Amundsen-Winnington Ingram 1955, 28, according to whom Themison, like Satyros and the anonymous composer of P.Osl. inv. 1413, "may have exercised his art on the iambic or 'recitative' parts of the tragedies, *without turning them into lyrics*" (italics are mine).

probabilities. In fact, on the basis of evidence both epigraphic and literary collected here for the imperial age, it seems more likely that we are dealing with re-performances of single scenes rather than with a consistent re-writing of whole works, whether tragic or lyric. What Themison has set to music by himself would likely have been "Glanzstücke," *pièces de résistance* perceived as fit to please the audience's predilection for well-known highlights.[365]

Once granted these premises, in order to understand which part of a poetic work might have been selected by Themison for his own musical resetting, it may be useful to turn our attention to the fact that the subject of Themison's performance is not only Attic tragedy (Euripides, Sophocles) but also lyric compositions (Timotheus). From this perspective, since Timotheus is an author of purely lyric works (dithyrambi, citharodic nomoi), and since he is set on equal terms with the tragedians Euripides and Sophocles, the most likely solution seems to be to posit a performative homogeneity: that is, we are probably dealing with a selection of tragic lyric passages (choral songs, duets, monodies) and of Timotheus' lyric airs, all performed monodically by Themison.[366]

If this is taken to be the correct interpretation of Εὐρειπίδην Cοφοκλέα καὶ Τιμόθεον ἑαυτῶι μελοποιήϲαντα, how should we understand μόνον καὶ πρῶτον at ll. 7–8?[367] A faithfully literal interpreta-

---

[365] See Latte 1954, 126–7, Cockle 1975, 63, Xanthakis-Karamanos 1993, 125 and Hall 2002, 14–8.

[366] Differently Fassino 1997–98, 223–4 argues for a "riesecuzione ad una voce di canti già in origine monodici" for the tragic excerpts as well on the basis of the fact that "per quanto riguarda Timoteo, però, i canti su cui Temisone è intervenuto non potevano che essere fin da principio monodie astrofiche." The only inference that the mention of Timotheus together with Euripides and Sophocles allows us to draw is that the performance was a lyric one and monodically *performed* by Themison. The possibility of citharodic (that is, monodic) adaptation of Timotheus' (choral) dithyrambs cannot in fact be ruled out *a priori*: see the case of the famous third century BC citharode Nikokles from Taras who won the first prize at the Lenaia 'with a dithyramb' (διθυράμβωι: *IG* II² 3779. 7–8): cf. Wilson 2002, 63. On this kind of 'perverted' performance of dithyrambs in Hellenistic time (especially by members of the technitai of Dionysus), see more generally Bélis 1995, 1053–5 (even if the instance of Pylades of Megalopolis is wrong) and the Tean inscriptions now re-edited by Le Guen 2001, I, 241–2 (cf. also Wilson 2000, 391 n. 155).

[367] Broneer 1953, 193 traced back this formulation to Themison's outstanding talent, that is, to the huge number of his victories (ninety-four in all, if the reading of ΠΘ [89] at l. 7 is correct), yet Robert 1954, 215 already argued that "le chiffre de 89 victoires n'est pas spécialement 'un record'; on a des chiffres bien plus élevés dans les inscriptions de ce genre." Furthermore, Broneer's explanation does

tion of Themison as πρῶτος εὑρετής of such a performative practice would of course be false, as is clearly shown by the instances previously examined. On this ground Bélis has recently proposed to relate Themison's outstanding uniqueness to the supposition that he had set to music "*tous* les textes d'Euripide, de Sophocle et de Timothée. Personne avant lui ne l'avait fait, personne avant lui n'avait osé le faire."[368] Yet, contemporary imperial evidence on which we have dwelt before strongly supports 'anthological' rather than integral performances of tragedies, and the same lack of the article before Εὐρειπίδην Cοφοκλέα καὶ Τιμόθεον that is regarded by Bélis as a clue supporting her hypothesis, seems to point in the opposite direction just because of the vagueness of the formulation. The most reasonable explanation of μόνον καὶ πρῶτον, one which does not entail a historical lie or assume a practice hard to be performed, is instead that indirectly suggested by Latte himself. "Der lokalpatriotische Stolz" might well resort to hyperbolic eulogistic formulae in order to praise a fellow-citizen.[369]

---

not take account of the word order: μόνον καὶ πρῶτον must be linked syntactically to what follows (that is, to Εὐρειπίδην Cοφοκλέα καὶ Τιμόθεον ἑαυτῶι μελοποιήcαντα) and not to what comes before.

[368] Bélis 1999, 176 (author's italics); the same position is defended by ead. 2001, 43–6.

[369] See Latte 1955, 75, followed by Pöhlmann 1960, 15; for boasts of this kind among athletes see Dickie 2003, 242–3 with nn. 32–5. Moreover, Latte, on the basis of *IDidyma* 181 (ca. 213/250 AD: the Milesian δῆμος honours Aurelios Hierocles, winner at the Great Didymeia as τιμοθεαcτής and ἡγηcιαcτής), believes that Themison had actually inaugurated a musical fashion of "composing in the manner of Timotheus" (that is, τιμοθεάζειν), a fashion which would have persisted because of local chauvinism, since Timotheus was himself from Miletos. Yet, Latte's conclusions seem to me to go a step too far. Themison's fame, at least as attested by *SEG* XI 52c, is not linked exclusively or even predominantly with Timotheus' poetry: μόνον καὶ πρῶτον does not refer to performing monodically only highlights of Timotheus but also pieces of Euripides and Sophocles. The Didyma inscription is instead interesting from another point of view. The very fact that at ll. 5 ff. Aurelios Hierocles is said to have defeated both τειμοι[θε]αcτάc and ἡγηcιαι[c]τάc testifies to the close resemblance (and, we should add, to the spatial contiguity as regards the place of the performance) between lyric performances (τειμοθεάζειν: Rehm in *IDidyma*, 145 suggests a citharodic performance) and rhetorical epideixeis (ἡγηcιάζειν: 'writing in the manner of Hegesias', that is, writing pamphlets and discourses in Asian style, and thus, probably, in a noticeably rhythmic prose; for this *hapax* see Rehm 1954, 179–80); see also Hordern 2002, 78–9. Once again, we are facing an instance of "ein vielseitiges Talent" (Rehm *ibid.*) like Satyros and Themison. One could quote *à propos* also the evidence of Dio Chr. 16. 68, where Dio is complaining about the degeneration of contemporary literary taste by claiming that πάντεс δὴ ἄιδουcι καὶ ῥήτορεс καὶ cοφιcταί, καὶ πάντα περαίνεται δι' ὠιδῆc· ὥcτ' εἴ τιc παρίοι δικαcτήριον, οὐκ ἂν γνοίη ῥαιδίωc πότερον ἔνδον πίνουcιν ἢ δικάζονται.

Summing up, the *Themisoninschrift* thus testifies to the persistence, in the second half of the second century AD, of the agonal practice consisting of re-setting to new music tragic and lyric excerpts by converting them, if necessary, to a monodic performance. As we shall see later, also in the Vienna papyrus, that is already in the third century BC, there seem to be clues which point in the same direction of a monodic, astrophic performance of an originally strophic choral song.

I.9.2 *What alternative? The 'paths' of texts*
After this general and somewhat meandering survey of the main performative contexts that frame the various methods of re-adaptation and re-appropriation of the past poetic tradition in Hellenistic and post-Hellenistic times, the next step is to apply in a more detailed way the interpretative frame here roughly sketched to the direct evidence provided by those musical papyri which can be compared with the medieval manuscript tradition. We shall thus temporarily narrow the focus to minute textual analysis, examining musical papyri in order to understand whether and to what extent it is possible to single out in these scores some hints of a broader cultural practice.

A useful starting point is again trying to respond to Fleming-Kopff's suggestive literary archaeology, looking for possible alternatives that enable us to outline a more diversified scenario. In particular, we have already seen that one of the major shortcomings underlying Fleming-Kopff's hypothesis is that their legitimate insistence upon revising on new bases Wilamowitz's notorious negative judgment on the Hellenistic period as a Dark Age for music and poetry has led them to dismiss some still useful remarks present in Wilamowitz's treatment (cf. point (2) at I.9.1). In fact, Fleming-Kopff seem to have undervalued, if not completely neglected, the possibility of considering musical papyri as one potential source, among many others, of *textual* variants (and, secondarily and occasionally, colometrical variants) for Alexandrian ἐκδόϲειϲ.[370]

---

[370] See Wilamowitz 1889, 132–3: "das freilich war ganz natürlich, dass auch Schauspielerexemplare in die Bibliotheken kamen und die antiken Philologen auch solche einsahen [. . .]. Auch das ist sicher, dass sie sich über die Verwilderung des Textes durch die Schauspieler keinerlei Illusionen gemacht und mit der Möglichkeit gerechnet haben, dass der Text unter deren Einwirkung gelitten hätte."

As already observed before, this is also the most conspicuous limitation of Pöhlmann's opposite hypothesis, that is, a sharp separation between *Bühnenexemplare* provided with musical notation and Alexandrian learned *Lesetexte*. Especially telling in this regard is the rough equivalence established by Pöhlmann 1960, 12 between P.Vind. G 2315 and Dion. Hal. *De comp. verb.* 11. 19–21 Auj.-Leb. (Pöhlmann, as we have previously seen, believes that Dionysius' remarks on the parodos of *Orestes* have to be traced back to a musical score, see I.1 n. 78). According to Pöhlmann both the Vienna papyrus and the copy (provided with musical notation) underlying Dionysius' quotation must be regarded "als von der alexandrinischen Textredaktion unabhängig [. . .]. Denn auch in seinen [i.e. Dionysius'] Euripideszitaten finden sich Varianten, die nicht in der handschriftlichen Euripidesüberlieferung auftreten." Granted that Pöhlmann's statement is partially true as regards the Vienna papyrus,[371] Dionysius' quotation from Eur. *Or.* 140–2, on the other hand, does not seem to exhibit any kind of idiosyncratic 'otherness', in terms of textual tradition, with respect to the alleged Alexandrian edition as reconstructed on the basis of the papyrological and manuscript tradition. If we compare Usener-Radermacher's apparatus (more minutely descriptive than that of Auj.-Leb.) with that of Diggle *OCT* III, 198 as regards *Or.* 140–2, we can see that all the alternative readings (some of them obviously mistaken) provided by Dion.'s manuscript tradition can actually be found also in the Euripidean one. For instance, the oscillation between cίγα cίγα and cῖγα cῖγα is present in both traditions (in Dion., as confirmed by the following commentary at 11. 20 Auj.-Leb. ἐν γὰρ δὴ τούτοιc τὸ cίγα cίγα λευκὸν ἐφ᾽ ἑνὸc φθόγγου μελωιδεῖται, καίτοι τῶν τριῶν λέξεων ἑκάcτη βαρείαc τε τάcειc ἔχει καὶ ὀξείαc, the correct reading is the former, that is, cίγα cίγα),[372] and the same can be said for readings such as λευκόν, τιθεῖτε, ἄπο πρόβατε. Analogously, Dionysius' omission of μηδ᾽ ἔcτω κτύποc at 141 has recently found a parallel in P.Köln VI 252 (= Π⁴ Diggle): it is

---

[371] P.Vind. does actually provide a textual (and not colometrical) variant unknown to medieval tradition, that is, the inverted order of lines at *Or.* 338–9 (i.e. 339 before 338), together with an instance of an alternative rhythmic scansion which is likely to be traced back to the performative context.

[372] Usener-Radermacher's cίγα cῖγα, defended on the basis of the Σ^MTAB to Eur. *Or.* 140 (πρόcφοροc τῶι πάθει ἡ τοῦ ῥυθμοῦ ἀγωγὴ δοχμιάζουcα), is wrong whether in regard to the Dionysian tradition or to the Euripidean one. A dochmiac scansion - - - - ⌣ - of cίγα cῖγα λευ(κόν) would in fact entail interpreting the whole sequence cίγα cῖγα . . . ἀρβύληc (140) as two dochmiacs, creating a problematic responsion δ~hypδ with the first colarion of 152 (πῶc ἔχει; λόγου κτλ.). On the debated admissibility in tragedy of the responsion δ~hypδ see Barrett 1964, 325 on Eur. *Hipp.* 850 and more recently Medda 1993, 184 and 222–3 with n. 287 on Aesch. *PV.* 576~95 (the case of Eur. *Med.* 1252~62 quoted by Parker 1997, 166 as an instance of hypδ corresponding with normal dochmiacs is not convincing: see cf. Dale *MATC* III, 44). As regards comedy, a case of responsion δ~hypδ would be, according to the manuscript tradition, that of Ar. *Ach.* 494~570 (τειχόμαχὸc ἀνὴρ codd.: τειχόμαχᾶc ἀνὴρ Dobree), but see Elliott 1914, 159 and Parker 1997, 134–5.

thus highly likely that Dionysius' variant κτυπεῖτ' should also be assumed
in the corresponding lacuna of P.Köln VI 252 l. 8, see Diggle 1991, 132,
Gronewald 1987, 130 and also O'Callaghan 1981, 16–7. Furthemore, even
more interesting is Dionysius' explicit attribution of the first lines of *Orestes*
parodos to Electra and not to the Chorus (cf. 11. 19 Auj.-Leb. τὴν Ἠλέκτραν
λέγουcαν ἐν Ὀρέcτηι πρὸc τὸν χορόν). Whatever solution one prefers to adopt
for this *vexata quaestio*,[373] it is worth noticing that Dionysius' evidence is in
keeping with the second hypothesis of *Orestes* ascribed to Aristophanes of
Byzantium (= Diggle *OCT* III, 189 *arg.* II ll. 40–1): ἔcτι δὲ ὑπονοῆcαι τοῦτο
ἐξ ὧν φηcιν Ἠλέκτρα τῶι χορῶι· Cῖγα cῖγα κτλ.[374] These data seem thus to
suggest quite reasonably that both traditions, the scenic and the Alexandrian
one, are not to be regarded as completely detached from each other: mutual
overlaps must have been more frequent than we might actually guess.

At present, the possibility of regarding texts provided with musical
notation also as potentially collecting basins of textual variants seems
to me the most productive approach. There is in fact no reason to
exclude *a priori* that Alexandrian philologists resorted to the musical
scores they occasionally happened to possess, nor to believe that

---

[373] Diggle *OCT* III, 198, preceded by Murray, Biehl, Willink and West, ascribes
ll. 140–1 to the Chorus according to the *notae personarum* of the medieval tradition,
whereas the Aristophanic second hypothesis, Dion. Hal. *De comp. verb.* 11. 19, Diog.
Laert. 7. 172 and Psell. *De Eur. et Georg. Pis. Iud.* = 46 ll. 72–4 Dyck (most likely
resting on Dion. Hal., cf. Dyck 1986, 33) assign them to Electra (see Di Benedetto
1961, 312–4, id. 1965, 34–5, and Medda 1989, 100–3). Two minor observations
may be made here on the documentary value to be ascribed respectively to Tzetzes'
excerpt from περὶ τραγωιδίαc as recorded in *Anecd. Par.* I, 19–20 Cramer and to
P.Köln VI 252. Diggle 1991, 126 classes Tzetzes' excerpt among the evidence supporting the attribution of ll. 140–1 to the Chorus. Yet, the looseness of the expression ὠιδὴ χοροῦ γινομένη ἅμα τῆι εἰcόδωι does not seem to me to allow any certain
inference about the speaking character at 140–1, especially if we pay attention to
the context of the quotation. Tzetzes quotes the Euripidean lines as an instance of
the parodos *tout court*, that is as a structural constituent of the tragedy, leaving out
of consideration the identity of the speaking character (for another example of kom-
matic parodos opened by an actor see e.g. Eur. *Hel.* 191 ff.). As regards the Köln
papyrus, on the basis of the explanation advanced by Gronewald 1987, 130 for the
ekthesis of l. 8= *Or.* 142 (that is, a "Rollenwechsel" between 141/2; cf. also Diggle
1991, 132 and more recently Savignago 2003, 8–9 with n. 36), I believe that P.Köln
VI 252 can reasonably be listed among the evidence supporting the attribution of
ll. 140–1 to the Chorus, so that the textual arrangement may thus be traced back
at least to the second/first century BC. Musso's conclusion that "si può ipotizzare
con qualche fondamento che, cosí come in Dionigi, anche nel papiro i versi in
questione venissero attribuiti a Elettra" (id. 1982, 46) is actually wrong: it does not
explain the re-alignment of l. 9 of the Köln papyrus with the iambic trimeters at
ll. 1–6.

[374] For the Aristophanic authorship of the second hypothesis of *Orestes* see Medda
2001, 85–6 n. 14 and more generally id. 1989, 100–1.

these copies carrying musical notation were ignored as textual evidence. From this perspective, then, Fleming-Kopff's initial suggestion (that is, Alexandrian philologists resorting to musical scores), once stripped of its alleged systematic consistency, is certainly a valuable one.

What instead needs specifying is *what* kind of use of those musical scores by Alexandrian γραμματικοί we can likely guess. In fact, despite the scantiness of our evidence, in the very few cases where we can compare these scores with the manuscript tradition (that is, P.Vind. G 2315 as to Euripides' *Or.* and P.Leid. inv. 510 as to *IA*), musical papyri, besides providing in some cases *variae lectiones* that could be argued to be originally Euripidean or, better, in the case of the suspected passages of *IA*, at least to go back to an early date,[375] show also peculiar divergences.[376] It is therefore in these idiosyncratic divergences, once we have reasonably shown that they are not merely mechanical slips, that we ought to search for any possible evidence for the different degrees of rhythmic and textual re-adaptation that lyric texts (quite often of anthological origin) intended for performance may actually undergo.

An interesting term of comparison and, in a sense, an indirect confirmation for such phenomena involving metrical and textual re-adaptations is provided by P.Stras.W.G. 304–7, a lyric (eminently Euripidean) anthology of the third century BC, which, although not provided with musical notation, was nevertheless conceived for performance.[377] The Strasbourg papyrus in fact warns us against any easy automatism and forces us to ask how many of the *errores singu-*

---

[375] Cf. P.Leid. inv. 510 as to Eur. *IA* 793: compared with the text transmitted by L πατρίδοϲ οὐλομέναϲ ἀπολωτιεῖ (‿ ‿gl^d), P.Leid. has]ιν[. . (.)]ϲ γαϲ πατριαϲ ολο[μεναϲ απολωτιει], ολο[μεναϲ confirming the soundness of Burges' emendation (ὀλομέναϲ ἀπολωτιεῖ ‿ ‿gl), see Diggle 1994, 412. For a detailed analysis of the text offered by the Leiden papyrus as regards *IA* 792–3 see II.2.2.

[376] See e.g. in P.Vind. G 2315 ll. 5–6 the scansion cr ia mol instead of 2δ for κατέκλυϲεν δεινῶν πόνων ὡϲ πόντου (= *Or.* 342–3), a rhythmic interpretation that entails a consequent atomization of what is reasonably supposed to be the right syntactic structure of these lines (cf. further II.1.3); or the inverted order of 339 *ante* 338.

[377] The performative nature of this *Tragödienliederpapyrus*, already argued by Zuntz 1965, 250 and Gentili 1977, 12 on the basis of typological elements (an anthological organization of the material) has been persuasively advocated by Fassino 2003, 33–50 through a systematic analysis of variants in *Medea* and *Phoenissae* provided by the Strasbourg papyrus.

lares of musical papyri may be considered as the result of a conscious process of rhythmic and textual adaptations required ultimately
by the different performative practice and context. The true basis
on which to graft a proper link between P.Stras.W.G. 304–7 and
the Euripidean musical papyri (P.Vind. G 2315 and P.Leid. inv. 510)
is therefore to be sought within this broader resemblance in respect
to processes of re-adaptation and not, as has recently been claimed
by Lomiento, in a closer similarity of their alleged roughly rhyth-
mical-colometrical layout.[378] It may be useful to quote here at full
length some of Lomiento's conclusions inasmuch as they are representative of a certain modern critical trend which indeed deserves
further consideration:

> Their layout [that is, that of P.Vind. G 2315 and P.Leid. inv. 510]
> does not correspond to the criteria of prose but, at least in some cases,
> as it has convincingly been argued, to a scansion that, even if not
> properly 'colometric', seems to be linked with the rhythmic-melodic
> phrasing.[379] In this regard it is telling that a not dissimilar disposition
> of the text can perhaps be found also in the contemporary P.Strasb.W.G.
> 304A–307 [. . .]. This papyrus is devoid of musical notation but its
> particular *mise en page* lets us posit that it derives *recta via* from a musi-
> cal score similar to those of *Orestes* and *Iphigenia*.[380]

Speaking for the Strasbourg papyrus of "a not dissimilar disposition
of the text," that is, one comparable to the layout of the Euripidean
musical papyri, as well as suggesting for it a straightforward derivation "from a musical score similar to those of *Orestes* and *Iphigenia*,"[381]
runs the risk of diverting our attention from the right perspective by

---

[378] See Lomiento 2001, 308.

[379] At this regard Lomiento 2001, 340 n. 58 quotes Comotti 1978 and Marino
1999a.

[380] Lomiento 2001, 308: "La disposizione del testo non risponde in essi ai criteri
della prosa ma, almeno in qualche caso, come è stato con buoni argomenti ipo-
tizzato, a una scansione che, anche se non propriamente 'colometrica', sembra con-
nessa con il fraseggio ritmico melodico. È significativo in tal senso che una disposizione
non dissimile del testo si trovi forse anche nel coevo P.Strasb.W.G. 304A–307 [. . .].
È privo di indicazioni musicali, ma la particolare *mise en page* lascia ipotizzare che
discenda *recta via* da una partitura analoga a quelle dell'*Oreste* e dell'*Ifigenia*."

[381] Lomiento 2001, 340 n. 59 states that this hypothesis has already been sketched
by Zuntz 1965, 250 and Irigoin 1997, 266. Yet, both scholars do not seem in fact
to suppose such a direct derivation. Zuntz 1965, 250 simply claims that P.Stras.
represents "the repertory, so it seems, of an actor who specialized in Euripidean
lyrics," whereas Irigoin 1997, 266 traces the physical resemblance between P.Stras.
and P.Vind./P.Leid. back to the mere "présentation du passage lyrique en lignes

focusing on a potentially misleading datum, at least in terms of *Textgeschichte*. Actually, the only physical element concerning the *mise en page* shared by these papyri is the unusual width of the column,[382] likely to be ascribed to practical needs, that is, that of visualizing ahead, while performing, a portion of the score as broad as possible, in order to be able to catch at once a view of the whole melodic line.[383] But apart from this common feature, the Strasbourg papyrus (in *scriptio continua*) does not present a peculiar physical layout that may in itself suggest possible alternative rhythmic scansions and so on. That is to say, if in P.Stras. we can find instances of metrical scansions different from those attested by the medieval tradition,[384] this, quite differently from the case of P.Vind. ll. 5–6 (where we find the scansion cr ia mol instead of 2δ for κατέκλυϲεν δεινῶν πόνων ὡϲ πόντου [= *Or.* 342–3] embedded between two instrumental clusters), happens only inasmuch as these colometrical scansions are primarily the result of alternative *textual* readings, which have nothing to do with the *mise en page* of P.Stras.

The following pages are thus an attempt to fathom in a more detailed way any possible evidence of these phenomena of re-adaptation as attested by P.Vind. G 2315 and P.Leid. inv. 510.

---

longues." For the outstanding column width as characteristic of the typology of such texts see Fassino 1999, 4–5 with nn. 23 and 27.

[382] Ca. 23–4 cm as to P.Stras. (cf. Fassino 1999, 4) and 15·5 cm as to P.Vind. G 2315 (cf. Johnson 2000a, 67). Johnson's previous reconstruction of a column "approximately 21–27 cm wide" for P.Leid. inv. 510 (Johnson 200a, 67) is wrong: a more precise reconstruction of the lineation leads to significantly different values, that is, the length of lines varies between 14·4 cm at l. 6 and 19·5 cm at l. 8. See II.2.1.

[383] See Johnson 2000a, 68 and id. 2000b, 25.

[384] That is, *errores singulares* that disrupt the strophic responsion and thus are not to be considered as real variants actually competing with the readings of the original Euripidean text (cf. Fassino 2003).

CHAPTER 2

THE EURIPIDEAN MUSICAL PAPYRI

II. *Papyrus evidence: musical practice and textual transmission*

As we have already seen in the previous chapter, phenomena of partial (oral) memory, musical re-setting, rhythmic and/or textual adaptations co-existed from a relatively early date onwards: the crosscheck
of epigraphic and literary evidence has enabled us to recover, at
least partially, a consistently heterogeneous picture of the main performative typologies orienting the Hellenistic and late-Hellenistic
entertainment culture. Such an analysis, although rather erratic and
selective, has allowed us to cast a glance at the different degrees of
re-elaboration and performative adaptation to which tragic and lyric
texts of the fifth century BC were subject in the renewed context of
Hellenistic performances.

Let us now turn to a more fine-grained approach by temporarily
focusing on the minute data conveyed by the actual scores we possess. The next step to be taken is thus that of applying this broader
interpretative frame to the direct evidence provided by those papyri
carrying musical notation that may be compared with medieval manuscript tradition, that is, P.Vind. G 2315 for Eur. *Or.* 338–44 and
P.Leid. inv. 510 for Eur. *IA.* 1500?–09 and 784–93).[1] The present

---

[1] It may be worth remembering that according to epigraphic evidence (see *IG*
II² 2320 = *TrGF* I, DID A 2a, ll. 2–3, 17–8, 32–3) the most successful Euripidean
plays as regards the revival of old tragedies in Hellenistic times actually turn out
to be the *Orestes* (408 BC) and *Iphigenia* (we do not know whether the *IT*, that is,
ca. 414 BC, or the posthumous *IA*, that is, 405 BC): see Pickard-Cambridge 1968²,
99–100, 286–7, Smith 1993, 15–6 and Falkner 2002, 356 n. 55. That could hardly
be a mere accident: the musical virtuosity displayed by the last stage of Euripides'
theatrical production (see Csapo 1999–2000, 409–15) perfectly suits the increasing
demand for professional performers in the fourth/third century BC (on the increasingly professionalism required in acting in the fifth and fourth century BC see now
Csapo 2004b). As regards the high degree of spectacularity inherent in the *Orestes*,
in terms both of stage directions and emotional impact, as already recognized (or,
better, criticised) by ancient scholiasts, see Falkner 2002, 355–61. The very high
percentage of lyric parts of *Orestes* conceived for actors (respectively 47.1% as regards

aim is to verify if and to what extent we can discover in these scores, by means of a minutely philological analysis, some traces of those processes of textual and rhythmic re-adaptation usually examined in their macroscopic aspect of cultural phenomena.[2]

Once again, the starting point will necessarily be the major issue underlying our inquiry up to now, that is, the attempt at ascertaining what kind of relationship, if any, may exist between musical scores and Alexandrian editing technique. We should then keep constantly in mind the inherently precarious identity of such scores, permanently oscillating between their status as documents testifying to a concrete performative practice and their somewhat marginal role as conveyers of a textual transmission. It is by means of comparison between these two different and yet contiguous fields, by focusing on their overlaps and divergences, that we can ultimately try to grasp the very nature of the papyrological evidence here at stake.

Actually, one of the main shortcomings inherent in the previous investigations devoted to the issue lies in having dismissed the idiosyncratic nature of the documentary typology provided by musical scores. Differently from modern practice, writing down a score was not meant, in ancient Greece, to ensure its spread and faithful re-performability by each potential user and/or performer but it rather served a performance precisely circumscribed in space and time.[3] To

---

the song alone and 52.2% for song + recitative: cf. Csapo 1999–2000, 412–3) can well have contributed to its survival as a tragic play performed in its full length (cf. *arg.* II l. 43 = Diggle *OCT* III, 189 τὸ δρᾶμα τῶν ἐπὶ ϲκηνῆϲ εὐδοκιμούντων) as well as a privileged source for anthological highlights. If we turn our attention to the first translations of Euripidean dramas into modern European languages from the sixteenth century onwards, it is interesting to see that *IA* seems to have been a favourite *pièce de résistance* already in the Renaissance: see Bolgar 1954, 441, 512–3 and Burian 1997, 229–33.

[2] For an updated survey of the manifold scenarios offered by the various typologies of performance culture in Hellenistic times see Hall 2002 and Lightfoot 2002. Most recently, for a critical approach to fourth-century BC dramatic re-performances of 'classic' tragic texts (that is, the emergence of non-classical "performance practices, attitudes towards actors, possibly even theories of acting") see Duncan 2005 (esp. 55–6). For the role played by second-rate artists like γελωτοποιοί, θαυματοποιοί and πλάνοι, whose performances were generally referred to under the loose, catch-all heading of ἀκροάματα, see Milanezi 2004.

[3] See Barker 1995, 59–60, claiming that "when a written notation, melodic or rhythmic, was added to a text in Greek antiquity, it was never designed as the vehicle of the music's publication to a wide readership, as it is in the modern world. It served precisely as an aide-mémoire for performers." Cf. also Comotti 1988, 24. For the modern concept of musical transcription see the references quoted in I.9.1 n. 334.

apply indiscriminately to these texts, which do not present themselves as merely textual evidence (at least not pre-eminently), the
otherwise sound Maasian criteria may sometimes be misleading. As
we shall see further, at least in one case the Vienna papyrus provides us with a reading clearly mistaken if traced back to Euripides'
'normative' textual tradition (that is, the metrically wrong ὀλεθρίοιϲ
attested also by codd. VACLPXT[t3]—a trifling slip—at *Or.* 343 instead
of the correct ὀλεθρίοιϲιν, which ensures the strophic responsion
between the dochmiacs of 344 (-)ϲιν ἐν κύμαϲιν and 328 ὀρεχθεὶϲ
ἔρρειϲ) but that can paradoxically turn out to be the 'true' one (and
in any case the actually 'performed' reading) if framed within these
processes of re-adaptation (the disruption of strophic responsion and
so on).[4]

To come close to defining the nature of these performances and
of the dynamics underlying such traditional processes represents a
first step towards a more critical approach to these texts regarded
in their peculiar documentary value.

II.1 *P.Vind. G 2315: the material evidence*

The first thing to be done in order to evaluate properly the contribution to our question provided by the P.Vind. G 2315 is of course
to establish the most likely physical layout (colometric or non-
colometric) to be reconstructed for the Vienna papyrus. Fleming-
Kopff's major working hypothesis will thus be challenged once again.
This preliminary survey represents in fact the only certain ground
for considering in an unbiased perspective the possible metric, rhythmic, or textual divergences and idiosyncrasies, if any, to be found
in P.Vind. compared with the medieval manuscript tradition.

The most valuable edition recently provided by Pöhlmann-West
correctly claims "a non-colometric reconstruction of the lineation"
for the Vienna papyrus.[5] Yet, since the issue is a long-lasting vexed
question[6] and also in recent times the hypothesis of a colometric *mise*

---

[4] For a more detailed analysis of this phenomenon see II.1.4. This limited perspective is still operating in Marino 1999a, Landels 1999 and Willink 2001.

[5] Pöhlmann-West *DAGM*, 15.

[6] For the alleged colometric layout displayed by P.Vind. (that is, the material
end of the writing column coinciding with colon end) see what has been argued
by Jourdan-Hemmerdinger 1973, 293, Pöhlmann 1976, 70 n. 126 and Mathiesen
1981, 23. Against this interpretation see Turner 1980, 29–30 and id. *GMAW*[2], 150

en page of the Vienna papyrus has proven to be still resilient in current scholarship,[7] it may be worth re-discussing once and for all the evidence the two contrasting statements rely on. A systematic revision of the issue is all the more welcome inasmuch as recently Marino, arguing for a colometric layout of P.Vind.,[8] has adduced this alleged evidence as a positive proof of the broader validity of Fleming-Kopff's hypothesis. In particular, Marino has advocated a close dependency of the scholium to Eur. *Or.* 340 on the instrumental notational clusters to be found at ll. 5–6 of the Vienna papyrus.[9] Marino's hypothesis, strongly relying on Solomon's reconstruction of the physical layout of P.Vind., entails, if accepted, consequences in terms both of general processes of transmission (a close relationship between the Alexandrian and musical tradition) and, on a more specific level, of the *Textgeschichte* of Euripides' *Orestes*. It is in fact on such a basis that Marino eventually argues for the textual soundness (that is, the original Euripidean text) of the inverted verse order 339/338/340 attested by P.Vind.[10] A detailed analysis of these data thus represents the first step towards a broader comprehension of the relevance of P.Vind. with regard both to the Euripidean textual tradition of *Orestes* and to the typologies of re-performances enacted in Hellenistic times.

n. 79, followed by West 1992, 1, Johnson 2000a, 67 and more recently Pöhlmann-West *DAGM*, 15. Solomon's position in this respect (id. 1977, 71–83), with all its further implications, will receive separate treatment below.

  [7] See Marino 1999a and, independently, also Landels 1999, 250 (both of them are not discussed by Pöhlmann-West *DAGM*). Cf. now also Giannini 2004.

  [8] Marino 1999a and ead. 1999b: as regards the more assertive nature of Marino 1999a see below.

  [9] That is, the *diastolé* ⸓ followed by the instrumental notes ⸂⸃: in both cases the signs are inserted within (and not above) the line of the text. As regards the relevance of such a notational cluster for the metrical interpretation of the passage, see already Dale *LMGD²*, 207 and ead. *MATC* III, 128–9. A full treatment of Marino's peculiar interpretation of the scholium to Eur. *Or.* 340 as dependent on a musical score like that transmitted by P.Vind. can be found in II.1.3.

  [10] See Marino 1999a, 155. A convincing defence of the soundness of the manuscript order 338/339/340 as the 'true' Euripidean text has recently been offered by Willink 2001, 131–3. However, as we shall see further, both Marino and Willink do not take account of Crusius' suggestion, taken up later by Turner, that the transposition of l. 339 κατολοφύρομαι κατολοφύρομαι before l. 338 may be intended as a parenthetic interjection (cf. respectively Crusius 1894, 179 and Turner 1956, 96).

II.1.1 *P.Vind. G 2315: the visual formatting. Something to do with Alexandrian colometry?*

Marino's proposal to ascribe to the sign $\dot{\mathsf{L}}$ in P.Vind. the specific function of a colon mark,[11] together with the supplementary task of outlining the rhythmic structure underlying the whole Euripidean passage,[12] re-opens the issue of the physical reconstruction of the lineation of P.Vind. and, consequently, of the metrical value, if any, to be assigned to its line-ends. Before tackling directly the problems involved by the reconstruction of lineation, I provide here a new transcription of P.Vind. resulting from a re-examination by autopsy.[13]

Paleographic description

Dimensions: $8 \times 9 \cdot 2$ cm,[14] interlinear space ca. 6/7 mm, original column width ca. 15·5 cm. Provenance: Hermoupolis Magna, cartonnage.[15] *Recto* written along the fibres, *verso* blank. The upper margin of the scrap seems to have been neatly cut, which suggests, together with the unwritten space (ca. 1·3 cm wide) at the top of our fragment, that we are dealing here with the upper margin of a papyrus-roll. The handwriting, a largish, roughly bilinear, well-rounded capital style, is to be assigned to the first half of the third century BC, that is, it belongs to the so-called group C among the Ptolemaic bookhands identified by Turner 1980, 29–30 no. 22: see Turner 1956, 95.

---

[11] Marino 1999a, 150. In the same direction see also Landels 1999, 250, according to whom the sign $\dot{\mathsf{L}}$ "is nothing more than a colon mark, to indicate to the singer where one metrical unit ends and the next begins." In P.Vind. this sign appears at least three times within the line of the text (that is, at ll. 1, 2, 3; for its likely presence at l. 7 see below) and one time *supra lineam* at l. 4. For a brief survey of the previous interpretations provided for this sign see Marino 1999a, 149 with nn. 14–6. However, Marino does not discuss the most recent bibliography on the issue, that is, West *AGM*, 206–7, Anderson 1994, 217 and Barker 1995, 45–7.

[12] Leaving aside the question of the alleged strictly colometric function of $\dot{\mathsf{L}}$, we may still welcome Marino's theoretical claim that the rhythmic function of $\dot{\mathsf{L}}$ is not to be understood as mutually exclusive of its potentially musical value (that is, as an instrumental note): see Marino 1999a, 149 with n. 15. Cf. also Marzi's previous remark that "questa stessa funzione (i.e. rhythmic), è ovvio, resta pertinente al segno anche se lo si consideri σῆμα della notazione musicale" (id. 1973, 319). Willink 2001, 126 n. 5 still seems to be bound to an antagonistic interpretation of the two possible functions of $\dot{\mathsf{L}}$; in this direction cf. also Giannini 2004, 102–3 (on which see note 63 in II.1.2).

[13] I inspected the papyrus at the *Österreichische Nationalbibliothek* of Vienna in August 2002.

[14] See Turner *GMAW²*, 70 and id. 1980, 30. Surprisingly different are the measurements recorded by Wessely 1892, 269 (cf. also id. 1892a, 66 and Crusius 1894, 174), that is, 8·5 × 9·2 cm.

[15] See Wessely 1892a, 67 and Pöhlmann-West *DAGM*, 14 n. 2.

Transcription

	]π̄ P C Ṗ Φ Π [	
1	]φυρομαι Ⳑ ματεροϲ[	339–38
	]Ζ̣ Ι Z E Δ̣[	
2	]ακχευει Ⳑ ο μ εγαϲ[	338–40
	] π̄ P C Ι Z [	
3	]ϲ εμ βροτοιϲ Ⳑ ανα [	340–41
	] C P π̄ C PⳐ Φ̇C–[	
4	]ϲ ακατου θοαϲ[ ]τινα[	342
	]Φ̇ Π P π̄ ?[	
5	]κατεκλυϲεν ꓶꓶꓷδ[	343
	] Ζ̇ Ι Z [	
6	]γ ꓶꓶꓷ ω ωϲ ποντ [	343
	] P Ċ P Z π̄ Φ[	
7	] Ⳑ….[	344

7 …. [: very uncertain readings. Below the C belonging to the *Notenschrift* there are apparently short high traces of ink: most likely the top of a circular letter, ΕΘΟC[16] equally possible. Then traces of a back and upper curve of a rounded letter: more likely C or E than O. What follows is a high point (top of an upright or curve?) and after ca. 1 mm there is an oblique stroke sloping to the right. G. Messeri suggested to me that we can be dealing here with the back and upper curve (distinctly drawn in two different movements) of E, cf. both E of κατεκλυϲεν at l. 5. Then a descending diagonal and the top of an upright projecting above the line-level: possibly N, cf. the second upright of N projecting beyond the line-level also at ll. 3, 4, 5. Finally, just before the lacuna, there seems to be the almost completely erased top of an upright: Γ, Η, Ι, Κ all possible

Notation

5 ? : very uncertain reading. A low point of ink above what seems to be the junction of two obliques (that is, the underlying Δ): P̣ Pöhlmann, P̣ Wessely   7 P̣: upper part of a closed loop, most likely P (Wessely, Crusius, Pöhlmann, Pöhlmann-West)   Ⳑ: almost entirely in the gap: the trace is no more than the upper sign of the ϲτιγμή as in the previous instances of that sign

---

[16] Crusius' skepticism, according to which "ist nichts zu erkennen, höchstens ein Schatten des obern Randes, der aber jede andere Deutung zulässt," seems to be exaggerated. The optical microscope clearly reveals traces of ink for an extension of ca. 2/3 mm.

Textual apparatus

7 ⸉ ϲεεν[Messeri: ⸉ [ϲι]ενκ[Pöhlmann-West: ⸉ τινα[Solomon:]ϲιν͐[Crusius: ο]ϲων Wessely

Since Marino's conclusions about the colometric layout displayed by P.Vind. strongly rely on Solomon's textual reconstruction of ll. 6–7 of the Vienna papyrus,[17] it may be useful to start by directly considering Solomon's argumentation. For the sake of clarity, I reproduce here the text of P.Vind. as edited by Pöhlmann,[18] at that time the standard edition of reference before Pöhlmann-West's recent *DAGM*:

⌐κατολοφύρομαι⌐	/339
]π̄ Ρ Ϲ Ρ̇ Φ Π [	
1 ⌐κατολο⌐φύρομαι ⸉ ματέροϲ ⌐αἷμα ϲᾶϲ⌐	339/38
] Ζ ι̇ Ζ Ε [	
2 ⌐ὅ ϲ᾽ ἀναβ⌐ακχεύει. ⸉ ὁ μέγαϲ ⌐ὄλβοϲ οὐ⌐	338/40
] π̄ Ρ Ϲ ι̇Ζ[	
3 ⌐μόνιμο⌐ϲ ἐμ βροτοῖϲ, ⸉ ἀνὰ ⌐δὲ λαῖφοϲ ὥϲ⌐	340/41
] ϹΡ π̄ Ϲ Ρ ⸉ Φ̇Ϲ-[	
4 ⌐τιϲ ἀκάτου θοᾶϲ τινά⌐ξαϲδαίμων⌐	342
Φ̇Π Ρ π̄ ?[	
5 κατέκλυϲεν ⌐⌐ϲ δ⌐εινῶν⌐	343
] ζ̇ ι̇ Ζ [	
6 ⌐πόνω⌐ν ⌐⌐ϲ ὡϲ πόντ⌐ου⌐	343
] Ρ Ϲ̇ ΡΖ ?̇ Φ [	
7 ⌐λάβροιϲ ὀλεθρίοι⌐ ⸉ ϲιν ⌐εέν κύμαϲιν⌐	344

A preliminary observation is necessary here. Although Solomon in his paper focuses almost exclusively on *Or.* 343–4 (that is, ll. 5–7 of the Vienna papyrus), as regards *Or.* 338–42 he seems to accept the colometry transmitted by the Euripidean medieval tradition, that is, he interprets ll. 338–42 as series of dochmiac dimeters linked by synapheia.[19] According to Solomon, who assigns to ⸉ the function

---

[17] See Marino 1999a, 147–8 (at 148 Marino misquotes Solomon's colometry of ll. 6–7, which is in fact πόνων ὡϲ πόντου λάβροιϲ ὀλεθρίοιϲιν ἐν κύμαϲιν κτλ. and not πόνων ὡϲ πόντου λάβροιϲ ὀλε‖θρίοιϲιν ἐν κύμαϲιν: see Solomon 1977, 78).

[18] Pöhlmann 1970, 78.

[19] Solomon 1977, 71, 73, 78. As regards ll. 338–42, Solomon indeed seems to accept the text edited by Di Benedetto 1965, 73–4, which is substantially faithful

both of an instrumental note and of a "dividing point between the two dochmii of each line,"[20] this same metrical articulation is reproduced also by P.Vind., although exhibiting a different physical layout of the lineation (suffice it here to note the hiatus—not coinciding with the material end of the lineation—, and therefore verse end, between ἀναβακχεύει and ὁ μέγας within l. 2). Once granted this premise, let us turn to the new reading advanced by Solomon for l. 7 of the Vienna papyrus.[21] This is Solomon's own deciphering of the desperately uncertain traces of ink at l. 7:

-μασιν] ɿ τινᾳ [γαρ ετι

Thus, according to Solomon, the colometric layout transmitted by P.Vind. as regards its last two lines would be the following:[22]

6 πόνων ὡς πόντου ɿ λάβροις ὀλεθρίοι-
7 σιν ἐν κύμασιν ɿ τίνα γὰρ ἔτι πάρος[23]

Yet such a textual arrangement entails conspicuous difficulties, both paleographic and metrical. As regards the reading proper, although

---

to the medieval manuscript colometry, apart from the dochmiac ἀνὰ δὲ λαῖφος ὥς (341), interpreted by the Italian scholar as a dochmiac monometer. Lines 338–44 are in fact understood by medieval tradition as a sequence of dochmiac dimeters linked by synapheia: cf. the correct word division ἐκιλαθέσθαι at 325 shared by HMOVACrFGKPPrRRySaξZcT, and φοιταιλέου at 326 preserved by HMBOVACGKξZc (see Diggle 1991, 135). The only element of discontinuity within an otherwise uniform manuscript colometry is an occasional instance of word division accidentally running on or stopping short: see Diggle 1991, 134–6 and more recently Willink 2001, 128–9 with n. 11. The colometric consistency of the manuscript tradition as regards the first stasimon of *Orestes* has been convincingly advocated by Willink 2001, 128–30 also on the basis of the papyrus evidence (neglected by Marino) provided by P.Berol. inv. 17051 + 17014 (= Π⁷ Diggle). See especially Diggle's reconstruction of the physical layout of P.Berol. (id. 1991, 134 with n. 10), which restores a full coincidence between the colometry transmitted by the Berlin papyrus and that of the medieval tradition (that is, the word division ἐκιλαθέσθαι at 325 and φοιταιλέου at 326). Diggle's textual arrangement rectifies Lenaerts' previous claim of a diverging colometry for *Or.* 325–6 (id. 1977, 21–3: see also O'Callaghan 1981, 19–24 and Luppe 1980, 241). It is worth noticing that Ioannidou 1996, 111–2 no. 83 still reproduces Lenaerts' *mise en page* of the Berlin papyrus. A synoptic view of the manuscript colometry transmitted for first stasimon of *Orestes* can be found in Marino 1999a, 145–6. As regards the colometry displayed by the Triclinian autograph Ang. gr. 14 cf. now Faveri 2002, 51–3 and 163–5.

[20] Solomon 1977, 77.
[21] Solomon 1977, 81.
[22] Solomon 1977, 78–9.
[23] Solomon 1977, 80 scans πάρος, that is, he assumes here a break in the synapheia and thus verse end. For this metrical device see below.

any effort to make sense of the scanty traces of ink at l. 7 is most welcome and deserves serious consideration, Solomon's suggestion of reading]τίνα̣ [γὰρ ἔτι πάροc as the second dochmiac at l. 7 is unconvincing for several reasons.

First of all, Solomon's interpretation of what he considers to be "the first horizontal stroke" as the high horizontal bar of a]τ̣ is quite unsatisfactory. The parallel of the bar of tau in τινά[ξαc] (l. 4) adduced by the scholar is only an alleged one: at l. 4, immediately below the suprascript sign ⌐, there are clearly traces of the left stroke of the high horizontal with medial junction, which is not the case at l. 7.[24] As for Solomon's objection to the previous reading]ς accepted by Pöhlmann,[25] although the instrumental note c at l. 7 is all but rounded, another instance of a sigma with a quite straight upper curve can be found in θοας̣ at l. 4.[26] Thus, *pace* Solomon, the only readings suiting the traces of ink at this point still remain either ς or ε̣.[27]

Secondly, the final α̣ of]τ̣ι̣ν̣α̣[as suggested by Solomon is also a very doubtful reading[28] since it entails a marked slope to the left of the first oblique of alpha.[29] Equally problematic is the ν̣ of]τ̣ι̣ν̣α̣[, a reading already proposed by Crusius, who suggested]ς̣ι̣ν̣ʸ[and regarded the vanishing trace of ink after ν̣ (a trace deciphered by Solomon as the apex of α̣) as an otherwise unspecified "Vortragszeichen."[30]

---

[24] Cf. recently also Willink's criticism against Solomon's reading]τ̣, claiming the necessity of returning to the previous reading consisting of "the top of a sigma, as it had been taken by every one before Solomon" (id. 2001, 129).

[25] According to Solomon 1977, 77 "his *sigma* would seem to have a top that is not rounded enough."

[26] The high horizontal stroke underlying the low horizontal bar of ⌐ *supra lineam* at l. 4 can only be the top of the sigma of θοας̣.

[27] The reading ε̣ had already been suggested initially by Crusius: see Crusius 1894, 178.

[28] Solomon himself is well aware of that: "in my reconstruction the oblique stroke of the next letter would have to be the apex of the alpha. But unless the ink and its underlying papyrus fibers have been damaged because of their position at the edge of the fragment, the reading of an alpha here must remain in doubt" (id. 1977, 80).

[29] Equally unlikely is the *disemon* read by Solomon above the alleged α of]τ̣ι̣ν̣α̣[: it would be set too much above the line-level, cf. the *disemon* above the α of τινα̣[ξαc at l. 4.

[30] See Crusius 1894, 178 ("der offenbar von oben nach unten gezogene schräge Strich in der Mitte wird ein Vortragszeichen sein, wie bei dem letzten C in Zeile 7 [= that is, l. 4: Crusius is referring to the disemon above the α of τινα̣[ξαc at l. 4]").

Finally, Solomon considers as one of the main difficulties in accepting the reading]ϲ at l. 7, the fact that "here the musical note *sigma*
falls too far to the left of the supposed *sigma* of ϹΙΝ [i.e. the reading accepted by Pöhlmann 1970 for l. 7]—a displacement not observed
elsewhere in either this papyrus or any of the other extant musical
papyri."[31] Yet this objection is not conclusive. Although this phenomenon is much more conspicuous at l. 7, a similar displacement
may be found also in the case of the vocal note ρ put above the
underlying α of θοαϲ at l. 4. In this case the note ρ appears in fact
to be slightly displaced to the left if compared with the position of
the same letter at l. 1 above the ρ of κατολοφυρομαι or above the
μ of ματεροϲ.

However, the missing central alignment of the ρ, if compared with the
underlying α of θοαϲ at l. 4, can be well explained if we keep in mind that
the whole suprascript musical notation corresponding to the underlying textual sequence αϲτ at l. 4 reveals a clearly squashed appearance, which is
especially evident if we focus on the sign ⅃. If compared with its other
instances *intra lineam* in the Vienna papyrus, this time the sign ⅃ presents
not only a significant lessening in size but also a marked compressing of
the vertical upright. All these elements seem to suggest that the copyist,
once aware of having forgotten to leave the necessary space for adding *intra
lineam* the sign ⅃ as in the previous cases, tried to gain space.[32] So I do
not agree with Pöhlmann who, in order to explain the insertion of ⅃ *supra
lineam* at l. 4, refers to the copyist's intention of singling out the corresponding point of the strophe where the phenomenon of verbal synapheia
occurs, that is, the word division ἐκ|λαθέϲθαι at ll. 325–6.[33] Since we are
dealing with a score underlying an actual performance, to mark the presence of the synapheia in the corresponding lines of the strophe (which

---

[31] Solomon 1977, 79–80.
[32] Even if we suppose that the sign ⅃ was to be inserted *intra lineam* at the same
time as the copyist was writing down the text, that omission could have been
favoured by the graphic resemblance between ⅃ and the following τ of τινα[ξαϲ (I
owe this suggestion to L. Battezzato). For the failed placement *intra lineam* of ⅃ at
l. 4 see also Marino 1999a, 147 and Willink 2001, 126 n. 5.
[33] See Pöhlmann 1970, 82: "Die Erklärung für diese hier sinnwidrige Notenstellung
bringt die Strophe. An der Parallelstelle zu Z. 4 mit dem hochgestellten ⅃, Vers
326, zeigt sich nämlich Synaphie mit γόνον ἐάϲατ᾽ ἐκ|λαθέϲθαι λύϲϲαϲ. [. . .] Man
sieht also, dass die Notenstellung der Antistrophe den Wortenden der Strophe
Rechnung trägt und, was bei scriptio continua naheliegt, mechanisch auf die an
einigen Stellen anders gegliederte Antistrophe übertragen wurde." Cf. also the similar remarks by Pöhlmann-West *DAGM*, 16, Pöhlmann 2005, 136–7. Pöhlmann-
West's explanation relies on the assumption (still to be proved) that P.Vind. does
represent a faithfully strophic performance of the first choral song of Euripides'
Orestes.

we must suppose *already* sung and performed) while writing down the text and music of the antistrophe, seems, at least to me, devoid of any practical purpose.[34]

Summing up, a closer examination of the traces of ink at l. 7 strongly leads to rejecting Solomon's new reading]τ̣ι̣ν̣α̣[. Equally unsatisfactory is Crusius' previous suggestion]ϲι̣ν̣ˊ[, a reading which, also leaving aside the awkwardness of the alleged *Vortragszeichen* above the last letter, reproposes the same difficulty already acknowledged as regards the ν of Solomon's]τ̣ι̣ν̣α̣[.[35] Among the readings suggested by previous scholars, Wessely's ο]ϲ̣ω̣ν[[36] still seems to me to deserve serious consideration, notwithstanding some elements of perplexity. Above all, with Wessely's reading, we would be forced to accept an ω too high within the level-line. On the other hand, the fact that Wessely's reading would provide us with a somewhat obscure textual variant not otherwise attested by the medieval tradition[37] is not in itself a conclusive argument for rejecting it. Fassino's recent re-examination of P.Stras.W.G. 304–307 (another Ptolemaic papyrus) has clearly shown that the earliest tradition of *Medea* knew textual variants deeply diverging from those attested by medieval manuscripts.[38]

To sum up, as regards l. 7 of the Vienna papyrus, if we decline to accept Wessely's ο]ϲ̣ω̣ν[, the only valid paleographic alternative

---

[34] See Anderson's skepticism about the possibility that P.Vind. does actually preserve the original Euripidean strophic correspondence (id. 1994, 219–22).

[35] Crusius' proposal]ϲι̣ν̣[has been partially taken up by Pöhlmann 1970, 78, who however does not speak any longer of *Vortragszeichen*. West's]ε̣ν̣κ̣[(cf. id. 1992, 1 and id. in Pöhlmann-West *DAGM*, 12 and 16) is also problematic: if we interpret the high point of ink after the first letter (that is, ε̣ according to West) as the first upright of a ν, we have still to explain the unusual gap between this upright and the following oblique. Furthermore the resulting ν would be much wider than the other instances we can observe in P.Vind.: ca. 7 mm wide against the 4–5 mm otherwise attested.

[36] Wessely 1892, 270–1 and id. 1892a, 68.

[37] Wessely 1892, 272 suggested tentatively for *Or.* 343–4 a quite unlikely κατέκλυϲεν κύμαϲιν ἐν ὡϲ πόντου λάβροιϲ ὀλεθρίοιϲ ὅϲων ϲυμφορῶν. See also Wessely 1892a, 68.

[38] See Fassino 1999. This theoretical possibility remains valid independently of the fact that Wessely's textual reconstruction for l. 7 (see note above) cannot be right inasmuch as it does not take account of the column length. Solomon 1977, 82 does not consider the possibility of having here a *varia lectio*: he limits himself to observe that at l. 7 a reading diverging from that attested by the manuscript tradition would entail "the unattractive implication that the papyrus is a musical anthology that proceeds to a new piece of music without having finished out the last one."

seems to me that suggested by G. Messeri, that is, we should read
at l. 7 ϲεεν[. That is to say, the curving stroke interpreted up to
now as the oblique of a ν would fit well the upper curve of an ε.
Furthermore, the final ν read by Messeri before the lacuna (ϲεεν[)
is the only reading that suits the traces of ink described above (that
is, the top of an upright) and is consistent with the dimension positively attested for such a letter (ca. 4–5 mm). If we therefore accept
Messeri's reading and understand εεν[as most probably a melism
for the prepositive ἐν (κύμαϲιν) of the original Euripidean text,[39] the
problem still remains of explaining why we cannot detect in the
papyrus any extant trace of the final ν of the previous ὀλεθρίοιϲιν,
a letter whose second upright usually projects beyond the upper margin of the line-level.[40] A possible explanation for such an 'absence',
an explanation which makes sense within a musical score, is that of
supplementing at l. 7 (λά)|[βροιϲ ὀλεθρίοι] ⅂ ϲ ἐεν [κύμαϲιν. That is,
we have to suppose that P.Vind. has here ὀλεθρίοιϲ in spite of the
transmitted ὀλεθρίοιϲιν, a variant preserved also by part of the
Euripidean medieval tradition.[41]

It is worth noting that Solomon's reconstruction of the lineation for ll. 6–7
(= *Or.* 344–5), that is, his reading (ὀλεθρίοι)ϲιν ἐν κύμαϲιν ⅂ τίνα γὰρ ἔτι
πάροϲ, is doubtful also from a metrical point of view. Starting from the
premise that ⅂ has necessarily to divide two identical metrical cola, Solomon
claims that "therefore we can be certain that line 7 had at least two dochmii
divided by this instrumental note," and suggests an unlikely scansion of τῑνᾱ
γᾰρ ἔτῐ πᾰρο̄ϲ as a dochmiac with "a tribrach third beat" consisting of "the
three short syllables of the adverbial (and relatively insignificant) γὰρ ἔτι."[42]
This is clearly an unconvincing device designed to avoid the rare pyrrhic
implementation of the fourth element of the alleged second dochmiac at
l. 7.[43] Furthermore, Solomon's scansion πᾱρο̄ϲ (that is, assuming verse-end),

---

[39] See also the previous melism ὤωϲ at l. 6.

[40] This difficulty is clearly perceived by Pöhlmann-West *DAGM*, 12, 16, who supplement at l. 7 ὀλεθρίοι] ⅂ [ϲι] ἐν κ[ύμαϲιν (thus apparently hiatus between ὀλεθρίοιϲι
and the ἐν), by observing that "the nu in ὀλεθρίοιϲιν was omitted in the papyrus."

[41] That is, the codd. VACLPXT[13], see Diggle *OCT* III, 210. For the different
value to be ascribed to this *varia lectio* in the medieval tradition (a mechanical slip
disrupting the responsion) and in P.Vind. (a potential performative variant), see
II.1.4.

[42] Solomon 1977, 81–2 (see also *ibid.* 77 and 80).

[43] See Martinelli 1997[2], 270 with n. 18 and Medda 1993, 108–9 n. 13. The case
of Aesch. *Ag.* 1176 quoted by Solomon 1977, 80 n. 20 can also be differently understood, see the metrical appendix *ad loc.* in West 1998[2]. Even if we interpret τῑνᾱ

even if theoretically possible,[44] does not allow us to gain a consistent colometry for the following problematic lines 345–6.[45] In fact we would be forced to scan them as a trochaic-dochmiac sequence (οἶκὄν ᾰλλὄν| ἔτὲρὄν ἢ τὄν ᾰπὄ θὲὄγὄνῶν γᾰμῶν: tr + 2 δ), an unparalleled series in tragedy. The only two tragic instances partially comparable, that is, Aesch. Ag. 1123–4~1134–5 and Eur. Phoen. 187, besides presenting the reverse order δ + tr, are more likely to be traced back to a different metrical interpretation.[46]

Finally, according to Solomon's reconstruction of the physical layout exhibited by P.Vind., l. 6 would have originally contained "33 letters and instrumental notes, one character longer than line 3, the longest line attested elsewhere in the fragment."[47] We would then have here a much wider line-length than we can reconstruct for the previous lines.[48] The comparison drawn by Solomon with l. 3 (= 29 letters + the sign ‑ι) is of no avail: the beginning of l. 3 (μόνιμο]ϲ) is perfectly aligned with that of ll. 1–2, whereas this alignment to the left margin is completely lacking for l. 6 (cf. the beginning in *eisthesis* of πόνω]ν according to Solomon's hypothesis).

Besides, according to Solomon's textual arrangement of ll. 338–43 (substantially the same text as edited by Pöhlmann), we should have a remarkable indentation at the beginnings of ll. 4–5 of the Vienna papyrus. His attempt at defending such a *mise en page* by arguing that "in other strophic poetry preserved on papyri, line lengths often vary, with resulting irregular left or right margins. Consequently a variation in line-length in this papyrus should not disturb us, nor should extension of a line farther to the right or left of the other lines," is quite unconvincing.[49] The examples quoted by Solomon

γᾱρ ἔτῐ πᾱρὄϲ as kδ, the problem still remains of finding an acceptable colometry for the following lines 345–6 Diggle (see below).

[44] See Medda 1993, 122–3 with n. 48 and id. 2000, 115–42.

[45] The same objection against Solomon can be found also in Willink 2001, 129.

[46] Cf. Medda 1993, 198–9. We could also scan ἔτὲρὄν ἢ τὄν ᾰπὄ θὲὄγὄνῶν γᾰμῶν as cr ia cr or 2tr 2cr (a syncopated trochaic tetrameter?), but the metrical context would still remain obscure. Granted the difficulty of making sense of the series 345–6~329–30 (cf. Diggle 1981, 20, id. 1991, 135–6 with n. 13 and recently Kopff 1999, 87), Solomon's purely dochmiac interpretation of Or. 345~329 has rightly been neglected by subsequent scholars, see Marino 1999a, 154 and Diggle 1991, 135.

[47] Solomon 1977, 78 with n. 17.

[48] Line 7 as reconstructed by Solomon (that is, (ὀλεθρίοι]ϲιν ἐν κύμαϲιν ‑ι τίνα γὰρ ἔτι πάροϲ) would restore again a line-length compatible with that of the previous lines: l. 6 would represent thus an isolated exception.

[49] Solomon 1977, 78. Marino 1999a, 147 follows entirely Solomon's argumentation in this regard.

are in fact only alleged parallels:[50] both P.Oxy. 1175 and P.Oxy.
2369 (respectively scraps from Sophocles' *Eurypylos* and *Inachos*) show
eisthesis coinciding with change of metre. That is, in both cases the
indentation marks a change from iambic trimeters to lyric metres
and this editorial device never appears within a section which is
already lyric and metrically homogeneous, as would be the case here
for *Or.* 338–44.[51] Furthermore, in P.Oxy. 2369 fr. 1 col. I l. 22 the
eisthesis is followed by the *diplé obelismene*, according to a well-attested
ancient editorial practice of marking the change to a lyric section.[52]

Summing up, neither the excessive length of l. 6[53] nor the supposed indentation of the beginnings of ll. 4–6 as reconstructed by
Solomon seems to find a reasonable explanation, at least within
Solomon's broader outline. In fact, Solomon seems to believe in a
real colometric layout of the Vienna papyrus as regards ll. 5–7 (that
is, line-end coinciding with colon or verse-end for ll. 343–5),[54] a belief

---

[50] Solomon 1977, 78 n. 17.

[51] P.Köln VI 252 l. 8 (= Eur. *Or.* 142) does not represent an exception to the
rule: the *ekthesis* marks a change of speaker at *Or.* 141–2, that is, within the dochmiac
section of the parodos, see Gronewald 1987, 130 (cf. I.9.2 n. 373). For similar
instances of *eisthesis*/*ekthesis* denoting change of speaker within amoibaic sections in
the Euripidean tradition see recently Savignago 2003, 2 n. 11, 9 n. 36. Also P.Laur.
III/908 (= Eur. *Or.* 196–216) cannot be adduced as a parallel supporting Solomon's
argumentation: the presence of *eisthesis* + *paragraphos* at l. 5 (= *Or.* 202, that is,
within the second antistrophe of the parodos) marks a change of rhythm from the
dochmiac dimeter of 201 (cύ τε γὰρ ἐν νεκροῖc, τὸ δ᾽ ἐμὸν οἴχεται) to the prosodiac of 202 (βίου τὸ πλέον μέροc ἐν) and the following cola: see Pintaudi 1985, 15.
The same can be said of the musical papyrus P.Oxy. 2436 (a lyric passage perhaps drawn from a satyr drama): the indentation of ll. 7–8, which are linked by
verbal synapheia, corresponds to a change of rhythm (that is from a iambo-trochaic
rhythm to a cretic one). Similarly, in another musical papyrus recently edited by
West, that is, P.Oxy. 4461, the *ekthesis* marks the beginnings of new excerpts composed according to different notation-keys and metres, see M.L. West, *The Oxyrhynchus
Papyri*, LXV, London 1998, 83.

[52] See the several instances quoted by E. Lobel in *The Oxyrhynchus Papyri*, XXIII,
London 1956, 59. As regards the use of the *eisthesis*, either with the *diplé obelismene*
or alone, as denoting "a change in drama from trimeters to lyrics [...] or from
lyrics to tetrameters and back" see Turner *GMAW*[2], 12 with n. 60.

[53] What is puzzling is not the greater length of a single line in itself (P.Leid. inv.
510 also exhibits different line-lengths: see II.2.1) but the difficulty of matching this
alleged datum with the other physical features of P.Vind. (in P.Leid. inv. 510 all
the lines are in fact justified to the left).

[54] See the papyrus colometry as reconstructed by Solomon 1977, 78 for *Or.*
343–5: κατέκλυcεν δεινῶνl πόνων ὡc πόντου λάβροιc ὀλεθρίοιcιν ἐν κύμαcιν. τίνα
γὰρ ἔτι πάροcl, that is, a sequence of δl 2 δ 2 δ || (at 345 Solomon scans, as we
have already seen, παρōc, supposing verse-end).

that, as we have seen, cannot be extended to ll. 1–4 (= 338–42).[55]
Thus Solomon's somewhat contradictory hypothesis can confidently
be ruled out.

Let us turn to Marino's main proposal (that is, assigning a specifically
colometric function to ꞈ⏌), which rests entirely on Solomon's reconstruction of ll. 6–7 of the Vienna papyrus. A preliminary observation is necessary here. We have already seen that the colometry
advanced by Solomon for ll. 6–7 of P.Vind., even if inherently contradictory, does show however an inner explanation consisting of the
(wrong) belief that line-end concides with colon and/or verse-end. If
we ascribe a specifically colometric function to the sign ꞈ⏌ (as Marino
does), we would expect the line-length to be determined only by the
material space actually available. In other words, once we have
denied the physical line-end its colometric function and assigned this
task to the sign ꞈ⏌,[56] it would be reasonable to assume that we are
dealing with a case of continuous writing.[57] Therefore Solomon's
reconstruction, once embedded in Marino's own hypothesis, turns
out to be doubly unlikely.[58]

Thus, once granted that we are not to assign a strictly colometric function to the sign ꞈ⏌, the most appropriate layout reconstructed
for P.Vind. is that brilliantly suggested by West[59] (partially preceded
by Marzi):[60]

[55] See the presence of hiatus in the midline between ἀναβακχεύει and ὁ at l. 2.
[56] Marino 1999a, 147–8.
[57] A usual practice for musical papyri: see Johnson 2000a, 67–8.
[58] The same objections can be raised against Landels 1999, 250–1. Even though
Landels accepts for P.Vind. the text edited by Pöhlmann (that is, without the anomalous extension of l. 6 as suggested by Solomon), the problem still remains of explaining the indentation of ll. 4–6.
[59] West in Pöhlmann-West *DAGM*, 12 (a revised version of the layout suggested
by West 1992, 1; for the differences between the two transcriptions see Pöhlmann-
West *DAGM*, 15–6). For my different reading of l. 7 see what has been argued
above.
[60] Marzi 1973, 316–7. The text here reproduced follows the layout of Pöhlmann-
West 2001, 12, which is the most correct representation of the Vienna papyrus.
For different readings of single letters and a possible different word-division see the
transcription above and what already suggested in Prauscello 2002, 94.

```
                    ⌊κατολοφυρομαι⌋              339
        ]π̅  P  C        Ṗ Φ Π [
1  ⌊κατολο⌋φυρομαι ⸂ ματεροϲ ⌊αιμα ϲαϲ⌋        339–38
        ]Ẓ             ị Z E Δ[
2  ⌊οϲ αναβ⌋ακχευει ⸂ ο μεγαⲓϲ ολβοϲ ου⌋       338–40
      ]  π̅  P  C         ịZ[
3  ⌊μονιμοⲓϲ εμ βροτοιϲ ⸂ αναⲓ δε λαιφοϲ⌋     340–1
      ]  CP π̅    C P⸂ΦC̣–[
4  ⌊ωωϲτιⲓϲ ακατου  θοαⲓϲ⌋ τιναⲓ̣ξαϲ δαι⌋      342
      ]Φ Π P  π̅            ?[
5  ⌊μωων⌋κατεκλυϲεν  ⸌⸍ϲⲼ  δ⌊εινων⌋           343
      ]        Ż ị  Z   [
6  ⌊πονωω⌋ν  ⸌⸍ϲⲼ  ωωϲ ποντⲓου ου λα⌋         343
        ]Ṗ    C   PZ π̅ Φ [
7  ⌊βροⲓϲ ολεθριοⲓ⌋ ⸂ ⌊ⲓϲⲓ⌋ εγ̣κ̣⌊ⲩμαϲιν⌋      344
```

West's layout represents a great improvement inasmuch as it assumes a column width perfectly suiting the bibliological data otherwise attested by the musical scores at our disposal,[61] and avoids the awkward eisthesis of ll. 4–6 we should be forced to accept according to Solomon's reconstruction of the lineation. Leaving aside the problematic reading of the scanty traces of ink at l. 7, a first certain datum on which to graft further observations can be achieved with a reasonable degree of confidence: the Vienna papyrus provides us with a "non-colometric reconstruction of the lineation."[62] Once again, the fascinating hypothesis of a straightforward link between Alexandrian editing technique (colization) and texts carrying musical notation turns out to rest on feeble ground.

II.1.2   *P.Vind. G 2315: reading signs. Looking for a performative explanation of* ⸂ *and* ⸌⸍ϲ

The next step to be taken is to try and explain the function and meaning of ⸂ within the musical frame of the Vienna papyrus. First of all, Marino's skepticism on the musical nature of this sign seems unjustified.[63] As already pointed out by Pöhlmann, this very same

---

[61] See Johnson 2000a, 67 arguing, on the basis of West 1992, for a column ca. 15·5 cm wide for P.Vind.

[62] Pöhlmann-West *DAGM*, 15.

[63] See Marino 1999a, 148 n. 12, arguing that "un segno simile, *ma non puntato*, pare ricorrere anche in Pöhlmann 1970, nr. 24" (= P.Vind. G 29825 [c] l. 7 = Pöhlmann-West *DAGM*, no. 11; italics are mine). The same skepticism is now restated by Giannini 2004, 102–3 without adding any additional argument against the musical interpretation of ⸂: the *stigmé* can accompany both musical notes and

sign can be found in another musical score, that is, P.Vind. G 29825 (c) l. 7, where we can detect a "punktierte Instrumentalnote(n) . . . in der schon vom Euripidesfragment bekannten Form ⌐L, und zwar wie dort in Z. 4 zwischen Notenzeichen."[64] Although we cannot rule out *a priori* the possibility of a non-systematic use of the same sign in different scores, at least in this second case it is indeed quite difficult to assign to ⌐L a specifically colometric function, following Marino's suggestion for P.Vind. G 2315.[65] In fact in P.Vind. G 29825 (c) l. 7 the sign ⌐L is written above the second syllable of a word starting a new line (η φιλ[). That is, the supra-linear ⌐L is comparable, in terms of alignment and spacing, with the preceding vocal note C written above the first syllable of the line (that is, η, most likely the prepositive ἠ). Secondly, Marino's implicit assumption that the sign ⌐L, inasmuch as it is not preceded by the *diastolé*, cannot be an instrumental note like those written within the line at ll. 5 and 6 (which are accompanied by such a division mark),[66] is an argument drawn *e silentio*. Instead, the very acknowledgment of this difference may lead us to reflect further on the likely different modes of performance underlying the signs ⌐L and ⌐Ɔ.[67]

Recently Willink 2001, 126 n. 5, although with reason disagreeing with Marino's strictly colometric interpretation of ⌐L,[68] still seems to be rather too skeptical about the instrumental nature of ⌐L: "whether or not it (that

---

rhythmical signs (*pace* Giannini, the 'vocal' [and not instrumental] nature of the letter Z in the instances quoted in Prauscello 2002, 90 n. 44 was already recognized by the author). The instrumental nature of the note ⌐L in P.Vind. is strongly advocated by Pöhlmann-West *DAGM*, 15. For a slightly different interpretation see Bélis 2001, 35, 41. Psaroudakes 2004, 477 argues for a vocal note.

[64] Pöhlmann 1970, 91; cf. recently also Pöhlmann-West *DAGM*, 51. The autopsy of P.Vind. G 28295 (c) l. 7 does confirm the presence of the ϲτιγμή: ca. 1 mm to the right of the upper horizontal stroke of the Z, at the very edge of the scrap, there is clearly a dot of ink comparable with that above Γ at ll. 1 and 8.

[65] Marino 1999a, 150.

[66] See Marino 1999a, 150.

[67] Marino's claim that the explanation of the mid-line position of ⌐L as a colon-divider must be sought in "una disposizione utile per l'esecuzione musicale" (ead. 1999a, 150–1) is unconvincing. Johnson 2000a, 68 has correctly shown that the only practical aid provided by the unusual column length of musical scores is that of enabling the performer to visualize ahead a portion of the score as broad as possible, in order to be able to see at a glance the whole melodic line. The mid-line position of a colon-divider is an unnecessary corollary of this reasonable explanation.

[68] Marino 1999b, 23–4 with n. 36 seems to be in any case less assertive in arguing for a merely colometric function of this sign, yet the substance of her argumentation remains unchanged.

is, $\dot{L}$) had some *other/additional* musical connotation, it cannot be fortuitous
that it occurs only at the end of a dochmiac measure, behaving thus like
a bar-line in a modern musical score" (my italics). Even if we leave aside
the documentary evidence previously discussed, to ascribe a musical/instru-
mental function to $\dot{L}$ does not mean at all to deny its inherent rhythmic
value: both functions must be understood not as mutually exclusive but as
closely complementary. In other words, the fact that at the beginning of a
new metrical unit (namely dochmiac) the need was felt to mark the recur-
sive occurrence of the correspondent rhythmic pattern also by means of a
performative counterpart, is a datum nowadays shared by the most varied
musical traditions, which of course is different from ascribing to $\dot{L}$ a
specifically colometric function.[69] Also Willink's other statements on the issue
call for further comment. According to Willink "it is surely easier to believe
(1) that P.Vind. simply gives the dochmiac measures (and the superscribed
musical notes) with an appropriate divider wherever two measures are written uno versu. It *may* descend from a 'colometrised' ancestor with more
rational lineation. But it seems equally likely (2) that it was lineated according to a convention whereby the dochmiacs were colometrised only in the
sense that the end of each dochmius was shown *either* by line-end *or* by a
'divider' symbol between a pair of measures, the dividers thus analogous
to the 'bar-lines' in modern musical scores, while also serving to *articulate*
the (possibly unfamiliar) rhythm" (author's italics). First, both hypotheses
suggested by Willink somehow or other rest on the still unproven assumption of a close relationship between musical scores and Alexandrian colization (cf. e.g. the "colometrised 'ancestor'" of [1]). Secondly, as regards
the alleged analogy drawn between $\dot{L}$ and "(the) bar-lines in modern musical scores," this remark relies again on the same basic misunderstanding
previously noticed, that is, a supposed incompatibility between the instrumental role and rhythmic function of $\dot{L}$. Furthermore, series of recurrent
dochmiac dimeters seem to have been a relatively easily recognizable pattern: see e.g. Barrett 1964, 84 n. 3 on the non-significant agreement of the
colometry (in dochmiacs) between P.Oxy. 2224 and the medieval manuscript tradition of Eur. *Hipp.* 579–95.

A very interesting re-evaluation of the instrumental function conveyed by $\dot{L}$ within the musical frame of the Vienna papyrus has
instead been advanced by West and even if not unanimously shared
by current scholars[70] deserves serious consideration. According to
West, the occurrence between words, in the Vienna papyrus, of "a

---

[69] Giannini's statement that "la valenza ritmica del segno $\dot{L}$ non esclude la funzione colometrica" (id. 2004, 103 with n. 22) is partially right inasmuch as it recognizes the complementary nature of the rhythmical value underlying $\dot{L}$, but still
relies on the questionable assumption that $\dot{L}$ does not represent a musical note.

[70] See Anderson 1994, 215 and Landels 1999, 251.

small number of instrumental (aulos) notes" (among them, thus, also
the sign ⌐Ꞁ) must be meant "to sound simultaneously with the following word, possibly continuing as a drone throughout the phrase,"
in order to avoid an intolerable disruption of the rhythm itself.[71]
West's original insight (a simultaneous performance of both vocal
and instrumental melodies) may perhaps be further developed. As
we have already seen, West extends this simultaneousness to ⌐Ꞁ as
well as to the instrumental clusters ⌐Ɔ preceded by the *diastolé* at
ll. 5 and 6.[72] That is to say that in terms of actual performance no
particular rhythmic value is ascribed to the *diastolé*, whereas it is
just as likely that this sign, usually employed in musical scores as a
mark of punctuation dividing what precedes from what follows,[73]
conveys here a meaning of a minor performative pause, which is
not necessarily to be regarded as disrupting the rhythmic frame of
the whole melody. If we pay due attention to the separative function of the *diastolé*, the very absence of this sign before ⌐Ꞁ, that is,
exactly where we find, so to speak, the rhythmic 'joints' of the
dochmiac dimeters as transmitted by the medieval tradition and, vice
versa, its presence at ll. 5–6 before ⌐Ɔ, that is, not coinciding any
longer with the colon ends of the underlying metrical frame attested

---

[71] West *AGM*, 206–7 (see also 104). This suggestion had been already advanced
by the scholar in id. 1987, 204 and has been taken up in Pöhlmann-West *DAGM*,
15. See also Johnson 2000b, 17.

[72] In particular, as regards these last clusters, West *AGM*, 207 suggests that "it
looks as if the two auloi here diverged to blow the chord of a fourth," that is, we
would have here a precious instance of the much-debated possibility that the two
reeds of the aulos pair may in fact diverge, see also Johnson 2000b, 18, Hall 2002,
19 n. 48 and especially Barker 1995, 45–7. For an alternative explanation to that
offered by West (that is, the instrumental notes as marking the beginning of a drone
accompanying the whole musical phrase), see Barker 1995, 47, according to whom
those notes could just mark "only the initial and principal note of a more complex
piece of accompaniment to the phrase, whose details the aulete was expected to
extemporize."

[73] For the *diastolé* as *Trennungszeichen* see Anon. *Bell.* 11 = 4 ll. 7–10 Najock ἡ διαστολὴ
ἐπί τε τῶν ᾠδῶν καὶ τῆς κρουματογραφίας παραλαμβάνεται ἀναπαύουσα καὶ
χωρίζουσα τὰ προάγοντα ἀπὸ τῶν ἐπιφερομένων ἑξῆς. ἐστὶ δὲ αὐτῆς σχῆμα ⟨καὶ⟩
(con. Najock) σημεῖον τόδε 7 (for the shape of the sign cf. Najock 1972, 72 *ad loc.*).
Cf. also West *AGM*, 269. The other instances of that sign in the extant musical
scores are those of P.Vind. G 29825 a/bᵛ (= no. 10 Pöhlmann-West *DAGM*) ll. 3
(at the end of the line after the postpositive τις), 7 (apparently after the word-end,
that is ἐνδ]ρομίδος Ɔ α[) and P.Vind. G 29825 f (= no. 14 Pöhlmann-West *DAGM*)
l. 4 (likely at the word-end, followed in its turn by an instrumental note:]ουσα
Ɔ Γ[).

by the manuscripts, but disrupting from within the boundaries of the dochmiac measure,[74] seem indeed to support the hypothesis that 'ᒪ sounded simultaneously and without discontinuity with the vocal melody[75] and that there is a break in continuity between music and song at ll. 5–6 in correspondence with ⅂Ɔ.[76]

Now, the delivery of the song, the performative pause before δεινῶν and after πόνων might suggest a rhythmic interpretation of κατέκλυϲεν δεινῶν πόνων ὡϲ πόντου as a syncopated iambic trimeter (that is, cr ia mol) rather than 2δ,[77] but this does not necessarily mean that this rhythm must rely on a different 'transmitted' colometry in the technical meaning usually assigned to this term by modern scholars.[78] In other words, granted the substantial agreement and proven unity displayed by the medieval tradition as regards the colometry of the first stasimon of *Orestes*,[79] and granted that we are dealing with a musi-

---

[74] Cf. Bélis' statement that the *diastolé* followed by ⅂Ɔ occur "à la séparation des deux parties du dochmiaque" (ead. 2001, 41).

[75] Which is something different from assigning to 'ᒪ a specifically colometric function.

[76] That is, at ll. 5–6 (respectively between κατέκλυϲεν and δεινῶν first and between πόνων and ὡϲ the second time) the *diastolé* would mark the temporary arrest of the song and the accompanying starting of the instrumental melody. If this is the case, the presence of a separative sign would have been all the more necessary inasmuch as the pause-like effect does not fall at the beginning or at the end of the underlying dochmiac frame but cuts the dochmiac measure in the middle.

[77] That is, the 'correct' Euripidean colometry preserved by the medieval tradition. If we suppose a strophic performance of the whole first stasimon (see Pöhlmann-West *DAGM*, 16), the performative isolation encompassing at ll. 5–6 the syntagm δεινῶν| πόνων (= *Or.* 342–3), embedded as it is between instrumental clusters, would single out in the strophe the word φοιταλέου (= *Or.* 326–7), thus observing the word-boundaries. Yet, it is worth noticing that whereas in the antistrophe the iambic rhythm of δεινῶν πόνων involves a textual tessera that, at a certain stage of the textual transmission, has been perceived, although misleadingly, as syntactically isolable (that is, as a parenthetic exclamatory genitive: see the next section), this is not the case for the corresponding φοιταλέου in the strophe.

[78] What I mean by 'transmitted' colometry is, in this very precise case, the existence of a different branch of tradition (obviously lost to us) preserving an equally well-attested colometric interpretation of the passage going back at least to the Ptolemaic age. I am aware of using here the label 'colometry' somehow 'under erasure' for the sake of brevity. An iambic scansion of ll. 5–6 of the Vienna papyrus has been argued by Dale *LMGD²*, 207 and ead. *MATC* III, 128–9. Yet Dale's argumentation rests largely on a misleading interpretation of the scholium to *Or.* 340 (see below).

[79] See II.1.1 n. 19. The fact that at *Or.* 343 BVAbFMnRSSaξZcT divide (wrongly) at κατέκλυϲεν, that is, interpreting τινάξαϲ δαίμων κατέκλυϲεν as δ + cr, cannot be adduced as positive proof for the existence of an antagonistic colometry. Most probably we are dealing here with a colometric slip: see Diggle 1991, 135.

cal score, it seems to me more likely to regard the iambic interpretation of κατέκλυϲεν δεινῶν πόνων ὡϲ πόντου as an improvised device of a Hellenistic performer than as positive evidence of another competing colometry, strictly understood, for the Euripidean textual tradition of the *Orestes*. That is, if the interpretation outlined above for the musical signs at ll. 5–6 of P.Vind. is correct, I do not believe that the iambic rhythm of κατέκλυϲεν δεινῶν πόνων ὡϲ πόντου has to be considered as the ultimate proof testifying to a colometric tradition radically diverging from that attested by the medieval tradition for the first choral song of the *Orestes*. The evidence collected here seems to suggest, more cautiously, that we are dealing with minor isolated variations likely to be ascribed to the performance itself.

II.1.3 *P.Vind. G 2315 ll. 5–6 and the scholium to Eur.* Or. *340*

Another piece of evidence adduced by Marino to support Fleming-Kopff's general outline is the allegedly direct derivation of the scholium to Eur. *Or.* 340 from a musical score virtually exhibiting the same notational clusters as those to be found in P.Vind. G 2315 at ll. 5–6, that is, the instrumental notes singling out the syntagm δεινῶν πόνων (= *Or.* 342–3). This is the text of the scholium to Eur. *Or.* 340 as edited by Schwartz:

> ὁ μέγαϲ ὄλβοϲ: περιϲϲὸν τὸ ἓν ὡϲ: -MᶦTA
> οὐ μόνιμοϲ ὁ μέγαϲ ὄλβοϲ. κατέκλυϲε γὰρ αὐτὸν δαίμων τιϲ, ὡϲεὶ λαῖφοϲ
> ἀκάτου θοᾶϲ τινάξαϲ κατέκλυϲε τοῖϲ ὀλεθρίοιϲ καὶ λάβροιϲ κύμαϲι πόντου.
> τὸ δὲ δεινῶν πόνων ἐν μέϲωι ἀναπεφώνηται. ἢ οὕτωϲ· ὡϲ δὲ πόντου
> λάβροιϲ ὀλεθρίοιϲ ἐν κύμαϲι δαίμων τιϲ ἀκάτου θοᾶϲ λαῖφοϲ κατέκλυϲεν,
> οὕτωϲ καὶ τὸν μέγαν ὄλβον κατέκλυϲε τινάξαϲ ὑπὸ δεινῶν πόνων:
> -MᶦTAB

A great prosperity: one instance of ὡϲ[80] is superfluous. A great prosperity is not lasting. In fact some god submerged it in the same way that it shook and submerged the sail of a swift ship in the evil, violent waves of the sea. The words "δεινῶν πόνων" ἐν μέϲωι ἀναπεφώνηται. Or differently: as a god overwhelmed the sail of a swift ship in the evil, violent waves of the sea, in the very same way it overwhelmed also great prosperity by shaking it by means of awful pains.

---

[80] The brachylogy of the scholiastic remark does not allow us to establish whether the ὡϲ mentioned is that at 341 (perhaps the most likely hypothesis) or at 343.

Marino, commenting on the sentence τὸ δὲ δεινῶν πόνων ἐν μέϲωι ἀναπεφώνηται, explicitly claims that "nothing, from a syntactic point of view, can have satisfactorily engendered such an observation. It is clear that the scholium can be traced back to a tradition that knew the disposition of the instrumental notations embedding the words δεινῶν πόνων as between brackets."[81] As we shall soon see, Marino's statement largely rests on the interpretation of the scholium previously advanced by Dale[82] and then taken up by subsequent scholars without further inspection.[83]

Before focusing on Marino's own conclusions, we must re-examine Dale's original proposal. Actually Dale, on the basis of this scholium, of the evidence offered by [Arist.] *Probl.* 918a 10–12 (= XIX, 6)[84] and of the remark that in the Vienna papyrus "there are no notes above the words δεινῶν πόνων," suggests regarding the syntagm δεινῶν πόνων as "unsung words." According to Dale we would have here a rare instance of "mixed delivery in choral lyric":[85] at

---

[81] Marino 1999, 152–3 "ora, nulla dal punto di vista sintattico può aver generato con sufficiente motivazione un'osservazione del genere. È chiaro che lo scolio può essere fatto risalire ad una tradizione che conosceva la disposizione della notazione strumentale che chiude le due parole δεινῶν πόνων come fra parentesi." Marino's argument has been followed also by Redondo Reyes 2001, 69. In the same direction see already Crusius' remark that "man möchte fast vermuten, dass der Gewährsmann, nach dem diese Worte ἐν μέϲωι ἀναπεφώνηται [. . .], noch ein Exemplar mit solchen Zeichen benutz habe" (id. 1894, 185).

[82] Dale *LMGD*[2], 207–8; although Marino does not eventually accept the iambic scansion suggested by Dale for *Or.* 342–3, she entirely sticks to Dale's interpretation of τὸ δὲ δεινῶν πόνων ἐν μέϲωι ἀναπεφώνηται as a musical stage direction.

[83] Pöhlmann 1970, 80 with n. 11 correctly claims that "durch diese Instrumentaleinwürfe werden die Worte δεινῶν πόνων, die auch ein Scholion als Parenthese bezeichnet, abgegrenzt," but he goes on to include our scholium in the "Scholien zur Vertonung des Orestes" together with the Σ to *Or.* 176 and 1384, only these last ones being really concerned with musical issues, that is, respectively, Electra's apostrophe to the night, a song to be performed ἐπὶ ταῖϲ λεγομέναιϲ νήταιϲ and thus very high-pitched, and the vocal delivery of the Phrygian slave's melody (see Falkner 2002, 345–6 on the issue). Still entirely relying on Dale's 'musical' interpretation of the Σ to *Or.* 340 (although accepting a dochmiac scansion of 342–3) are Marzi 1973, 327, Basta Donzelli 1974, 99 with n. 31 and Van Akkeren 1983, 264 with n. 5.

[84] [Arist.] *Probl.* 918a 10–12 (= XIX, 6) διὰ τί ἡ παρακαταλογὴ ἐν ταῖϲ ὠιδαῖϲ τραγικόν; ἢ διὰ τὴν ἀνωμαλίαν; παθητικὸν γὰρ τὸ ἀνωμαλὲς καὶ ἐν μεγέθει τύχηϲ ἢ λύπηϲ. τὸ δὲ ὁμαλὲς ἔλαττον γοῶδεϲ. For a more detailed discussion of the pseudo-Aristotelian passage see below.

[85] Partially in this direction see also Sedgwick 1950, 222–3, who, relying on the observation that "the papyrus apparently had no musical notation over δεινῶν πόνων" and on the evidence of [Arist.] *Probl.* 918a 10–12 (= XIX, 6) provided by

ll. 342–3 of the first stasimon of *Orestes* there would be an imperceptible shifting, in terms of vocal delivery, from song to recitative (ἀναπεφώνηται) and then again back to song.

The passages quoted by Dale *LMGD²*, 208 as parallels for the insertion of "recitative in songs" within an otherwise metrically homogeneous choral section are unconvincing. In Eur. *Hipp.* 817–51 the alternation of dochmiacs and iambics is a basic, recurrent pattern of Theseus' whole lament. In fact Theseus' grief at the sight of Phaidra's corpse consists of a single system of strophe and antistrophe (separated by the iambic trimeters spoken— and not sung—by the Chorus at 834–5: see Halleran 1995, 219), where each stanza presents a regular series of 2 δ | 2 δ | 2 ia trim| 2 δ | 2 δ | 2 ia trim| 2 δ | 2 δ | 2 ia trim| 7 δ, in order to bring out the inner contrast between Theseus' violent emotion (δ) and control (ia). It should then be added that the iambic trimeters show a tendency to be constructed as syntactically and rhythmically self-contained sections (Barrett 1964, 319 already observed that the "pauses in sense" are arranged so to be "heavy after the iambics, light before them"): according to Stinton's criteria of identifying syntactic units (Stinton 1977), we have 'light' syntactic pause after both ὦ τύχα at 817 and εἰσορῶ at 822.

Equally unsuited as a parallel for the supposed instance in *Orestes* is the second *kommos* of Soph. *OT* 1313–68. In this case the contrast between lyric metres (basically dochmiacs) and iambics mirrors the emotive difference between Oedipus and the Chorus: to Oedipus' song the Thebans reply in iambic trimeters at 1319–20~1327–8, 1347–8~1367–8 and dimeters at 1336~56.[86] Likewise, the parallel drawn by Dale with Eur. *HF* 875–921 is misleading: the long astrophic section in enoplian dochmiacs is structurally intermingled with iambic metres, spoken as well as sung (see Bond 1981, 295–6 and 305 *ad* ll. 910–21), alternately assigned to the Chorus, Amphitryon and the messenger.

Similar remarks can be made also for Eur. *Ion* 1439–1509 (lyric astrophic duet between Ion and Kreusa immediately following their mutual recognition) and *Hel.* 625–99 (another well-known *Anagnorisisamoibaion*, that between Helen and Menelaus). In both cases the alternation of lyric metres (principally dochmiacs) and iambics reproduces the distribution of the lines between female and male character (with a greater degree of flexibility in the case of *Hel.*, where, at least as regards the first section of the duet, that

---

Dale, suggests that the words δεινῶν πόνων were "merely intoned." More recently Dale's interpretation has apparently been taken up also by Richter 2000, 71.

[86] See Scott 1996, 146: "Significantly Oedipus sings while the chorus speaks [. . .]. The intermingling of choral iambic trimeters with Oedipus' animated music sharply separates the mood and the perceptions of the king from those of the chorus [. . .] the opposition between song and speech also marks a breakdown in communication as the Thebans fail to understand Oedipus."

is, ll. 625–59, Menelaus too yields to lyric metres, and only the second
part, that is, ll. 660–97, is structured as a proper "punctuated monody."
See Willink's observations [id. 1989, 46–7] on Kannicht 1969, II, 175–6).
Furthermore, all the instances quoted by Dale consist of a mixed delivery
that is dramatically motivated. That is, it takes place either within the monody of an actor (as in *Hipp.* 817–51) in order to bring out his/her emotional distress, or within a duet between actor and Chorus or actor and
actor in order to emphasize the different emotional stances of the speak-
ers. The alleged instance of mixed delivery posited by Dale for *Or.* 342–3[87]
does not fall within these categories: the shifting from song to recitative
and back would take place (1) within a choral song (the first stasimon:
therefore there is no change of speaker) and (2) in a metrically homogeneous section.

    In contrast, cases of alternation of song and recitative within the same
line can actually be found in comedy, cf. e.g. the holodactylic series (leaving aside the iambic trimeters of 1284–5) in Ar. *Pax* 1270–87.[88] Twice
(1270b and 1286b) the hexameter that the first παῖς begins singing is inter-
rupted by Trygaeus, who shifts to a bare delivery (see the last metron
παῦσαι at 1270b and the final segment ἄςμενοι, οἶμαι immediately after the
bucolic diaeresis at 1286b). Yet, once again the Aristophanic passage is not
comparable with *Or.* 342–3 as interpreted by Dale. The precise context
(Trygaeus inviting the boy to perform in advance the songs he will later
sing at the wedding dinner) and the change of speaker within the same
line allow us to measure the striking difference between the Aristophanic
passage and the case of *Or.* 342–3.

Let us turn to the direct evidence provided by the Vienna papyrus.
First of all, the claim that at ll. 5–6 upon δεινῶν πόνων there are
no notes is an inference drawn *e silentio* which cannot be positively
verified. In fact the words δεινῶν πόνων fall almost entirely within
the gap (that is, δ[εινῶν] πόνω]ν).[89] Secondly, above the δ[at the

---

[87] See Dale *LMGD*², 208: "if this interpretation of the δεινῶν πόνων in the *Orestes*
papyrus is correct, Euripides sometimes sought the emotional irregularity of mixed
delivery in choral lyric too." This last remark clearly relies on the unproven assumption that the music transmitted by the Vienna papyrus is the original Euripidean
one.

[88] For the manner of delivery of this Aristophanic passage (alternation of song/recita-
tive) see Pretagostini 1995a, 168–70 supplemented by Martinelli 1999, 383–4 (especially convincing is Martinelli's suggestion that we regard as sung also ll. 1280–1,
except the words καὶ τὰ τοιαυτί at 1280b: Trygaeus would himself here be showing the boy what kind of song to perform. The objections of Napolitano 1999, 121
seem to me far-fetched).

[89] See J.F. Mountford's observation that "it is impossible to know whether there
was musical notation or not" in the lost part of the fragment (id. *apud* Sedgwick
1950, 222 n. 2).

end of l. 5 traces of ink can be clearly seen, traces which, although uncertain, may reasonably be interpreted as the remains of a musical note above the underlying delta.[90]

As regards the literal meaning of τὸ δὲ δεινῶν πόνων ἐν μέσωι ἀναπεφώνηται, a more detailed attention paid to the context of the expression can provide some useful insight leading to an alternative explanation to that provided by Dale. Now, the scholium, if considered in its full length, presents a well-structured argumentative frame that follows an inner consistency. We are in fact provided with two alternative explanations of *Or.* 340–4[91] (which are to be regarded as mutually exclusive: note the disjunctive ἤ), whose only divergence consists of the different syntactic function ascribed to δεινῶν πόνων within the structure of the whole sentence.

Let us start from the second explanation, whose understanding is less problematic. Here the words δεινῶν πόνων are understood as an instrumental/causal genitive strictly related to the upsetting action conveyed by κατέκλυcε (ἀνα)τινάξαc. According to this interpretation, in the poetic brachylogy of the Euripidean text we should regard δεινῶν πόνων as equivalent to the prosaic prepositional syntagm ὑπὸ δεινῶν πόνων.[92] But what is the first explanation offered by the anonymous scholiast? The keystone depends on the meaning we assign to the verb ἀναφωνέω in this context and, consequently, on how we interpret the expression ἐν μέcωι ἀναπεφώνηται. Among the various possible meanings of the verb ἀναφωνέω, Dale singles out for ἀναπεφώνηται the specific sense of 'declaiming, reciting aloud',[93] claiming that we are dealing here with an instance of recitative delivery

---

[90] Pöhlmann 1970, 78 put a question mark above δ, while Crusius read P. Also according to West *AGM*, 207, above the δ[can be read what is likely to be "(a) concurrent vocal note," see now Pöhlmann-West *DAGM*, 12.

[91] Both of them are most likely mistaken: see Di Benedetto 1965, 74 and Willink 1986, 143.

[92] For similar cases of ὑπό to be understood in scholiastic exegesis see e.g. Matthaios 1999, 601 with n. 4 (on Aristarchus' fr. 201). As regards specifically our case, see also the Σ[MTB] to *Or.* 343 κατέκλυcεν δεινῶν: κλύζεcθαι παρεcκεύαcεν. ἄcτατον ὄντα ὑπὸ δεινῶν πόνων, τουτέcτιν ἔργων [. . .] ὡc γὰρ κλύζεται ναῦc ἐν θαλάccηι, οὕτω καὶ ἡ τῶν ἀνθρώπων τύχη ὑπὸ ἀcτάτων ἔργων. τὸ γὰρ τῆc τύχηc ῥεῦμα μεταπίπτει ταχύ. For the use of ὑπό + gen. of abstract nouns expressing cause or agency see Mastronarde 2002, 169 ad Eur. *Med.* 34.

[93] See LSJ's entry s.v. ἀναφωνέω 1, also referred to by Sedgwick 1950, 223 n. 3. It is worth noting that Sedgwick's reference to Rutherford 1905, 58 n. 7 quoting the scholium to Eur. *Med.* 228 τοῦτο ἐν ἤθει ἀναπεφώνηται as evidence supporting

(παρακαταλογή) embedded in an otherwise entirely lyric context. Yet a systematic examination of the instances of ἀναφωνέω/ἀναφώνηϲιϲ in the epic, tragic and Pindaric scholia strongly points in another direction.[94] A significant number of cases suggests in fact that the pertinent meaning here is the strictly grammatical and rhetorical one of 'exclamatory utterance'.[95] In particular, as clearly emerges from the evidence collected below, beside a broader, generic meaning of 'uttering, speaking aloud',[96] the scholiastic instances of these words convey pre-eminently the sense of a parenthetic utterance syntactically separate from the main clause and always delivered in an emotionally charged tone of exclamation (whether it is a monosyllabic interjection, an apostrophe, a self-address or an even wider segment of text). I have found the following instances:

Σ to Eur. *Med.* 228 (ia) τοῦτο ἐν ἤθει ἀναπεφώνηται (Medea's words once she has become fully aware of Jason's κακία), 764 (ia) ὦ Ζεῦ· τοῦτο μόνον ἡ Μήδεια αὐτὴ καθ' ἑαυτὴν ἀναφωνεῖ κτλ., 1273 (lyr.) ἀκούειϲ βοάν· τοῦτο πρὸϲ ἀλλήλαϲ αἱ ἀπὸ τοῦ χοροῦ φαϲι κατ' ἐρώτηϲιν· τὸ δὲ ὦ κακοτυχὲϲ γύναι ἰδίωϲ πρὸϲ τὴν Μήδειαν ἀναπεφώνηται κτλ. (the Chorus replying to the chil-

---

the meaning of 'declaiming, intoning' for ἀναφωνέω is incorrect. In fact Rutherford correctly understands ἀναπεφώνηται of the scholium as an "interjectional exclamation." What indicates the mood is ἐν ἤθει, while ἀναφωνέω denotes the mere exclamation: see Rutherford 1905, 135.

[94] Especially telling is the fact that such occurrences of ἀναφωνέω/ἀναφώνηϲιϲ spread all over the tragic scholia refer indistinctly to both iambic and lyric sections, which significantly decreases the possibility of a univocally technical sense of 'recitative' for such terms. It may be of interest to notice that the only scholiastic instance of ἀναφωνέω which carries the meaning of 'declaiming aloud' referring to tragic actors is that of the Σ to Pind. *Nem.* 8. 32c Drachm. (without distinction, of course, between recitative and song): ἄλλωϲ· οἱ μέγα φωνεῖν θέλοντεϲ οἷον τραγωιδοί, προαναπνέουϲιν ἐπιπολύ, ἵν' ὅταν ἀναφωνήϲωϲιν, ἐξαρκέϲηι ἐπιπλέον ἡ φωνή κτλ.

[95] LSJ's entry s.v. ἀναφωνέω is unfortunately of no help: the scholiastic literature is entirely neglected and the meaning of 'exclamation' is erroneously restricted to the mere ἀναφώνημα. More correctly Bécares Botas 1985, 36 s.v. ἀναφώνηϲιϲ/-έω records such a meaning but does not cite the passages I shall quote below.

[96] See e.g. Σ^Hsl to Soph. *Aj.* 887 (lyr.) <ἀπύοι:> ἀ<να>φωνῆϲαι καὶ ἀπαγγεῖλαι (the hendiadys points to regarding ἀ<να>φωνῆϲαι as a synonymic variant of ἀπαγγεῖλαι), Σ to *OC* 1211 (lyr.) κατάδηλός ἐϲτιν ὁ χορὸϲ ἐν ταὐτῶι ἀναφωνῶν καὶ ἀλληγορῶν περὶ τῆϲ τῶν ἀνθρώπων ἀπληϲτίαϲ κτλ., Σ to Pind. *Pyth.* 2. 115 Drachm. νεότατι μὲν ἀρήγει· τῆι νεότητι μὲν βοηθεῖ ἡ περὶ τὸ πολεμεῖν θραϲύτηϲ· τοῦτο δὲ ἐν τῶι καθόλου γνωμικῶϲ ἀναπεφώνηκεν. In Σ to Pind. *Pyth.* 2. 36b Drachm. the hendiadys ἀναφωνεῖ καὶ ἀνυμνεῖ strongly suggests for ἀναφωνεῖ the meaning of 'invoking'. Finally in Σ to Soph. *Tr.* 643 (lyr.) ἀναφωνέω is used for denoting the sound produced by two musical instruments, that is, the aulos and the lyre (ἀφ' οὗ δηλοῦται <ὅτι> ὁμοῦ αὐλὸϲ καὶ λύρα ἀναφωνήϲουϲιν).

dren's cries off stage), 1371 (ia) οἴδ᾽ εἰςίν, ὤμοι· μεταξὺ ἀναπεφώνηκεν εἰς
ὑπόμνηςιν τῶν τέκνων ἐλθών (Jason claiming the existence of haunting
demons); *Hipp.* 812 (lyr.) τὸ δὲ αἰαῖ τόλμας διὰ μέςου ἀναπεφώνηται καὶ
οὕτως τὸ ἐξῆς ἵςταται; *Andr.* 1036 (lyr.) ὦ δαῖμον, ὦ Φοῖβε· ὦ δαῖμον ὁ χορὸς
θαυμάζων ἀνεφώνηςεν εἰ Ἀπόλλων τοῦτο προςέταξεν, 1273 (ia) ὦ πότνια ὦ
γενναῖα· τὸ ἐξῆς· ὦ πότνια Νηρέως γένεθλον χαῖρε· ὥςτε τὸ ὦ γενναῖα
ςυγκοιμήματα κατὰ ἀναφώνηςιν ἰδίαν ἐξενήνεκται κτλ.; *Hec.* 626 (ia) †ἄλλως
φροντίδων· τοῦτο κατ᾽ ἰδίαν ἀναπεφώνηται· μάτην εἰςὶ τὰ βουλεύματα καὶ τὰ
τῆς γλώττης καυχήματα (κατ᾽ ἰδίαν emphasizing here the syntactic continuity with what follows rather than with what precedes: see Diggle 1981, 102
and Gregory 1999, 105); *Phoen.* 550 (ia) ὑπέρφευ· ὑπεράγαν. διὰ μέςου μετὰ
ςχετλιαςμοῦ τὸ ὑπέρφευ ἀναπεφώνηται (the scholiast's interpretation is most
likely wrong: ὑπέρφευ is here not a parenthetical interjection but an adverb
used predicatively and governed by τιμᾶις), 1520 (lyr.) μονάδ᾽ αἰῶνα· τοῦτο
ἰδίαι ἀναπεφώνηται; *Or.* 327 (lyr.) τοῦτο (that is, τὸ φεῦ μόχθων) κατ᾽ ἰδίαν
ἀναπεφώνηται. ἢ τὸ φεῦ ςυντέτακται ἵν᾽ ἦι· φεῦ [ἰὼ Ζεῦ] οἵων μόχθων ὁ τάλας
ὀρεχθεὶς ἔρρειc (the second alternative clearly shows that the problem is a
syntactic one: exclamatory genitive or genitive governed by ὀρεχθείς), 332
(lyr.) ἰὼ Ζεῦ· πρὸς τὸ ἄνω τοῦτο ςχετλιαςτικῶς μετὰ ἤθους ἀναπεφώνηται (H
bears the intralinear scholium τ⟨οῦ⟩το κατὰ δ⟨ία⟩ ἀναπεφώνηται or at least
this is the text as edited by Daitz 1979, 47 l. 11. Yet I wonder whether
in the light of the instances previously quoted we should emend here κατὰ
⟨ἰ⟩δ⟨ίαν⟩. In this case we would achieve a more consistent meaning as well
as a plausible paleographic *ratio*: haplography).

As regards the Aeschylean scholia see Σ to *Se.* 106d (lyr.) ἠθικὸν τὸ δὶς
(that is, the anadiplosis ἔπιδ᾽ ἔπιδε) ἀναφωνῆςαι κτλ.; *Su.* 166–7 (lyr.) [. . .]
τὰ δ᾽ ἄλλα διὰ μέςου ἀναπεφώνηται (referring to the apostrophe to Zeus at
162–3); *Choe.* 44 (lyr.) ⟨ἰὼ γαῖα μαῖα⟩] ὦ γῆ μῆτηρ· τοῦτο δὲ διὰ μέςου
ἀναπεφώνηται, 378 (an.) ⟨ςτυγερῶν τούτων⟩] τοῦτο ἰδίαι ἀναπεφώνηται τῶν
ἄγαν ςτυγερῶν τούτων· τοῦτο δὲ μᾶλλον Ἀγαμέμνονος τοῖς παιςὶν αὐτοῦ
ςυμβέβηκεν, πρὸς ὃ ἐπάγει Ἠλέκτρα ὅτι ὡς βέλος μου ὁ λόγος ἥψατο (ll.
378–9 are a well-known *crux*: the scholiast however interpreted the genitive
as syntactically independent, cf. ἰδίαι); *Eum.* 785c ἰώ] τοῦτο διὰ μέςου
ὀλοφυρόμεναι ἀναφωνοῦςιν (that is, the Chorus), 839 [. . .] τὸ δὲ φεῦ διὰ
μέςου ἀναφωνεῖ (I disagree here with West 1998², 289–90, and I regard as
more likely a purely dochmiac scansion of 837–47, with φεῦ *extra metrum*).

As regards the Sophoclean scholia see Σ to *Aj.* 173a (lyr.) ὦ μεγάλα φάτις·
[. . .] ἔςτι δὲ διὰ μέςου ἡ ἀναφώνηςις, 340b (ia) [. . .] λεληθότως δὲ ἀνεφώνηςε
καὶ τὸ τοῦ παιδὸς ὄνομα (Tecmessa accidentally exclaiming Eurysaces' name);
Ant. 31 (ia) τὸ δὲ λέγω γὰρ κἀμὲ διὰ μέςου μετὰ πάθους ἀνεφώνηκεν κτλ.;
OC 1683 (lyr.) τὸ τάλαινα διὰ μέςου ἀναπεφώνηται.

For the epos[97] the most significant instances are Σ to Θ 236 Ζεῦ πάτερ·
διὰ τῆς ἀναφωνήςεως καὶ ὀνειδίζει καὶ ψυχαγωγεῖ, τὴν αἰτίαν εἰς θεοὺς ἀνάγων,

---

[97] I owe D.J. Mastronarde the observation that the occurrences of ἀναφώνηςις/

M 113 νήπιος, οὐδ᾿ ἄρ᾿ ἔμελλε: cημαντικωτάτωι ὀνόματι χρῆται τῶι νήπιος
ἐν ταῖc ἀναφωνήcεcιν, N 603 coί, Μενέλαε: ἀναφώνηcιc τοῦ ποιητοῦ κτλ., O
365b ἤïε: [. . .] ἔcτι δὲ περιπαθὴc ἡ ἀναφώνηcιc κτλ., X 297 <ὦ πόποι:>
ἐλεεινοτάτη ἡ ἀναφώνηcιc καὶ εἰc οἶκτον κινοῦcα, Ω 201a ὤ μοι: ἡ ἀναφώνηcιc
ἐξιcταμένηc ἐπὶ τῶν τηλικούτων τολμῶν, 255–60 ὤ μοι ἐγὼ ⟨πανάποτμοc,
ἐπεί—πάντα λέλειπται⟩: ἠθικὴ ἡ μεταξὺ ἀναφώνηcιc.

An apparently problematic case, which deserves more detailed consideration, is that of the scholium to *Or.* 183 (lyr.) καὶ τοῦτο κατὰ
ἀναφώνηcιν λέγει ἡ Ἠλέκτρα. At first glance, also on the basis of
what the scholium to *Or.* 176 claims,[98] it might seem that in this
case too the scholiast meant to emphasize the manner of vocal delivery performed by the actor (that is, a hypothetical shift from song
to recitative), but this is only an apparent impression. First, as regards
καὶ τοῦτο, at least two interpretations are possible: (1) either τοῦτο
refers to the exclamatory interjection cῖγα cῖγα at 183–4: to stress
the parenthetic exclamatory value of such an expression could seem
necessary to the scholiast in the light of the following hyperbaton
οὐχὶ [. . .] παρέξειc;[99] (2) or τοῦτο refers to Electra's whole apostrophe to the Chorus (ll. 182–6),[100] an apostrophe uttered in an exclamatory tone.[101] Secondly, it is worth observing that l. 182, that is, a
prosodiac and thus a lyric metre, is in responsion with l. 203 of the
antistrophe (βίου τὸ πλέοc μέροc ἐν), which ends with the prepositive ἐν and is therefore linked together with the following line by

---

ἀναφωνέω in the Homeric scholia mostly refer to second-person addresses or apos-
trophes to a character, suggesting an even more restricted use of such terms.

[98] Namely [. . .] τοῦτο τὸ μέλοc ἐπὶ ταῖc λεγομέναιc νήταιc ἄιδεται καί ἐcτιν
ὀξύτατον. ἀπίθανον οὖν τὴν Ἠλέκτραν ὀξείαι φωνῆι κεχρῆcθαι, καὶ ταῦτα
ἐπιπλήccουcαν τῶι χορῶι. ἀλλὰ κέχρηται μὲν τῶι ὀξεῖ ἀναγκαίωc, οἰκεῖον γὰρ τῶν
θρηνούντων, λεπτότατα δὲ ὡc ἔνι μάλιcτα.

[99] See Willink 1986, 115.

[100] For a defence of the attribution of ll. 174–81 to the Chorus see Medda 1989,
101.

[101] It is worth noticing that the καὶ at the beginning of the Σ to *Or.* 183 seems
to assume the presence of another antecedent exclamatory utterance, but which
one? The most reasonable solution satisfying the requested premises (exclamation
+ Electra as the utterer of such an exclamation) seems to be that of seeing here a
reference to the apostrophe to the πότνια νύξ delivered at 174 ff. (the scholia assign
these lines to Electra). I would rule out the possibility that the antecedent mentioned by the scholiast (καὶ τοῦτο) is the alleged ἆ at 182 (Willink's emendation of
the transmitted text): the contrived nature of such an emendation, accepted by
Willink and Diggle, is emphasized by Medda 1989, 101.

means of verbal synapheia. A shifting from song to recitative coinciding with verbal synapheia seems to me most unlikely.

Finally, in the scholiastic literature we can find precise parallels for the syntagm κατὰ ἀναφώνηϲιν meaning 'by way of exclamation': see the Σ to β 272 τὸ "οἶοϲ ἐκεῖνοϲ" κατὰ ἀναφώνηϲιν εἴρηται εἰϲ ἔπαινον τοῦ Ὀδυϲϲέωϲ τοῦ πατρὸϲ Τηλεμάχου[102] and to α 242 ἀπὸ ἄλληϲ ἀρχῆϲ τὸ "οἴχετ᾽ ἄιϲτοϲ" κατὰ ἀναφώνηϲιν.[103] Therefore it seems reasonable to include the scholium to *Or.* 183 in those instances that testify to the technical meaning of 'exclamatory utterance' for ἀναφώνηϲιϲ. Dale's peculiar interpretation of the Σ to *Or.* 340 turns out to be unparalleled and has to be rejected.

As regards then the evidence of [Arist.] *Probl.* 918a 10–12 (= XIX, 6) διὰ τί ἡ παρακαταλογὴ ἐν ταῖϲ ὠιδαῖϲ τραγικόν; ἢ διὰ τὴν ἀνωμαλίαν; παθητικὸν γὰρ τὸ ἀνώμαλὲϲ καὶ ἐν μεγέθει τύχηϲ ἢ λύπηϲ. τὸ δὲ ὁμαλὲϲ ἔλαττον γοῶδεϲ ("Why is parakalogé in songs tragic? Is it because of contrast? For contrast is emotionally affecting in extremities of calamity or grief, while uniformity has a less mournful effect": the translation is that of Barker *GMW*, I, 191 no. 165), I do not think that it represents a problem. Pseudo-Aristotle is more likely to refer here to instances like the *kommos* of the fifth stasimon of *Medea* (ll. 1273–92): that is, passages where strophes sung by the Chorus are intermingled with iambic trimeters or anapaests spoken by actors, see Martinelli 1997², 32, Hall 1999, 107 (Dale herself mentioned this possibility in ead. *LMGD²*, 208). Furthermore, the presence in the pseudo-Aristotelian passage of such a generic term as ὠιδαί does not allow us to ascertain with absolute certainty whether the author is referring here to astrophic or strophic songs. In *Probl.* 918b 13 ff. the term ὠιδή refers to the astrophic νόμοϲ, while the strophic songs are called (ὠιδαὶ) χορικαί. In any case, it seems quite clear that the ἀνωμαλία mentioned by [Arist.] is to be understood as referring to the contrast engendered by the alternation of παρακαταλογή and μέλοϲ in lyric songs (ἐν ταῖϲ ὠιδαῖϲ) and not to

---

[102] As F. Pontani has brought to my attention, the codd. MᵃSYs significantly gloss οἶοϲ as θαυμαϲτικόν. The explicit mention of the exclamatory value to be assigned to οἶοϲ ἐκεῖνοϲ accomplishes in this case also a function of syntactic divider similar to that of the ϲτιγμή: see in fact the exegetic difficulty noted by the Σ to β 271 as regards the syntactic structure of the Homeric sentence (that is, ὁ ϲτίχοϲ καὶ τοῖϲ ἑπομένοιϲ καὶ τοῖϲ ἡγουμένοιϲ δύναται ϲυνάπτεϲθαι). It is not by accident that already Carnuth 1875, 30 traced this scholium back to Nicanor.

[103] Also for this scholium Carnuth 1875, 24 suggests a Nicanorean authorship. These two instances, together with the Σ to Eur. *Andr.* 1273 (see above) are the only occurrences of the syntagm κατὰ ἀναφώνηϲιν in the tragic, epic and Pindaric scholia.

the "Widerstreit von sprachlicher Deklamation und musikalischer Begleitung" within the παρακαταλογή alone, as argued by Flashar 1962, 602. Flashar's misunderstanding is clearly shown by his own translation of the passage, that is, "Warum wirkt das Rezitieren mit musikalischer Begleitung tragisch? etc." (Flashar 1962, 158). The textual segment ἐν ταῖϲ ᾠδαῖϲ is in fact omitted: that "das Rezitieren mit musikalischer Begleitung" translates only the term παρακαταλογή and is not a hendiadys for the whole syntagm ἡ παρακαταλογὴ ἐν ταῖϲ ᾠδαῖϲ seems to be confirmed by Flashar, 1962, 602 who specifies that under the label παρακαταλογή "verstand man das Rezitieren von Versen unter musikalischer Begleitung." For a correct interpretation of [Arist.] *Probl.* 918a 10–12 (= XIX, 6) see Barker *GMW*, I, 191 n. 5.

Let us return now to the starting point, that is, the scholium to *Or.* 340: what does τὸ δὲ δεινῶν πόνων ἐν μέϲωι ἀναπεφώνηται precisely mean? On the basis both of the evidence previously collected and of the specific context to which this sentence belongs (that is, a discussion of the possible syntactic interpretations of the words δεινῶν πόνων), it seems to me more likely that what the scholiast is saying here is that δεινῶν πόνων is to be understood as a parenthetic (ἐν μέϲωι) exclamation (ἀναπεφώνηται),[104] or, to put it better, as a parenthetic exclamatory genitive.[105] Therefore, notwithstanding Marino's skepticism on the issue, this syntactic observation on the part of the anonymous scholiast can only have been engendered by reflecting on the complexity of the phrasal structure displayed by Eur. *Or.* 340–4. Thus, what we have is an attempt to clarify the syntactic structure of the Euripidean sentence, an effort perfectly comparable, in terms of inner consistency and logical thread, with that attested by the Σ to *Or.* 327.[106]

---

[104] Cf. especially the Σ to Eur. *Phoen.* 550, *Hipp.* 812, to Aesch. *Eum.* 839, to Soph. *OC* 1683; as to διὰ μέϲου ~ ἐν μέϲωι as a technical term for designating rhetorically the tropos of the parenthetic clause see e.g. Hdn. περὶ ϲχημάτων III, 95, ll. 14–5 Spengel.

[105] See already Paley 1860, 252, who, without specifying to which scholium he was referring, observed that "the Scholiasts explained δεινῶν πόνων by either ὑπὸ or φεῦ understood, one excepted, who rightly says, ὀλεθρίοιϲ ἐν κύμαϲι πρὸϲ τὸ δεινῶν πόνων ϲύναπτε." See also Pöhlmann-West *DAGM*, 15, who correctly interpret the scholium to *Or.* 340 as alleging "a parenthetical exclamation." That exclamations, even mono- or bisyllabic interjections, could be set to music and therefore sung is confirmed by P.Ashm. inv. 89B/31, 33 fr. 1 ll. 1–2 (third/second century BC) that provides typically tragic exclamations like ἰώ μοι, ἒ ἔ, and ἰὼ πόποι accompanied by the relevant vocal notation: cf. Pöhlmann-West *DAGM*, 25.

[106] Σ to *Or.* 327 (lyr.) τοῦτο (that is, τὸ φεῦ μόχθων) κατ᾽ ἰδίαν ἀναπεφώνηται. ἢ τὸ φεῦ ϲυντέτακται ἵν᾽ ἦι· φεῦ [ἰὼ Ζεῦ] οἵων μόχθων ὁ τάλαϲ ὀρεχθεὶϲ ἔρρειϲ.

Summing up, Marino's hypothesis of a direct derivation of the scholium to *Or.* 340 from a musical score similar to that of P.Vind. turns out to be unnecessary, if not strongly misleading. On the contrary, the fact that the words δεινῶν πόνων in P.Vind. (a piece of evidence going back to the third century BC) are isolated from what precedes and follows by instrumental notes, can instead be interpreted as supporting the antiquity of the (erroneous) first explanation offered by the anonymous scholiast (that is, δεινῶν πόνων as a parenthetic exclamation). That is, the text of P.Vind. rests on a similar misinterpretation of the Euripidean words δεινῶν πόνων.

As we have already seen, the *Orestes* seems to have achieved considerable success on the Hellenistic stage as well as to have attracted, from an early date onwards, the attention of scholars. According to the list of the Euripidean papyri recorded by Bouquiaux Simon-Mertens 1992, to be now supplemented by the new data provided by D. Obbink in *The Oxyrhynchus Papyri*, LXVII, London 2001, 2–15, the figure for the extant papyri of *Orestes* (26) is second only to that for the *Phoenissae*. In particular, 5 out of these 26 papyri go back to the Ptolemaic age (third/second century BC: beside P.Vind. see P.Stras.W.G. 307ᵛ, P.Laur. inv. III/908, P.Ross.Georg. I 9, P.Duke inv. MF 74. 18) whereas 4 papyri can be dated to second/first century BC (P.Oxy. 1178, P.Köln VI 252, P.Columb. inv. 517A, P.Oxy. 3716). Likewise, also the erudite material of Hellenistic origin preserved by the scholia to *Or.* is particularly noteworthy. The scholia to *Or.* 1038 and 1287 testify to precise textual discussions going directly back to the mastery of Aristophanes of Byzantium (respectively the defence of the variant δόμον, as reported by Callistratos, against the transmitted γόνον at 1038 and of the reading ἐκκεκώφωνται against ἐκκεκώφηται, attested by most of the medieval tradition [= ΩXZTᵗ³] at 1287). More generally, the scholia to *Or.* allow us, however episodically, to detect traces of the philological work on tragic texts accomplished by Aristophanes' contemporaries. The scanty remnants of this exegetic activity we can still recover from the scholia seem indeed to suggest the existence of specific ὑπομνήματα on the play rather than derivation from more broad-ranging treatises.[107] Suffice it here to report some instances. Callistratos, Aristophanes' pupil and contemporary,[108] is

---

[107] The likely existence of ὑπομνήματα on the *Or.* in the third/second century BC agrees with what we know about the history of this genre: for commentaries on papyri dating back to the third century BC see Del Fabbro 1979, 131. Furthermore, the second century BC was the heyday of Aristarchus' exegetical activity: see Pfeiffer 1968, 212 ff.

[108] See Wilamowitz 1889, 151 n. 56, A. Gudeman, *RE* X (1919) s.v. Kallistratos 38, coll. 1738–48 (especially col. 1743 as regards the text of Euripides' *Orestes*) and Pfeiffer 1968, 190–1.

mentioned in the scholia to *Or.* 314, 434 and 1038 with regard to textual
matters: that is, respectively, the defence of νοϲῆ(ι), the right reading preserved only by a minority of the medieval tradition (see Diggle 1991, 160)
vs. νοϲῆ(ι)ϲ at 314; the explanation of the expression διὰ τριῶν δ' ἀπόλλυμαι
at 434 (with explicit reference to his commentary: ἐν δὲ τοῖϲ Καλλιϲτράτου
γέγραπται· ἐπιζητήϲειεν ἄν τιϲ πῶϲ διὰ τριῶν εἴρηκεν, κτλ.); as to 1038 see
above. In all these instances we are dealing with precise remarks circumscribed to textual matters or to the explanation of rather obscure expressions, a fact that had already led Wilamowitz to assess that "in den Scholien
zum *Orestes* ist ein ὑπόμνημα des Aristophaneers Kallistratos benutzt"
(Wilamowitz 1889, 151). Besides Callistratos, we also find the name of
Apollodoros of Cyrene (certainly prior to Pamphilos—first century BC—
see recently the relative chronology advanced by Dyck 1981, 106), quoted
by the Σ to *Or.* 1384 for regarding the verse as an interpolated marginal
note, and that of an otherwise unknown Aeschines, mentioned by both the
Σ to *Or.* 12 and 1371 as regards etymological remarks (*Or.* 12: τὰ ἔρια
would be called ϲτέμματα since they stem ἀπὸ τοῦ ϲτέφειν τὰϲ ἠλακάταϲ) as
well as syntactic (*Or.* 1371: the use of the preposition ὑπέρ ἀντὶ τῆϲ πρό).
In view of the evidence, it is not difficult to suppose the existence, already
in the third century BC, of exegetical activity on an inherently difficult passage like *Or.* 340–4.

Summing up, the comparison between P.Vind. ll. 5–6 and the scholiastic remark τὸ δὲ δεινῶν πόνων ἐν μέϲωι ἀναπεφώνηται (Σ to *Or.*
340) does not tell us anything about the alleged direct derivation of
the Alexandrian editorial tradition from texts carrying musical notation, but can perhaps cast some further light on the constant cross-
fertilization between textual tradition and performance onstage.

II.1.4 *P.Vind. G 2315. Textual and/or performative variants: some considerations*

The next question to be asked regards the value to be assigned to
the textual and/or metrical variants provided by the Vienna papyrus.
To what extent do the data at our disposal allow us to regard these
variants just as 'normal' alternative readings provided by a source
that presents itself primarily as textual evidence of the original
Euripidean words? Or, conversely, does the idiosyncratic nature of
P.Vind. as a musical score affect in some way our understanding of
these variants if compared with those attested by a purely textual
tradition? Is it possible to make sense, within a performative dimension that, by that time, showed significant deviations from the 'standard' performance of fifth-century tragedy, of features that seem to
be nonsensical if understood within a strictly Maasian perspective?

Let us turn to focus once again on the data offered by P.Vind. Marino's emphasis on the substantial agreement, in terms of colometric articulation, between medieval tradition and P.Vind. turns out to be basically right, once the necessary corrective is made that P.Vind. does not exhibit a colometric layout and that therefore, except for the case of ll. 5–6 (where we are aided by the musical notation), nothing can be inferred in that respect.[109]

What is, however, more debatable in Marino's argumentation is her claim that it is possible to observe a "clear increment of the colometric variants" within the medieval tradition as regards *Or.* 325–7~341–3 and her consequent inference of a close relationship between Alexandrian textual criticism and texts provided with musical notation (Marino 1999a, 151–2). More precisely, Marino observes that this alleged breaking up of the tradition significantly coincides with the absence, in P.Vind., of the sign ⌐ and with the appearance of the instrumental notes preceded by *diastolé*. Therefore, according to Marino, the coincidence of these elements would have engendered, in the very shift from texts carrying musical notation (that is, conceived for performance) to texts devoid of musical notes and written down in a unique column (that is, texts conceived for reading), "an interpretative confusion as regards the cola in synapheia and the musical and metrical-rhythmical signs."[110] Moving from these premises, Marino finally concludes that "at this point we can confidently suppose that at ll. 325–7~341–3 of the *Orestes* there must have been modifications of the transmitted colometry on the basis of the comparison drawn with musical copies carrying musical, rhythmical and thus colometric notations similar to those of the Vienna papyrus [. . .]. This presupposes that texts carrying musical notation were available to those who dealt with the colometric disposition" (Marino 1999a, 152). Before discussing Marino's own conclusions, it may be useful to dwell briefly on her methodological premises.[111] First, her peculiar use of the term 'variant'. The claim that "it is fair here to speak of variants and not of errors inasmuch as in this context we do not take into account the correctness of the colometry but its processes of transmission" seems to me partially misleading. Both aspects, the processes of transmission and the correctness of colometry, are indeed strictly related and it is not rare for the 'traditional' history of a passage to be determined by our correct or incorrect understanding of its colometry. Secondly, Marino's statement that "the criterion that the colometry of the strophe should be compared with that of the antistrophe in order to establish the actual colometry preserved by the codex, is useful but not always cogent," if occasionally

---

[109] For the iambic interpretation of ll. 5–6 (= *Or.* 342–3) see above.
[110] Marino 1999a, 152.
[111] See esp. Marino 1999a, 151. n. 22.

true, does not exempt us, whenever possible, from trying to reconstruct the likely original colometry exibited by the codex. Once granted these premises, it seems to me more correct to regard what Marino calls a "clear increment of colometric variants in the medieval tradition for ll. 325–7∼341–3" as simply the result of antecedent colometric mistakes (as is clarified by the strophic responsion), that is, mistakes that, certainly not by chance, occur in correspondence with the first appearence of verbal synapheia in the strophe, that is, ἐκἰλαθέϲθαι at 325 and φοιτᾱλέου at 326, a phenomenon which does not involve the corresponding lines of the antistrophe. Therefore the fact that these 'variants', or, better, mistakes, are concentrated in the final lines has a precise internal textual explanation and is not to be traced back to an alleged comparison with musical scores.

The only certain[112] *textual* (and not colometric) variant provided by P.Vind., that is, l. 339 of the medieval tradition transposed before l. 338, does not alter the manuscript colometry: whether we have the order 339/340 (codd. + Π[7] Diggle)[113] or 338/340 (P.Vind.), in both cases between 339 and 340 or between 338 and 340 there is always hiatus and thus verse-end between cola consisting of two dochmiacs.[114] What is perhaps worth asking, of course with due caution, is whether the order 339 before 338 can tell us something about the particular nature and destination of the Vienna papyrus.

The exegetical tradition of *Or.* 334–9 is notoriously a long-standing and vexed one[115] and there have been repeated attempts at proving the Euripidean authenticity of the verse order 339–338–340 transmitted by P.Vind.[116] In particular, from Longman onwards, the supporters of the verse order of P.Vind. have unanimously denied the anadiplosis κατολοφύρομαι κατολοφύρομαι (339) the value of a

---

[112] Given the difficulty of interpreting the scanty traces of ink at l. 7, Messeri's reading ὀλεθρίοιϲ (against ὀλεθρίοιϲιν of the manuscript tradition) has to be considered separately.

[113] Π[7] Diggle (= P.Berol. inv. 17051 + 17014) presents in fact the same order 338/339 as the manuscript tradition: see Willink 2001, 128–9.

[114] The barely metrical criterion is unfortunately of no avail in the choice of the verse order. Given the extreme flexibility exhibited by dochmiacs in responsion, the coincidence, in terms of word boundaries, we observe between the first and second metron of 322 and 328 (respectively τανᾱὸν αἰθέρ᾽ἰ ἀμὶ-(πάλλεϲθ᾽) and μᾱτέροϲ αἷμᾱἰ ϲᾱϲἱ) cannot be considered as conclusive, see Dale in Turner 1956, 96 n. 8.

[115] See e.g. Di Benedetto 1965, 72–4, Willink 1986, 141–3 and id. 2001, 131–3, West 1987, 206.

[116] In this direction see already Crusius 1894, 179, Turner 1956, 96, Feaver 1960, 9, 14–5, Longman 1962, 64 ff., Griffith 1967, 14.

parenthetic clause that is presupposed by the order of the medieval tradition.[117] Consequently they understand κατολοφύρομαι κατολοφύρομαι as governing the accusative ματέροc αἷμα cᾶc of 338,[118] thus disrupting the whole architecture of the sentence. Yet inherent in all these instances is the same syntactic difficulty which is hard to overcome: the lack of a direct object governed by the transitive πορεύων (337).[119]

Such a difficulty is clearly perceived by Longman, who is consequently forced to adopt a somewhat contrived textual arrangement for *Or.* 334–9.

---

[117] Turner 1956, 95 correctly stresses that the medieval tradition assigns to 339 "the status of an independent clause." The very object of the Chorus's complaint is in fact Orestes: the accusative governed by κατολοφύρομαι is in fact easily obtainable from the previous line (that is, c' ἀναβακχεύει at 338), regardless of what textual arrangement one is inclined to accept for the beginning of the second dochmiac of 338 (that is, ὅc c' ἀναβακχεύει, with ὅc c' transmitted by GLO^lcV^2/3 and ^γρΣ^mc and accepted by Diggle *OCT* III, 210, Willink 1986, 142, id. 2001, 131–2 and Kovacs 2002, 446, or ὅ c' ἀναβακχεύει of the remaining manuscript tradition, advocated by Di Benedetto 1965, 73, West 1987, 82, Medda 2001, 184). For the transitive use of (κατ)ολοφύρομαι + acc. of person see Di Benedetto 1965, 73.

[118] See Longman 1962, 63, Griffith 1967, 147 (the attempt at justifying ματέροc αἷμα cᾶc as a metonymy for μητέρα and thus as "a fair equivalent" to the acc. of person, has been convincingly confuted by Willink 1986, 143 and id. 2001, 131: the shift of the dramatic focus from Orestes to Clytaemestra is not contextually motivated and is not in keeping with the Chorus's previous attitude towards Orestes' misfortune: see also Di Benedetto 1965, 41–2). The most recent contribution in support of κατολοφύρομαι + ματέροc αἷμα cᾶc is that of Marino 1999a, 155–6, but her approach raises further difficulties. First, the claim that "the construction of κατολοφύρομαι becomes less ambiguous if referring to ματέροc αἷμα cᾶc" seems to me debatable: just this consideration could indeed have led to a banalization of the text, by favouring the transposition of 339 before 338, as already pointed out by Crusius 1894, 179. Secondly, if we conserve the manuscript reading πορεύων at 337 and at the same time consider ματέροc αἷμα cᾶc as the direct object of κατολοφύρομαι (as Marino did), thus regarding 335–337 as a self-contained clause, the problem still remains of identifying the object of πορεύων. To treat the distant pronoun cε of 335 as its object (see Marino 1999a, 156 with n. 32, taking up a suggestion advanced by Weil 1868, 711, who, however, accepted Kirchhoff's transpostion of 339 after 340, inverted the sequence of the two dochmiacs of 338, and regarded ματέροc αἷμα cᾶc as an apposition to δάκρυα at 335) strains the syntax of the whole passage. In fact the personal pronoun cε belongs to a syntactic clause other than that of cυμβάλλει κτλ. See also Longman's objections (id. 1962, 63) against Weil's textual arrangement.

[119] The same problem (the transitive value of πορεύων, a reading transmitted by almost the whole manuscript tradition) persists even if, following Willink 1986, 142 and Diggle *OCT* III, 210, we accept for the second dochmiac of 338 the textual arrangement ὅc c' ἀναβακχεύει, regarding ματέροc αἷμα cᾶc as an accusative of respect governed by ἀναβακχεύει. Hence the various emendations of πορεύων to the intransitive πολεύων (Willink) or χορεύων (Diggle; a variant attested by G, Σ^g and Σ^c).

In order to explain the transitive value conveyed by πορεύων, Longman is in fact compelled to emend the unanimously transmitted τιc at 337 in τέ c᾽(ε), with the postpositive τε thus coordinating the two participles θοάζων (335) and πορεύων (337), both governed by ὅδ᾽ ἀγών at 333.[120] This textual arrangement lends itself to detailed criticism. To the objections already raised by Di Benedetto (that is, the unlikelihood of identifying ἐc δόμον ἀλαcτόρων with the House of the Erinyes, that is, Hades)[121] we can also add further syntactic remarks. Now, if we coordinate θοάζων and πορεύων and consequently regard πορεύων too as belonging to the direct interrogative clause τίc ἔλεος, τίc ὅδ᾽ ἀγών/φόνιος ἔρχεται (333–4), it follows that the relative clause ὧι δάκρυα δάκρυcι cυμβάλλει becomes a self-contained parenthetical sentence, whose subject cannot any longer be τιc [. . .] ἀλαcτόρων. Longman tries to avoid this difficulty by translating ὧι δάκρυα δάκρυcι cυμβάλλει "for whom tears vie with tears," that is, by regarding δάκρυα as the subject (and not the object) of the verb cυμβάλλει.[122] Yet, to assign to cυμβάλλει the meaning of 'to vie with', even granted that such an overtone may be justified as an expansion of the original meaning of 'coming together' (see LSJ s.v. cυμβάλλω II. 4), seems to me to be misleading.[123] The image conveyed by the passage is that of adding tears to tears according to a well-employed Euripidean stylistic pattern: see e.g. Eur. *Hel.* 195 δάκρυα δάκρυcί μοι φέρων.

In order to explain the text provided by the Vienna papyrus, it thus seems more fruitful to pay attention to a suggestion first advanced by Crusius and then taken up by Turner. That is, the only way of making sense of the syntax underlying the verse order 339/338/340 is actually to preserve the original value of κατολοφύρομαι κατολοφύρομαι as parenthetic interjection (the main reason for its textual fluctuation) even if it is transposed before 338.[124]

---

[120] Longman 1962, 64–6.
[121] Di Benedetto 1965, 73–4.
[122] Longman 1962, 65.
[123] Griffith 1967, 147 does not take account of this difficulty.
[124] See respectively Crusius 1894, 179 ("ich wenigstens meine, dass der Klagruf, dazwischen geworfen, wie in dem Papyrus, wirkungsvoller ist, als nachschleppend, wie in den Handschriften") and Turner 1956, 96. This possibility is neglected by Willink 2001, 131 according to whom "with κατολοφύρομαι [. . .] preceding ματέροc αἷμα ⟨ἃc ὅ c᾽ ἀναβακχεύει there is no possible construction for 'your mother's blood' except as objective to 'I lament'." Marino 1999a, 156 misunderstands Turner's argumentation: his re-evaluation of the verse order 339/338/340 as *varia lectio* going back to the third century BC (and not as a merely mechanical slip) does rely on the interpretation of 339 as parenthetic interjection. In other words, according to Turner ll. 337 and 338, even if separated by 339, have to be understood as syntactically interlocked.

It may be worth asking whether the parenthetic nature of 339 can be explained in an easier way if we take account of the very nature and destination of P.Vind., that is, that of a performance which, as we have seen, can entail rhythmic-textual re-adaptations. That is, in this case too we always have to be aware of the possibility that the verse order 339/338/340 transmitted only by P.Vind. may not have been meant to convey the original Euripidean verse order[125] but may have been the result of a re-adaptation aiming at increasing the pathos of the performance. If the order 339 before 338 can be saved, from a syntactic point of view, only as an emotionally charged parenthetic interjection and if we pay attention to the idiosyncratic nature of P.Vind. as a musical score conceived for an immediate performance, the emotional emphasis resulting from atomizing the syntactic structure of the sentence and from the consequent break of continuity is a device that fits well the hypothesis of a virtuoso performance on the part of some τραγωιδός.[126]

Another element that deserves to be framed within this perspective is Messeri's reading (λά-)[βροις ὀλεθρίοι] ͵ ϲ ἐεγ[κύμαϲιν at l. 7 of P.Vind. What we would have in the Vienna papyrus is thus ὀλεθρίοιϲ and not ὀλεθρίοιϲιν, the reading otherwise attested by the majority of Euripidean manuscripts. If we were facing just a 'normal' textual witness, we could confidently assess that the reading ὀλεθρίοιϲ is a commonly mechanical slip for the correct ὀλεθρίοιϲιν assured by strophic response.[127] But the musical notation at l. 7 in P.Vind. assures us that the text with ὀλεθρίοιϲ should be regarded as performable and actually performed, even if this textual arrangement breaks down the strophic response with ὀρεχθεὶϲ ἔρρειϲ at 328. Once again, the specific nature of the Vienna papyrus at least

---

[125] The *a priori* premise that the presence of musical notation, regarded as reproducing the authentic Euripidean music, is in itself a guarantee that the textual arrangement also reflects the Euripidean original has been correctly criticized by Willink 2001, 130–1: see also Parker 2001, 36–8.

[126] The theoretical possibility that in P.Vind. "the scribe had erroneously written κατολοφύρομαι only once" (Willink 2001, 128 with n. 8) does not affect this interpretation.

[127] The wrong reading ὀλεθρίοιϲ (I mean 'wrong' within the Euripidean textual tradition) is attested in fact also by VACLPXT[t3]: see the apparatus of Diggle *OCT* III, 210. For the ease and frequency of the exchange, within the manuscript tradition, of the endings in -οιϲ, -οιϲι, -οιϲιν, even in passages covered by response, see the instances quoted by Diggle 1994, 118.

suggests that we could regard ὀλεθρίοιϲ not as a copyist's mistake perverting the strophic responsion but rather as an alternative (and what is more important actually performed) rhythm, divergent from the 'right' one transmitted by the Euripidean manuscript tradition. In fact we would no longer have a purely dochmiac scansion (λάβροιϲ ὀλεθρίοιϲιν ἐν κύμαϲιν 2 δ) but a sequence consisting of δ + ia (λάβροιϲ ὀλεθρίοιϲ ἐν κύμαϲιν).[128] This scansion would suit well the syncopated iambic interpretation of ll. 5–6 exhibited by P.Vind. and add further weight to the notion of an astrophic performance of the originally strophic song of Euripides.[129]

Summing up, P.Vind. provides two cases (the verse order 339–338 and the probable ὀλεθρίοιϲ at l. 7) that deserve to be re-thought and that seem in fact to suggest an interpretative possibility other than that advocated by Fleming-Kopff and Marino: a process of textual transmission that involves, unfortunately or not, more fluid and contaminated inner dynamics.

II.2 *P.Leid. inv. 510: the limits of the tradition*

As we have seen, by adopting a more flexible interpretative approach to this typology of text, in the case of P.Vind. we can positively follow, although sporadically and of course with margins of uncertainty, the remaining traces of processes of rhythmic re-adaptation, which allow us to glimpse the possible 'openings' of a tradition no longer conceived as a merely textual vehicle. The traditional status of the musical anthology of P.Leid. inv. 510,[130] as we shall now show,

---

[128] I owe this suggestion to M.C. Martinelli.

[129] The suggestion of regarding P.Vind. as an anthological excerpt, and thus likely free from the ties of the original strophic responsion, has been variously formulated: see e.g. Van Akkeren 1983, 270–1, Willink 1986, liv–v and Anderson 1994, 220–1. Differently, Pöhlmann-West *DAGM*, 16 believe in a faithful strophic performance (see also Csapo 2004a, 223–5).

[130] Out of the 10 ll. of text transmitted by P.Leid. (I adopt here Pöhlmann-West's numeration: see below), only lines 7–10 (= Eur. *IA* 784–93) bear traces of musical notation above the lines of writing. The extension of the term 'musical' anthology also to the first excerpt, that is, to ll. 1–6 (= Eur. *IA* 1500?–09) is justified by the fact that the interlinear space we can reconstruct for ll. 1–6 (ca. 5–6 mm) is basically the same as that of ll. 7–10 (ca. 4–5 mm). This seems to suggest that also for ll. 1–6 the copyist has left the necessary space for writing down, evidently at a later stage, the corresponding musical notation: see Mathiesen 1981, 24–5 and Pöhlmann-West *DAGM*, 20. For speculation on the reason for the absence of musical notation above the first excerpt (it is worth remembering that both text and

requires even more caution and in a sense resists, at least partially, more detailed investigation in this respect because of its idiosyncratic features.[131]

Once again, the most reliable starting point from which to check whether and to what extent P.Leid. allows us to find vestiges of re-adaptation is the attempt to reconstruct the original column width and consequently the visual layout of the papyrus. It has often been suggested that P.Leid. provides, if not a properly colometric arrange-ment, at least a rhythmic disposition in 'systems' or 'metric periods', that is, by assigning to its line ends a metrical value.[132] In its turn, this issue again raises the question of the existence or not of a closer relationship between musical scores and Alexandrian colization. But before turning to these interpretative problems let us focus first on the material data provided by P.Leid, looking for some safe point of reference.

II.2.1 *P.Leid. inv. 510: the material evidence*
The first thing to be done is to establish the precise column width of P.Leid., an aspect which is strictly related to a possible colomet-ric interpretation of its line ends. The value of the column width of P.Leid. usually referred to by scholars is that established by Johnson,[133]

---

notation of the second Euripidean excerpt are written by the same hand: cf. Jourdan-Hemmerdinger 1981a, 36) see II.2.3.

[131] This of course is not tantamount to questioning the performative nature of that score: P.Leid. provides interesting insights into the performance of tragic high-lights in Hellenistic times. What I want to emphasize here is that the tools of a philological analysis in this case often do not allow us to ascertain with a reason-able degree of confidence what can be directly traced back to a performative re-adaptation, at least not at the level of the textual frame.

[132] See Jourdan-Hemmerdinger 1973, 292–3, ead. 1981a, 36–7, followed by Comotti 1978, 148 (esp. "nel nostro papiro [. . .] la disposizione del testo si ispira al criterio colometrico di far coincidere la fine della linea con la fine del colon o verso"), Mathiesen 1981, 23 with n. 27, Ferrari 1984, 20, Tessier 1995, 15, Lomiento 2001, 308, 340 n. 58 (for a detailed discussion of Lomiento's argumentation see I.9.2) and Concilio 2002. For a different evaluation see Günther 1988, xi, Parker 2001, 36 n. 21 and Pöhlmann-West *DAGM*, 20, correctly claiming that in P.Leid. "there is no colometry; we should not expect to find any at such an early date, and it is in any case not characteristic of texts carrying musical notation." Yet Pöhlmann-West's reconstruction of the column width of P.Leid. (cf. esp. iid. *DAGM*, 20 n. 2) unfortunately still relies on the erroneous data provided by Johnson 2000a, 67: see below.

[133] Johnson 2000a, 67: up to now the only estimate, to my knowledge. Jourdan-Hemmerdinger 1973, 292 and ead. 1981a, 36–7 limits herself to recording the

one recently accepted also by Pöhlmann-West in their authoritative
edition of the Leiden papyrus.[134] According to Johnson's reconstruction, the column of writing is thus "approximately 21–27 cm
wide": that is, remarkably high values even within the particular
typology provided by musical papyri, which normally features an
unusual column width[135] probably for practical reasons.[136]

Now Johnson's reconstruction, although it encompasses theoretically acceptable values, is unfortunately wrong. As admitted by
Johnson himself, he derived these data from "a rough estimate inferred
from the photo in Mathiesen 1981, 24 and the report of the papyrus
dimensions given in Jourdan-Hemmerdinger 1981,"[137] but the reproductions provided by both these sources turn out to be somewhat
inadequate. In fact, although Jourdan-Hemmerdinger correctly states
that the dimensions of P.Leid. are respectively 7·5 cm wide × 6 cm
high,[138] the photo she provides[139] is conspicuously enlarged if compared with the original scrap (we are not told about the scale of the
enlargement). Likewise, Mathiesen provides us with another enlarged
photo,[140] which this time is not accompanied by a scale.[141] It is the
sum of these factors that has determined Johnson's mistaken evaluation.

---

dimensions of the scrap (7·5 cm wide × 6 cm high). Likewise, Mathiesen 1981, 15
and id. 1999, 111 quotes Jourdan-Hemmerdinger's data without checking the real
length of the single lines of writing.

[134] See Pöhlmann-West *DAGM*, 20 n. 2.

[135] See Johnson 2000a, 67: out of the eight instances examined by Johnson (that
is, P.Vind. G 2315, P.Zen. 59533, P.Oxy. 2436, P.Oslo inv. 1413, P.Mich. inv.
2958, P.Oxy. 3704, P.Berol. inv. 6870 and P.Oxy.1786) the only one providing values comparable, if even not higher, with Johnsons' reconstruction of the P.Leid.
layout is P.Oxy. 1786 (a Christian hymn of the third/fourth century AD) whose
lines of writing are ca. 29·5 cm wide (cf. also Hunt in B.P. Grenfell-A. Hunt, *The
Oxyrhynchus Papyri*, XV, London 1922, 23 and Pöhlmann-West *DAGM*, 192). However,
in the case of P.Oxy. 1786 it must be noticed that we are dealing with anapaests
(that is, not a properly polymetric lyric as in P.Leid.), a metric measure comparable, in a sense, with stichic verses like hexameters and trimeters, that is, verses written down in *scriptio continua* in every age: see Fassino 1999, 4 n. 25.

[136] See Johnson 2000a, 68 and id. 2000b, 25.

[137] Johnson 2000a, 67.

[138] Jourdan-Hemmerdinger 1973, 292 and ead. 1981a, 36.

[139] Jourdan-Hemmerdinger 1973, 295.

[140] Mathiesen 1981, 24.

[141] All the other photos of papyri reproduced in Mathiesen 1981 are provided
with a graduated scale which allows one to recover the real dimensions of the scraps
(in this case, those of P.Oxy. 3161 frr. 1–4): the only exception in this respect is
P.Leid. inv. 510. It is perhaps worth noticing that the excellent photo reproduced
on the frontispiece by Pöhlmann-West *DAGM* is an enlargement of the original (this
is not the case of the photo reproducing P.Vind. G 2315).

A new photo of the Leiden papyrus kindly provided by the *Papyrologisch Instituut* of the *Rijksuniversiteit* of Leiden and a consequent autopsy of the papyrus conducted in January 2003 has allowed me, by adopting as a standard point of reference the transcription of Pöhlmann-West,[142] to re-calculate the actual width of the column layout. The length of the single lines of writing turns out to oscillate between ca. 14·4 cm for l. 6 (40 letters = *IA* 1508–09) and ca. 19·5 cm for l. 8 (62 letters = *IA* 787–90):[143] that is, remarkably lower values than Johnson's, but still fully compatible with the data provided by other musical papyri.

Before discussing the colometric or non-colometric value to be assigned to the verse ends, I provide here a new transcription of P.Leid. inv. 510 resulting from re-examination by autopsy.

In order to avoid further confusion in the quotations and cross-references I reproduce the numeration of the lines adopted by Pöhlmann-West *DAGM*, 18. It is however worth emphasizing that lines 2 and 4 of Pöhlmann-West have to be regarded simply as the supralinear space reserved for the musical notation. In fact a more detailed examination of the interlinear space does not allow, as regards the first excerpt, the reconstruction of 6 lines of text with the corresponding 6 lines carrying musical notation. As regards the second excerpt (that is, ll. 7–10), the interlinear space is ca. 4–5 mm. wide (respectively 4 mm between ll. 7–8, 4 to 5 mm between ll. 8–9, 4 mm between ll. 9–10). The interlinear space between ll. 1–3, 3–5, 5–6, 6–7 of Pöhlmann-West (that is, the extension of the first excerpt) is respectively ca. 5 mm, 6·5 mm, 5 to 6 mm, 5 to 6 mm: very slightly higher values than we can reconstruct for ll. 7–10. Thus, while adopting the Pöhlmann-West numeration for the sake of clarity, in this edition of P.Leid. lines (2) and (4), whenever mentioned, are to be understood as referring to the interlinear space between ll. 1–3 and 3–5, which are indeed the only real lines of the text of the first excerpt.

---

[142] Pöhlmann-West *DAGM*, 18: basically the most correct transcription inasmuch as regards the *usus scribendi* to be assumed in the gap (that is, the regular adoption of the *scriptio plena* notwithstanding the inconsistency of P.Leid. in marking the instances of elision: cf. ταδεεϲαλληλαϲ at l. 9 and μη]τεμοιμητεμοιϲ[at l. 7).

[143] Here and thereafter the verses I refer to are those in Diggle's OCT edition. Fortunately, the unwritten space before the beginning of l. 9 does assure that ταδε at l. 9 and γ[at l. 10 are most likely the very beginning of the left margin of the column. As regards the uncertain original length of l0 see below. All the figures I quote, if not otherwise specified, rely on the new autopsy.

Paleographic description

Dimensions: 7·5 × 6 cm, interlinear space ca. 5/6 mm for ll. 1–6 and ca. 4/5 for ll. 7–10, original column width oscillating between ca. 14·4 cm of l. 6 and ca. 19·5 cm of l. 8. Provenance: unknown. *Recto* written along the fibres, *verso* blank (with some occasional spots of ink). The unwritten space before the beginning of l. 9 indicates that ταδε at l. 9 and γ[at l. 10 are most likely to be regarded as the very beginning of the left margin of the column. The handwriting is an upright, roughly bilinear capital style, generally written with a thick blunt pen (see esp. ll. 1–6) and it is marked by a conspicuous alternation of remarkably large-sized letters (ΑΔΛ, ΜΝ, ΓΠΤ) and remarkably thin ones (ΕΟС). Both the musical notation, limited to ll. 7–10, and the text belong to the same hand. The most immediate parallel is provided by P.Lit.Lond. 73 (= Pack² 397, dated to the first half of the third century BC and containing Eur. *Hipp.* 1165–79, 1194–204: see Turner 1980, 28 no. 12),[144] especially as regards the shape of the tau with the "pen-entry of cross-bar [...] usually retrogressive from above," see Turner *GMAW²*, 126 and already Roberts 1956, 3, referring to P.Lit.Lond. 73. All these features confirm Jourdan-Hemmerdinger's dating to the first half of the third century BC: the papyrus may be labelled under Turner's group C among the Ptolemaic bookhands, see Turner 1980, 27–30.

Transcription[145]

1]..[	
(2)	
3]. γ .[	1501–02
(4)] [ ] [	
5].λιπη[ ]λαμπ[	1504–07
] [ ] [	
6]ωνακαιμοιραγοικη[	1508–09
]! . ? · I ? ? ?[	
7]τεμοιμητεμοις[	784–6
] С. Т СТ.? ?[	
8 ο[.]αναιπολυχρυссοιllλυδαι[	787–90
? ? _ · +⊥ [	
9 ταδεεсαλληλαстιςα[	790–2
Π Т С ⊥ С Т ΠТ [	
10 γ[...]ςγαсπατριαсολο[	792–3
]? IΟ [	
11	

---

[144] This comparison had first been suggested by Jourdan-Hemmerdinger 1973, 292.

[145] The description of the traces is limited to the cases where the autopsy has allowed me to gain some advancement in the reading. The numeration of the lines of *IA* follows that of Diggle *OCT* III, *ad loc.*

Text

1]. : very uncertain reading: irregular traces of ink apparently suiting the upper and lower curve of a rounded letter, ΕΘΟϹ all possible .[: very uncertain reading: legible low and high points of ink   3]. : uncertain reading: low point of ink, then at the middle of the line-level a curving rising stroke, apparently incompatible with West's reading N. More likely the right curve of an Ω γ : a descending diagonal oriented NW-SE, followed by a joining, slightly rightwards curved upright projecting above the line-level, cf. the second leg of the first N at l. 6. The descending diagonal, strongly flattened to the low line-level, does not suit the descending oblique of an A (Mathiesen, West), which usually exhibits an acute angle slope. Equally unlikely is West's interpretation of the second upright of the N as I, which in this case would show an unusually curved shape: elsewhere I is always strictly vertical and usually projects below the line-level, cf. I of πατριαϲ at l. 10   .[: uncertain reading: low point of ink, then, apparently along the same vertical axis but slightly to the right, high point of ink compatible with the tip of an upright. N (West) seems unlikely: there is no trace of the joining oblique. The traces above described are compatible with the back curve of E, cf. the first E of ταδεε at l. 9 5 The gap between λιπη[and]λαμπ is ca. 2·3/2·4 cm wide: too long for the only interjection ἰὼ ἰώ transmitted by the manuscripts, even assuming the presence of the iota for λιπη[ι.[146] To assume dicolon and/or unwritten space after λιπη[ι and before the interjection as a marker of change of speaker is one possible solution (1), although this does not seem to be the case at l. 3 χερ]ῶν ἐ[θρεψ- (= IA 1501–02), if the reading]ωγε[above suggested for this line is correct. Possible alternatives are: (2) to assume in the gap a threefold anaphora of the interjection ἰώ, that is, λίπη[ι ἰὼ ἰὼ ἰώ] λαμπ[, which is not, however, attested in Eur.:[147] a slip of the copyist by dittography or a rhetorical expansion *ad usum tragoedi*? or (3) to supplement λίπη[ι ἰὼ μοι]λαμπ[,[148] ἰὼ μοι being scanned as a bacchiac: cf. Eur. *El.* 1208   10 γ[: upright followed by a joining oblique descender: traces compatible with the first leg and the

---

[146] As correctly do Pöhlmann-West *DAGM*, 18.

[147] The only tragic instance of a threefold repetition of ἰώ can be found in Aesch. *Su.* 125–6 ἰώ, ἰώι, ἰὼ δυϲάγκριτοι πόνοι (ia | 2 ia); for the interjection ἰὼ ἰώ within anapaestic series in Eur. see Diggle 1974, 23–4. Metrically ἰὼ ἰὼ ἰώ can be scanned either as a molossus (with a semiconsonant iota), or, perhaps more likely, as a trochaic monometer (with ω shortening in hiatus, resolution of the long elements and anceps implemented by a *longum*: ˘ ˘ ˘ ˘ ˘ -), an interpretation that would assure a rhythmic continuity with the following lekythion at *IA* 1506 (for this reason a possibly iambic scansion of ἰὼ ἰὼ ἰώ seems to me less probable). Finally, we cannot rule out the possibility that the performer re-interpreted ἰὼ ἰὼ ἰώ as an interjection *extra metrum*.

[148] λίπη[ι ἰὼ ἰώ μοι]λαμπ[(cf. Eur. *Su.* 1198) is unfortunately too long: see the length of the sequence μοι at ll. 6 and 7 (ca. 1.1 cm wide).

diagonal of a N, cf. the N of]ωνα at l. 6. The previous reading T suggested by Jourdan-Hemmerdinger[149] is definitely to be rejected: the horizontal of T never exhibits such a serifed stroke as we would be forced to accept for the the initial part of the horizontal γ: Γ more likely than Π (West):[150] the high horizontal does not project to the left beyond the point of junction with the upright

Paleographic apparatus

1]..[West *DAGM*:]λε[Jourdan-Hemmerdinger 1981a:]ος[Mathiesen 1981 (= 1999):]εθ[Diggle *OCT* III, 417 app. ad *IA* 1502   3]ωνε[Jourdan-Hemmerdinger 1981a:]. ας[Mathiesen 1981 (= 1999):]γαιν[West *DAGM* 10 ν[...]ϲ: Günther 1988, corrig. ad app. crit., Diggle *OCT* III, 389, West *DAGM*: γυςας: Van Akkeren 1983 (sic): τ[. .]ϲ Jourdan-Hemmerdinger 1973, Comotti 1978, Mathiesen 1981 (= 1999), Jouan 1983a, Ferrari 1984, Stockert 1992, Willink 2001, Gentili 2001: ⌐[...]ϲ Jourdan-Hemmerdinger 1981a πατριαϲ Van Akkeren 1983, Günther 1988, corrig. ad app. crit., Diggle *OCT* III, 389, West *DAGM*: πατ·ριαϲ Jourdan-Hemmerdinger 1973 and 1981a, Comotti 1978, Mathiesen 1981 (= 1999), Jouan 1983a

Textual apparatus

1]..[West *DAGM*: κα]λε[ῖϲ πόλιϲμα Jourdan-Hemmerdinger 1981a (= *IA* 1500):]ος[Mathiesen 1981 (= 1999):]ἐθ[ρέψ- Diggle *OCT* III, 417 (= *IA* 1502)   3 χερ]ῶν ἐ[θρέψαϲ Jourdan-Hemmerdinger 1981a (= *IA* 1501–02):]. ας[Mathiesen 1981 (= 1999): ἀ]γαίν[ομαι West *DAGM* (= *IA* 1503)   5 λίπη[ι· ἰὼ ἰὼ]λαμπ[vel λίπη[ι ἰὼ ἰὼ ἰώ]λαμπ[vel λίπη[ι ἰὼ μοι]λαμπ[malim: λίπη[ι ἰὼ ἰώ]λαμπ[West *DAGM* 10 τα]ιν[ύϲα]ϲ: Günther 1988, corrig. ad app. crit. (praeeunte Van Akkeren 1983 τα]ινύϲαϲ), West *DAGM*: τα]ιν[ύϲα]ϲ vel δακρυόε]ιν [τᾶ]ϲ Diggle *OCT* III, 389: τ[αα]ϲ Jourdan-Hemmerdinger 1973, Comotti 1978, Mathiesen 1981 (= 1999), Jouan 1983a, Ferrari 1984, Stockert 1992, Willink 2001, Gentili 2001: ⌐[ταα]ϲ Jourdan-Hemmerdinger 1981a (sic)

II.2.2   *P.Leid. inv. 510: layout and variants. Which tradition?*

On the basis of these data, if for the time being we leave aside the problematic ll. 1–3, the more correct reconstruction, in terms of layout, of ll. 5–10 of the Leiden papyrus is that recently advanced by Pöhlmann-West.[151] As regards ll. 5–10, the text of P.Leid. is thus the following:

---

[149] See Jourdan-Hemmerdinger 1973, 294, followed by Comotti 1978, 153, Mathiesen 1981, 26 (= id. 1999, 112), Jouan 1983a, 91, 139, Ferrari 1984, 19, Stockert 1992 II, 128, and Gentili 2001, 134.
[150] West in Pöhlmann-West *DAGM*, 19.
[151] Pöhlmann-West *DAGM*, 18.

5 ιμͅηλιπῃ ͺ¹⁵²λαμπͺαδουχοϲαμεραδιοϲτεφεγγοϲετερονετερονͺ 1504–7
6 ͺαιͺωνακαιμοιραγοικηͺϲομενχαιρεμοιφιλονφαοϲͺ 1508–9
7 ιμηͺτεμοιμητεμοιϲͺιτεκνωντεκνοιϲελπιϲαδεποτεελθοιͺ 784–6
8 οιͺιαγαιπολυχρυϲοιͺ‖λυδαιͺκαιφρυγωναλοχοιϲτηϲουϲιπα-
  ραιϲτοιϲμυθευϲαιͺ 787–90
9 ταδεϲϲαλληλαϲτιϲͺαͺραμεευπλοκαμουκομαϲϲερυμαδακρυοενταͺ 790–2
10 γͺιυϲαͺϲγαϲπατριαϲολͺιμεναϲαπολωτιειͺ 792–3

If, from a merely editorial point of view, the visual formatting of the lineation as suggested by Pöhlmann-West for ll. 5–10 is in itself correct, unfortunately the missing evaluation of the actual length of each line of writing prevents them from giving a reasonable explanation of the apparently "irregular length" they are forced to acknowledge for ll. 5–10.[153] In other words, a reconstruction of the line length which relies exclusively on the abstract figure of the letters of each line (a figure oscillating between 40 letters for l. 6 and 62 for l. 8), turns out to be rather misleading since it ignores the characteristic and conspicuous alternation of remarkably large-sized (ΑΔΛ, ΜΝ, ΓΠΤ) and thin (ΕΘϹ,[154] ΙΥ) letters to be found in P.Leid.

In fact this very belief in the alleged "irregular length" of the P.Leid. lineation leads Pöhlmann-West to argue that l. 8 (IA 787–90= 62 letters), if supplemented on the basis of medieval tradition, seems to be exceedingly long and, consequently, that "perhaps the papyrus had a shorter text here,"[155] thus suggesting an unnecessary textual variant. Actually, a reconstruction of the lineation which takes account of the remarkably different size of the letters allows us to establish already for l. 5 a line length of ca. 19 cm (that is, IA 1504–07= ± 51 letters,[156] 21 of which are small-sized [i.e. ΕΘϹ, ΙΥ]).[157] Likewise,

---

[152] For the possible supplements of the gap see above.

[153] Pöhlmann-West DAGM, 20: "There is no colometry [. . .]. Instead the text is written in long lines of irregular length, usually ending with a complete word, though τανύϲαϲ in 791 appears to have been broken between lines 9 and 10."

[154] P.Leid. does not provide us with sure instances of Θ: Diggle's reading]ἐθ[ρέψ- at l. 1 (id. OCT III, app. ad IA 1502) is far from certain and it entails serious problems as regards the physical layout to be reconstructed for ll. 1–3: see below). Nevertheless, it is reasonable to assume that also Θ, along with ΕΘϹ, should probably be a small-sized letter.

[155] Pöhlmann-West DAGM, 19.

[156] This in the case we suppose that in the gap between λιπη[and]λαμπ we supplement the interjection ἰὼ ἰώ preceded by dicolon and unwritten space.

[157] I agree with Pöhlmann-West in supplementing at the end of l. 5 the anadiplosis ἕτερον ἕτερον (1507) transmitted by the medieval tradition. Notwithstanding the

l. 9 (that is, *IA* 790–2= 51 letters, 19 of which are small-sized) is
also ca. 19·3 cm wide. Thus in both cases we are not dealing with
values significantly diverging from the length that we can reconstruct
for l. 8, that is, ca. 19·5 cm (62 letters, 31 being small-sized): the
alleged 'excessive' length of l. 8 is ultimately only apparent. The percentage of small-sized letters at l. 8 is about 50%: we can reasonably understand now why the actual length of this line made of 62
letters (at first sight an impressive number) is not remarkably longer
than the one we can reconstruct for ll. 5 and 9, which consist of
'only' 51 letters (the percentage of small letters is ca. 41.2% for l.
5 and 37.2% for l. 9).[158] There is therefore no reason to suppose
that l. 8 of P.Leid. should be affected by some textual omission
potentially ascribable to the anthological nature of the papyrus.

Jourdan-Hemmerdinger's previous reading τ[αα]c at the beginning of l. 10
(ead. 1973, 294) had led some scholars to see at work in P.Leid. "the colometric criterion of making line end coincide with colon or verse end,"[159]
with the resulting belief in a disposition of the text according to metrical
'systems' or 'major metrical units'.[160] Such a belief has ultimately been
proved wrong by Van Akkeren's new reading for the beginning of l. 10,
that is,]γ[. . .]ς (id. 1983, 261: see also Günther 1988, corrigendum ad
app. crit. 790–2, Diggle *OCT* III, 389 app. *ad loc.* and Pöhlmann-West
DAGM, 18–9). Yet, Gentili 2001, 135 has recently advocated once again
Jourdan-Hemmerdinger's τ[αα]c, regarding it as "a certain transcription of
the *editio princeps*" and objecting to the syntactic difficulties pointed out by
Willink 2001.[161] Nevertheless, the reading]τ[αα]c, accepted among others
also by Mathiesen 1981, 26 (= id. 1999, 112) and Stockert 1992, can be

---

metrical perplexity which could be raised by the iteration of ἕτερον (see Diggle
1994, 410; but differently Günther 1988, 56) we are not entitled to assume *a priori* that P.Leid. had here a different reading.

[158] Furthermore, the need of a nominative participle of a *verbum dicendi* at the
end of l. 8 (the transmitted μυθεῦςαι) is guaranteed by the very beginning of the
following line, that is, ταδε ες αλληλας at l. 9.

[159] Comotti 1978, 148 "nel nostro papiro invece, nel quale come si è visto le
linee non hanno eguale lunghezza [. . .], la disposizione del testo si ispira al criterio colometrico di far coincidere la fine della linea con la fine del *colon* o del verso."

[160] Jourdan-Hemmerdinger 1973, 292–3.

[161] See Willink 2001, 130 n. 14: "When an adjective unaccompanied by definite
article either follows or precedes an article-plus-noun phrase, the adjective has pred-
icative force." As to the apparent exceptions allowed by the possessive adjective
ἐμός in Eur. *Hipp.* 683 (Ζεύς ς' ὁ γεννήτωρ ἐμός codd.: Ζεύς ςε γεννήτωρ ἐμός
Wolff) and Soph. *Aj.* 573 (μήθ' ὁ λυμεὼν ἐμός codd.: μήτε λυμεὼν ἐμός Schaefer)
see Barrett's justifiable skepticism (id. 1964, 290).

confidently ruled out: see the description of the traces of ink given above. Van Akkeren's]ν̣[. . .]ς̣ is thus to be regarded as conclusive and the supplement τα]ιν̣[υ‹α]ς̣ suits the gap's width best,[162] and moreover allows us to reconstruct at the same time a coherent layout. Now, the reading τα]ιν̣[υ‹α]ς presents a word division between ll. 9 and 10 which cannot be traced back to any reasonably colometric interpretation of *IA* 792–3. In other words, if we keep in mind that the longest line we can reconstruct for P.Leid. is l. 8, that is ca. 19·5 cm, and that ll. 5 and 9 range from ca. 19 to 19·3 cm, it seems reasonable to infer that the width of l. 8 (~19·5 cm) should represent the physical limit of the column length. It seems thus more likely to assume that the reason for the word division τα]ιν̣[υ‹α]ς is not to be sought in an alleged colometric interpretation of the Euripidean text but in this extrinsic physical feature.

The 'irregular' length of the remaining lines of writing in P.Leid. (that is, ll. 6, 7 and 10) can also be consistently explained within the picture sketched here. The scanty length of l. 6 (40 letters, ca. 14·4 cm) is easily explained if we consider that l. 6 is the very final line of the first excerpt (that is, *IA* 1509 χαῖρε μοι, φίλον φάος): it is thus reasonable to suppose that the copyist marked the end of the excerpt by starting the following Euripidean passage in a new line. The same can be said for l. 10: since the last word of the line might well be ἀπολωτιεῖ (thus 32 letters, ca. 11·8 cm),[163] this line, which ends a syntactically self-contained clause, can perfectly suit, from a typological point of view, the end of the second excerpt. Of course,

---

[162] Diggle's δακρυοε]ιν̣ [τα]ς (see id. *OCT* III, 389) is slightly too short and above all it assumes for ll. 9–10 an unnecessary (and hard to motivate) word division δακρυοε]ιν, the column width of l. 9 allowing the copyist to write δακρυοεν in full. Besides, Diggle's supplement δακρυοε]ιν̣ [τα]ς γα‹ πατριασ ολο̣[μενα‹ απολωτιει] lends itself to the same syntactic objections already raised by Willink 2001, 130 n. 14 against Jourdan-Hemmerdinger's]τ̣[αα]ς γα‹ πατριασ as regards the word order. Gentili's recent attempt at defending the syntagm τᾶς γᾶς πατρίας (id. 2001, 135) is unconvincing. Although the noun-plus-adjective γᾶ πατρία is "perceived in classical times as a whole syntagm tantamount to the bare πατρίς, the adjective following and not preceding the noun," the passages of Soph. *Ant.* 806 ὦ γᾶς πατρίας πολῖται and Eur. *Med.* 653 ἢ γᾶς πατρίας ‹τέρεσθαι (πατρώας V) are not cogent. The word order noun + adjective, given the absence of the definite article, cannot be regarded as a real parallel. Furthermore, if we look at all the Euripidean instances of γῆ/γᾶ πατρία (with the adjective following the noun: 5 ×, i.e. *Med.* 653, *El.* 1315 [πατρίας Schaefer: πατρώας L, see Denniston 1939, 73 ad l. 209], *Tr.* 857, *Ion* 483, [*Rh.*] 932) the article is never attested (the same is true for Soph. *Ant.* 806).

[163] Of course, the precise length of l. 10 is not recoverable any longer. Mathiesen's hypothesis that at l. 11 the quotation from the epode should go on is not verifiable (id. 1981, 30).

the problem still remains of explaining the somewhat puzzling length of l. 7 (46 letters, ca. 15·9 cm): in this case we are really dealing with line end coinciding with verse end (cf. the hiatus between ἔλθοι at l. 7 and οἵαν at l. 8). There are no easy explanations for such an exception but since we have here the beginning of a new excerpt, we might suppose that the line length of l. 7 has been influenced by that of the preceding l. 6 (ca. 14·4 cm), or perhaps the fact itself that l. 7 (that is, *IA* 784–6 μήτ' ἐμοὶ μήτ' ἐμοῖcι τέκνων τέκνοιc ἐλπὶc ἅδε ποτ' ἔλθοι) is a semantically and syntactically self-contained clause might have played an important role.

Summing up, on the basis of the data collected here (that is, the copyist's tendency to write continuously through the column length, up to a limit of ca. 19~19·5 cm), to ascribe a specifically colometric value to the P.Leid. line ends on the basis of the single instance of l. 7 (hiatus after ἔλθοι), seems to be quite hazardous[164] and above all it does not suit the papyrus layout above reconstructed. This is all the more evident if we pay attention to the fact that also as regards the first excerpt, at least for those lines we can confidently reconstruct, that is ll. 5–6, a coincidence of line end with colon or verse end cannot be positively attested.

The same can be said also as regards ll. 3 and 5. According to the medieval tradition, line 5, that is, μ]η λιπη[ι κτλ.,[165] begins with the first long of the second iambic metron of 1504 (i.e. cε μὴ λίπηι). The word to be supplemented at the end of l. 3 is thus the second person pronoun cε, that is to say that l. 3 ends with the anceps of the very same iambic metron. In other words, the word division cεἰ μὴ λίπηι between ll. 3 and 5 does not suit any reasonable colometric interpretation. Besides, according to manuscript tradition there is hiatus between λίπηι (1504) and the following interjection ἰὼ ἰώ (1505). This means thus that whatever supplement we may choose to fill in the gap μ]η λιπη[ι]λαμπ at l. 5 (see above), we have verse end in the middle of the line of writing, that is, a verse end not coinciding with line end. As regards then the final part of l. 5, correctly supplemented by Pöhlmann-West *DAGM*,18 with the transmitted anadiplosis ἕτερον ἕτερον, it must be said, theoretically speaking, that this line end could make sense metrically (Tr¹ in L and Tr⁽¹⁾ in P[166] divide after the first ἕτερον, see

---

[164] See e.g. the presence of hiatus (and thus verse end) in the middle of l. 5, that is, μ.ηλιπη.ιιωιωͺ (= *IA* 1504–5).

[165] The alignment of the lines to the left margin rules out Jourdan-Hemmerdinger's supplement cε μ]η λιπη[ι at the beginning of l. 5 (ead. 1981a, 61).

[166] I am adopting here the *sigla* suggested by Günther 1988, xxi. I have inspected L and P on the reproductions provided by Spranger 1920 and id. 1939–46.

Günther 1988, 56 and Stockert 1992, I, 147). In fact we could scan λαμ-
παδοῦχος ἀμέρα Διός τε φέγγος ἕτερον ἕτερον αἰῶνα καὶ μοῖραν οἰκήϲομεν (*IA*
1506–8) either as 2tr ∫ 2tr ⏐ 3 tr sync?⏐ (sic Stockert 1992, II, 611) or as
lk ⏐ pe ‖[167] 2ia ⏐ 2cr ⏐ (cf. Günther 1988, 67; but see also Diggle's objections in id. 1994, 410).[168] Yet, the fact that the line length of l. 5 is about
19 cm wide, a value indeed closest to the maximum width of the column
we can reconstruct for P.Leid. (19·5 cm of l. 8), does not allow us to rule
out the possibility that we are simply dealing here with the physical end
of the column of writing. For the non-relevance of the end of l. 6, inasmuch as coinciding with the end of the first excerpt, see above.

Close scrutiny of l. 3 leads in the same direction too, that is, towards
a non-colometric reconstruction of the lineation. As we have already
seen (cf. II.2.1), West's α]ϝαιν[ομαι at l. 3 (= *IA* 1503) is to be
rejected on paleographic grounds: the reading best suiting the traces
of ink is still that originally suggested by Jourdan-Hemmerdinger,
that is,]ΩΝΕ[,[169] a sequence of letters perfectly overlapping with the
text χερῶν ἐ[θρεψ- of *IA* 1501–2. On the basis of this overlap, if
we keep in mind that the standard column width of P.Leid. (that is,
whenever we are not faced with the beginning or ending of an
excerpt) is about 19~19·5 cm, the most likely column layout to be
reconstructed for l. 3 (= *IA* 1501–3) is the following:

3 χερ]ῶ̣ν̣ ἐ̣[θρεψαϲ Ἑλλάδι μέγα φάος θανοῦϲα δ(ὲ) οὐκ ἀναίνομαι κλέος γὰρ
οὔ ϲε[170]

The resulting line entails 59 letters (24 of which small-sized, that is,
an overall percentage of 40%),[171] the total length being ca. 19·3 cm
wide: that is, values perfectly matching the data otherwise reconstructed for the remaining lines of P.Leid.

---

[167] That is, with *brevis in longo* in φέγγōϲ.
[168] We could also interpret this sequence as lk⏐ ia∫ δ ‖ ia 2cr, that is, if we assume
brevis in longo in the second ἕτερōν.
[169] Jourdan-Hemmerdinger 1981a, 60–1.
[170] The text here supplemented is that transmitted by the medieval tradition;
Diggle *OCT*, III, 417 accepts Elmsley's emendations ἐθρέψαθ' (ἔθρεψαϲ L) and με
(μέγα L) at l. 1502. Even if we accept Diggle's text (57/8 letters: in the case of
ἐθρέψαθ' we have to take into account the possibility of *scriptio plena*), the line length
remains substantially unchanged.
[171] Granted the not surprising inconsistency of the papyrus in marking the elision, whenever possible I assume *scriptio plena* (in this case δε ουκ at 1503).

Even apart from paleographic reasons, West's α]γαιγ[ομαι entails for l. 3 a layout that is hardly acceptable: we would be compelled to reconstruct a line of only 21 letters (that is, the second iambic metron of 1503, i.e. ἀναίνομαι, and the first part of 1504, i.e. κλέος γὰρ οὔ ϲε). Likewise, Diggle's reading]ε̣θ[at l. 1 (that is, to be supplemented]ε̣θ[ρεψ-, cf. 1502) is quite problematic. According to that reconstruction, the resulting 52 letters (that is, the textual segment from ἐθρεψ- at 1502 to οὔ ϲε at 1504) should be distributed along three lines of writing. If we read]ΩΝΕ̣[at l. 3 and supplement χερ]ῶν ἐ[θρέψ- (= IA 1501–2), it is instead possible to gain for l. 3 a column layout perfectly compatible, in terms of line width and number of letters, with the *mise en page* of P.Leid as reconstructed above. Furthermore, if we go backwards in calculating the preceding lines of text, the first possible beginning for the first Euripidean excerpt (that is, an *incipit* [1] starting at a new line, [2] allowing us to reconstruct for the previous lines a column ca. 19·5 cm wide, and [3] making sense both syntactically and semantically) is IA 1491 ἰὼ ἰώ.[172] Thus, the first Euripidean excerpt should probably begin at least at 1491 (that is, Iphigenia's apostrophe to the Chorus: ἰὼ ἰὼ νεάνιδεϲ).

The data considered here seem to lead in the same coherent direction. The re-evaluation of the column layout allows us to reconstruct also for P.Leid. a *mise en page* consistent with that attested by the extant musical papyri at our disposal (that is, continuous writing, absence of a colometric layout). The physical criterion of the line end cannot thus be adduced any longer as evidence that P.Leid. displays a different colometry from that of medieval tradition.

The erroneous belief in a colometric layout of P.Leid. has led some scholars to regard the participle μυθεῦϲαι][173] to be supplemented at the very end

[172] I accept here Hermann's emendation ἰὼ ἰώ instead of the transmitted ὦ (Tr¹): see Stockert 1992, II, 614, commenting that "doch hat Hermann [. . .] wohl richtig das für Iph. charakteristische doppelte ἰώ eingesetzt." We should then suppose four lines of writing before χερ]ῶν ἐ[θρέψ- of l. 3. For the sake of clarity I name these lines 3a, 3b, 3c and 3d; wherever possible, I have always assumed the use of *scriptio plena*. This is thus the tentative reconstruction I suggest: 3a ιω ιω νεανιδεϲ—αντιπο(-) (= IA 1491–3; 45 letters, 20 of which small-sized; line length ca. 18·7 cm); 3b (-)ρον—αυλιδοϲ (= IA 1493–5; 43 letters, 17 of which small-sized; line length ca. 18·8 cm); 3c ϲτενοποροιϲ—μυκηναιαι (= IA 1496–8; 46 letters, 20 of which small-sized; line length ca. 18·8 cm); 3d τεεμαι—πονον (= IA 1498–501; 48 letters, 19 of which small-sized; line length ca. 18·9 cm).
[173] For a convincing defence of the transmitted μυθεῦϲαι against Matthiae's emendation μυθεύ⟨ου⟩ϲαι (adopted also by Stockert 1992, II, 428) see Ferrari 1984, 20–1. As to the Ionic contraction ευ in Euripides see Mastronarde 2002, 243 ad *Med.* 423 ὑμνεῦϲαι.

of l. 8 as coinciding with colon end, which would suggest for *IA* 789–90 a remarkably different colometry from that transmitted by medieval tradition. Actually both L and P divide cτήcουcι παρ' ἱcτοῖcι μυθεῦcαι τάδ' ἐc ἀλλήλαcι, a sequence to be interpreted as reiz | gl dragged | (only P² tries to create a contrived responsion between 773–83 and 784 ff. by dividing at 788/9 cτήcουcι παρ' ἱcτοῖc μυ|θεῦcαι τάδ' ἐc ἀλλήλαc, that is, 2^gl dragged in synapheia: see Günther 1988, ix–x with n. 1 and the colometric apparatus *ad loc.*). By ascribing a specifically colometric value to the line end at l. 8 (that is, colon end after μυθεῦcαι), various scholars have repeatedly argued that P.Leid. exhibits an alternative metrical interpretation to that transmitted by LP for *IA* 789–90. Suffice it here to quote, for example, Comotti 1978, 153–4, who, while adopting Matthiae's μυθεύ<ου>cαι, interprets the sequence cτήcουcι παρ' ἱcτοῖc μυθεύ<ου>cαι τάδ' ἐc ἀλλήλαc as ^pher | anl anl and Ferrari 1984, 21, scanning cτήcουcι παρ' ἱcτοῖc μυθεῦcαι τάδ' ἐc ἀλλήλαc as 2an | anl. More recently also Stockert 1992, I, 66, although adopting a different textual arrangement for ll. 789–90 (that is, cτήcουcι παρ' ἱcτοῖc μυθεύ<ου>cαι τάδ' ἐc ἀλλήλαc regarded as ^pher | 2anl: see id. 1992, II, 419–20), observes that "Dieser Papyrus (i.e. P.Leid.) [...] weist noch nicht die später obligate Kolometrie des Aristophanes v. Byzanz auf. So wird z.B. v. 789 μυθεύ<ου>cαι zum Vorhergehenden gezogen." The very fact that the physical layout displayed by P.Leid. does not allow us to infer for cτήcουcι παρ' ἱcτοῖc μυθεῦcαι a diverging colometric disposition as compared with that of the manuscript tradition, is of course not to say that the metrical interpretation of this textual segment as anapaestic dimeter is to be regarded as inherently wrong.[174] What I should like to emphasize here is only the fact that, granted that the anapaestic scansion of cτήcουcι παρ' ἱcτοῖc μυθεῦcαι is, theoretically speaking, one possible metrical interpretation among others, P.Leid. cannot be adduced as positive evidence supporting this anapaestic interpretation.

Summing up, the purely physical data conveyed by P.Leid. (continuous writing, absence of rhythmic-notational clusters suggesting, as for P.Vind., alternative metrical interpretations) do not allow us to detect in this lyric anthology any traces of metrical re-adaptations ascribable to performance itself.

In addition, a closer examination of the textual (and *consequently* colometric)[175] variants provided by P.Leid. seems to lead to similar 'open-ended' conclusions. At l. 10 P.Leid. has γᾶc πατρίαc ὀλο[μένας

---

[174] For the presence of anapaests associated with choriambic cola in the Euripidean lyric see Ferrari 1984, 21.

[175] From this point of view the resemblance of P.Leid. to P.Stras.W.G. 304–7 is more striking, cf. I.9.2.

against the transmitted πατρίδος οὐλομένας of L and P (= *IA* 793).
The papyrus reading ὀλο[μένας confirms the soundness of Burges'
emendation[176] and is most likely to be regarded as the 'original' reading for *IA* 793 (and that quite apart from the vexed question of the
Euripidean authenticity of the whole epode).[177] The variant ὀλο[μένας
provided by P.Leid. is in fact to be preferred for both linguistic and
metrical reasons. As regards the middle aorist participle of ὄλλυμι,
the Euripidean usage shows a clear predominance of the normally
Attic form ὀλομ- (18 ×)[178] against the epicism οὐλομ- (1 ×: *Phoen.*
1529 οὐλόμεν' αἰκίσματα νεκρῶν).[179] Furthermore, the reading ὀλομένας
is metrically preferable inasmuch as it allows one to interpret πατρίδος
ὀλομένας ἀπολωτιεῖ (a textual segment unanimously transmitted by
L and P as a metrically self-contained unit) as a sequence of ia∫ δ,[180]

---

[176] Burges 1807, 183: see Diggle 1994, 412.

[177] See Diggle 1994, 503–6. ὀλομένας had already been accepted by Dindorf
1869, 272, and in modern times also by Jouan 1983, 91, Günther 1988, 30 and
Diggle *OCT* III, 389.

[178] That is, *Med.* 1253 (lyr.) (ὀλ- of ΩLP² being metrically assured by responsion
with 1263), *Hipp.* 869 (lyr.), *El.* 154 (lyr.), *HF* 1061–2 (lyr.), *Tro.* 1079 (lyr.) (ὀλ-
being metrically protected by responsion with 1069), 1313 (lyr.) (ὀλ- being metrically assured by responsion with 1329), *IT* 1109 (lyr.) (ὀλομένων LP; Triclinius and
Erfurdt's emendations, respectively οὐλομένων [= Tr²] and ὀλλυμένων, in order to
assure an exact responsion gl ~ gl between 1109 and 1092 are not necessary: for
the responsion dim cho ~ gl cf. Itsumi 1982, 59, 69, 70–1), *Hel.* 178 (lyr.) (ὀλ-
being guaranteed by the responsion with 190), 232 (lyr.), 385 (lyr.), 1245 (ia), 1545
(ia) (ὀλόμενον is Stephanus' emendation *metri causa* of the transmitted ὀλούμ-), *Phoen.*
1029 (lyr.) (ὀλ- being metrically assured by the responsion 1053), 1295 (lyr.) (ὀλ-
being metrically guaranteed by responsion with 1307), *Or.* 1307 (lyr.) (2 ia; ὀλομ-
MBOVaALX: ὀλλομ- FGKPZ: ὀλλυμ- cett.), 1364 (lyr.) (ὀλ- of ΩT¹³ and K¹ᶜ being
metrically assured by responsion with 1547), 1383 (lyr.), P.Stras.W.G. 306ʳ col. IV
r. 9 (see Fassino 1999, 27 and 30).

[179] This is the only certain Euripidean instance of οὐλ-, see Mastronarde 1994a
ad loc. In fact Eur. fr. 915. 1 *TrGF* (that is, Clem. Alex. *Strom.* 6. 2. 12. 4 Descourtieux
= *PG* 9. 224) νικᾶι δὲ χρεία μὲν κακῶς τε οὐλομένηι γαςτήρ (this is the transmitted text) is certainly to be emended *metri causa*: see Casaubon's emendation νικᾶι
δὲ χρεία μ', ἡ κακῶς τ' ὀλουμένηι γαςτήρ on the basis of Diph. 60. 1–3 K-A
(Casaubon 1621², 422), the use of the future participle ὀλουμ- being attested also
in Eur. *Cyc.* 474 (ia) and *Hcld.* 874 (ia). Most likely the ionic form οὐλομένη in
Clem. Alex. must be explained as a slip induced by the previous Homeric quotation of ρ 286–7 γαςτέρα δ' οὔ πως ἔςτιν ἀποκρύψαι (ἀποπλῆςαι Clem. Alex.)
μεμαυῖανǀ οὐλομένην κτλ. at *Strom.* VI 2. 12. 3 Descourtieux.

[180] This seems to me the most likely scansion; for similarly iambo-dochmiac
sequences within choriambic contexts see e.g. Eur. *Ion* 496–8 (dim cho Bǀ 2 ial δ).
Another possibility is to interpret πατρίδος ὀλομένας ἀπολωτιςῖ as glᵈ (assuming πᾱ
τρι- as aeolic base). Yet, in this latter case we would have an isolated dactylic
expansion (see below) together with the split resolution of the first long belonging

thus avoiding what would otherwise be the only instance of dactylic expansion (πατρίδος οὐλομένας ἀπολωτιεῖ: ‿‿gl^d) to be found among the aeolo-choriambic metres of the strophic stanzas and epode of the second stasimon.[181]

Dindorf 1869, 272, accepted for *IA* 792 the athetesis of τανύςας originally advanced by Hermann 1848, 5–6 (who considered the aorist participle a later interpolation) and divided ἔρυμα δακρυόεν πατρίδō‹ ὀλομένας ἀπολωτιεῖ, that is, dim cho B‖ ‿‿gll).[182] Yet, it seems to me better to avoid splitting the segment πατρίδος ὀλομένας ἀπολωτιεῖ, which is transmitted as a metric unit by the medieval tradition. In fact as regards *IA* 792–3 L and P have colon end after τανύςας and not after πατρίδος (that is, ἔρυμα δακρυόεν τανύςας ‿‿‿‿‿‿‿‿‿, probably dim cho B); this colometry is apparently accepted by Jouan 1983a, 91, cf. also Diggle *OCT* III, 389 (with ἔρυμα δακρυόεν τανύςας between *cruces*).

Whereas the ὀλο[μένας provided by P.Leid. can confidently be considered a better reading than the transmitted οὐλομένας and be accepted as the 'correct' text for *IA* 793, the evaluation of the variant γᾶς πατρίας (P.Leid.) against πατρίδος (LP) is more problematic.[183] In this case the linguistic criterion is not conclusive: the syntagm γῆ/γᾶ πατρία occurs quite frequently in Euripides[184] and it is not

---

to choriambic core of the glyconic: see Diggle 1994, 470–1 ad *Ba*. 865 (for a less skeptical view as regards glyconic with the resolution of "the 'left' side of the 'choriambic nucleus'" cf. Itsumi 1984, 78: among the instances quoted by Itsumi of, the more persuasive ones are Eur. *El*. 126, *Su*. 978 and Soph. *OC* 186~205).

[181] See Dale *LMGD*², 158 (in *MATC*, II, 151 Dale maintains the scansion ‿‿gl^d but accepts for *IA* 793 Erfurdt's emendation ὀλλυμένας against the transmitted οὐλομένας (in this direction see already Weil 1868, 374 and Wecklein 1899, 34; cf. also Kovacs 2002, 250). *Contra* see Comotti 1978, 153.

[182] See similarly also Hermann 1848, 6, who however emended the transmitted ἔρυμα in ῥῦμα.

[183] The erroneous reading τ[αα]ς γας πατριας at l. 10 had previously led some scholars to regard τανύςας (already suspected by Hermann) as a corruption of the alleged τᾶς γᾶς, a process that would have triggered in its turn the substitution of γᾶς with πατρίδος: see in this direction Jourdan-Hemmerdinger 1973, 297, Comotti 1978, 153, Ferrari 1984, 19 and Stockert 1992, II, 428. Provided that at l. 10 of the Leiden papyrus we must read τα]ν̣[υςα]ς and not τ[αα]ς γας πατριας, the participle τανύςας, if spurious, must however have been an ancient interpolation already widespread in the third century BC. If we athetize τανύςας the only means of making sense of the syntax would be that suggested by Ferrari 1984, 20 with n. 5, who interprets εὐπλοκάμου [Duport] κόμας ἔρυμα δακρυόεν as "apposizione 'libera' al colon principale τίς ἄρα μ(ε) . . . ἀπολωτιεῖ."

[184] 9 x: *Med*. 653 (lyr.) ἢ γᾶς πατρίας ςτέρεςθαι (πατρώας V), *Hipp*. 1148 (lyr.) ἐκ πατρίας γᾶς, *Hec*. 946–7 (lyr.) ἐπεί με γαίας‹ ἐκ πατρίας ἀπώλεςεν (γαίας Diggle:

possible to single out some preferential use of γῆ/γᾶ πατρία against πατρίς or γῆ/γαῖα πατρίς,[185] since both expressions are felt to be basically equivalent.[186] Moreover, since we are dealing with an astrophic section, a similar uncertainty of judgment encompasses the metrical level too. Both πατρίδος (LP) and γᾶς πατρίας (P.Leid.) allow plausible metrical scansions of *IA* 792–3 (that is, the segment ἔρυμα— ἀπολωτιεῖ). In fact, with ὀλομένας accepted, the text transmitted by the medieval tradition (that is, ἔρυμα δακρυόεν τανύσασ] πατρίδος ὀλομένας ἀπολωτιεῖ) would present a sequence interpretable as dim cho B| ia∫ δ |, whereas according to P.Leid. (ἔρυμα δακρυόεν τα]|γ[ύσα]ς γᾶς πατρίας ὀλο[μένας ἀπολωτιεῖ) we would have either (1) dim cho B| chol ⁓gl | or (2) dim cho B| 2 δ |,[187] both sequences being perfectly compatible with the aeolo-choriambic context of the second stasimon of *IA*.

What new elements, then, either textual or colometric, does P.Leid. allow us to gain as compared with the manuscript tradition of *IA* 1500?–09 and 784–93? And how are we to interpret these contributions? What conclusions may be drawn in terms of *Textgeschichte* as regards the transmission of *IA* in the third century BC? Let us try to gain some safe point of reference.

First of all, we have seen that the apparently 'irregular' distribution of the line lengths of P.Leid. is not to be traced back to an alleged colometric disposition but must instead be linked to the physical features displayed by the column layout of our papyrus (that is, continuous writing). Thus, the *mise en page* alone of P.Leid. does not entitle us to draw any inference, positive or negative, as regards the

γᾶς codd.; πατρίας Dindorf: πατρωιας fere omnes codd.; see Diggle 1994, 319 and Stinton 1975, 91 [= id. 1990, 123]), *El.* 1315 ἢ γῆς πατρίας ὅρον λείπειν [πατρίας Schaefer: πατρώας L, see Denniston 1939, 73 ad l. 209], *Tro.* 162 (lyr.) πατρίας ἐκ γᾶς (Burges: πατρώ(ι)ας VPQ), 857 (lyr.) ἐλπίδα γᾶι πατρίαι μεγάλαν, *Ion* 483 (lyr.) δορί τε γᾶι πατρίαι φέρει, *Hel.* 522 (lyr.) οὔπω λιμένων| ψαύσειεν πατρίας γᾶς, [*Rh.*] 932 ἀμφὶ γῆν μὲν πατρίαν.

[185] 10 x: *Su.* 1037 ἐς γῆν πατρίδα (Hermann: τὴν L) *HF* 620 γῆς πατρίδος, *Ion* 261 πατρίς γῆ, *Hel.* 16 γῆ μὲν πατρίς, 273 πατρίδος [. . .] γῆς, *Phoen.* 280 γῆ πατρίς, 1738 (lyr.) πατρίδος ἀποπρὸ γαίας, *IA* 1558 πατρίδα τ᾽ ἐξίκοισθε γῆν, [*Rh.*] 869 ὦ γαῖα πατρίς, fr. 696. 1 *TrGF* ὦ γαῖα πατρίς.

[186] Cf. *Tro.* 857 where V has the metrically wrong πατρίδι instead of the correct γᾶι πατρίαι (assured by the responsion with l. 837, that is D + reiz).

[187] See e.g. *IT* 897–8 (πόρον ἄπορον ἐξανύσασ] δυοῖν τοῖν μόνοιν Ἀτρείδαιν φανεῖ) cr| chol 2 δ (differently Dale *MATC*, III, 89, scanning cr | δ | cr| δ; cf. also Sansone 1981, 34).

colometric frame of the two Euripidean excerpts if compared with
the manuscript tradition. As already shown for P.Vind., also in the
case of the Leiden papyrus Fleming-Kopff's hypothesis of a close
relationship between Alexandrian editorial technique and texts carrying musical notation turns out ultimately to be unproven. Secondly,
if there are good reasons for regarding ὀλο[μένας (793), among the
lectiones singulares provided by P.Leid., as linguistically and metrically
preferable to the transmitted οὐλομένας, in the case of γᾶς πατρίας
we cannot rely on sure inner criteria to ascertain whether we are
dealing with the original reading (1), with a merely textual variant
produced by the processes of transmission (2) or with some kind of
textual re-arrangement ascribable to actual performance (3) (which
seems to me in this case the least probable explanation).

Likewise, the fact that the beginning of the second Euripidean
excerpt preserved by the Leiden papyrus coincides with *IA* 784 ff.,
or, to put it differently, the fact that it reproduces only a segment
of the whole epode of the second stasimon of *IA* (that is, ll. 773–800),
does not allow us to draw any further conclusions about the perceived authenticity, in the third century BC, of lines 773–83.[188] In
the light of the anthological nature of P.Leid.[189] we cannot confidently
rule out the possibility of an intentional process of selection.[190]

Thus, while in the case of P.Vind. it is possible to detect some
traces of processes of rhythmic re-adaptation and take a look at the
possible 'openings' of a tradition no longer conceived as a merely
textual vehicle, P.Leid. makes us aware of the unavoidable limits

---

[188] These lines had already been suspected by Hartung; see also Diggle 1994,
503–6.
[189] The anthological features displayed by P.Leid. are unanimously acknowledged
by current criticism on the issue. The only idiosyncratic exception is, to my knowledge, that of Jourdan-Hemmerdinger 1981a, 37, according to whom the verse order
preserved by P.Leid. (that is, ll. 1500–9 before 784–93) represents "en raison de
son ancienneté et de la cohérence de son texte [...] l'ordre authentique" of the
Euripidean text, whereas the medieval tradition would have undergone "un déplace-
ment accidentel." The reason for such an alleged displacement adduced by Jourdan-
Hemmerdinger, that is, the fact that some musical papyri have been written in
reverse order ("tête-bêche"), is in itself implausible.
[190] Which seems indeed to be the case for the first excerpt. In fact, of the long
astrophic section represented by *IA* 1475–531 P.Leid. quotes only the central portion, omitting thus both the Chorus's final words (1510–31) and most likely also
the beginning of Iphigenia's initial monody (for the first excerpt starting possibly at
1491 see above).

inherent in such an inquiry. Some important points have been established (continuous writing, non-colometric layout), but the idiosyncratic
features of P.Leid. do not allow us (at least not they *alone*) to go farther and reconstruct the details of the underlying actual performance.

Once again the resulting scenario turns out to be, both in its documentary evidence and absence of evidence, manifold and pluralistic: we are not faced with an antihistoricist *reductio ad unum* (a
straightforward derivation of Alexandrian colometry from musical
scores) but with an erratic interlacing, separating and crossing again
between textual tradition and performative dimension. Alexandrian
editions and live theatrical performances must have interplayed in
more than a single way,[191] and it is up to us to reconstruct, as far
as possible, the paths of these textual 'journeys'.

II.2.3 *P.Leid. inv. 510: which kind of performance?*
Notwithstanding the inherent limitations pointed out above, it is possible to advance some tentative hypotheses on the possible modes of
performing the two Euripidean excerpts transmitted by P.Leid.
Fortunately, where the philological analysis exhibits its limits, the
comparison with the broader cultural scenario of the Hellenistic entertainment industry briefly sketched in chapter one suggests some possibilities. Evidence like that provided by *SIG*[3] 648B (Satyros of Samos)
and *SEG* XI 52c (Themison of Miletus) allows us in fact to fathom
the flexibility inherent in the processes of re-adaptation of tragic texts
according to defined common practices.[192] In particular, the instance
of *SEG* XI 52c points, most likely, towards a solo performance for
the second excerpt of P.Leid. (that is, *IA* 784–93: originally a choral
astrophic lyric), while the comparison with both *SIG*[3] 648B and Plut.
Crass. 33. 3–6 lets us entertain the possibility of a two-part performance for the first excerpt, in its double amoibaic variant encompassing both a lyric duet between actors (soloist/soloist) or between
actor and secondary Chorus.[193] Although the fragmentary status of

---

[191] See especially Easterling 1997, 225, speaking of "repeated cross-fertilisation
between performance and the production of texts."
[192] See I.9.1.
[193] For a similar case of two-part performance of the astrophic duets drawn from
Eur. *Phoen.* 1530–81 and 1710–36 as preserved by P.Stras.W.G. 307[r] see Fassino
2003, 49 n. 62 (see note 354 in I.9.1).

P.Leid. does not allow one to establish with certainty at what point the first Euripidean excerpt should actually begin,[194] it is hard to avoid the impression that the process of anthological selection has here consciously aimed at a particular goal. Specifically, of the long astrophic section represented by *IA* 1475–531 the Leiden papyrus has selected just those lines which represent not only the most pathetic point of the whole section but also the only part where a lyric exchange takes place between the Chorus and Iphigenia.[195] Of course, the hypothesis of a solo performance also for this first excerpt cannot be completely ruled out. The evidence provided by Ar. *Th.* 101–29 (Agathon singing an astrophic song by imitating the alternating voices of the female chorus-leader and chorus-members) guarantees that already at the end of the fifth century BC an especially skilful actor was able to perform a 'duet' by exploiting vocal mimicry.[196]

The increasing importance of vocal mimicry on the tragic and comic stage at the end of the fifth/beginning of the fourth century BC has recently been stressed by Sifakis 1995 (esp. 21 with n. 37), Vetta 1995, 68–78, Rispoli 1996, 4 n. 6, 6 with n. 19 and above all by Csapo 2002, 135–40 (the most up-to-date survey on the issue; but see also Griffith 2001, 118 and Foley 2003, 5–6). More to the point, Csapo persuasively argues against a persistent trend in recent scholarship which denies that ancient acting

---

[194] For a possible beginning of the first excerpt at *IA* 1491 see above II.2.2. In any case, of the long astrophic section consisting of ll. 1475–531 P.Leid. certainly omitted the Chorus's conclusive lines (1510–31). Even apart from the question where the first Euripidean excerpt should actually begin, the habit usually displayed by anthologies of cutting originally long textual sections suggests that P.Leid. could also have omitted part of Iphigenia's initial monody (1475–99).

[195] From a strictly dramatic point of view this exchange between the Chorus and Iphigenia does not entail an actual dialogical interaction: Iphigenia is completely absorbed in her painful thoughts and thus already entirely detached from the Chorus. Nevertheless just this emotional detachment emphasizes the dramatic pathos of the situation.

[196] As regards the Aristophanic scene of the *Thesmophoriazusae*, it is unnecessary to suppose the presence on stage of an actual chorus. The words delivered by Euripides and Mnesilochus both before and after Agathon's solo performance clearly show that the effeminate tragedian is to be regarded as alone on the stage; see Prato 2001, 169, Csapo 2002, 136–7 and Austin-Olson 2004, 87. Mnesilochus' hesitation in recognizing Agathon οὐκκυκλούμενος (that is, l. 96 καὶ ποῖός ἐςτι;) is not to be interpreted as a clue to the actual presence on stage of more *personae* than Agathon himself. Mnesilochus' difficulty in grasping immediately the tragedian's identity is to be traced rather to Agathon's ostentatiously female garments, cf. *Th.* 97–8 ἀλλ᾽ ἦ τυφλὸς μέν εἰμ᾽; ἐγὼ γὰρ οὐχ ὁρῶ | ἄνδρ᾽ οὐδέν᾽ ἐνθάδ᾽ ὄντα, Κυρήνην δ᾽ ὁρῶ.

involved verbal mimicry, the main representatives of this strand being
Pavloskis 1977, Jouan 1983b and Damen 1989. Csapo correctly points out
that this view greatly overstates the alleged difficulty, on the part of the
audience, of following an actor playing multiple roles. Furthermore, he
makes a strong case against the traditional assumption that "the actor's
interest in winning the competition prevented him from altering his natural speaking voice to suit any particular role." This commonly held opinion turns out to rest on quite feeble ground if we keep in mind that not
the single actor but the entire acting troupe competed for the prize (see
Csapo 2002, 136).[197] In support of Csapo's main argumentation it may be
added that the assumption that, because of the use of masks, actors were
generally identified by the audience by their distinctive vocal tones (which
are to be regarded as substantially unchanging), relies, at least partially, on
a misleading interpretation of Plut. *Lys.* 23. 6 (see especially Jouan 1983b,
74, 76, followed by Damen 1989, 318 with nn. 10, 12 and, more cautiously, by Kaimio 1993, 25 n. 33, 26). This is the text of the Plutarchan
passage: οἷον ἐν τραγωιδίαιϲ ἐπιεικῶϲ ϲυμβαίνει περὶ τοὺϲ ὑποκριτάϲ, τὸν μὲν
ἀγγέλου τινὸϲ ἢ θεράποντοϲ ἐπικείμενον πρόϲωπον εὐδοκιμεῖν καὶ πρωταγωνιϲτεῖν,
τὸν δὲ διάδημα καὶ ϲκῆπτρον φοροῦντα μηδ᾽ ἀκούεϲθαι φθεγγόμενον, οὕτωϲ
περὶ τὸν ϲύμβουλον ἦν τὸ πᾶν ἀξίωμα τῆϲ ἀρχῆϲ, τῶι δὲ βαϲιλεῖ τοὔνομα τῆϲ
δυνάμεωϲ ἔρημον ὑπελείπετο (Plutarch is commenting on the rivalry between
Agesilaus and Lysander on the occasion of the Asian expedition of 396
BC). It is in fact on the basis of this passage that Jouan 1983b, 74 argues
that if the first actors (πρωταγωνιϲταί: cf. also Plut. *Mor.* 816 f.) could perform minor roles successfully, then their being successful onstage (εὐδοκιμεῖν
καὶ πρωταγωνιϲτεῖν) when playing such 'humble' characters "prouve que le
public reconnaissait sous leurs masques la vraie personnalité des acteurs."[198]
This interpretation does not take account of at least two elements: (1) first
of all, the words πρωταγωνιϲτήϲ/-εῖν refer primarily to the dramatic excellence of the performer (which is not dependent on the social status of the
character he embodies on stage), cf. Pickard-Cambridge 1968², 132–3 and
more recently Kaimio 1993, 19–20 with n. 5, 27–8; (2) secondly, the first
actor (πρωταγωνιϲτήϲ), given the convention of playing multiple roles, necessarily acted different characters, some of which were socially eminent
while others were not, but this did not affect his qualification of πρωταγωνιϲτήϲ *tout court.*[199]

---

[197] Cf. also Sifakis 1995, 17–8 on the issue.

[198] The same misleading argumentation is repeated also by Damen 1989, 318 n.
10, who translates the passage οἷον ἐν τραγωιδίαιϲ—εὐδοκιμεῖν καὶ πρωταγωνιϲτεῖν
"in tragedies it happens fairly often that the actor who plays some messenger or
servant is *a well-known protagonist*" (my italics).

[199] As regards the alleged convention of assigning certain roles to the protagonist (e.g. the messenger) and others to the deuteragonist and/or tritagonist (e.g. the
tyrant and so on) see Kaimio 1993, 27–8.

Although both possibilities, the solo and two-part performance, deserve serious consideration and are not to be considered as mutually exclusive,[200] the absence of musical notation above the first excerpt, the one encompassing a dialogic section, can perhaps speak in favor of an amoibaic performance of *IA* 1500?–9. That is, P.Leid. could well be a soloist's score,[201] the copyist (maybe the performer himself?) having written down the musical notation only of the parts he would have performed monodically (that is, the second excerpt).

The existence of selective prompt-books as *aide-mémoires* for both sung and spoken performances is not unparalleled. Notwithstanding remarkable differences (first of all the absence of musical notation) a quite interesting parallel is that provided by P.Oxy. 4546 (first century BC/first century AD), an *Alcestis* papyrus (ll. 344–82) which preserves only Admetus' lines by omitting both the dialogue between Chorus and Alcestis at 369–73 and Alcestis' lines in stichomythia at 375, 377, 379 and 381. As suggested by Obbink in *The Oxyrhynchus Papyri*, LXVII, London 2001, 1, we are probably faced with "a private copy for someone learning his lines in the local play."[202] Granted the substantial differences in terms of diffusion, use and authorial control that apply to operatic scores, a somewhat similar function of didactic support for professionals can be found in modern times in the arrangement of single operatic roles as piano-vocal scores: see the engaging historical survey by Christensen 1999b.[203]

---

[200] The wide range of flexibility of ancient acting and the prompt-book-like nature of musical scores do not allow us to rule out the possibility of a two-part reperformance of what was originally understood as a monody and vice versa.

[201] I owe this suggestion to M.S. Funghi. To assume here a mere negligence on the part of the copyist, and thus a fortuitous break in the process of writing, is of course another possibility, yet the problem would still remain of explaining why the excerpt devoid of musical notation is the first and not the second one.

[202] See recently Marshall 2004 (esp. 30 ff.), establishing a comparison with the use of the so-called 'parts' to be found in the English medieval and renaissance theatre. D.J. Mastronarde points out to my attention that also the so-called *Adulteress* mime on the verso of P.Oxy. 413 seems to be a transcription of just the words of that one role, the / symbols seeminlgy indicating where another performer would speak words omitted by the copyist.

[203] Cf. esp. Christensen 1999b, 76: "such consumers (i.e. of the so-called *partitions reduites*) first arose among those professional singers, conductors, directors, stage designers, and intendants who wanted them for rehearsing and learning parts of opera scores." Of course, these professional customers represent only one recipient of such *partitions reduites* in the eighteenth and nineteenth century, the other great core consisting of the broader world of the private amateurs (mostly middle-class people). This aspect, that is, democratizing opera music by favouring the diffusion of *partitions reduites* is of course totally foreign to the ancient Greek world.

II.3   *Some concluding remarks*

The analysis of P.Vind. G 2315 and P.Leid. inv. 510 confirms the
existence of processes of transmission and reception less strongly consistent and univocal than those reconstructed by Fleming-Kopff. The
scenario which offers itself to our eyes is a manifold and pluralistic
picture, where the continuity is almost never the result of straightforward automatic derivations but the product of a more complicated overlapping of different modes of transmission, the textual and
musical tradition. What we can occasionally glimpse is the accomplished result of this interlacing, very often without the possibility of
recovering the intermediate stages underlying the process.

As we have seen, a telling instance of this cross-fertilization is provided by
the Leiden papyrus, a documentary typology that by its very nature was
potentially liable to a double process of alteration as compared with the
original Euripidean text, since it is first an anthology and secondly also a
musical score conceived for a performance greatly diverging from the 'original' one.[204] Nevertheless, on closer examination this papyrus turns out to
be the only bearer of what is most likely the 'right' reading for the text of
Eur. *IA* 793 (ὀλομέναc vs. οὐλομέναc). In other words, in this case it is a
musical score, that is, a source which does not present itself, at least not
primarily and certainly not only, as merely textual evidence, that alone preserves the correct reading. Once again, the boundaries between *Bühnenexemplare*
and *Lesebücher* are more fluctuating and blurred than suggested by Fleming-
Kopff or, on the opposite side, by Pöhlmann. Points of intersection between
the two traditions, points more or less intermittent and recognizable, must
certainly have existed, even if we cannot trace them back to standardized
protocols once and for all. Every single case will require a minute analysis on its own.

The arbitrariness of the papyrus discoveries has left us only these
two texts carrying musical notation which are susceptible to a comparison with the medieval tradition, yet, if properly investigated, even
this scanty survival is able to rescue from the opacity of a broader
documentary shipwreck some isolated tesserae which enable us to
observe more general dynamics.

But, summing up, what have we achieved? In the case of the
Vienna papyrus, we see that it gives evidence of the existence of

---

[204] The high degree of instability, in terms of textual identity, of a text set to
music (and all the more if of anthological origin) has been stressed by Christensen
1999b, 67–8.

variants most likely to be abscribed to actual performance: the words
δεινῶν πόνων framed by notational clusters; an iambic-dochmiac
rhythm for *Or.* 343–4 λάβροις ὀλεθρίοις ἐν κύμασιν suggesting in its
turn an astrophic performance of the Euripidean text; and perhaps
also the displacement of l. 339 before l. 338. We have also realized
that these variants, if properly contextualized, are not to be judged
only on the basis of strictly Maasian criteria: the renewed Hellenistic
context could in fact entail a whole range of modes of performance
different from those codified by classical theatrical practice. The evidence provided by P.Leid. seems instead to be more silent and elusive: the 'openings' of this 'enlarged tradition' suggested by P.Vind.
are not verifiable here. Yet, also as regards the Leiden papyrus, some
general observations impose themselves. First, the limits pointed out
above in our attempt at interpreting the evidence provided by P.Leid.
are to be regarded primarily as *our* limits, that is, as limits imposed
by the tools we adopt or are forced to adopt. Secondly, given the
documentary gap which has swallowed up most of the Greek musical microcosm, even apparently negative certainties can help us to
match the tesserae of an otherwise entirely lost mosaic. In this specific
case the possibility of reconstructing a new column layout does allow
us to confirm an important point of reference for the tradition of
musical scores, that is, a generally non-colometric disposition of the
lineation. This, in its turn, helps us to rescue Alexandrian critical
editions from the ghost of a straightforward derivation from texts
carrying musical notation.

The lessons conveyed by both P.Vind. and P.Leid, the positive as
well as the negative, are thus mutually complementary and allow us
to cast some new light on the possibilities and limits inherent in the
Hellenistic performance of classical tragic texts. Both aspects belong
to a coherent picture that we have attempted here, although only
partially, to reconstruct.

CHAPTER 3

THE 'OTHER' PATHS OF THE SONG:
THEOCRITUS' IDYLL 29

III. *The 'other' paths of the song: musical mimicry 'without music' in*
Theocritus' Idyll 29

The evidence (literary, epigraphic and papyrological as well) investigated in previous chapters has allowed us to outline, although partially and selectively, some of the main typologies of performance
orienting the re-use of tragic texts within the renewed space, both
public and private, of the Hellenistic entertainment industry. Up to
now, we have examined the jagged archipelago of the fourth/third-
century spectacularity by focusing on the possible re-adaptations of
lyric (tragic) texts conceived from the very outset for an actual
performance.[1] As we have already seen, the processes of re-arrangement can be more or less deep and the resulting degree of 'otherness' of the end-product can range widely in form, content and aim.
Nevertheless, the lowest common denominator underlying such dynamics is the very fact that, no matter how drastic the transformation
may have been, the final product still presents itself as primarily conceived for musical performance.

In the following pages the magnifying glass of our analysis will
instead shift to another apparently less conspicuous typology of literary re-appropriation enacted by the Hellenistic performance culture.
We shall now focus on the reverse process, that is, on the other
major guideline shaping the renewed space of the Hellenistic musical

---

[1] Especially telling, within a broader pragmatic perspective, is the accompanying, widespread trend in Hellenistic times of converting to music texts originally
conceived for a spoken or recitative delivery. Both the increasing display of theatricality and high degree of visual impact that tragic texts, often detached from
their original context, undergo in the Hellenistic period, go along with an ever
increasing sound effect. In other words, at least as regards the forms of entertainment more socially 'open' and less élitist, it is the strand from speech to song that
turns out to be the leading one: see Pretagostini 1998, 625–6, and Rossi 2000a,
154.

microcosm: the guideline leading from song (the glorious heritage of both choral and monodic poetry of the sixth and fifth-century BC) to reading and, presumably, to recitation (lyric lengths re-used in repeated stichic series).[2] The aim here is to cast some new light on the inner dynamics triggered by the absence (an intentional one) of a strictly musical dimension in re-shaping a past poetic tradition where, in contrast, music was still a leading feature.[3]

Many interlocking questions immediately arise. Are we to assume in such an appropriative process a complete effacement of the original musical aspect? Or does the musical dimension inherent in the model (that is, both the instrumental accompaniment and vocal melody), even if it has actually vanished, still somehow affect the authorial memory and inner structure of a poetic text that was by that time conceived for mere reading? And, if so, what devices and what slightly 'perverting' unfaithfulness facilitates this process of re-appropriation of a text already perceived as classic? Or, to put it differently, how can musical mimicry survive 'without music'?[4]

In this connection, an especially interesting sample is provided by Theocritus' *Idyll* 29, a paederastic love song composed in so-called aeolic pentameters (the 'Sapphic fourteen-syllable' of Hephaestion: cf. Sapph. 227 V), that is, a poem which is clearly modelled, both metrically and linguistically (just note the use of the aeolic dialect),

---

[2] A still valuable starting point for understanding the Hellenistic practice of innovating the past poetic tradition by converting lyric verses in iterated stichic series is provided by Leo 1897: see also Rossi 1971, 85–6, 94 n. 92, id. 2000a, 153–4 and Hunter 1996, 4–5. That ancient Greeks were perfectly aware of the 'perverted' nature of this phenomenon (an *abusio*, rhetorically speaking) is clearly shown by Heph. 58, 16 ff. Consbr. (referring in particular to the pherecratean: κατὰ ϲτίχον μὲν ὅϲα ὑπὸ τοῦ αὐτοῦ μέτρου καταμετρεῖται, ὡϲ τὰ Ὁμήρου καὶ τῶν ἐποποιῶν ἔπη· καταχρηϲτικῶϲ δὲ κἄν ὑπὸ κώλου ἢ κόμματοϲ, ὡϲ τὸ Καλλιμάχειον τοῦτο ποιημάτιον [that is, Call. fr. 401. 1–2 Pfeiffer] καταμετρεῖται γὰρ ὑπὸ κόμματοϲ ἀντιϲπαϲτικοῦ, καλουμένου Φερεκρατείου.

[3] For a balanced assessment of the spreading in Hellenistic times of poetical and musical performances investigated in their manifold variants in different social milieus, see against Cameron's challenging overstatement (id. 1995, 44–6, 71–103) Hunter 1996, 3–13 and Bing 2000.

[4] If, as Rossi says, "the very nature of a phenomenon is better recognized while being transformed" (Rossi 2000a, 154: "la natura di un fenomeno la si riconosce meglio nel momento in cui quel fenomeno si trasforma"), then such an analysis may perhaps cast some light also on the starting point of the process examined here, that is, on the original model itself, or, at least, on the ways this model was perceived in Hellenistic times.

on Lesbian monodic lyric and whose subject-matter is largely drawn from widespread τόποι in archaic and classical homoerotic poetry.[5] Hence, at first sight *Idyll* 29 offers itself, among the so-called 'aeolic poems' of Theocritus, as a privileged test-bed for the present inquiry. In fact, although Theocritus' other aeolic poems, that is, *Idylls* 28 and 30,[6] both share the same 'archaeological' exploitation of lyric verses which are basically to be traced back to the same Lesbian tradition (in this specific case, the greater asclepiad, that is, gl^{2c}),[7] *Idyll* 29 is the only one which consciously takes up a metre (that is, gl^{2d}) entirely neglected outside Sapphic and Alcaic tradition.[8] Likewise, also as regards subject-matter, *Idyll* 29 displays an intentionally archaic and archaizing content, reducing to a minimum features and developments peculiar to Alexandrian poetry.[9]

In sum, the uniqueness of the underlying metrical model (the aeolic pentameter), Theocritus' clear intent to re-shape archaic homoerotic poetry (Alcaeus and Theognis) and, above all, the explicitly antiquarian recovery of a tradition perceived as unavoidably lost contribute to making of *Idyll* 29 the most appropriate subject for the present investigation. We shall thus try to verify how such an explicitly declared formal faithfulness to the past lyric tradition can interpret

---

[5] A sophisticated formal analysis of Theocritus' aeolic *Idylls* 28–30 can be found in Pretagostini 1995b, 40–2. For an outline of the intertextual frame sketched by *Id.* 29 and 30 cf. Pretagostini 1997 and above all Hunter 1996, 167–86.

[6] The fragmentary condition of *Idyll* 31, which is composed in aeolic dialect and metre too (most likely in gl^{2c}: the slight emendation of the transmitted]αλλευ at l. 31 to β]άλλεο [Hunt] or ἀγ]άλλεο [Gow] is not problematic) and is preserved only by the Antinoe papyrus codex (= Π³ Gow), prevents us from taking the poem into account for the present survey.

[7] See Pretagostini 1995b, 41–2, Hunter 1996, 172 ff. and Rossi 2000a, 153.

[8] The Hellenistic *Nachleben* of the greater asclepiad (gl^{2c}) has, in contrast, been more successful: see below n. 41.

[9] Pretagostini 1997, 17 has convincingly pointed out the 'double' nature of the archaism underlying *Idyll* 29: "L'*Idillio* 29 si presenta dunque come un componimento di impianto arcaico, sia dal punto di vista strutturale [. . .] sia dal punto di vista dell'impiego di *topoi* e immagini propri della poesia arcaica. Solo in alcuni sporadici particolari affiorano tratti tipici della nuova sensibilità poetica alessandrina o, più precisamente, teocritea." Quite differently, notwithstanding the apparently homogeneous subject-matter (paederastic love), the structural frame of *Idyll* 30 (a solipsistic dialogue between the poet-ἐραϲτήϲ and his own θυμόϲ) clearly reveals the adoption of a genuinely Alexandrian compositional technique; see Pretagostini 1997, 21 and Hunter 1996, 181–6. Similarly, also *Idyll* 28 is to be regarded as "un epigramma dedicatorio di netto stampo alessandrino" (Pretagostini 1997, 42; see also Cairns 1977).

on itself and reflect upon its own performative distance from the model (namely, the absence of music).[10]

III.1 *The Lesbian models of* Idylls *28–30*

The first step to be taken is briefly to survey the literary horizon underlying Theocritus' antiquarian recovery of the past as displayed by his aeolic poems: that is, the tradition of Lesbian monody, where the musical aspect (song and instrumental accompaniment) was inherently linked to the modes of composition and performance of the poetic text itself and to the recipients' experience.

Of course, such an inquiry has to confront the almost complete shipwreck of Greek music at large (and not only of the Lesbian lyric in particular), yet, fortunately, as we shall soon see, the documentary evidence at our disposal (both papyrological and literary) provides us with some indirect conclusions on which to graft further observations with a reasonable degree of confidence. We need to analyze, as far as possible, the very nature of the relationship between the syntactic structure of the poetic text (that is, in our case, the Sapphic and Alcaic odes composed in gl^{2d} and gl^{2c}) and its rhythmic-musical frame (the supposedly recurrent two-line melodic pattern).[11]

---

[10] For Theocritus' *Idylls* as reading texts and recitation as their most likely performative context see Gow 1952, II, 495 and Pretagostini 1995b, 41 n. 26. As regards the long-standing vexed question of the editorial arrangement underlying the Theocritean bucolic collection, see Gutzwiller 1996, esp. 137–9. However, in the past there have been repeated attempts at arguing for an actual musical performance of Theocritus' *Idylls*: cf. e.g. Stark 1963, 380–1 with n. 61, suggesting that *Idylls* 29 and 30 should have been performed to the Hypodoric tune. A balanced assessment of the question (that is, reading as the normal rule, which of course does not exclude the possibility of some isolated lyric performance) can be found in Hunter 1996, 4–6 and id. 1999, 11. What is even more interesting to us is the fact that previous Theocritean scholarship has mostly linked the missing musical performance of the *Idylls* with their stichic nature (that is, the absence of a strophic frame reproducing quasi-stanzaic effects) and, consequently, the fact that this assumption has been indiscriminately applied also to those poems (*Idd.* 28–30) whose relationship with the past lyric tradition is far more explicit. Suffice it here to quote, e.g., Gow's statement (id. 1952, II, 495) "if, as seems likely, T. meant his lyrics [. . .] not for singing but for reading, it is conceivable that he should have deliberately discarded stanza-form as no longer relevant or necessary." Such a biased perspective has prevented scholars from seeing in Theocritus' *Idylls* quasi-strophic effects re-created by means of "a lyric verbal style" (Hunter 1996, 4).

[11] The very nature of such a rhythmic-musical recurrence is of course a much debated issue. The most balanced opinion still seems to be that of Koller 1956, 24–5. It is reasonable to assume that the recurrent musical pattern underlying

We shall try to check to what extent this recurrent melodic pattern may have influenced the syntactic structure of the phrasing at that very crucial boundary represented by the end of one strophe and the beginning of the next. Therefore, once the presence of a structure κατὰ cύcτημα for the Lesbian odes composed in aeolic pentameters and greater asclepiads has been ascertained, at least as far as the fragmentary nature of the texts allows us, we shall focus on the resulting correspondence (or lack thereof) between sense-break at the end of a syntactic segment and metrical pause at period-end.[12] This will allow us to see whether or not the syntactic articulation of these odes reveals a tendency to coincide with a distichic frame, thus avoiding enjambements across stanza-boundaries.

In this latter inquiry, it must be admitted from the outset that the very nature of such an analysis and the scantiness of the evidence we have to rely on do not allow us to go beyond the bare acknowledgment of a preferential trend. In other words, we are not entitled to draw strictly normative conclusions from such data. The criteria here adopted in order to check a possible match between syntactic and distichic units are basically those formulated by Stinton 1977 (= id. 1990, 310–61) for tragic lyric. They allow us to verify whether or not the metrical pause breaks off the syntactic unit understood as articulated in rhetoric cola or sense-groups, which in their turn can be isolated in performance without heavily disrupting the verbal delivery. The choice of Stinton's criteria rather than the more restrictive methods orienting this strand of studies within oral hexametric poetry (see e.g. Higbie 1990) has been determined by the nature of the subject-matter involved: a poetry that still pretends to be lyric without being so any more.

III.1.1 *The Lesbian models: series of gl²ᵈ and gl²ᶜ and strophic structure*
What was, then, the formal structure of Sappho and Alcaeus' odes consisting of series of aeolic pentameters (gl²ᵈ) and greater asclepiads (gl²ᶜ)? Or, to put it better, what did their Greek successors believe it to be? What are the documentary data we may rely on in such an inquiry? Can we grasp some safe point of reference as a basis for further investigations?

---

strophic compositions did not entail an exact and unchangeable reproduction of the very same musical phrase but that we are dealing with something more like a contained improvisation within a standard set of rules to be observed (e.g. the musical mode).

[12] I am using here the term 'period' according to Stintonian criteria, see Stinton 1977, 77 (= id. 1990, 323).

Let us start first with Sappho. Our main source (and unavoidable starting point) is provided by indirect tradition. In fact, as regards the second and third book of the Alexandrian edition of Sappho (books totally consisting of odes, respectively, in gl^{2d} and gl^{2c}),[13] Hephaestion, the metrician, repeatedly testifies to their distichic strophic structure. The passages relevant to our discussion are the following:[14]

> Heph. 59, 7–10 Consbr. κοινὰ δὲ ὅϲα (that is, ποιήματα) ὑπὸ ϲυϲτήματοϲ μὲν καταμετρεῖται, αὐτὸ δὲ τὸ ϲύϲτημα ἔχει πληρούμενον, οἷά ἐϲτι τὰ ἐν τῶι δευτέρωι καὶ τρίτωι Ϲαπφοῦϲ· ἐν οἷϲ καταμετρεῖται μὲν ὑπὸ διϲτιχίαϲ, αὐτὴ δὲ ἡ διϲτιχία ὁμοία ἐϲτί

Those poems are called *koiná* whose metrical unit of reference is a system, and this very system is fully accomplished in itself, as for instance the poems to be found in the second and third book of Sappho. These poems are measured according to a distichic pattern, and the distich itself is of identical parts.

> id. 63, 4–8 Consbr. ϲύϲτημα δέ ἐϲτι μέτρων ϲυναγωγή, ἤτοι δύο ἢ πλειόνων, ἢ ὁμοίων ἢ ἀνομοίων· [. . .] τὸ δὲ ἐξ ὁμοίων, ὡϲ τὸ δεύτερον Ϲαπφοῦϲ, ὡϲ προϊόντεϲ δείξομεν

A system consists of a combination of metra, metra which can be two or more, the same or not the same; [. . .] an instance of a system consisting of the same metrical measures is Sappho's second book, as we shall see later.

> id. 63, 15–24 Consbr. κοινὰ δὲ [ϲυϲτηματικά], ἅπερ καὶ ὁ κατὰ ϲτίχον γεγράφθαι φάϲκων ὑγιῶϲ ἂν λέγοι καὶ ὁ κατὰ ϲύϲτημα, ὡϲ τὸ δεύτερον καὶ τρίτον Ϲαπφοῦϲ. διὰ μὲν γὰρ τὸ ἐν τοῖϲ παλαιοῖϲ ἀντιγράφοιϲ κατὰ δύο ὁρᾶν παραγεγραμμένον ἕκαϲτον ᾆϲμα, καὶ ἔτι διὰ τὸ μηδὲν εὑρίϲκεϲθαι ἀριθμοῦ περιττοῦ, κατὰ ϲυϲτήματα νομίζομεν αὐτὰ γεγράφθαι· πάλιν δὲ, τῶι ὅμοιον ἑκάτερον εἶναι τῶν ἐν τῆι δυάδι ϲτίχων, καὶ τῶι δύναϲθαι τὴν ποιήτριαν κατὰ τύχην τινὰ ἀρτίου πάντα ἀριθμοῦ πεποιηκέναι, φαίη τιϲ ἂν κατὰ ϲτίχον αὐτὰ γεγράφθαι[15]

---

[13] See Heph. 23, 14–6 Consbr. (= Sapph. 227 V) τῶν δὲ ἀκαταλήκτων (that is, δακτυλικῶν) τὸ μὲν πεντάμετρον καλεῖται Ϲαπφικὸν τεϲϲαρεϲκαιδεκαϲύλλαβον, ὧι τὸ δεύτερον ὅλον Ϲαπφοῦϲ γέγραπται and id. 34, 11–3 Consbr. (= Sapph. 229 V) τὸ δὲ ἀκατάληκτον (ἀντιϲπαϲτικὸν τετράμετρον) καλεῖται Ϲαπφικὸν ἑκκαιδεκαϲύλλαβον, ὧι τὸ τρίτον ὅλον Ϲαπφοῦ γέγραπται, κτλ.

[14] All these passages are collected by Voigt in Sapph. 228.

[15] For a critical survey of this third passage see Bohnenkamp 1972, 115 with n. 465. Hephaestion's claims about the distichic nature of the second and third book of Sappho's odes are rather obscurely paraphrased by I. Tzetzes, *De metris Pindaricis* 14. 21–15. 12 Drachmann.

Those poems are called *koiná* which one could equally well say are written stichically and strophically, as for instance the second and third book of Sappho. In fact, since we see that in ancient copies each song is marked by a marginal stroke [i.e. a *paragraphos*] every two lines and since we do not find poems consisting of an odd number of lines, we believe that they are written strophically. On the contrary, since the verses of the couplets are exactly alike and since it might have been a mere accident that the poetess composed only poems consisting of an even number of lines, one could say that they are written stichically.

The reasons that Hephaestion adduces to support a strophic structure of Sappho's aeolic pentameters and greater asclepiads are twofold: the recurrence of *paragraphos* every two lines in ancient copies (ἐν τοῖϲ παλαιοῖϲ ἀντιγράφοιϲ) and the invariably even number of the lines of each ode.[16] Unfortunately, because of the scanty evidence we have to rely on, Hephaestion's second statement is not verifiable any longer, yet the ever increasing contribution offered by papyri discoveries allows us, at least partially, to check the reliability of Hephaestion's first claim, if not within the boundaries of the Sapphic tradition, however within those of Alcaeus'.

In fact, if we turn our attention to Sappho's second book, the only ode in gl²ᵈ preserved to us by direct tradition and which can consequently be taken as a test-bed for our inquiry,[17] is Sapph. 44 V (= P.Oxy. 1232 fr. 1 coll. ii–iii + fr. 2, P.Oxy. 2076 col. ii), which does not in fact present marginal *paragraphoi* marking the strophic boundaries.[18] Nevertheless, as will be argued later, I do not believe

---

[16] As regards the possibility (seemingly a secondary one according to Heph. 63, 22–4 Consbr.) that the even number of lines of Sappho's poems belonging to the second and third book is to be ascribed to a mere accident (κατὰ τύχην τινά), see Bohnenkamp's remark that "er (i.e. Hephaestion) will dabei Zufall gelten lassen; aber die strophische Gliederung ist sicher beabsichtigt; denn sie war ja nur möglich, wenn die Gedichte wirklich aus einer geraden Versanzahl bestanden, und diese wiederum wird nur verständlich, wenn Strophen intendiert waren" (id. 1972, 115 n. 465).

[17] Sapph. 43 V (= P.Oxy. 1232 fr. 1 col. i) escapes this analysis inasmuch as the left margin of the column is completely lost. Equally unverifiable according to our criteria is Sapph. 44Aa V (= P.Fouad 239 col. I), whose authenticity has been variously questioned by modern scholars. Fragmentary as it is, Sapph. 44Ab V (= P.Fouad 239 col. ii), whose Sapphic authorship has also been a matter of debate, shows traces compatible with a scansion in gl²ᵈ but does not present *paragraphoi* (the left margin is preserved). All the other fragments that can confidently be traced back to the second book, that is, Sapph. 45–52 V, are preserved only by indirect tradition.

[18] The only *paragraphos* to be found in Sapph. 44 V (recorded by Lobel-Page

that this datum may be taken as conclusive proof for questioning
the evidence provided by Hephaestion as regards both Sappho's second book in general and Sapph. 44 V in particular, and this even
if we recognize (as we do) the eccentric nature of this last ode within
the extant Sapphic production.

Differently Page 1955, 68–9, who mostly relies on Lobel 1925, xxv ff., singles out as a standard feature of the so-called "abnormal poems" (a critical label relying on a perception of Sapphic poetry partially rejected by
the most up-to-date criticism: see Yatromanolakis 1999, 194 with n. 62 for
bibliography on the issue), and thus also of Sapph. 44 V, a structure organized "not in stanzas or pairs of lines, but with the single line as the unit."
Yet, due attention must be paid first to the fact that Sapph. 44 V is composed in the same measure as the whole second book (which we know to
have been metrically homogeneous: see Sapph. 227 V), and secondly to
the equally important fact that this poem is the very final ode of this book,
as clearly confirmed by the colophon Cαπφο[ῦc μελῶν]/ β̄ [to be found
in P.Oxy. 2076 col. ii, 25–6.[19] Now, although both papyri preserving Sapph.

1955 but omitted by Voigt 1971) is that of P.Oxy. 1232 fr. 1 col. iii, 6, where the
paragraphos is accompanied by coronis and marks the end of the ode. As to the possible editorial nature of P.Oxy. 1232, see below.

[19] In current studies of Sapphic *Textgeschichte* the ongoing debate on the epithalamic nature of Sapph. 44 V is strictly related to the much discussed possibility of
its double classification, on the part of Alexandrian scholars, within both the second book and the so-called 'book' of the *Epithalamians* (the alleged ninth? Cf. Sapph.
234 V): see esp. Page 1955, 125–6, followed recently by Pardini 1991, 261–2. In
particular, according to Page, the alleged book of the *Epithalamians* did not include
all Sappho's epithalamic odes but only those which Page calls "the miscellaneous
remainder," that is, the epithalamians composed in metres other than those included
in the metrically homogeneous books of the Alexandrian edition. Yet Page's label
of "miscellaneous remainders" and the very existence of a separate book inscribed
Epithalamians have strongly been questioned more recently by Yatromanolakis 1999
(esp. 193–4), who has convincingly argued for the possibility that "some of our
papyrus fragments come from 'collected poems' editions that were not direct descen-
dants of the Alexandrian ones" (id. 1999, 183); criticism against the catch-all label
of "miscellaneous reminders" has been expressed also by Ferrari 2003, 56–9. Partially
in the same direction, see also by Pernigotti 2001, 14–20, who, as regards fr. 44
V, has correctly separated the two poles of the debate, emphasizing the possibility
of a non-epithalamic (at least not directly epithalamic) context for Sapph. 44 V and
suggesting that "the ode was conceived for a performance within the Sapphic circle, as both a symbolic and at the same time preparatory representation of the aim
toward which the whole training of the Sapphic school strove: the wedding."
Moreover, Pernigotti has further developed Hunt's suggestion (id. *The Oxyrhynchus
Papyri*, XVIII, London 1927, 50) of regarding the lack of a numeral in the *sub-
scriptio* at col. iii Cαπφ[ο]ῦcι μέλη[as a clue to the anthologic nature of P.Oxy. 1232,
which would have thus contained "a selection from Sappho's work." In fact, according to Pernigotti, P.Oxy. 1232 shows material features which can be fully explained

44 V (that is, P.Oxy. 1232 and P.Oxy. 2076) omit the *paragraphoi*, one may question whether this necessarily entails a different rhythmic-melodic scansion of the poem as a whole. That is, it seems unreasonable to posit, on this basis, an opposition within the same book (the second of the Alexandrian edition) between gl²ᵈ κατὰ cτίχον and gl²ᵈ κατὰ cύcτημα, an opposition which in any case Hephaestion never mentions. Somewhat more cautious in this regard is Bohnenkamp 1972, 114, who, although still recognizing "die stichische, d.h. astrophische Komposition" as "eines der Merkmale der 'abnormen', unter epischem Einfluss stehenden Gedichte" and, thus, also of Sapph. 44 V, claims that with its absence of *paragraphoi* "angesichts der Evidenz der übrigen Beispiele hat dieses Stück in seiner Sonderstellung keine normbrechende Bedeutung" (see esp. id. 1972, 114 n. 463). Moreover, it may be worth noticing that Bohnenkampf's statement that P.Oxy. 1232 untypically omits *paragraphoi* for Sapph. 44 V, while it "sonst durchgängig Paragraphen schreibt" (id. 1972, 114), is misleading. P.Oxy. 1232 preserves only Sapph. 43–44 V, and we have already seen that as to Sapph. 43 V the presence (or absence) of the *paragraphos* is a datum that cannot be positively recovered (see above n. 17) since the left margin of the column is lost. In other words, we cannot rule out *a priori* the possibility that this papyrus omitted indiscriminately *all* the *paragraphoi* (that is, also those of poems other than Sapph. 44 V), and this quite apart from the contrived label of the "abnormal poems" (for a similar omission and discontinuity in the use of *paragraphoi* see e.g. P.Oxy. 2165 for Alc. 129 and 130 V). Furthermore, an additional distinction is to be drawn as regards the different typologies to which P.Oxy. 1232 and P.Oxy. 2076 belong. Whereas P.Oxy. 2076 does represent a philologically accurate product (cf. the presence, however problematic, of marginal scholia) and thus its lack of *paragraphoi* is somewhat puzzling, the seemingly derivative nature of P.Oxy. 1232 (likely a Sapphic anthology: see Pernigotti 2001, 12–3) makes the absence of *paragraphoi* marking stanza-end less startling.

Similarly, also as regards Sappho's third book we are not able to draw a direct comparison between Hephaestion (arguing for a distichic structure of the odes composed in gl²ᶜ) and the editorial practice attested by papyri, inasmuch as all the fragments which can be

---

only within the hypothesis of an anthological nature and the difference between the two final subscriptions of P.Oxy. 2076 col. ii and P.Oxy. 1232 col. iii "probably allows us to posit a clear-cut splitting of the textual tradition, a twofold path which, although displaying just minor—but significant—textual divergences, testifies to a more complicated situation than that which looks at the Alexandrian tradition as the single monopolizing point of reference for the history of the text." Cf. also the anthological nature of Sapph. 103 V as argued by Yatromanolakis 1999, 190–2 (a selection of *incipits* from Book 8); on the debated editorial nature of the 'new Sappho', whether anthological or not, see Gronewald-Daniel 2004a, 2 and more compellingly Luppe 2004.

confidently traced to the third book (that is, Sapph. 53–7 V) are preserved exclusively by the indirect tradition.[20]

The Sapphic tradition thus seems to lead us to a documentary impasse, but the Alcaic tradition gives us a valuable aid in this regard. An important indication of the reliability of Hephaestion's claims about the distichic structure of Sappho's odes belonging to the second and third book is provided by the occurrence of *paragraphos* every two lines in some Alcaic odes composed in the same metres. These poems are respectively Alc. 38a V for gl²ᵈ,[21] Alc. 50 and most likely also 44 V[22] for gl²ᶜ. Thus, for Alcaeus, the direct tradition provides us with positive instances testifying to a distichic structure for those odes composed in the same metres as Sappho's second and third book.

If we turn our attention, still within the boundaries of Lesbian lyric, to those poems composed in metres other than gl²ᵈ and gl²ᶜ but still consisting of dactylic or choriambic expansions, we gain the following data. The occurrence of *paragraphos* every two lines can be found also in some poems transmitted by P.Oxy. 1787 and by other fragments to be traced back to the same papyrus roll: these poems are usually ascribed to the alleged fourth book of Sappho as reconstructed by Page 1955, 114–5 on the basis of Heph. 36, 13 ff. Consbr. (= Sapph. 154 V *apud* test. I). Although no ancient source explicitly specifies the metrical composition of the fourth book, this would seem to consist, at least partially, of two-line stanzas of greater parasclepiads (^hipp²ᶜ || ^hipp²ᶜ |||), a metre certainly attested by P.Oxy. 1787 (cf. e.g. Sapph. 58 and 81 V). The poems that are provided with *paragraphoi* are Sapph. 59, 62, 63, 67a, 82b V, to which we can add also some minor fragments omitted by Voigt, that is, P.Oxy. 1787 frr. 21–5, fr. 35 col. ii (cf. *The Oxyrhynchus Papyri*, XXI, 136), P.Oxy. 2166 (d) fr. 9a (cf. *ibid.*, 138). However, it is worth remembering that the alleged fourth book of Sappho seems to have contained also three-line stanzas consisting of two

---

[20] As to Sapph. 57 V Di Benedetto 1982, 13–6 correctly claims that only ll. 1 and 3 can actually belong to the third book, since the quotation of Maximus of Tyrus (that is, l. 2 τίς δὲ ἀγροΐωτιν ἐπεμμένα ϲτόλαν) shows, *pace* Blomfield, a metrical shape which cannot be assimilated to gl²ᶜ without being seriously emended (Di Benedetto *ibid.*, 16 argues for a dactylo-epitritic scansion). Nothing certain can be said about Sapph. 120 and 150 V, whose metre remains uncertain. Finally, ll. 2, 8 and 9 of Sapph. 103 V (= P.Oxy. 2294) also escape our inquiry since they are quotations of the beginnings of various odes entirely lost to us. For the most probable reconstruction of ll. 14–7 of P.Oxy. 2294 see Yatromanolakis 1999, 188–92.

[21] The only other evidence of an Alcaic compositions in gl²ᵈ preserved, at least partially, by direct tradition is Alc. 141 V, whose fragmentary status does not allow one to verify the presence (or not) of *paragraphoi*.

[22] While the positive presence of marginal *paragraphoi* every two lines guarantees

greater parasclepiads followed by a lesser asclepiad ($\wedge$hipp^{2c} || $\wedge$hipp^{2c} || $\wedge$hipp^c |||): among the instances quoted by Voigt 1971, 97, the most convincing are Sapph. 65, 86 and 88 V. As regards Alc. 48 V (= P.Oxy. 1233 fr. 11) and 61 V (= P.Oxy. 2166 (c) 42), both of them composed in greater parasclepiads, nothing can be said about the presence of *paragraphoi* since the left margin of the column is lost.

Finally, in the 'new Sappho' recoverable from the two Köln papyri (= P.Köln inv. 21351 + 21376, early third century BC) most recently published by Gronewald-Daniel (iid. 2004a and 2004b), we find the remnants of two poems (the second one apparently preserved in its full length: see now West 2005) in two-line stanzas of greater parasclepiads marked off by *paragraphos* and the beginning of a new one in a different metre. As regards the second of the poems in greater parasclepiads, strophic and syntactical boundaries coincide.

As to the Alcaic poems composed in lesser asclepiads (gl^c), the presence of a strophic structure or, on the contrary, of an inner organization κατὰ cτίχον is even more difficult to evaluate. The only certain instance transmitted by the direct tradition, that is, Alc. 112 V (= P.Berol. 9569 col. i, 1–18 + P.Aberd. 7), is unfortunately of no help: the left margins of both papyri are lost. It is however telling that both Alc. 113 and 114 V show almost constantly marginal *paragraphos* every two lines: although the metre cannot be established with absolute certainty, the material contiguity of these fragments, both of them transmitted by P.Berol. 9569 too (col. ii, 1–9 and col. ii, 10–23), with Alc. 112 V (= gl^c) suggests that also for them we are dealing with series of gl^c.[23]

Summing up, if we focus on Lesbian poems consisting of series of aeolic pentameters and greater asclepiads, the evidence provided

---

a distichic frame for Alc. 44 V, its metre cannot be recovered beyond doubt because of its fragmentariness. Yet, on the basis both of the textual supplements accepted by Voigt and of the fact that P.Oxy. 1233 preserves also other sure instances of odes in gl^{2c} (e.g. Alc. 50 V), to suppose for Alc. 44 V a metrical frame consisting of iterated greater asclepiads strophically organized seems to be the most reasonable hypothesis. The interpretation of Alc. 34A, 39 and 120 V (that is, the remaining possible instances of Alcaic odes in gl^{2c} preserved by direct tradition) is even more uncertain: to the impossibility of ascertaining the metron (gl^{xc}) must be added also the loss of the left margin of the column.

[23] See also Bohnenkamp 1972, 117. Differently, Barabino 1978, 165 argues also for a clearly stichic use of gl^c in Alcaeus: yet, to quote only one instance among others, Alc. 50 D.^{2}= Alc. 350 V (cited by ead. 1978, 165 n. 13) cannot be assumed as positive evidence for such a hypothesis since it is transmitted by indirect tradition.

by both direct and indirect tradition (respectively, the papyri of Alcaeus and Hephaestion on Sappho) complement each other. It thus seems reasonable to assume that the second and third book of the Alexandrian edition of Sappho and Alcaeus' poems composed of series of gl^{2d} and gl^{2c} alike[24] did actually display a distichic strophic structure.[25]

III.1.2   *The Lesbian models: syntactic structure and distichic articulation in odes composed of series of gl²ᵈ and gl²ᶜ*

The two-line strophic pattern underlying such poems should certainly entail also a performative counterpart. If we turn our attention to the merely musical aspect, the distichic pattern framing the odes should most likely mean that the melody accompanying these strophic couplets repeated itself, with a limited set of variations, every two lines. This practice, for obvious material reasons, cannot be verified any longer, but the recurrent nature of the melodic phrasing should certainly orient the audience towards a proper understanding of the strophic structure of the poem in performance. What the evidence at our disposal does, however, allow us to verify with a reasonable degree of confidence is, as we have mentioned before, whether this practice has left behind any textual traces. The next step to be taken, then, is to investigate whether or not the syntac-

---

[24] The Alexandrian edition of Alcaeus' odes, as already acknowledged by Bergk, was arranged according to thematic and not metrical criteria: see recently Pardini 1991, esp. 265–84.

[25] Modern misunderstandings about the distichic nature of Sappho and Alcaeus' odes composed in series of gl^{2d} and gl^{2c} mostly go back to Leo's authoritative statement that "Die einzigen nach einem hellenistischen oder allenfalls in die hellenistische Epoche zu ziehenden Dichter benannten Masse, die nachweislich nicht von diesem Dichter zuerst stichisch verwendet worden sind, sind die Asclepiadeen, die beide bei Alkaios (und Sappho) stichisch auftreten" (id. 1897, 68–9. Leo *ibid.*, 69 extends this stichic use also to the Lesbian poems gl^{2d}). In this regard see also recently Pretagostini 1995b, 42 n. 29. It is, however, worth noticing that Leo's usage of the term "stichisch" seems to denote, more than once (or not only) a specifically astrophic structure κατὰ ϲτίχον but, perhaps somewhat imprecisely, a generic iterated repetition of the same metrical measure. Finally, we must keep in mind that at that time (1897) the papyrological evidence was still to come. As regards then Lobel's peculiar position in this regard (id. 1925, xvi: that is, his belief in the presence of a "four-lined stanza" in Alcaeus' odes in gl^{2c} on the basis of the biased assumption that "the four-lined stanza was a fundamental element in Alcaeus's method of composition"), the feeble documentary ground of his reconstruction has convincingly been shown by Bohnenkamp 1972, 115–6 and n. 468 (some isolated clue in this direction can be found already in West 1967, 84 n. 3; see below).

tic articulation of odes composed of series of gl²ᵈ and gl²ᶜ reveals an underlying tendency to coincide with a distichic strophic structure, or, to put it differently, whether or not there is enjambement across stanza-boundaries.[26]

Let us start again with the Sapphic tradition. As regards the second book of the Alexandrian edition (gl²ᵈ), the only poem susceptible to such an inquiry (that is, a poem that provides us with a sufficient number of lines)[27] is the well-known Sapph. 44 V. This is the text of the fragment as edited by Voigt:

Κυπρο.[−22−   ] αϲ·
κᾶρυξ ἦλθε θε[− 10 −]ελε[. . .]. θειϲ
Ἴδαοϲ ταδεκα. . .φ[. .]. ιϲ τάχυϲ ἄγγελοϲ
3ᵃ   <"   >
      τάϲ τ᾽ ἄλλαϲ ᾽Αϲίαϲ.[.]δε, αν κλέοϲ ἄφθιτον·
5   Ἔκτωρ καὶ ϲυνέταιρ[ο]ι ἄγοιϲ᾽ ἐλικώπιδα
      Θήβαϲ ἐξ ἰέραϲ Πλακίαϲ τ᾽ ἀπ᾽ [ἀϊ]ν⟨ν⟩άω
      ἄβραν ᾽Ανδρομάχαν ἐνὶ ναῦϲιν ἐπ᾽ ἄλμυρον
      πόντον· πόλλα δ᾽ [ἐλί]γματα χρύϲια κἄμματα
      πορφύρ[α] καταΰτ[με]να, ποίκιλ᾽ ἀθύρματα,
10   ἀργύρα τ᾽ ἀνάριι.θμα ιποτή.ρια. κάλέφαιϲ".
      ὢϲ εἶπ᾽· ὀτραλέωϲ δ᾽ ἀνόρουϲε πάτ[η]ρ φίλοϲ·
      φάμα δ᾽ ἦλθε κατὰ πτόλιν εὐρύχορον φίλοιϲ.
      αὔτικ᾽ Ἰλίαδαι ϲατίναι[ϲ] ὑπ᾽ ἐυτρόχοιϲ
      ἆγον αἰμιόνοιϲ, ἐπ[έ]βαινε δὲ παῖϲ ὄχλοϲ

---

[26] As to the admissibility, in Lesbian lyric, of enjambements across stanza-end, see Slings' rather negative conclusions (Slings 1991): his analysis is however restricted to three-line and four-line stanzas. In fact Slings explicitly excludes from his survey "poems consisting of stanzas with two identical lines in papyri" (ibid. 408 n. 19). As regards then two-line strophes composed in metrically different lines, Slings 1991, 405 observes anyway that "Alcaeus' two-line stanzas seem to form a class of their own (of Sappho's two-line stanzas too little is left), which behaves exactly like the two- and three-line stanzas of iambus (i.e. epodes) and elegy of this period." The issue had previously been tackled, although marginally, also by Gow 1952, II, 495 (surprisingly enough, as regards the "metres in which the lines are uniform throughout" Gow quotes as instance of enjambements across stanza-end Sapph. 69 D.², that is, Sapph. 67 V. Yet, the words οὐ μάν at l. 4 can well be considered as the beginning of a syntactically self-contained distich and the same can be said for τὸ δ᾽ αἴτιον at the outset of l. 6).

[27] In Sapph. 44Aa V the papyrus has punctuation marks at the end of ll. 7, 8, 10, 11 and 12; yet the fragmentary condition of the ode, together with the impossibility of establishing its beginning and/or end, does frustrate any attempt at further evaluations. Equally unverifiable are Sapph. 43 and 45–52 V (both Sapph. 48 and 50 V could be a syntactically self-contained distich but, since we are not able to assess where the stanza should end, we cannot draw any inference on the issue).

15   γυναίκων τ᾽ ἄμα παρθενίκα[ν] τ . . [. .]. cφύρων,
     χῶρις δ᾽ αὖ Περάμοιο θυγ[α]τρες[
     ἵππ[οιc] δ᾽ ἄνδρες ὔπαγον ὐπ᾽ ἄρ[ματα
     π[   ]εc ἠίθεοι, μεγάλω[c]τι δ[
     δ[   ]. ἀνίοχοι φ[. . . . .].[
20   π[᾽]ξα. ο[
     ⟨   desunt aliquot versus   ⟩
                                        ἴ]κελοι θέοι[c
                                        ] ἄγνον ἀολ[λε
     ⌊ὄρμαται⌋[   ]νον ἐc Ἴλιο[ν
     ⌊αῦλοc δ᾽ ἀδυ[μ]έληc⌋[   ]τ᾽ ὀνεμίγνυ[το
25   ⌊καὶ ψ[ό]φο[c κ]ροτάλ⌋[ων   ]ωc δ᾽ ἄρα πάρ[θενοι
     ⌊ἄειδον μέλοc ἄγγ⌋[ον, ἴκα]νε δ᾽ ἐc αἴθ[ερα
     ⌊ἄχω θεcπεcία γελ⌋[
     ⌊πάνται δ᾽ ἦc κὰτ ὄδο⌋[ιc
     ⌊κράτηρεc⌋ φίαλαί τ᾽ ὀ⌋[. . .]υεδε[. .] . . εακ[.]. [
30   ⌊μύρρα κα⌋ὶ καcία λίβ⌊ανόc τ᾽ ὀνεμείγνυτο
     ⌊γύναικεc δ᾽ ἐλέλυcδο⌋ν ὄcαι προγενέcτερα[ι
     ⌊πάντεc δ᾽ ἄνδρεc ἐπήρατον ἴαχον ὄρθιον
     ⌊πάον᾽ ὀνκαλέοντεc⌋ Ἐκάβολον εὐλύραν
     ⌊ὔμνην δ᾽ Ἔκτορα κ᾽Α⌋νδρομάχαν θεο⟨ε⟩ικέλο[ιc. ⊗

Cypros [. . .] the herald came [. . .] Idaeus [. . .] swift messenger [. . .]
"and of the rest of Asia [. . .] undying fame. (5) Hector and his companions are bringing the lively-eyed one, graceful Andromache from
holy Thebe and ever-flowing Placia in their ships over the salt sea;
(conveyed) by the breath of the wind are coming[28] many golden bracelets
and purple robes, ornate trinkets and (10) countless silver drinking-
cups and ivory." So he spoke; and nimbly his dear father leapt up,
and the news went to his friends throughout the spacious city. At once
the sons of Ilus yoked the mules to the smooth-running carriages, and
(15) the whole crowd of women and (tender?-) ankled maidens climbed
on board. Apart the daughters of Priam [. . .] and unmarried men
yoked horses to chariots, [. . .] and greatly [. . .] charioteers [. . .] (20)
[. . .] like gods (21) [. . .] holy, all together (22) [. . .] set out [. . .] to
Ilium (23), and the sweet-sounding pipe and (cithara?) were mingled
(25) and the sound of castanets, and maidens sang a (high pitched)
holy song, and a marvellous echo reached the sky [. . .] and every
where in the street was [. . .] bowls and cups [. . .] (30) myrra and cas-
sia and frankincense were mingled. The elder women cried out joy-
fully, and all the men let forth a lovely high-pitched strain calling on
Paean, the Archer skilled in lyre, and they sang in praise of the god-
like Hector and Andromache.' (Campbell 1990, 89–91 adapted)

---

[28] Following Lobel' suggestion I read at l. 9 κὰτ ἀύτμενα: see Ferrari 1986, 446–7
n. 7.

Even though we cannot establish any longer the precise position within the original poem (whether the very beginning, some lines after the *incipit*, or in the middle) of 'our' first lines and even though the exact width of the gap at ll. 21 ff. cannot be recovered, the coronis preserved by both the papyri (= P.Oxy. 1232 col. iii and P.Oxy. 2076 col. ii) guarantees that l. 34 of Voigt's edition actually was the last line of our poem. Following Stinton's criteria, we can gain the following data about enjambement:

l. 1:   P.Oxy. 1232 has high stop at the end of the line: it is reasonable to assume here a sense-break.

ll. 2–3:   the segment introducing the messenger speech seems to be a syntactically self-contained distichic.

ll. 3ᵃ-10:   The direct speech of the messenger encompasses 8 lines. The first two lines (3ᵃ–4)²⁹ consist of a semantically independent segment (the papyrus bears high stop at the very end of l. 4). In the following lines the adoption of a more dilated tempo and rhythm of writing, quite in keeping with the strongly narrative feature of the poem, blurs the boundaries of the three distichs (ll. 5–10) by means of two enjambements: the first one, less strongly emphasized, at ll. 6/7, the direct object of the participle ἄγοις' (l. 5), that is, Andromache, having already been anticipated by ἐλικώπιδα;³⁰ the latter at ll. 8/9, with the noun separated from the attribute (κάμματα| πορφύρ[α]). The direct speech ends at l. 10 (high point after κἀλέφαιc in the papyrus).

ll. 11–12: the papyrus has high stop both at the end of l. 11 and of l. 12. Nevertheless, a 'distichic' structure seems to be intentionally sought by the quasi-rhyme effect φίλοc ~ φίλοιc.

ll. 13 ff.: the description of the Trojans' reaction to the arrival of Andromache rests on a binary frame: ll. 13–16 focus on the women's reaction: see the enjambement, however not especially marked,³¹ at ll. 14/15 (ὄχλοc| γυναίκων τ' ἄμα παρθενίκα[ν] τ . . [. .]. cφύρων). Ll. 17 ff. record the men's reaction.

ll. 23–30: this section seems to be more complicated. The serial paratactic co-ordination, a distinctive feature of Sappho's poetry (see

---

²⁹ I assume here, together with Page 1955, 63, the omission of only one line of text; see also Grenfell-Hunt, *The Oxyrhynchus Papyri*, X, London 1914, 48.

³⁰ See Slings 1991, 408 n. 15: "It seems more in line with Sappho's practice to take 44, 5–7 ἐλικώπιδα . . . ἄβραν Ἀνδρομάχαν not as a case of hyperbaton of attribute and Head but of apposition ('the round-eyed one, [. . .] dainty Andromache'; so Page 1955, 64) [. . .] appositions behave more freely in terms of word order than attributes."

³¹ The genitives governed by ὄχλοc occupy the length of a full verse: they have, in terms of Stinton's criteria, a remarkable rhetorical weight.

already ll. 8–10), is intermingled with a series of enjambements which disrupt the boundaries of the distichs. It is difficult to avoid the impression of being faced here with highly sophisticated enjambements, resulting from a deliberate expressive choice: see the enjambement at ll. 24/5 (ὀνεμίγνυ[το]| καὶ ψ[ό]φο[ϲ κ]ροτάλ[ων), ψ[ό]φο[ϲ κ]ροτάλ[ων being the third subject governed by the verb ὀνεμίγνυ[το] (the previous two subjects—the second lost in the gap—have already been expressed in the preceding line); and at ll. 26/7 (ἴκα]νε δ᾽ ἐϲ αἴθ[ερα]| ἄχω θεϲπεϲία). A similar instance of enjambement separating the verb (to be supplemented in the gap of l. 28) from the subjects of l. 29 (κράτηρεϲ φιάλαί τ᾽) is likely also at ll. 28/9: the general syntactic trend of the ll. 23 ff. and Sappho's fondness for polysyndetic co-ordination by means of the postpositive δέ[32] strongly suggest that we posit in the lacuna of l. 28 the verb governing κράτηρεϲ φιάλαί τ᾽ of the following line. For similar reasons it seems to me more probable to assume enjambement (this time not across stanza-end, but within the boundaries of the distich) at ll. 29/30 (with μύρρα as subject of a preceding finite verb) rather than to posit a threefold subject governed by the single verb ὀνεμείχνυτο at l. 30. In the latter case the polysyndetic co-ordination would be disrupted and we should assume asyndeton between ll. 29 and 30.[33]

ll. 31–4: the last four lines of the poem consist each of a syntactically autonomous segment and can most likely be traced back to two self-contained distichs (that is, ll. 31–2, 33–4).[34]

Summing up, although Sapph. 44 V seems indeed to reveal an underlying distichic pattern, equally self-evident are the frequent violations of this binary frame by means of enjambements.[35] We cannot

---

[32] See ll. 24 αὖλοϲ δ᾽ ἀδυ[μ]έλης, 25]ωϲ δ᾽ ἄρα πάρ[θενοι, 26 ἴκα]νε δ᾽ ἐϲ αἴθ[ερα, 28 πάνται δ᾽ ἦϲ, and perhaps also 29 ὀ[...]υεδε[(ὀ[νέθυ]ε δὲ [πόϲ]ϲακ[ιϲ] suppl. Körte e.g.), 31 γύναικεϲ δ᾽ ἐλέλυϲδον, 32 πάντεϲ δ᾽ ἄνδρεϲ, and 34 ὔμνην δ᾽ Ἔκτορα.

[33] It seems thus more reasonable to regard καί at l. 30 as co-ordinating two clauses and not two nouns (that is, μύρρα καὶ καϲία).

[34] According to Stinton's criteria, the syntactic autonomy of ll. 33–34 remains unchanged whether we understand the problematic ὔμνην at l. 34 as a third person plural imperfect (see Hamm 1958², 163), or as an epexegetic infinitive governed by ἴαχον in l. 32 (see Snell 1931, 73 n. 1 and 368).

[35] For a different approach to this topic see A.C. Volgers 1997 (MA thesis at the Vrije Universiteit of Amsterdam, still unpublished. The title is the following: *Wat is daarop uw antwoord? Zes studies naar het hoe, wat en waarom van Sapph's fragment 44*), adopting a strictly pragmatic perspective. According to what is reported by Slings 1999, 67 (= id. 2000, 120), the only enjambement Volgers accepts for Sapph. 44 V is that of ll. 7/8 ἐπ᾽ ἄλμυρον| πόντον.

thus find a consistent and systematic coincidence between syntactic structure and distichic scansion.

A similarly heterogeneous picture emerges if we cast a glance at Sappho's odes in greater asclepiads (gl^{2c}). The only extant fragments which belong to Sappho's third book and which can be taken as a test-bed for our inquiry are Sapph. 55 and 56 V. The former seems to lead to the same conclusions as Sapph. 44 V (we have enjambements at ll. 1/2, 2/3 and 3/4),[36] while in Sapph. 56 V there is only one enjambement at ll. 2/3.[37]

A parallel survey of the Alcaic tradition offers similar results. Among the odes composed of series of gl^{2d} the only extant fragment which is long enough to allow such an investigation, that is, Alc. 38a V, has enjambement across stanza-end at ll. 2/3 and most likely also at ll. 8/9,[38] whereas as regards the odes in series of gl^{2c} we have a lack of coincidence between syntactic structure and distichic unit in Alc. 50, ll. 2/3, 4/5 V[39] and 346, ll. 4/5 V.[40]

---

[36] 1/2 μναμοϲύνα ϲέθενl ἔϲϲετ', 2/3 βρόδωνl τὼν ἐκ Πιερίαϲ, 3/4 ἀλλ' ἀφάνηϲ κἀν Ἀίδα δόμωιl φοιτάϲηιϲ. This fragment is preserved only by indirect tradition. The ways in which ancient authors quote it (that is, Plutarch, Stobaeus and Clement of Alexandria), together with the adversative tone (κατθάνοιϲα δὲ κείϲηι) of what represents *our* beginning of Sapph. 55 V, seem to suggest that the text we know should not coincide with the actual beginning of the ode. Yet, the very fact that in Sapph. 55 V we can find enjambements both between even and odd lines, allows us to claim that in any case, wherever the original boundaries of the strophe could be, there was not a straightforward coincidence between syntactic structure and distichic frame.

[37] 2/3 ἔϲϲεϲθαι ϲοφίαν πάρθενον [. . .]l τεαύταν. The rhetorical weight of the participial clause προϲίδοιϲαν φάοϲ ἀλίω suggests that we consider it a syntactically self-contained sense-group.

[38] The object governed by ζάβαι[ϲ (l. 3) is most likely to be supplemented at the end of l. 2. For the possibility of supplementing the gap of l. 8 with a finite verbal form whose subject would be Κρονίδαιϲ βα[ϲίλευϲ (l. 9), see Page 1955, 301. In the case of Alc. 38a V the *paragraphos* and coronis to be found in P.Oxy. 1233 fr. 1 col. ii ll. 7/8 assure us that we are dealing with the actual beginning of the ode.

[39] See πωνώντων, κάκα[at l. 3 (the papyrus, that is, P.Oxy. 1233 fr. 32 l. 4, has high stop after πωνώντων) and ἀ]νθ[ρ]ώπων, ὁ δὲ μὴ φ[at l. 5 (this time the papyrus does not bear punctuation mark after ἀ]νθ[ρ]ώπων, but the postpositive δέ makes clear that we are dealing with a new syntactic clause). Luckily enough, also in this case the material data at our disposal (remnants of coronis legible in P.Oxy. 1233 fr. 32 l. 3: see Grenfell-Hunt, *The Oxyrhynchus Papyri*, X, London 1914, 70) guarantee that κὰτ τὰϲ πολλὰϲ κτλ. at l. 1 is the real first line of the poem.

[40] 4/5 ἔγχεε κέρναιϲ ἔνα καὶ δύοl πλήαιϲ κὰκ κεφάλαϲ. The fragment is preserved only by indirect tradition. The initial exhortation and the way Athenaeus quotes the Alcaic passage seem, however, to suggest that we have the actual beginning of

Therefore, on the basis of the data collected here, in Sappho and Alcaeus' odes consisting of series of gl^{2d} and gl^{2c} we can see at work a rather clear-cut tendency to avoid a mechanical coincidence between sense-break at stanza-end and distichic boundaries. This lack of a systematic correspondence favours an ongoing alternation and variety of the poetic rhythm without jeopardizing at the same time the strophic nature of the poems themselves. In other words, a straightforward, rigorous correspondence between strophic unit and syntactic structure does not seem to have been an absolute leading feature of archaic Lesbian lyric, at least not in the poems consisting of series of gl^{2d} and gl^{2c}. The recurrent nature of the musical accompaniment was most likely a sufficient aid for orienting the audience to a comprehension of the strophic structure of the odes in performance.

III.2 *Aeolic pentameters and greater asclepiads: looking for a tradition*

Now that we have ascertained the distichic structure underlying Sappho and Alcaeus' odes in gl^{2d} and gl^{2c} and have cast a glance at the possible 'openings' and boundaries that such a strophic performance could enact in organizing the poetic text from within, the next step before focusing on a direct comparison between Theocritus' aeolic poems (*Idylls* 28–30) and Lesbian monodic lyric is to verify the precise nature of the model re-created by Theocritus himself. To put it better: did some other authoritative tradition apart from Sappho and Alcaeus exist which could have influenced, from a metrical point of view, the Syracusan poet in his archaeological recovery of the past? And, if so, is there any difference, in terms of further success and diffusion, between aeolic pentameters and greater asclepiads?

---

the ode. As to Alc. 44, 6/7 V (see above n. 22), the presence or not of enjambements across stanza-end depends on the supplement we accept for l. 6. With Wilamowitz's Νά[ϊδα the following syntagm νύμφ[αν ἐνν]αλίαν could be regarded as an apposition and thus it would not disrupt the syntactic unity of the preceding couplet. Differently, if we accept Page's νά[ϊδ᾽ ὑπερτάταν (id. 1955, 281), the adjective ὑπερτάταν must be linked with the following νύμφ[αν ἐνν]αλίαν, that is, we should assume here enjambement (Page translates "the Naiad, queen of the Nymphs of the sea"). The same can be said also as regards Diehl's Να[ϊάδων. Equally uncertain is the case of Alc. 348 V. Since we cannot determine either the beginning or the end of the ode, it is not possible to establish whether the enjambement at ll. 2/3 (πόλιος τὰς ἀχόλω καὶ βαρυδαίμονος ἐστάσαντο τύραννον) falls within the strophe or across stanza-end (at ll. 1/2 the name Φίττακον is to be regarded as apposition to the preceding τὸν κακοπατρίδα⟨ν⟩: see Stinton 1977, 32 = id. 1990, 317).

That is, what survival or oblivion, what process of re-writing did these metres undergo after the Lesbian experience? Which frame of reference must be assumed as the most likely for a poet like Theocritus?

A fully detailed diachronic analysis of the literary genealogy of these verses, together with a wide-ranging survey of the diffusion of dactylic and choriambic expansions in aeolic metres, has already been provided elsewhere:[41] suffice it here to mention briefly the main guidelines in order to provide the reader with a concise overview of the phenomenon.

A first basic distinction allows us, from the very beginning, considerably to restrict the range of the data to be investigated in mapping the literary pedigree of *Idylls* 28–30: that is, we must distinguish between lyric texts in which 'expanded' aeolic metres are embedded in a properly polymetric frame (choral lyric, drama) and those consisting entirely of series of gl^{2d} and gl^{2c}.

If we keep in mind this typological distinction, the first (metrically homogeneous) instances we can find after the Lesbian experience are the greater asclepiads of the late-archaic 'sympotic chain' transmitted by Athen. 15. 694c ff., that is, *PMG* 897, 902–5 and 908.[42] All these skolia consist of two lines, *PMG* 903 partially excepted, since the scholium to Ar. *Th.* 529 quotes, among the songs ascribed to Praxilla (τῶν εἰϲ Πράξιλλαν ἀναφερομένων), also a monostichic version of this (*PMG* 750). How is this two-line length to be regarded? Should we assume that these skolia still reflect, in some way, in the inner organization of their contents a somewhat blurred consciousness

---

[41] See Fassino in Fassino-Prauscello 2001, 19–32. As to the criteria orienting such an investigation, that is, the exclusion from the label 'dactylic expansions' of those cases, especially frequent in Attic drama, where we have dactyls ending with a cretic or trochaic foot (i.e. series like - ⌣ - - - ⌣ . . . - ⌣ - or even the hypercatalectic variant - ⌣ ⌣ - - ⌣ . . . - ⌣ - ⌣ -) which were as correctly regarded by Theocritus as real dactylic measures (that is, without aeolic base) see Fassino *ibid.*, 26–9. That Theocritus did not perceive these dactylic series as properly aeolic is clearly confirmed by *Epigr.* 20. 2. The instance of Arch. 190 West² allowed him in fact to let the sequence Μήδειοϲ τὸ μνᾶμ' ἐπὶ τᾶι ὁδῶι κἠπέγραψε Κλείταϲ (l. 2: 4da⁻ ⁻| ith |||) respond with ὧν τὸν κῶρον ἔθρεψε· τί μάν; ἔτι χρηϲίμα καλεῖται (l. 4: 4da⁻⁻| ith |||).

[42] Both *PMG* 897 (the well-known 'skolion of Admetus' quoted also by Ar. *V.* 1238) and 903 (the skolion of 'the scorpion') bear a text mostly overlapping with *PMG* 749–50, traditionally ascribed to Praxilla of Sicyon (cf. respectively the scholium to Ar. *V.* 1239, Eust. *ad Il.* 326, 38–9 = I, 509 ll. 12–3 van der Valk as to *PMG* 749 and the scholium to Ar. *Th.* 529 as to *PMG* 750).

of the distichic nature of the Lesbian couplets? Most probably the right explanation is to be sought elsewhere. Paying attention to the distinct communicative media underlying sympotic songs may lead to the opposite conclusion. In fact, it seems more reasonable to assume that the concise, semantically self-contained nature of these two-line skolia is the result of broader practical reasons ascribable to the performative context itself (that is, the symposium). Furthermore, it is worth noticing that 'our' skolia (that is, the skolia as we have them) strongly tend to structure each line as an autonomous rhetorical colon or sense-group:[43] it is thus more appropriate to speak of monostichs as a standard unit of reference.

After the Attic skolia, we must wait till the Hellenistic age before finding other songs consisting only of iterated gl^{xc}:[44] the only extant fragment in 'expanded' glyconics ascribed to Asclepiades of Samos, that is, *SH* 215 ἀφεγγέϲϲι φαείνοιϲα κέλευθον αὖ (= Trichas 6 ap. Heph. 390. 2 Consbr.: gl^c, a lesser asclepiad[45]) is of uncertain authorship but the very name of the colon strongly suggests that Asclepiades was, if not the first, at least the most important Alexandrian poet who composed poems in this measure κατὰ ϲτίχον.[46] Apart from Asclepiades' own poetic production (almost completely lost to us),[47] in Hellenistic times there are, as far as we can see, the following instances of metrically homogeneous series of glyconics with choriambic expansions, presumably conceived κατὰ ϲτίχον:

Callim. fr. 400 Pfeiffer[48]	gl^{2c} | gl^{2c}
Simias of Rhodes, *CA*, p. 114, fr. 16	$hipp^{2c}$

---

[43] For one of the (very few) exceptions to this rule see e.g. the enjambement in *PMG* 908 μεγάλην ἔχει| τιμήν.

[44] Although no certainty can be obtained about the original context, the hypothesis of a song composed entirely in greater asclepiads for Phryn. *TrGF* I 3 F 6 gl^{2c}? gl^{2c} || gl^{2c} seems quite unlikely. Moreover, Phrynichus' first two asclepiads are linked by verbal synaphia, which does not happen to be the case for the Attic skolia.

[45] The term 'greater asclepiad' is of relatively late coinage: according to ancient metricians, the only 'true' Ἀϲκληπιάδειον was the 'lesser,' whereas the 'greater' was usually named Ϲαπφικὸν ἑκκαιδεκαϲύλλαβον (isolated exceptions in this regard are Diom., *GL* I, 527. 19 Keil, Mar. Plot., *GL* VI, 536. 23 ff. and 539. 4 Keil). See West 1982, 192 s.v. Asclepiad.

[46] See Leo 1897, 68–9.

[47] Theocritus certainly knew it, see the praise of Asclepiades in *Id.* 7. 39–41.

[48] For the likely paederastic overtone of Callimachus' propemptic fragment see Hunter 1996, 173.

Seleucus, *CA*, p. 176   gl²ᶜ | gl²ᶜ
Ps.-Stesich. *PMG* 278[49]   gl²ᶜ | gl²ᶜ

As often happens, what strikes one most in this picture is a conspicuous absence, namely that of gl²ᵈ. For series of gl²ᶜ, Theocritus
could rely, for *Idd.* 28 and 30, also on a tradition other than Lesbian
lyric, that is, on models he could perceive as chronologically closer
to him and his world (we should say more 'modern'), models which
converted to a stichic use a lyric measure previously organized strophically in the Lesbian experience. Quite differently, such an alternative and, in a sense, rival tradition for the aeolic pentameters (gl²ᵈ)
seems to have been non-existent, at least as far as the evidence at
our disposal allows us to verify.[50]

The 'antiquarian' recovery of an otherwise 'lost' metre (gl²ᵈ) displayed by Theocritus in *Idyll* 29 seems thus to be the result of a
self-aware marginal experiment within the Hellenistic literary scenario, at least from a reader-oriented perspective.[51] In fact, whether
we adopt a synchronic or diachronic view, Theocritus' actualization
of the past presents itself as an isolated exception, as an attempt at
re-vitalizing and at the same time, in a sense, creating a literary
'ghost' tradition. Not only Alexandrian poets, that is, the cultural
environment representing the most direct addressees and reader

---

[49] The authorship of this fragment has been a matter of debate since antiquity:
see Strab. 8. 3. 20 καὶ ἡ ᾽Ραδίνη δὲ [εἰϲ] ἣν Ϲτηϲίχοροϲ ποιῆϲαι δοκεῖ. Rose 1932
traces the fragment back to the Hellenistic period on the basis of both content and
metre; Page (*PMG*) and Davies (*PMGF*) consider the fragment spurious. For a real
Stesichorean authorship see *contra* Lehnus 1975 and D'Alfonso 1994, 89–103 (more
cautious Cassio 1997, 209).

[50] The only instance, at least to my knowledge, of 'isolated' gl²ᶜ ascribed to the
Hellenistic period, that is, the anonymous *PMG* 979 (= *SH* 1001), cannot be assumed
as a certain example inasmuch as it is the result of a highly hypothetical textual
emendation. The codd. bear in fact τὸ δὲ ἐκ Ϲαπφοῦϲ (-ῶϲ) ἀμελγόμενοϲ φέρω
μέντοι, emended by Ahrens in ἐκ Ϲαπφῶϲ τόδ᾽ ἀμελγόμενοϲ μέλι τοι φέρω. It is
indeed symptomatic that West suggested a Theocritean authorship for this line (West
in *SH*, 517, app. ad loc.). Nor can *PMG* 989 be listed beyond doubt among the
aeolic pentameters (notwithstanding West 1982, 150 n. 27). It seems indeed more
economical to regard it as a 'pure' dactylic pentameter: cf. Mar. Plot., *GL* VI, 510,
25 ff. Keil *metrum integrum pentametrum dactylicum, quod semper quinque dactylis constat* and
Bergk's remark that "Grammaticus cum dicit quinque dactylis versum constare, non
ex Aeolico poeta petivisse censendus est, sed fortasse ex heroico versu hunc pentametrum detruncavit" (id., *Poetae Lyrici Graeci*, Lipsiae 1914⁴, III, 726 ad fr. adesp.
119).

[51] For a balanced theory of reader-constructed authorial intention see Hinds 1998,
47–51.

communities of Theocritus' works, seem to have completely neglected
the dactylic expansions of aeolic metres in favour of the choriambic
ones, but between Sappho and Alcaeus' experience and Theocritus'
Idyll 29 there are three centuries in which Greek poets (and consequently their on-going self-reflexive construction of a literary archaic
past to be perceived and thus canonized as such) seem to have forgotten Lesbian aeolic pentameters.[52] Partial and, in a sense, subjective as every teleological literary history can be, in this very case the
absence of intermediate stages *en route* to Theocritus' *Idyll* 29 lets us
focus once again, and perhaps in an unusually concentrated way,
on Sappho and Alcaeus' poems consisting of series of gl.^{2d}

III.3   *Theocritus'* Idyll *29 between past and present: letting words sound
their 'music'*

The quite different, if not opposite, *Nachleben*, in terms of reception
and further poetic tradition, of poems consisting entirely of iterated
gl^{2d} and gl^{2c} can in fact allow us to cast some new light on a feature which up to now has usually been neglected by modern scholarship on the issue. In other words, this underlying different tradition
may turn out to be a valuable aid in analysing the inner structure,
in terms of stichic articulation or not, of *Idylls* 28, 30 (in gl^{2c}) on the
one hand and *Idyll* 29 (gl^{2d}) on the other. Indeed, having specified
the nature (and relative boundaries) of the possible models underlying Theocritus' aeolic poems, if we now focus on the extent to which
Idylls 28–30 tend to re-create the distichic (that is, strophic) frame
of the corresponding Sapphic and Alcaic poems,[53] we can gain quite

---

[52] The declining fortune of the aeolic pentameter *vs.* the increasing success of the
greater asclepiad has been emphasized also by Pretagostini 1995b, 41–2.

[53] The criteria here adopted are obviously the same as for Sappho and Alcaeus:
we shall look for correspondence (or lack of such) between sense-break at the end
of a syntactic segment and metrical pause at period end, focusing especially on
stanza-boundaries. This approach thus differs from that adopted by Hunter 1996,
174–5, who, while recognizing that in Sappho and Alcaeus' odes "sense-breaks do
not, however, necessarily correspond with any division into distichs or quatrains,
any more than there is a necessary sense break at the end of a stanza in the stanzaic poems," yet in his detailed analysis of *Idylls* 28–30 adopts as the only valid
criterion the syntactic unit, regarded as a self-contained item which cannot be dis-
mantled into minor rhetoric cola. In other words, Hunter does not verify whether
metrical pause infringes (or not) the minor sense-groups which can be isolated within
the syntactic unit.

a consistent picture. As we shall soon see, in *Idylls* 28 and 30, viz in poems for which Theocritus could resort *also* to models other than Lesbian lyric (just think of Asclepiades' contemporary practice of converting gl,[2c] that is a metre originally conceived to be sung, into a stichic-recitative measure), we can easily detect a clearly stichic use of the greater asclepiad. Differently, if we turn our attention to *Idyll* 29 (in gl[2d]), a metrical fossil whose only poetic antecedent is to be sought in the Aeolic monodic tradition, we can actually discover traces, faint as they may be, of a distichic (read strophic) inner organization.[54]

The present inquiry overlaps here the broader, long-lasting and much-debated issue of the admissibility of the so-called "hunt for strophes" (*Strophenjagd*) in Theocritus' poems and of the textual implications that such an approach entails: for a balanced survey of the terms of the question see Rossi 1971, 85–6, 94 n. 89 and id. 2000a, 152–3. What is worth stressing in our particular case is the difference, in terms of genre label, between *Idylls* 28–30 and Theocritus' extant hexametric production. As already pointed out by Wilamowitz 1906, 137–41, the legitimacy of looking for a "strophische Gliederung" in Theocritus' aeolic παιδικά is guaranteed by their very models (Lesbian lyric), models that explicitly entailed as a norm the presence of a strophic structure, which cannot be said for the Theocritus' remaining hexametric *Idylls* (see also Gow 1952, II, 16 n. 2). Some of the most recent critics on the issue have instead claimed the presence of "quasi stanzaic effects" also for Theocritus' hexametric poems: see e.g. Hunter 1996, 155–6 as regards *Idyll* 18.[55]

In particular, as regards the possibility of mapping *Idylls* 28–30 into a distichic frame, Gow 1952, II, 495 has come to rather negative conclusions, at least for *Id.* 28. In fact, Gow, who still depends largely on Lobel's argumentation (id. 1925, xvi), does not entirely rule out the possibility of some kind of strophic articulation for *Idylls* 29–30, but he loosely speaks of "four-lined stanzas" on the basis of Alcaeus' alleged predilection for such a metrical scheme. Yet, both West 1967, 84 n. 3 and Bohnenkamp 1972, 115–6 have convincingly shown the feeble documentary ground for Lobel's hypothesis.[56]

---

[54] This is of course not to deny Theocritus any creative impulse: on the contrary, as it shall be argued later, this declared faithfulness to the tradition can take place only at the cost of a subtle perversion of the model.

[55] For a different approach see e.g. Rossi 2000b, 176–7 and 2000c, who, precisely on the basis of the strophic 'disguise' to be found in *Idyll* 8 (a device created by alternating hexameters and elegiac couplets), suggests regarding this poem as an "apocrifo preterintenzionale."

[56] Specifically, according to Lobel, the stichic structure displayed by *Idyll* 28 is presumably to be ascribed to the fact that copies of Sappho available to Theocritus somehow did not present marginal *paragraphoi*. Yet, such an alleged rigid dichotomy,

Finally, on the basis of the odd number of lines of *Id.* 28 and, on the contrary, of the even number of both *Idylls* 29 and 30, West has suggested that Theocritus might have become aware of the distichic nature of the Lesbian poems in gl²ᵈ and gl²ᶜ "within the period covered by these poems" (West 1967, 82–4). Yet, West's argument that the scansion ὑπ' ἀπάλω of *Idyll* 28. 4 can be regarded as the conclusive proof that "when he wrote 28, Theocritus did not know the rare pyrrhich form of the Aeolic base, and was misled by a Sapphic case of it [that is, Sapph. 94. 22 V ἀπάλαν] into committing a false quantity" is unconvincing. Only a few lines before, viz in Sapph. 94. 16 V, we find indeed the scansion ἀπάλαι (assured by the metre). It seems thus quite unlikely that Theocritus was actually unaware of the pyrrhic base of Sapph. 94. 22 V.

But let us focus directly on the texts. As regards the metrical structure in which the greater asclepiads of both *Idylls* 28 and 30 can be mapped, we are clearly faced with a stichic re-use of a lyric metre, and the contemporary example of Asclepiades' experimentalism may be considered to have been authoritative.[57] In fact, the stichic structure of *Idyll* 28 is assured by both the odd number of lines[58] and inner distribution of enjambements, which are to be found indifferently at the end of the odd and even lines alike.[59] Likewise, the irregular presence of enjambements scattered throughout *Idyll* 30[60] suggests a stichic structure underlying the whole poem.[61]

---

in pre-Alexandrian editorial practice, between the text of Sappho (without *paragraphoi*) and that of Alcaeus (carrying *paragraphoi*) is an unproven assumption that lacks any documentary support: see now the two Köln papyri (early third century BC) of the 'new Sappho' exhibiting *paragraphoi* at stanza end. Furthermore, to posit implicitly for Theocritus such a mechanical dependency on material data means ultimately to deny him any awareness of the strophic nature of Lesbian lyric *tout court*.

[57] See Gow 1952, II, 495 and Pretagostini 1995b, 42 with n. 28.

[58] Repeated attempts at forcedly reducing *Idyll* 28 to an even number of lines by means of unnecessary atheteses have rightly been criticized by Gow 1952, II, 498 *ad* l. 4 (see already Wilamowitz 1906, 137).

[59] Respectively ll. 1/2 δῶρον[. . .]Ι γύναιξιν, 15/16 οὐ γὰρ εἰς ἀκίρας οὐδ' ἐς ἀέργω[. . .]Ι [. . .] δόμοις, 19/20 πόλλ' ἐδάη ςόφαΙ [. . .] φάρμακα, and 12/13 διὲ γὰρ μάτερες ἄρνων μαλάκοις [. . .] πόκοιςΙ πέξαιντ' αὐτοέτει.

[60] Enjambements at the end of odd lines: 3/4 ἀλλ' ὅποςον τῶι πόδι περρέχειΙ τᾶς γᾶς, 29/30 ταῦτα γὰρ ὦγαθοςΙ βόλλεται θέος. Enjambements at the end of even lines: 20/21 γλυκέρας ἄνθεμον ἄβας πεδ' ὑμαλίκωνΙ μένει, 26/27 τοὶς ὑπὲρ ἀμμέωνΙ [. . .] ἄςτερας.

[61] See already Wilamowitz 1906, 137, according to whom "Da lässt sich nun das 30. zwar durch zwei dividieren, aber die Sätze und Gedanken fügen sich einer Gliederung in Disticha durchaus nicht." More recently cf. also Hunter 1996, 175 and 181, claiming that as regards *Idyll* 30 "here the case is less clear than with

Remarkably different, however, is the inner structure displayed by
Idyll 29, whose only model, in terms both of metre and poetic tradition, is to be sought in the corresponding Sapphic and Alcaic production. This is the text of *Idyll* 29 as edited by Gow:

'Οἶνος, ὦ φίλε παῖ,' λέγεται, 'καὶ ἀλάθεα'·
κἄμμε χρὴ μεθύοντας ἀλάθεας ἔμμεναι.
κἄγω μὲν τὰ φρένων ἐρέω κέατ' ἐν μύχωι·
οὐκ ὄλας φιλέην μ' ἐθέληςθ' ἀπὺ καρδίας.
5   γινώςκω· τὸ γὰρ αἴμιςυ τὰς ζοίας ἔχω
ζὰ τὰν ςὰν ἰδέαν, τὸ δὲ λοῖπον ἀπώλετο·
κὤταν μὲν ςὺ θέληις, μακάρεςςιν ἴςαν ἄγω
ἀμέραν· ὄτα δ' οὐκ ἐθέληις ςύ, μάλ' ἐν ςκότωι.
πῶς ταῦτ' ἄρμενα, τὸν φιλέοντ' ὀνίαις δίδων;
10   ἀλλ' αἴ μοί τι πίθοιο νέος προγενεςτέρωι,
τῶι κε λώιον αὖτος ἔχων ἔμ' ἐπαινέςαις.
πόηςαι καλίαν μίαν ἐνν ἔνι δενδρίωι,
ὄππυι μηδὲν ἀπίξεται ἄγριον ὄρπετον.
νῦν δὲ τῶδε μὲν ἄματος ἄλλον ἔχηις κλάδον,
15   ἄλλον δ' αὔριον, ἐξ ἀτέρω δ' ἄτερον μάτης·
καὶ μέν ςευ τὸ κάλον τις ἴδων ῥέθος αἰνέςαι,
τῶι δ' εὐθὺς πλέον ἢ τριέτης ἐγένευ φίλος,
τὸν πρῶτον δὲ φίλεντα τρίταιον ἐθήκαο.
†ἄνδρων τὼν ὑπερανορέων δοκέης πνέην·
20   φίλη δ', ἆς κε ζόης, τὸν ὕμοιον ἔχην ἄει.†
αἰ γὰρ ὦδε πόηις, ἄγαθος μὲν ἀκούςεαι
ἐξ ἄςτων· ὁ δέ τοί κ' Ἔρος οὐ χαλέπως ἔχοι,
ὃς ἄνδρων φρένας εὐμαρέως ὑπαδάμναται
κἄμε μόλθακον ἐξ ἐπόηςε ςιδαρίω.
25   ἀλλὰ πὲρρ ἀπάλω ςτύματός ςε πεδέρχομαι
ὀμνάςθην ὅτι πέρρυςιν ἦςθα νεώτερος,
κὤτι γηράλεοι πέλομεν πρὶν ἀπύπτυςαι
καὶ ῥύςςοι, νεότατα δ' ἔχην παλινάγρετον
οὐκ ἔςτι· πτέρυγας γὰρ ἐπωμαδίαις φόρει,
30   κἄμμες βαρδύτεροι τὰ ποτήμενα ςυλλάβην.
ταῦτα χρή ςε νόεντα πέλην ποτιμώτερον
καί μοι τὠραμένωι ςυνέραν ἀδόλως ςέθεν,
ὄππως, ἄνικα τὰν γένυν ἀνδρείαν ἔχηις,
ἀλλάλοιςι πελώμεθ' Ἀχιλλέιοι φίλοι.

Idyll 29, and the chance that the observable structuring is accidental correspond-
ingly greater. This may add something to the case for at least caution in the matter of this poem's authenticity." Actually, the unhomogeneous grouping suggested
by Hunter for *Idyll* 30 (that is, a quatrain, followed by three distichs, a monostich,
three couplets again, a six-line stanza and finally a monostich) can be seen as a
different version of the irregular syntactic frame outlined above.

35 αἰ δὲ ταῦτα φέρην ἀνέμοιϲιν ἐπιτρέπηιϲ,
ἐν θύμωι δὲ λέγηιϲ 'τί με, δαιμόνι᾿, ἐννόχληϲ;'
νῦν μὲν κἀπὶ τὰ χρύϲια μᾶλ᾿ ἔνεκεν ϲέθεν
βαίην καὶ φύλακον νεκύων πεδὰ Κέρβερον,
τότα δ᾿ οὐδὲ κάλεντοϲ ἐπ᾿ αὐλείαιϲ θύραιϲ
40 προμόλοιμί κε, παυϲάμενοϲ χαλέπω πόθω.

In vino veritas, dear lad, as the saying goes; I am in my cups,
So I too must speak the truth. I shall tell you my inmost thoughts:
You will never love me with all your heart. I know this is true;
Your beauty gives meaning to half my life, while the other half is
Nothing. When you are good to me, I spend my day among the
   blessed,
But when you are not I'm plunged in darkness. Is this fair, to make
Your lover miserable? You are young, so listen to an older man;   10
When you see the benefit of my advice, you will thank me.
Keep to a single tree, and make one nest in it, where no wild
Creeping thing can reach you. You perch on one branch today,
And another tomorrow, always looking for the next place to lodge.
If someone sees your handsome face and praises it, you make him
There and then a lifelong friend, while you treat your first lover as   20
Yesterday's man. You have grown too arrogant; the best rule is to
Stick to your own kind. This is the way to win respect in the town,
And moreover Love will treat you well—Love, which crushes
Men's hearts with ease, and has enfeebled even my iron will.
I beg you, by your soft mouth, to remember that one year ago
You were younger. Wrinkled old age creeps up on us more quickly
Than we can spit, and youth wears wings upon its shoulders—
Once lost, it cannot be recalled. We are not quick enough to capture
Things that fly. Consider this, be good to me, and love me equally   30
Without guile. Then, when your cheeks begin to show the beard
Of manhood, we can be friends, as Achilles was to Patroclus,
But if you cast my words to the winds, and say in your heart
'Stop! Why must you keep pestering me?', though now I'd go
And fetch you the golden apples, or bring back Cerberus, guardian
Of the dead, that would mean an end to my painful passion: I'd not
Come to my house door to see you, even if you summoned me   40
(Verity in Verity and Hunter 2002, 81–2)

A close examination of the overall distribution of enjambements
in *Idyll* 29 reveals a consistent and regular match between syntactic structure and distichic scansion, inasmuch as all the enjambements to be found in this paederastic poem invariably occur at the
end of the odd lines. In other words, we find enjambements only
within the boundaries of the supposed couplets and never across

stanza-end.[62] The only instance of enjambement at the end of an even line, and thus across stanza-end, would be that of ll. 28/29 νεότατα δ' ἔχην παλινάγρετον| οὐκ ἔcτι. Yet even in this case, the considerable length of the infinitive phrase, which is expanded to the point of occupying almost an entire line, its inverted order as compared with the main clause and, last but not least, its semantic pregnancy within the ideological frame of the poem make it reasonable to ascribe to the syntagm νεότατα δ' ἔχην παλινάγρετον, by Stinton's criteria, a remarkable 'rhetorical weight', that is, a significant syntactic autonomy.[63]

In other words, in *Idyll* 29 each rhetoric colon which turns out to be isolable within a major sense-group is never infringed by a rhythmic pause. Even when Theocritus introduces a syntactically self-contained line (e.g. πῶc ταῦτ' ἄρμενα, τὸν φιλέοντ' ὀνίαιc δίδων; l. 9), which might be regarded as a potential exception disrupting the distichic frame of the poem,[64] his taste for variety does not go so far as to break, from a rhythmic point of view, the syntactic unit of the underlying rhetorical cola. On the contrary, the very observance of this rule makes it possible for the potentially dangerous monostich to be fully re-absorbed, from l. 18 onwards, in the previous binary pattern.[65]

---

[62] See ll. 5/6 τὸ γὰρ αἴμιcυ τὰc ζοίαc ἔχω| ζὰ τὰν cὰν ἰδέαν, 7/8 μακάρεccιν ἴcαν ἄγω| ἀμέραν, 21/22 ἄγαθοc μὲν ἀκούcεαι| ἐξ ἄcτων, 37/38 νῦν μὲν κἀπὶ τὰ χρύcια μᾶλ' ἕνεκεν cέθεν| βαίην, 39/40 ἐπ' αὐλείαιc θύραιc| προμόλοιμί κε.

[63] See Stinton 1977, 31 (= id. 1990, 315–6).

[64] "A powerfully rhetorical monostich" according to Hunter 1996, 174.

[65] Differently Hunter 1996, 174–5, who sees at work in *Idyll* 29 an irregular alternation of one-line, two-line, three-line, four-line and six-line stanzas reproducing "the small verse-groupings of Lesbian lyric" (according to Hunter, the precise order of these groupings in *Idyll* 29 would be respectively four couplets, a monostich, three couplets, a triplet, then textual uncertainty at ll. 19–20, and finally again a quatrain, followed by a six-line stanza and by five distichs). Yet, such an irregular atomization of the text does not pay due attention to the specific nature of the underlying model, at least as regards *Idyll* 29: that is, not Lesbian lyric *tout court* but the Sapphic and Alcaic poems consisting of series of gl[2d] structured according to a distichic strophic pattern. A previous attempt to interpret *Idyll* 29 strophically (with results not very diverging from Hunter's) can be found also in Beckby 1975, 521: "Idyll XXIX ist z.T. strophisch gegliedert. Vers 1–8 sind zwei vierzeilige Strophen, auf die (mit 9) ein Einzeiler als den ersten Teil abschliessende Fermate folgt. Genau das gleiche wiederholt sich in den nächsten neun Versen (10–18). Daran setzt sich eine Strophe aus drei Distichen (19–24). Der Rest ist durchkomponiert."

The validity of the data here collected as regards the distribution of enjambements across stanza-end in *Idyll* 28–30 seems to be indirectly confirmed
also by a close examination of the other strophic structures to be found in
Theocritus' epigrams. In the epigrams susceptible to such analysis, that is,
in those which exhibit an inner strophic articulation, Theocritus shows a
strong tendency to avoid enjambements across stanza-boundaries.[66] These
are the resulting data. As regards the epigrams composed in elegiac couplets (*Epigr.* 1–16, 23, [25–27]), the only enjambements to be found across
stanza-end are those of *Epigr.* 4 ll. 6/7 and 8/9. In *Epigr.* 17 (couplets consisting of 3ia ‖ phal ‖‖) there are no enjambements. In *Epigr.* 18 (4tr^ ‖
reiz ‖ 3ia ‖ reiz ‖‖ 4tr^ ‖ reiz ‖ 3ia ‖ reiz ‖‖ 4tr^ ‖˘ ˘ reiz ‖‖) we
find enjambements at ll. 1/2, 3/4, (at l. 7 the text is uncertain), that is,
only within stanza-boundaries. The same can be said for both *Epigr.* 20
(distichs consisting of phal ‖ 4da ǀ ith ‖‖), where there is enjambement
only at ll. 1/2, and *Epigr.* 21 (three-line stanza: 4da ǀ ith ‖ 3ia ‖ 3ia^
‖‖), where the only enjambement we have is at ll. 2/3.

How are we then to explain Theocritus' conspicuous consistency in
structuring distichically the textual and syntactic frame of *Idyll* 29?[67]
Or, to put the question at its strongest, how should we interpret, at
least from a reception-oriented perspective, this phenomenon, which,
if compared with the stichic frame of *Idylls* 28 and 30, turns out to
be, paradoxically enough, a rhythmic hypercorrection (avoidance of
enjambements between distichs) so inherently 'unfaithful' to the true

---

[66] As to the presence of elegiac couplets in *Id.* 8, 33–60 see Rossi 2000c. Theocritus'
Epigr. 19 (four choliambs, presumably structured κατὰ cτίχον according to the
Hipponactean model) and *Epigr.* 22 (a series of eight phalaecians whose distichic
nature is far from certain) have been excluded from the present survey. For these
epigrams see Gow 1952, II, 541 n. 1 and Gow-Page 1965, II, 533. Rossi 2001
does not address the question of the stichic or distichic nature of *Epigr.* 19 and 22.

[67] The evidence here analyzed strongly suggests that Theocritus had a clear awareness of the structure κατὰ cύcτημα of the Lesbian poems in series of gl[2d] (and, most
likely, also of those consisting in series of gl[2c]: but as regards *Idylls* 28 and 30 the
contemporary experience of Asclepiades was likely more influential): see also Hunter
1996, 5–6 and more generally 155 with n. 60 on Theocritus' understanding of the
stanzaic nature of archaic lyric. The sympotic 'fortune' of Lesbian monodic lyric
seems, on the other hand, to have been quite long-lasting: still at the time of Aulus
Gellius we are told about a dinner-party organized by an ambitious young *eques*
where Sappho's songs were sung, cf. Aul. Gell. *Noct. Att.* 19. 9. 4 *ac posteaquam intro-
ducti pueri puellaeque sunt, iucundum in modum* Ἀνακρεόντεια *pleraque et Sapphica et poetarum quoque recentium* ἐλεγεῖα *quaedam erotica dulcia et venusta cecinerunt* (see also Cameron
1995, 83–4). There is thus no reason, at least not theoretically, for ruling out *a
priori* the possibility that Theocritus could derive his awareness also from such sympotic performances. It is then worth noticing that the two early third-century BC
papyri of the 'new Sappho' (= P.Köln inv. 21351 + 21376) have the two-line stanzas of greater parasclepiads already marked off by *paragraphos*.

poetic practice displayed by Sappho and Alcaeus' poems in gl^{2d}, which tends to avoid a mechanical coincidence between strophic unit and syntactic structure? Could all this be just a mere accident? The uniqueness of the models underlying Theocritus' antiquarian experiment, together with the high degree of inner consistency, in terms of distichic articulation, displayed by *Idyll* 29, seems to point strongly in a different direction.

The most likely (and economical) reason for this straightforward systematization, on the part of Theocritus, of what was just a merely preferential trend in Sappho and Alcaeus is first to be sought, I believe, in the different nature of the modes of performance and reception of the poetic text here at stake. In Lesbian monodic lyric, that is, in a product conceived, from its very outset, for an actual performance circumscribed in space and time, a performance whose musical dimension (vocal and instrumental alike) was a basic and essential feature, the strophic unit was most likely underlined above all by the recurrent melodic pattern. Quite differently, when the 'old' traditional literary genres became outdated and obsolete inasmuch as they are too linked to the single cultural occasion which could not be reproduced any longer in the renewed Hellenistic microcosm,[68] or, to put it better, in the very moment when the only conceivable form of survival for a lyric which proudly claims its modernity is its conversion into a 'reading text', the only tools Theocritus can still rely on to re-create without music (and make perceivable to his readers) the distichic frame underlying *Idyll* 29, are those of a *métrique verbale* sophisticatedly negotiating between the syntactic articulation of rhetorical cola.[69] Paradoxically, then, the only means available to Theocritus for exhibiting his full faithfulness turned out to be a deeper betrayal, that is, what I have previously called somewhat provisionally musical mimicry 'without music':[70] to make systematic and normative what in Sappho and Alcaeus was only one among many stylistic possibilities.

---

[68] See Rossi 2000a, 153.

[69] Likewise see Hunter's penetrating observations on the quasi-stanzaic effects detectable in *Id.* 18 which are interpreted as "a marked product of a culture which has, to an important extent, lost touch with the musical and rhythmical aspects of the archaic performance [. . .]; this 'over-determined' formal structure is indeed another kind of compensation for that loss."

[70] For other instances, in Theocritus, of lyric mimicry triggered by means of syntactic devices see e.g. also Hunter 1999, 109–10 and Rossi 2000a, 152 on *Idyll* 3.

BIBLIOGRAPHY

Ailloud, H. 1961. *Suétone, Vies des douze Césars*, vol. 2 (Paris).
Albano Leoni, F. 2001. "Il ruolo dell'udito nella comunicazione linguistica. Il caso della prosodia." *Rivista di linguistica* 13, 45–68.
Anderson, W.D. 1966. *Ethos and Education in Greek Music* (Cambridge, MA).
——. 1994. *Music and Musicians in Ancient Greece* (Ithaca-London).
Aneziri, S. 2003. *Die Vereine der dionysischen Techniten im Kontext der hellenistischen Gesellschaft. Untersuchungen zur Geschichte, Organisation und Wirkung der hellenistischen Technitenvereine*, Historia Einzelschriften vol. 163 (Stuttgart).
Asper, M. 1997. *Onomata Allotria. Zur Genese, Struktur und Funktion poetologischer Metaphern bei Kallimachus*, Hermes Einzelschriften vol. 75 (Stuttgart).
Audollent, A. 1904. *Defixionum tabellae quotquot innotuerunt tam in Graecis Orientis quam in totius occidentis partibus praeter Atticas in corpore Inscriptionum Atticarum editas* (Paris).
Aujac, G. and Lebel, M. 1981. *Denys d'Halicarnasse. Opuscules rhétoriques*, vol. 3 (Paris).
Austin, C. 1970. *CR* 20, 18–21 (review of Dover 1968).
Austin, C. and Olson, S.D. 2004. *Aristophanes. Thesmophoriazusae* (Oxford).
Barabino, G. 1978. "Nota sul verso asclepiadeo." In *Problemi di metrica classica. Miscellanea filologica* (Genoa), 163–77.
Barker, A. 1995. "Heterophonia and poikilia: accompaniments to Greek melody." In B. Gentili and F. Perusino (eds.), *Mousike, metrica ritmica e musica greca in memoria di G. Comotti* (Pisa-Rome), 41–60.
Barlow, S.A. 1986. *Euripides. Trojan Women* (Warminster).
Barrett, W.S. 1964. *Euripides. Hippolytos* (Oxford).
Bartsch, S. 1994. *Actors in the Audience. Theatricality and Doublespeak from Nero to Hadrian* (Cambridge, MA-London).
Basta Donzelli, G. 1974. "Note di metrica e critica testuale, Euripide Elettra 437, Aristofane Rane 1314 e 1318." *SicGymn* 27, 89–119.
Bataille, A. 1961. "Remarques sur les deux notations mélodiques de l'ancienne musique grecque." *Recherches de papyrologie* 1, 5–20.
Battezzato, L. 2003. "I viaggi dei testi." In L. Battezzato (ed.), *Tradizione testuale e ricezione letteraria antica della tragedia greca. Atti del convegno Scuola Normale Superiore, Pisa 14–5 giugno 2002* (Amsterdam), 7–32.
Beacham, R.C. 1991. *The Roman Theatre and its Audience* (London).
Beare, W. 1964³. *The Roman Stage* (London).
Bécares Botas, V. 1985. *Diccionario de terminología gramatical griega* (Salamanca).
Beckby, H. 1975. *Die griechischen Bukoliker. Theokrit-Moschos-Bion* (Meisenheim am Glan).
Bélis, A. 1984. "Un nouveau document musical." *BCH* 116, 53–9.
——. 1986. *Aristoxène de Tarente et Aristote: le Traité d'harmonique*, Études et commentaires vol. 100 (Paris).
——. 1988. "La trasmissione della musica nell'antichità." In F. Berti and D. Restani (eds.), *Lo specchio della musica. Iconografia musicale nella ceramica attica di Spina* (Bologna), 29–39.
——. 1991. "Aristophane, Grenouilles, v. 1249–1364: Eschyle et Euripide ΜΕΛΟΠΟΙΟΙ." *REG* 104, 31–51.
——. 1992. *Les Hymnes delphiques à Apollon*, Corpus des Inscriptions de Delphes, vol. 3 (Paris).
——. 1994. "Inscriptions grecques relatives a des compositeurs." In *La pluridisciplinarité en archéologie musicale*, I. IV Rencontres internationales d'archéologie musicale de l'ICTM, Saint Germain en Laye, 8–12 octobre 1990 (Paris), 43–55.

——. 1995. "Cithares, citharistes, citharôdes en Grèce." *CRAI*, 1025–65.

——. 1999. *Les musiciens dans l'Antiquité* (Paris).

——. 2001. "Euripide musicien." In G.-J. Pinault (ed.), *Musique et poésie dans l'antiquité, Actes du colloque de Clermont-Ferrand, Université Blaise Pascal, 23 mai 1997* (Clermont-Ferrand), 27–51.

Beta, S. 1992. *Luciano. La danza* (Venice).

Billerbeck, M. 1999. *Seneca. Hercules Furens* (Leiden).

Bing, P. 2000. "Text or performance/text and performance. Alan Cameron's Callimachus and His Critics." In R. Pretagostini (ed.), *La letteratura ellenistica. Problemi e prospettive di ricerca*, Atti del Colloquio Internazionale, Università di Roma "Tor Vergata", 29–30 aprile 1997 (Rome), 139–48.

Blum, R. 1977. *Kallimachos und die Literaturverzeichnung bei den Griechen. Untersuchungen zur Geschichte der Biobibliographie* (Frankfurt am Main).

Boegehold, A.L. 1972. "The establishment of a central archive at Athens." *AJA* 76, 23–30.

Bohnenkamp, K.E. 1972. *Die horazische Strofe. Studien zur 'Lex Meinekiana'* (Hildesheim-New York).

Bolgar, R.R. 1954. *The Classical Heritage and its Beneficiaries* (Cambridge).

Bond, G.W. 1981. *Euripides. Heracles* (Oxford).

Borthwick, E.K. 1965. "Suetonius' Nero and a Pindaric scholium." *CR* 15, 252–6.

——. 1971. "Aristophanes, Clouds 1371." *CR* 21, 318–20.

Bosnakis, D. 2004. "Zwei Dichterinnen aus Kos. Ein neues inschriftliches Zeugnis über das öffentliche Auftreten von Frauen." In K. Höghammar (ed.), *The Hellenistic Polis of Kos. State, Economy and Culture, Proceedings of an International Seminar organized by the Department of Archaeology and Ancient History, Uppsala University, 11–13 May, 2000*, Boreas vol. 28 (Uppsala), 99–107.

Bouquiaux-Simon, O. and Mertens, P. 1992. "Les témoignages papyrologiques d'Euripide: liste sommaire arrêtée au 1/6/1990." In M. Capasso (ed.), *Papiri letterari greci e latini*, Papyrologica Lupiensia vol. 1 (Galatina), 96–107.

Bowie, A.M. 1997. "Thinking with drinking: wine and the symposium in Aristophanes." *JHS* 117, 1–21.

Bowie, E.L. 1986. "Early Greek elegy, symposium, and public festival." *JHS* 106, 13–35.

Braund, D. 1993. "Dionysiac tragedy in Plutarch, Crassus." *CQ* 43, 468–74.

Broneer, O. 1953. "Isthmia excavations. 1952." *Hesperia* 22, 182–95.

Burges, G. 1807. *Euripidis Troades* (Cambridge).

Burian, P. 1997. "Tragedy adapted for stages and screens: the Renaissance to the present." In P.E. Easterling (ed.), *The Cambridge Companion to Greek Tragedy* (Cambridge), 228–83.

Butler, H.E. and Cary, M. 1927. *C. Suetoni Tranquilli Divus Iulius* (Oxford).

Cagnazzi, S. 1997. *Nicobule e Panfila. Frammenti di storiche greche*, Documenti e Studi vol. 21 (Bari).

Cairns, F. 1977. "The distaff of Theugenis-Theocritus Idyll 28." In id. (ed.), *Papers of the Liverpool Latin Seminar 1976* (Liverpool), 293–305.

Calame, C. 1977. *Les chœurs de jeunes filles en Grèce archaïque*, 2 vols. (Rome).

——. 1983. *Alcman* (Rome).

Cameron, A. 1995. *Callimachus and His Critics* (Princeton).

Campbell, D.A. 1964. "Flutes and elegiac couplets." *JHS* 84, 63–8.

——. 1990. *Greek Lyric I, Sappho and Alcaeus* (Cambridge, MA-London).

Capra, A. 2000. "Il mito delle cicale e il motivo della bellezza sensibile nel Fedro." *Maia* 52, 225–44.

Carnuth, O. 1875. *Nicanoris Περὶ Ὀδυσσειακῆς στιγμῆς reliquiae emendatiores* (Berlin).

Carson, J. 1969. "Greek accent and the rational." *JHS* 89, 24–37.

Casaubon, I. 1621². *Animadversionum in Athenaei Deipnosophistas libri XV* (Leiden).

Cassio, A.C. 1977. *Aristofane, Banchettanti (ΔΑΙΤΑΛΗΣ). I frammenti* (Pisa).

——. 1997. "Futuri dorici, dialetto di Siracusa e testo antico dei lirici greci." *A.I.O.N.(filol)* 19, 187–211.

Catenacci, C. 1999. "ἀπονέμειν/'leggere' (Pind. Isthm. 2, 47; Soph. fr. 144 Radt; Aristoph. Av. 1289)." *QUCC* 61, 49–61.

Ceccarelli, P. 2004. "Autour de Dionysos: remarques sur la dénomination des artistes dionysiaques." In Ch. Hugoniot, F. Hurlet and S. Milanezi (eds.), *Le statut de l'acteur dans l'Antiquité grecque et romaine. Actes du colloque qui s'est tenu à Tours les 3 et 4 mai 2002* (Tours), 109–42.

Chailley, J. 1967. "Nouvelles remarques sur les deux notations musicales grecques." *Recherches de papyrologie* 4, 201–16.

——. 1979. *La musique grecque antique* (Paris).

Chandezon, C. 1998. "La base de Satyros à Delphes: le théâtre classique et son public à l'époque hellénistique." *CGITA* 11, 33–58.

Chaniotis, A. 1988. *Historie und Historiker in den griechischen Inschriften. Epigraphische Beiträge zur griechischen Historiographie*, Heidelberger althistorische Beiträge und epigraphische Studien vol. 4 (Stuttgart).

Christensen, T. 1999a. "Four-hand piano transcription and geographies of nineteenth-century musical reception." *Journal of American Musicological Society* 52, 255–98.

——. 1999b. "Public music in private spaces. Piano-vocal scores and the domestication of opera." In K. van Orden (ed.), *Music and Cultures of Print* (Stuyvesant, N.Y.), 67–93.

Cingano, E. 1998². in B. Gentili, P. Angeli Bernardini, E. Cingano and P. Giannini (eds.), *Pindaro, Le Pitiche* (Milan).

Cockle, W.E.H. 1975. "The odes of Epagathus the choral flautist: some documentary evidence for dramatic representation in Roman Egypt." In *Proceedings of the XIV International Congress of Papyrology* (London), 59–65.

Comotti, G. 1978. "Parola, verso e musica nell'Ifigenia in Aulide di Euripide (P.Leid. inv. 510)." In *Problemi di metrica classica*. Miscellanea filologica (Genoa), 145–62 [= "Words, verse and music in Euripides' Iphigenia in Aulis." *MPhL* 2 (1977), 69–84].

——. 1988. "I problemi dei valori ritmici nell'interpretazione dei testi musicali della Grecia antica." In B. Gentili and R. Pretagostini (eds.), *La musica in Grecia* (Bari-Rome), 17–25.

——. 1991². *La musica nella cultura greca e romana* (Turin).

Concilio, C. 2002. "La colometria del secondo stasimo dell'Ifigenia in Aulide di Euripide." In C. Concilio, M. D'Aiuto and S. Polizio (eds.), *La tradizione metrica della tragedia greca* (Naples), 9–19.

Conybeare, F.C. 1912. *Philostratus. The Life of Apollonius of Tyana*, vol. 1 (London-New York).

Corbato, C. 1991. "Symposium e teatro: dati e problemi." In K. Fabian, E. Pellizer and G. Tedeschi (eds.), *OINHPA TEYXH. Studi triestini di poesia conviviale* (Alessandria), 43–55.

Cozzoli, A.T. 1998. "Callimaco e i suoi 'critici'. Considerazioni su un recente lavoro." *Eikasmos* 9, 135–55.

Cribiore, R. 1996. *Writing, Teachers and Students in Graeco-Roman Egypt*, American Studies in Papyrology vol. 36 (Atlanta).

Crönert, W. 1909. "Die Hibehrede über die Musik." *Hermes* 44, 503–21.

Crusius, O. 1894. "Zu neuentdeckten antiken Musikresten." *Philologus* 52, 160–200.

Csapo, E. 1999–2000. "Later Euripidean music." In M. Cropp, K. Lee and D. Sansone (eds.), *Euripides and Tragic Theatre in the Late Fifth Century*, ICS 24–25 (Champaign, IL), 399–426.

——. 2002. "Kallipides on the floor-sweepings: the limits of realism in classical acting and performance styles." In P. Easterling and E. Hall (eds.), *Greek and Roman Actors. Aspects of an Ancient Profession* (Cambridge), 127–47.

——. 2004a. "The politics of the New Music." In P. Murray and P. Wilson (eds.),

Music and the Muses. The Culture of Mousike in the Classical Athenian City (Oxford), 207–48.

——. 2004b. "Some social and economic conditions behind the rise of the acting profession in the fifth and fourth centuries BC." In Ch. Hugoniot, F. Hurlet and S. Milanezi (eds.), *Le statut de l'acteur dans l'Antiquité grecque et romaine. Actes du colloque qui s'est tenu à Tours les 3 et 4 mai 2002* (Tours), 53–76.

Csapo, E. and Slater, W.J. 1994. *The Context of Ancient Drama* (Ann Arbor).

Currie, B. 2004. "Reperformance scenarios for Pindar's odes." In C.J. Mackie (ed.), *Oral Performance and its Context* (Leiden-Boston), 49–69.

Cuvigny, M. 1981. *Plutarque, Œuvres morales*, vol. 12.1 (Paris).

Daitz, S.G. 1979. *The Scholia in the Jerusalem Palimpsest of Euripides* (Heidelberg).

——. 1990². *Euripides. Hecuba* (Leipzig).

D'Aiuto, M. 2002. "La colometria del primo stasimo dell'Ifigenia in Aulide di Euripide." In C. Concilio, M. D'Aiuto and S. Polizio (eds.), *La tradizione metrica della tragedia greca* (Naples), 22–57.

D'Alessio, G.B. 1994. "First-person problems in Pindar." *BICS* 41, 117–39.

——. 1997. "Pindar's prosodia and the classification of Pindaric papyrus fragments." *ZPE* 118, 23–60.

——. 2000. "'Tra gli dèi ad Apollo, e tra gli uomini ad Echecrate'. P. Louvre E 7734 + 7733 (Pind. fr. dub. 333 S.-M.)." In M. Cannatà Fera and S. Grandolini (eds.), *Poesia e religione in Grecia. Studi in onore di G. Aurelio Privitera* (Naples), 233–62.

D'Alfonso, F. 1994. *Stesicoro e la performance. Studio sulle modalità esecutive dei carmi stesicorei* (Rome).

Damen, M. 1989. "Actor and character in Greek tragedy." *Theatre Journal* 41, 316–40.

D'Arbela, E.V. 1958. *M. Tullio Cicerone, L'oratore* (Milan).

Da Rios, R. 1954. *Aristoxeni elementa harmonica* (Rome).

Davies, M. and Kathirithamby, J. 1986. *Greek Insects* (London).

Dearden, C. 1999. "Plays for export." *Phoenix* 53, 222–48.

Del Corno, D. 1978. *Filostrato. Vita di Apollonio di Tiana* (Milan).

Del Fabbro, M. 1979. "Il commentario nella tradizione papiracea." *Studia papyrologica* 18, 69–132.

De Lucia, R. 1997. "Corali infraepisodici: un problema ancora aperto." In U. Criscuolo and R. Maisano (eds.), *Synodia. Studia humanitatis Antonio Garzya septuagenario ab amicis atque discipulis dicata* (Naples), 245–54.

Denniston, J.D. 1939. *Euripides. Electra* (Oxford).

Dettori, E. 2000. *Filita grammatico. Testimonianze e frammenti*, Quaderni di SemRom vol. 2 (Rome).

Devine, A.M. and Stephens, L.D. 1991. "Dionysius of Halicarnassus, De compositione verborum XI: reconstructing the phonetics of the Greek accent." *TAPhA* 121, 229–86.

——. 1994. *The Prosody of Greek Speech* (New York-Oxford).

Di Benedetto, V. 1961. "Responsione strofica e distribuzione delle battute in Euripide." *Hermes* 89, 298–321.

——. 1965. *Euripidis Orestes* (Florence).

——. 1982. "Contributi al testo di Saffo." *RFIC* 110, 5–21.

Dickie, M.W. 2003. "The topic of envy and emulation in an agonistic inscription from Oenoanda." In E. Csapo and M.C. Miller (eds.), *Poetry, Theory, Praxis. The Social Life of Myth, Word and Image in Ancient Greece. Essays in Honour of William J. Slater* (Oxford), 232–46.

Diggle, J. 1974. "On the 'Heracles' and 'Ion' of Euripides." *PCPhS* 20, 22–4.

——. 1981. *Studies on the Text of Euripides* (Oxford).

——. 1991. *The Textual Tradition of Euripides' Orestes* (Oxford).

——. 1994. *Euripidea. Collected Essays* (Oxford).

———. 2004. *Theophrastus. Characters* (Cambridge).

Dihle, A. 1981. "Der Prolog der 'Bacchen' und die antike Überlieferungsphase des Euripides-Textes." *Sitzungberichte der Heidelberger Akademie der Wissenschaften*, Phil.-hist. Kl., Band 2, 1–38.

Dindorf, W. 1869. *Poetarum scaenicorum Graecorum Aeschyli Sophoclis Euripidis et Aristophanis fabulae superstites et perditarum fragmenta* (Leipzig).

Dobrov, G.W. 1995. *BMCR* 1995.07.05 (review of Devine-Stephens 1994).

Dover, K.J. 1968. *Aristophanes. Clouds* (Oxford).

———. 1993. *Aristophanes. Frogs* (Oxford).

Dué, C. 2001. "Poetry and the demos: state regulation of a civic possession." In G. Nagy (ed.), *Greek Literature*, vol. 5 (New-York), 368–75.

Dunbar, N. 1995. *Aristophanes. Birds* (Oxford).

Duncan, A. 2005. "Gendered interpretations: two fourth-century BCE performances of Sophocles' Electra." *Helios* 32, 55–79.

Duysinx, F. 1999. *Aristide Quintilien, La musique* (Genève).

Dyck, A.R. 1981. "On Apollodorus of Cyrene." *HSCPh* 85, 101–6.

———. 1986. *Michael Psellus, The Essays on Euripides and George of Pisidia and on Heliodorus and Achilles Tatius*, Byzantina Vindobonensia vol. 16 (Vienna).

Easterling, P.E. 1997. "From repertoire to canon." In ead. (ed.), *The Cambridge Companion to Greek Tragedy* (Cambridge), 211–27.

Easterling, P.E. and Hall, E. (eds.) 2002. *Greek and Roman Actors. Aspects of an Ancient Profession* (Cambridge).

Eitrem, S., Amundsen, L. and Winnington Ingram, R.P. 1955. "Fragments of unknown Greek tragic texts with musical notation (P.Osl. inv. no. 1413)." *SO* 31, 1–87.

Elliott, R.T. 1914. *The Acharnians of Aristophanes* (Oxford).

Engels, J. 1992. "Zur Stellung Lykurgs und zur Aussagekraft seines Militär- und Bauprogramms für die Demokratie vor 322 v. Chr." *AncSoc* 23, 5–29.

Erbse, H. 1961. "Überlieferungsgeschichte der griechischen klassischen und hellenistischen Literatur." In H. Hunger et alii (eds.), *Geschichte der Textüberlieferung der antiken und mittelalterlichen Literatur*, vol. 1 (Zürich), 207–84.

Fabbro, E. 1998. "Ar. Nub. 1357s." *Eikasmos* 9, 53–60.

Falkner, T. 2002. "Scholars versus actors: text and performance in the Greek tragic scholia." In P. Easterling and E. Hall (eds.), *Greek and Roman Actors. Aspects of an Ancient Profession* (Cambridge), 342–61.

Fantuzzi, M. and Hunter, R. 2002. *Muse e modelli. La poesia ellenistica da Alessandro Magno ad Augusto* (Rome-Bari) [= iid., *Tradition and Innovation in Hellenistic Poetry*, Cambridge 2004].

Faraguna, M. 1992. *Atene nell'età di Alessandro. Problemi politici, economici, finanziari* (Rome).

Fassino, M. 1997–98. *Il papiro di Strasburgo W.G. 304–307 e la fase più antica della trasmissione del testo di Euripide* (Pisa) [unpublished M.A. dissertation].

———. 1999. "Revisione di P.Stras.W.G. 304–307: nuovi frammenti della Medea e di un'altra tragedia di Euripide." *ZPE* 127, 1–46.

———. 2003. "Avventure del testo di Euripide nei papiri tolemaici." In L. Battezzato (ed.), *Tradizione testuale e ricezione letteraria antica della tragedia greca. Atti del convegno Scuola Normale Superiore, Pisa 14–5 giugno 2002* (Amsterdam), 33–56.

Fassino, M. and Prauscello, L. 2001. "Memoria ritmica e memoria poetica: Saffo e Alceo in Teocrito Idilli 28–30 tra ἀρχαιολογία metrica e innovazione alessandrina." *MD* 46, 9–37.

Faveri, L. de. 2002. *Die metrischen Trikliniusscholien zur byzantinischen Trias des Euripides*, Beiträge zum antiken Drama und seiner Rezeption vol. 18 (Stuttgart-Weimar).

Feaver, D.D. 1960. "The musical setting of Euripides' Orestes." *AJPh* 81, 1–15.

Ferrari, F. 1984. "P. Leid. inv. 510 e il testo di Euripide, Ifigenia in Aulide 783–92." *CCC* 5, 19–22.

——. 1986. "Formule saffiche e formule omeriche." *ASNP* s. III, 16, 441–7.

——. 1991. "Colometria nei papiri pindarici." *ASNP* s. III, 21, 757–63.

——. 2000. "Intorno all'ombelico del mondo: le prospettive del rito nelle Pitiche di Pindaro." *SemRom* 3, 217–42.

——. 2001. "Sul prosodio pindarico per gli Egineti (= 'Peana' 6, 123–183)." *SCO* 47, 149–58.

——. 2003. "Il pubblico di Saffo." *SIFC* 96, 42–89.

Fisher, N. 2000. "Symposiasts, fish-eaters and flatterers: social mobility and moral concerns in Old Comedy." In D. Harvey and J. Wilkins (eds.), *The Rivals of Aristophanes. Studies in Athenian Old Comedy* (London), 355–96.

——. 2001. *Aeschines. Against Timarchos* (Oxford).

Flashar, H. 1962. *Aristoteles. Problemata Physica* (Darmstadt).

——. 1972. *Aristoteles, Opuscula II und III* (Berlin).

Fleming, T.J. 1975. "Ancient evidence for the colometry of Aeschylus 'Septem'." *GRBS* 16, 141–48.

——. 1999. "The survival of Greek dramatic music." In B. Gentili and F. Perusino (eds.), *La colometria antica dei testi poetici greci* (Rome), 17–29.

Fleming, T.J. and Kopff, E.C. 1992. "Colometry of Greek lyric verses in tragic texts." In *Atti del Convegno Internazionale di Antichità Classica della F.I.E.C.*, Pisa 24–30 agosto 1989, *SIFC* s. III 10, 758–70.

Foley, H. 2003. "Choral identity in Greek tragedy." *CP* 98, 1–30.

Ford, A. 2004. "The power of music in Aristotle's Politics." In P. Murray and P. Wilson (eds.), *Music and the Muses. The Culture of Mousike in the Classical Athenian City* (Oxford), 309–36.

Fortenbaugh, W.W. et al. 1992. *Theophrastus of Eresus. Sources for His Life, Writings, Thoughts and Influence*, 2 vols. (Leiden-New York-Köln).

Fortson, B.W. 1995. *BMCR* 1995.10.09 (review of Devine-Stephens 1994).

Fowler, H.N. 1960. *Plutarch's Moralia*, vol. 10 (London-Cambridge, MA).

Fraser, P.M. 1972. *Ptolemaic Alexandria*, 3 vols. (Oxford).

Frazier, F. and Sirinelli, J. 1996. *Plutarque, Œuvres Morales*, vol. 9.3 (Paris).

Gabba, E. 1991. *Dionysius and the History of Archaic Rome* (Berkeley-Los Angeles-Oxford).

Gentili, B. 1977. *Lo spettacolo nel mondo antico. Teatro ellenistico e teatro romano arcaico* (Bari).

——. 1988. "Metro e ritmo nella dottrina degli antichi e nella prassi della performance." In B. Gentili and R. Pretagostini (eds.), *La musica in Grecia* (Bari-Rome), 5–16.

——. 1990. "Parola, metro e ritmo nel De compositione verborum di Dionigi di Alicarnasso (anapesti ciclici e dattili con lunga irrazionale)." In R.M. Danese, F. Gori and C. Questa (eds.), *Metrica classica e linguistica. Atti del colloquio, Urbino 3–6 ottobre 1988* (Urbino), 9–23.

——. 1992. "Pindarica III. La Pitica 2 e il carme iporchematico di Castore (fr. 105 a-b Maehler)." *QUCC* 40, 49–55.

——. 1995³. *Poesia e pubblico nella Grecia antica* (Rome-Bari).

——. 1998. "Ecdotica e colometria dei testi poetici nella Grecia antica." In A. Ferrari (ed.), *Filologia classica e filologia romanza: esperienze ecdotiche a confronto. Atti del Convegno Roma 25–27 maggio 1995* (Spoleto), 138–49.

——. 1998². in B. Gentili, P. Angeli Bernardini, E. Cingano and P. Giannini (eds.), *Pindaro, Le Pitiche* (Milan).

——. 2001. "Postilla." *QUCC* 68, 134.

——. 2002. "La memoria operativa e la colometria del testo poetico." (addendum to Willett 2002) *QUCC* 71, 21–3.

Gentili, B. and Lomiento, L. 2001. "Colometria antica e filologia moderna." *QUCC* 69, 7–22.

BIBLIOGRAPHY   221

——. 2003. *Metrica e ritmica: storia delle forme poetiche nella Grecia antica* (Milan).
Gentili, B. and Perusino, F. (eds.) 1999. *La colometria antica dei testi poetici greci* (Rome).
Georgiades, T. 1958. *Musik und Rhythmus bei den Griechen* (Hamburg).
Gerber, D.E. 2005. *CR* 55, 15–16 (review of Loscalzo 2003).
Giannini, P. 2004. "Alcune precisazioni sul papiro musicale dell'Oreste e sulla colometria antica." *QUCC* 78, 99–106.
Giordano Zecharya, M. 2003. "Tabellae auris: musica e memoria nella trasmissione della lirica monodica." In R. Nicolai (ed.), PΥΣΜΟΣ. *Studi di poesia, metrica e musica greca offerti dagli allievi a Luigi Enrico Rossi per i suoi settant'anni* (Rome), 73–92.
Goettling, C.G. 1822. *ΘΕΟΔΟΣΙΟΥ ΓΡΑΜΜΑΤΙΚΟΥ ΠΕΡΙ ΓΡΑΜΜΑΤΙΚΗΣ. Theodosii Alexandrini grammatica* (Leipzig).
Gorman, R. 2001. "*ΟΙ ΠΕΡΙ ΤΙΝΑ* in Strabo." *ZPE* 136, 201–13.
Gostoli, A. 1990. *Terpander* (Rome).
Gottschalk, H.B. 1980. *Heraclides of Pontus* (Oxford).
Gow, A.S.F. 1952. *Theocritus*², 2 vols. (Cambridge).
Gow, A.S.F. and Page, D.L. 1965. *The Greek Anthology, Hellenistic Epigrams*, 2 vols. (Cambridge).
Gregory, J. 1999. *Euripides. Hecuba* (Atlanta).
Grenfell, B.P. and Hunt, A.S. 1906. *The Hibeh Papyri*, vol. 1 (London).
Griffith, J.G. 1967. *JHS* 87, 145–47 (review of Di Benedetto 1965).
Griffith, M. 2001. "Antigone and her sister(s): embodying women in Greek tragedy." In A. Lardinois and L. McClure (eds.), *Making Silence Speak: Women's Voices in Greek Literature and Society* (Princeton-Oxford), 117–36.
Griffiths, F.T. 1997. *AJPh* 118, 340–3 (review of Cameron 1995).
Gronewald, M. 1980. "P. Köln III 131 adespotum: Euripides, Orestes 134–142." *ZPE* 39, 35–6.
——. 1987. "Euripides, Orestes 134–142." In M. Gronewald, B. Kramer, K. Maresch, M. Parca and C. Römer (eds.), *Kölner Papyri* VI, Papyrologica Coloniensia vol. 7 (Opladen), 129–30.
Gronewald, M.-Daniel, R.W. 2004a. "Ein neuer Sappho-Papyrus." *ZPE* 147, 1–8.
——. 2004b. "Nachtrag zum neuen Sappho-Papyrus." *ZPE* 149, 1–4.
Guarducci, M. 1929. "Poeti vaganti e conferenzieri dell'età ellenistica. Ricerche di epigrafia greca nel campo della letteratura e del costume." *Mem. Accad. Naz. Lincei*, Classe di Scienze morali etc., ser. 6, vol. 2, fasc. 9, 629–65.
Guidorizzi, G. 1996. *Aristofane. Le nuvole* (Milan).
Günther, H.C. 1988. *Euripides. Iphigenia Aulidensis* (Leipzig).
Gutzwiller, K. 1996. "The evidence for Theocritean poetry books." In M.A. Harder, R.F. Regtuit and G.C. Wakker (eds.), *Theocritus*, Hellenistica Groningana vol. 2 (Groningen), 119–48.
Hall, E. 1999. "Actor's song in tragedy." In S. Goldhill and R. Osborne (eds.), *Performance Culture and Athenian Democracy* (Cambridge), 96–122.
——. 2002. "The singing actors of antiquity." In P. Easterling and E. Hall (eds.), *Greek and Roman Actors. Aspects of an Ancient Profession* (Cambridge), 3–38.
Halleran, M.R. 1995. *Euripides. Hippolytus* (Warminster).
Hamm, E.M. 1958². *Grammatik zu Sappho und Alkaios* (Berlin).
Handley, E.W. 2002. "Acting, action and words in New Comedy." In P. Easterling and E. Hall (eds.), *Greek and Roman Actors. Aspects of an Ancient Profession* (Cambridge), 165–88.
Haslam, M.W. 1977. *The Oxyrhynchus Papyri*, vol. 45 (London), 1–6.
Henderson, J. 1998. *Aristophanes*, vol. 2 (Cambridge, MA-London).
Herington, J. 1985. *Poetry into Drama. Early Tragedy and the Greek Poetic Tradition* (Berkeley-Los Angeles-London).
Hermann, G. 1848. *De interpolationibus Euripideae Iphigeniae in Aulide dissertationis pars altera* (Leipzig) [= id., *Opuscula*, vol. 8, ed. T. Fritzsche (Leipzig, 1877)].

Higbie, C. 1990. *Measure and Music, Enjambement and Sentence Structure in the Iliad* (Oxford).

Hillyard, B.P. 1981. *Plutarch: De audiendo. A Text and Commentary* (New York).

Hinds, S. 1998. *Allusion and Intertext. Dynamics of Appropriation in Roman Poetry* (Cambridge).

Hordern, J.H. 2002. *The Fragments of Timotheus of Miletus* (Oxford).

Hubbard, T.K. 2004. "The dissemination of epinician lyric: pan-Hellenism, reperformance, written texts." In C.J. Mackie (ed.), *Oral Performance and its Context* (Leiden-Boston), 71–94.

Hunger, H. and Pöhlmann, E. 1962. "Neue griechische Musikfragmente aus ptolemäischer Zeit in der Papyrussammlung der Österreichischen Nationalbibliothek." *WS* 75, 51–78.

Hunt, A.S. and Johnson, J. 1930. *Two Theocritus Papyri* (London).

Hunter, R. 1996. *Theocritus and the Archaeology of Greek Poetry* (Cambridge).

——. 1999. *Theocritus. A Selection. Idylls 1, 3, 4, 6, 7, 10, 11 and 13* (Cambridge).

——. 2002. "'Acting down': the ideology of Hellenistic performance." In P. Easterling and E. Hall (eds.), *Greek and Roman Actors. Aspects of an Ancient Profession* (Cambridge), 189–206.

Huss, B. 1999. *Xenophons Symposium. Ein Kommentar*, Beiträge zur Altertumskunde vol. 125 (Stuttgart-Leipzig).

Ioannidou, G. 1996. *Catalogue of Greek and Latin Literary Papyri in Berlin (P.Berol. inv. 21101–21299, 21911)* (Mainz am Rhein).

Irigoin, J. 1952. *Histoire du texte de Pindare* (Paris).

——. 1958. *Les scholies métriques de Pindare* (Paris).

——. 1997. *Tradition et critique des textes grecs* (Paris).

Itsumi, K. 1982. "The 'choriambic dimeter' of Euripides." *CQ* 32, 59–74.

——. 1984. "The glyconic in tragedy." *CQ* 34, 66–82.

Janko, R. 1997. "The physicist as hierophant: Aristophanes, Socrates and the authorship of the Derveni Papyrus." *ZPE* 118, 61–94.

Jocelyn, H.D. 1967. *The Tragedies of Ennius. The Fragments* (Cambridge).

Johnson, W.A. 2000a. "Musical evenings in the early empire: new evidence from a Greek papyrus with musical notation." *JHS* 120, 57–85.

——. 2000b. "New instrumental music from Graeco-Roman Egypt." *BASP* 37, 17–36.

Jones, C.P. 2005. *Philostratus. The Life of Apollonius of Tyana*, 2 vols. (Cambridge, MA-London).

Jory, E.J. 1986. "Continuity and change in the Roman theatre." In J.H. Betts, J.T. Hooker and J.R. Green (eds.), *Studies in Honour of T.B.L. Webster*, vol. 1 (Bristol), 143–52.

Jouan, F. 1983a. *Euripide, Iphigénie à Aulis*, vol. 7.1 (Paris).

——. 1983b. "Réflexions sur le rôle du protagoniste tragique." In *Théâtre et spectacles dans l'antiquité. Actes du colloque de Strasbourg 5–7 novembre 1981* (Leiden), 63–80.

Jourdan-Hemmerdinger, D. 1973. "Un nouveau papyrus musical d'Euripide." *CRAI*, 292–302.

——. 1981a. "Le nouveau papyrus d'Euripide: qu'apporte-t-il à la théorie et à l'histoire de la musique?" In *Les sources en musicologie* (Paris), 35–65.

——. 1981b. "La date de la 'notation vocale' d'Alypios." *Philologus* 125, 299–303.

Kaimio, M. 1993. "The protagonist in Greek tragedy." *Arctos* 27, 19–33.

Kannicht, R. 1969. *Euripides. Helena*, 2 vols. (Heidelberg).

Kassel, R. 1991. *Kleine Schriften*, hrsg. von H.-G. Nesselrath (Berlin-New York).

Kelly, H.A. 1979. "Tragedy and performance of tragedy in late Roman antiquity." *Traditio* 35, 21–44.

Kierdorf, W. 1992. *Sueton, Leben des Claudius und Nero* (Padeborn-Munich-Vienna-Zürich).

Kilburn, K. 1959. *Lucian*, vol. 6 (London-Cambridge, MA).

Knox, B.M.W. 1985. "Books and readers in the Greek world." In P.E. Easterling and B.M.W. Knox (eds.), *Cambridge History of Classical Literature*, vol. 1 (Cambridge), 1–41.

Knox, P.E. 1995. *Ovid, Heroides. Select Epistles* (Cambridge).

Kokolakis, M. 1960. "Lucian and the tragic performances in his time." *Platon* 12, 67–109.

Koller, H. 1954. *Die Mimesis in der Antike. Nachahmung, Darstellung, Ausdruck* (Bern).

——. 1956. "Die Parodie." *Glotta* 35, 17–32.

Kopff, E.C. 1999. "Diggle's critique of Dale's canon of iambic resolution in tragic lyrics". In B. Gentili and F. Perusino (eds.), *La colometria antica dei testi poetici greci* (Rome), 85–93.

Korn, O. 1863. *De publico Aeschyli Sophoclis Euripidis fabularum exemplari Lycurgo auctore confecto* (Dissert. Bonn).

Koster, W.J.W. 1941. "Studia ad colometriam poëseos Graecae pertinentia." *Mnemosyne* 9, 1–43.

Kovacs, D. 1994. *Euripidea* (Leiden-New York-Köln).

——. 2002. *Euripides*, vol. 5 (Cambridge, MA-London).

Kroll, W. 1907. "Randbemerkungen." *RhM* 62, 86–101.

——. 1958. *M. Tullii Ciceronis Orator* (Berlin) [anast. reprint of 1913 edition].

Kugelmeier, C. 1996. *Reflexe früher und zeitgenössischer Lyrik in der Alten attischen Komödie*, Beiträge zur Altertumskunde vol. 80 (Stuttgart-Leipzig).

Kurke, L. 1991. *The Traffic in Praise. Pindar and the Poetics of Social Economy* (Ithaca-London).

Lai, A. 1997. "La circolazione delle tragedie eschilee in ambito simposiale." *Lexis* 15, 143–48.

Lallot, J. 1989. *La grammaire de Denys le Thrace* (Paris).

Lameere, W. 1960. *Aperçus de paléographie homérique. A propos des papyrus de l'Iliade et de l'Odyssée des collections de Gand, de Bruxelles et de Louvain*, Les publications de Scriptorium vol. 4 (Paris-Brussels-Anvers-Amsterdam).

Landels, J.G. 1999. *Music in Ancient Greece & Rome* (London-New York).

Lapini, W. 2003. "Osservazioni su PHibeh I. 13 anonimo De musica (Alcidamante?)." In id., *Studi di filologia filosofica greca* (Florence), 173–215.

Lasserre, F. 1959. *AC* 28, 346–8 (review of Irigoin 1958).

Latte, K. 1954. "Zur Geschichte der griechischen Tragödie in der Kaiserzeit." *Eranos* 52, 125–7.

——. 1955. "Noch einmal die Themisoninschrift." *Eranos* 53, 75–6.

Laum, B. 1928. *Das alexandrinische Akzentuationsystem* (Padeborn).

Lavecchia, S. 2000. *Pindari dithyramborum fragmenta* (Rome-Pisa).

Lee, K.H. 1976. *Euripides. Troades* (New York).

——. 1997. *Euripides. Ion* (Warminster).

Le Guen, B. 2001. *Les associations de technites dionysiaques à l'époque hellénistique*, 2 vols. (Nancy).

Lehnus, L. 1975. "Note stesicoree: i poemetti "minori" (frr. 277–9 PMG)." *SCO* 24, 191–6.

Lelli, E. 2001. "La polivalenza simbolica dell'opposizione asino/cicala nel prologo degli Aitia di Callimaco (fr. 1. 29 ss. Pf.)." *SemRom* 4, 247–52.

Lenaerts J. 1977. *Papyrus littéraires grecs*, Papyrologica Bruxellensia vol. 13 (Brussels).

Leo, F. 1897. *Die plautinischen Cantica und die hellenistische Lyrik*, Abh. kgl. Ges. Wiss. Göttingen, Phil.-Hist. Kl., N.F. 1.7 (Berlin).

Lesky, A. 1966. "Neroniana." In W. Kraus (ed.), *Gesammelte Schriften. Aufsätze und Reden zu antiker und Deutscher Dichtung und Kultur* (Bern), 335–51 [= *Mélanges Henri Grégoire*, 9 (1949) 385–407].

——. 1972³. *Die tragische Dichtung der Hellenen* (Göttingen).

Lightfoot, J.L. 2002. "Nothing to do with the technitai of Dionysus?" In P. Easterling and E. Hall (eds.), *Greek and Roman Actors. Aspects of an Ancient Profession* (Cambridge), 209–24.

Lobel, E. 1925. *ΣΑΠΦΟΥΣ ΜΕΛΗ* (Oxford).

Lobel, E. and Page, D.L. 1955. *Poetarum Lesbiorum fragmenta* (Oxford).

Lomiento, L. 2001. "Da Sparta ad Alessandria. La trasmissione dei testi nella Grecia antica." In M. Vetta (ed.), *La civiltà dei Greci. Forme, luoghi, contesti* (Rome), 297–355.

Longman, G.A. 1962. "The musical papyrus: Euripides Orestes 332–340." *CQ* 56, 61–6.

Loscalzo, D. 2003. *La parola inestinguibile. Studi sull'epinicio pindarico* (Rome).

Lowe, C.G. 1924. *The Manuscript Tradition of Pseudo-Plutarch's* Vitae decem oratorum. University of Illinois Studies in Language and Literature IX. 4 (Urbana).

Luppe, W. 1980. "Literarische Texte unter Ausschluss der Christlichen. Drama." *APF* 27, 233–250.

——. 1995. "Ein neuer früher 'Medeia'-Papyrus P. Berol. 21257." *APF* 41, 34–9.

——. 1997. "Literarische Texte. Drama." *APF* 43, 93–106.

——. 2004. "Überlegungen zur Gedicht-Anordnung im neuen Sappho-Papyrus." *ZPE* 149, 7–9.

Madvig, J.N. 1846. "Emendationes per saturam." *Philologus* 1, 670–7.

Malnati, A. 1992. "Revisione di PMil.Vogl. I 7 = Pack² 1898." In M. Capasso (ed.), *Papiri letterari greci e latini*, Papyrologica Lupiensia vol. 1 (Lecce), 321–3.

Marino, E. 1999a. "Il papiro musicale dell'Oreste di Euripide e la colometria dei codici." In B. Gentili and F. Perusino, *La colometria antica dei testi poetici greci* (Rome), 143–56.

——. 1999b. *Gli scolî metrici antichi alle Olimpiche di Pindaro*, Labirinti vol. 38, Dipartimento di Scienze Filologiche e storiche, Università degli studi di Trento (Trento).

Marrou, H.-I. 1965⁶. *Histoire de l'éducation dans l'antiquité* (Paris).

Marshall, C.W. 2004. "Alcestis and the ancient rehearsal process (P.Oxy. 4546)." *Arion* 11, 27–43.

Martin, E. 1953. *Trois documents de musique grecque* (Paris).

Martin, R.P. 2003. "The pipes are brawling." In C. Dougherty and L. Kurke (eds.), *The Cultures within Ancient Greek Culture. Contact, Conflict, Collaboration* (Cambridge), 153–80.

Martinelli, M.C. 1997². *Gli strumenti del poeta* (Bologna).

——. 1999. *Eikasmos* 10, 379–90 (review of M. Fantuzzi and R. Pretagostini, *Struttura e storia dell'esametro greco*, 2 vols. [Rome 1995–1996]).

Marzi, G. 1973. "Il papiro musicale dell'Oreste di Euripide." In *Scritti in onore di Luigi Ronga* (Milan), 315–25.

Mastromarco, G. 1983. *Aristofane. Le commedie* (Turin).

Mastronarde, D.J. 1994a. *Euripides. Phoenissae* (Cambridge).

——. 1994b. *BMCR* 5.4, 326–30 (review of Kovacs 1994).

——. 2002. *Euripides. Medea* (Cambridge).

Mastronarde, D.J. and Bremer, M. 1982. *The Textual Tradition of Euripides' Phoinissai* (Berkeley-Los Angeles).

Matelli, E. 2004. "Musicoterapia e catarsi in Teofrasto." *BICS* 47, 153–74.

Mathiesen, T.J. 1981. "New fragments of ancient Greek music." *Acta Musicologica* 53, 14–32.

——. 1983. *Aristides Quintilianus. On Music. In Three Books* (New Haven-London).

——. 1999. *Apollo's Lyre. Greek Music and Music Theory in Antiquity and the Middle Ages* (Lincoln-London).

Matthaios, S. 1999. *Untersuchungen zur Grammatik Aristarchs. Texte und Interpretation zur Wortartenlehre*, Hypomnemata vol. 126 (Göttingen).

Medda, E. 1989. "Un nuovo commento all'Oreste di Euripide." *RFIC* 117, 98–124.

——. 1993. "Su alcune associazioni del docmio con altri metri in tragedia (Cretico, Molosso, Baccheo, Spondeo, Trocheo, Coriambo)." *SCO* 43, 101–234.

——. 2000. "Osservazioni su iato e brevis in longo nei docmi." *SemRom* 3, 115–42.

——. 2001. *Euripide. Oreste* (Milan).

Milanezi, S. 2004. "À l'ombre des acteurs: les amuseurs à l'époque classique." In Ch. Hugoniot, F. Hurlet and S. Milanezi (eds.), *Le statut de l'acteur dans l'Antiquité grecque et romaine. Actes du colloque qui s'est tenu à Tours les 3 et 4 mai 2002* (Tours), 183–209.

Moore-Blunt, J. 1978. "Problems of accentuation in Greek papyri." *QUCC* 29, 137–63.

Morgan, T. 1998. *Literate Education in the Hellenistic and Roman Worlds* (Cambridge).

Most, G.W. 1985. *The Measures of Praise. Structure and Function in Pindar's Second Pythian and Seventh Nemean Odes* (Göttingen).

Mulliez, D. 2000. *Bulletin épigraphique* 113, 497 no. 364.

Murray, P. and Wilson, P. (eds.) 2004. *Music and the Muses. The Culture of Mousike in the Classical Athenian City* (Oxford).

Musso, O. 1982. "Euripide, Oreste, vv. 134–142 (= Pap. Köln III 131)." *ZPE* 46, 43–6.

Nagy, G. 1990. *Pindar's Homer. The Lyric Possession of an Epic Past* (Baltimore-London).

——. 2000. "Reading Greek poetry aloud: evidence from the Bacchylides papyri." *QUCC* 64, 7–24.

Najock, D. 1972. *Drei anonyme griechische Traktate über die Musik. Eine kommentierte Neuausgabe des Bellermannschen Anonymus* (Göttingen).

Napolitano, M. 1999. *RFIC* 127, 107–25 (review of M. Fantuzzi and R. Pretagostini, *Struttura e storia dell'esametro greco*, 2 vols., [Rome 1995–1996]).

Nauck, A. 1848. *Aristophanis Byzantii grammatici Alexandrini fragmenta* (Halle).

Negri, M. 2004. *Pindaro ad Alessandria. Le edizioni e gli editori* (Brescia).

Neubecker, A.J. 1977. *Altgriechische Musik: eine Einführung* (Darmstadt).

Nicosia, S. 1976. *Tradizione testuale diretta e indiretta dei poeti di Lesbo* (Rome).

Nilsson, M.P. 1906. *Zur Geschichte des Bühnenspiels in der römischen Kaiserzeit* (Lund).

O'Callaghan, J. 1981. "Dos nuevos papiros de Eurípides (Orestes 134–142 y 290–300. 321–330)." *Studia Papyrologica* 20, 15–24.

Page, D.L. 1955. *Sappho and Alcaeus* (Oxford).

Paley, F.A. 1860. *Euripides*, vol. 3 (London).

Pardini, A. 1991. "La ripartizione in libri dell'opera di Alceo. Per un riesame della questione." *RFIC* 119, 257–84.

——. 1999. "Note alla colometria dell'Aiace di Sofocle." In B. Gentili and F. Perusino (eds.), *La colometria antica dei testi poetici greci* (Rome), 95–120.

Parker, L.P.E. 1997. *The Songs of Aristophanes* (Oxford).

——. 2001. "Consilium et ratio? Papyrus A of Bacchylides and Alexandrian metrical scholarship." *CQ* 51, 23–52.

Pavloskis, Z. 1977. "The voice of the actor in Greek tragedy." *CW* 71, 113–23.

Pearson, L. 1990. *Aristoxenus. Elementa Rhythmica. The Fragment of Book II and the Additional Evidence for Aristoxenean Rhythmic Theory* (Oxford).

Pecorella, G.B. 1962. *Dionisio Trace. ΤΕΧΝΗ ΓΡΑΜΜΑΤΙΚΗ* (Bologna).

Perdicoyanni-Paléologue, H. 2002. "The interjections in Greek tragedy." *QUCC* 70, 49–88.

Pernigotti 2001, C. "Tempi del canto e pluralità di prospettive in Saffo, fr. 44 V." *ZPE* 135, 11–20.

Perrin, E. 1997. "Propagande et culture théâtrales à Athènes à l'époque hellénistique." In B. LeGuen (ed.), *De la scène aux gradins: théâtre et représentations dramatiques après Alexandre le Grand*, Pallas vol. 47 (Toulouse), 201–18.

Peruzzi, E. 1998. "ΜΟΥΣΙΚΗ." In id., *Civiltà greca nel Lazio preromano* (Florence), 139–56.

Pfeiffer, R. 1968. *History of Classical Scholarship from the Beginnings to the End of the Hellenistic Age* (Oxford).

Pfeijffer, J.L. 1999. *Three Aeginetan Odes of Pindar* (Leiden).

Pickard-Cambridge, A. 1968². *The Dramatic Festivals of Athens* (Oxford) [second edition revised by J. Gould and D.M. Lewis].

Pintaudi, R. 1985. "Un nuovo papiro tolemaico dell'Oreste di Euripide (PL III/908)." *SCO* 35, 13–23.

Pöhlmann, E. 1960. *Griechische Musikfragmente. Ein Weg zur altgriechischen Musik* (Nürnberg).

——. 1965. "Marius Victorinus zum Odengesang bei Horaz." *Philologus* 109, 134–40 [= id., *Beiträge zur antiken und neueren Musikgeschichte* (Frankfurt am Main 1988), 135–43].

——. 1970. *Denkmäler altgriechischer Musik* (Nürnberg).

——. 1976. "Die Notenschrift in der Überlieferung der griechischen Bühnenmusik." *WJA* 2, 53–73 [= id., *Beiträge zur antiken und neueren Musikgeschichte* (Frankfurt am Main 1988), 57–93].

——. 1986. "Zur Frühgeschichte der Überlieferung griechischer Bühnendichtung und Bühnenmusik." In *Festschrift für Martin Ruhnke* (Erlangen), 294–306 [= id., *Beiträge zur antiken und neueren Musikgeschichte* (Frankfurt am Main 1988), 23–40].

——. 1988. "Sulla preistoria della tradizione di testi e musica per il teatro." In B. Gentili and R. Pretagostini (eds.), *La musica in Grecia* (Rome-Bari), 132–44.

——. 1991. "Die Überlieferung der Musik in der antiken Welt." *Die Musikforschung* 44, 1–9.

——. 1994. *Einführung in die Überlieferungsgeschichte und die Textkritik der antiken Literatur*, vol. 1 (Darmstadt).

——. 1995a. "Metrica e ritmica nella poesia e nella musica greca antica." In B. Gentili and F. Perusino (eds.), *Mousike. Metrica ritmica e musica greca in memoria di Giovanni Comotti* (Rome), 3–15.

——. 1995b. s.v. "Griechenland A, Antike Musik." In *Die Musik in Geschichte und Gegenwart²* (= *MGG²*) 3, 1626–76.

——. 1997. s.v. "Notation II. Antike." In *MGG²* 7, 283–9.

——. 1998. "Frieder Zaminers 'griechische Singsprache': ein neuer Zugang zu altgriechischer Metrik und Rhythmik?" *WJA* 22, 9–19.

——. 2005. "Dramatische Texte in den Fragmenten antiker Musik." In S. Hagel and Ch. Harrauer (eds.), *Ancient Greek Music in Performance. Symposion Wien 29. Sept.–1.Okt. 2003*, Vienna, 130–45.

Prato, C. 2001. *Aristofane. Le donne alle Tesmoforie* (Milan).

Prauscello, L. 2002. "Colometria alessandrina e testi con notazioni musicali: per un riesame di P.Vind. G 2315 (= Eur. Or. 338–44)." *ZPE* 141, 83–102.

——. 2003. "La testimonianza di P. Leid. Inv. 510 (= Eur. I.A. 1500?-1509, 784–793?) fra prassi esecutiva e trasmissione testuale." *ZPE* 144, 1–14.

——. 2004. "A note on tabula defixionis 22 (a). 5–7 Ziebarth: when a performance enacts love." *CQ* 54, 333–39.

——. forthcoming in *CP*. "Looking for the 'other' Gnesippus: some notes on Eupolis fragment 148 K-A."

Pretagostini, R. 1995a. "L'esametro nel dramma attico del V secolo: problemi di 'resa' e di 'riconoscimento'." In M. Fantuzzi and R. Pretagostini (eds.), *Struttura e storia dell'esametro greco*, vol. 1 (Rome), 163–91.

——. 1995b. "L'autore ellenistico fra poesia e "filologia". Problemi di esegesi, di metrica e di attendibilità del racconto." *Aevum(ant)* 8, 33–46.

——. 1997. "La ripresa teocritea della poesia erotica arcaica e tardoarcaica (Idd. 29 e 30)." *MD* 38, 9–24.

——. 1998. "'Mousike': poesia e 'performance'." In S. Settis (ed.), *I Greci*, II. 3 (Turin), 617–33.

Pritchard, D. 2003. "Athletics, education and partecipation in classical Athens." In D.J. Phillips and D. Pritchard (eds.), *Sport and Festivals in the Ancient Greek World* (Swansea), 293–349.

Psaroudakes, S. 2004. "The Orestes papyrus: some thoughts on the dubious musical signs." In E. Hickmann and R. Eichmann (eds.), *Studien zur Musikarchäologie 4. Vorträge des 3. Symposiums der Internationalen Studiengruppe Musikarchäologie im Kloster Michaelstein, 9.–16. Juni 2002*, Deutsches Archäologische Institut, Orient-Abteilung (Berlin), 471–92.

Questa, C.-Raffaelli, R. 1990. "Dalla rappresentazione alla lettura." In G. Cavallo, P. Fedeli and A. Giardina (eds.), *Lo spazio letterario di Roma antica* III, *La ricezione del testo* (Rome), 139–215.

Redondo Reyes, P. 2001. "Eurípides y la música del drama ático: una revisión del papiro del Orestes." *Myrtia* 16, 47–75.

Rehm, A. 1954. "Neue Wörter aus Didyma." *IF* 61, 170–86.

Reinach, T. 1919. s.v. "Tibia." In C. Daremberg and E. Saglio (eds.), *DAGR* 5, 300–22.

Reitzenstein, R. 1893. *Epigramm und Skolion. Ein Beitrag zur Geschichte der alexandrinischen Dichtung* (Giessen).

Renehan, R. 1976. *Studies in Greek Texts. Critical Observations to Homer, Plato, Euripides, Aristophanes and Other Authors* (Göttingen), 88–92.

Reynolds, L.D. and Wilson, N.G. 1974². *Scribes & Scholars. A Guide to the Transmission of Greek & Latin Literature* (Oxford).

Ribbeck, O. 1897–8³. *Scaenicae Romanorum poesis fragmenta*, 2 vols. (Leipzig).

Richter, L. 2000. "Das Musikfragment aus dem Euripidischen Orestes." In L. Richter, *Momente der Musikgeschichte. Antike und Byzanz. Aufsätze*, Wort und Musik: Salzburger akademische Beiträge vol. 45 (Salzburg), 42–92.

Rispoli, G.M. 1996. "La voce dell'attore nel mondo antico: teorie e tecniche." *Acme* 49, 3–28.

Robert, L. 1954. *Bulletin épigraphique* 67, 128–9 no. 111.

Roberts, C.H. 1956. *Greek Literary Hands, 350 B.C.–A.D. 400* (Oxford).

Rocconi, E. 2001. "Il 'canto' magico nel mondo greco. Sulle origini magiche del potere psicagogico della musica." *SemRom* 4, 279–87.

———. 2003. *Le parole delle Muse. La formazione del lessico tecnico musicale nella Grecia antica*, Quaderni di SemRom vol. 5 (Rome).

Rolfe, J.C. 1997. *Suetonius*, 2 vols. (Cambridge, MA-London).

Rose, H.J. 1932. "Stesichoros and the Rhadine-fragment." *CQ* 26, 88–92.

Rossi, L.E. 1963. *Metrica e critica stilistica. Il termine 'ciclico' e l'ἀγωγή ritmica* (Rome).

———. 1971. "I generi letterari e le loro leggi scritte e non scritte nelle letterature classiche." *BICS* 18, 69–94.

———. 1993. "Lirica arcaica e scoli simposiali (Alc. 249, 6–9 V. e carm. conv. 891 P.)." In R. Pretagostini (ed.), *Tradizione e innovazione nella cultura greca da Omero all'età ellenistica. Scritti in onore di B. Gentili*, vol. 1 (Rome), 237–46.

———. 1998. "Orazio, un lirico greco senza musica." *SemRom* 1, 163–81.

———. 2000a. "La letteratura alessandrina e il rinnovamento dei generi letterari della tradizione." In R. Pretagostini (ed.), *La letteratura ellenistica. Problemi e prospettive di ricerca. Atti del Colloquio Internazionale, Università di Roma "Tor Vergata", 29–30 aprile 1997*, Quaderni di SemRom vol. 1 (Rome), 149–61.

———. 2000b. "L'autore e il controllo del testo nel mondo antico." *SemRom* 3, 165–81.

———. 2000c. "Origini e finalità del prodotto pseudoepigrafo. Pseudepigrafia preterintenzionale nel corpus Theocriteum: l'Idillio VIII." In G. Cerri (ed.), *La letteratura pseudepigrafa nella cultura greca e romana. Atti di un incontro di studi, Napoli 15–17 gennaio 1998*, A.I.O.N. (filol) 22, (Naples), 231–61.

Rossi, L. 2001. *The Epigrams Ascribed to Theocritus: A Method of Approach*, Hellenistica Groningana vol. 5 (Leuven).

Ruijgh, C.J. 2001. "Le Spectacle des Lettres, Comédie de Callias (Athénée X 453c–455b), avec un excursus sur les rapports entre la mélodie du chant et les contours mélodiques du langage parlé." *Mnemosyne* 54, 257–335.

Rutherford, I.C. 1997. "For the Aeginetans to Aiakos a prosodion: an unnoticed title at Pindar, Paean 6, 123, and its significance for the poem." *ZPE* 118, 1–21.

——. 2001. *Pindar's Paeans. A Reading of the Fragments with a Survey of the Genre* (Oxford).

——. 2003. "The prosodion: approaches to a lyric genre." In F. Benedetti and S. Grandolini (eds.), *Studi di filologia e tradizione greca in memoria di Aristide Colonna*, vol. 2 (Naples), 713–26.

Rutherford, W.G. 1905. *A Chapter in the History of Annotation being Scholia Aristophanica*, vol. 3 (London).

Sandys, J.E. 1885. *M. Tullius Cicero, Ad M. Brutum Orator* (Cambridge).

Sansone, D. 1981. *Euripides. Iphigenia in Tauris* (Leipzig).

Savignago, L. 2003. "Il sistema dei margini nei papiri di Euripide." In L. Battezzato (ed.), *Tradizione testuale e ricezione letteraria antica della tragedia greca. Atti del convegno Scuola Normale Superiore, Pisa 14–5 giugno 2002* (Amsterdam), 77–98.

Schmidt, M. 1860. ΕΠΙΤΟΜΗ ΤΗΣ ΚΑΘΟΛΙΚΗΣ ΠΡΟΣΩΙΔΙΑΣ ΗΡΩΔΙΑΝΟΥ, Jenae.

Schwartz, E. 1887–1891. *Scholia in Euripidem*, 2 vols. (Berlin).

Scott, W.C. 1996. *Musical Design in Sophoclean Theater* (Hanover-London).

Sedgwick, W.B. 1950. "A note on performance of Greek vocal music." *C&M* 11, 222–6.

Shackleton Bailey, D.R. 1965. *Cicero's Letters to Atticus*, vol. 2 (Cambridge).

——. 1977. *Cicero: Epistulae ad familiares*, vol. 1 (Cambridge).

Sicking, C.M.J. 1993. *Griechische Verslehre* (Munich).

Sickinger, J.P. 1999. *Publics Records and Archives in Classical Athens* (Chapel Hill-London).

Sifakis, G.M. 1967. *Studies in the History of Hellenistic Drama* (London).

——. 1995. "The one-actor rule in Greek tragedy." In A.H. Griffiths (ed.), *Stage Directions. Essays in Ancient Drama in Honour of E.W. Handley*, BICS Suppl. 66 (London), 13–24.

Slater, W.J. 1986. *Aristophanis Byzantii fragmenta* (Berlin-New York).

Slings , S.R. 1991. "Sappho fr. 1, 8 V.: golden house or golden chariot?" *Mnemosyne* 44, 404–10.

——. 1999. "Information unit and metrical unit." In I.L. Pfeijffer and S.R. Slings (eds.), *One Hundred Years of Bacchylides: Proceedings of a Colloquium held at the Vrije Universiteit* (Amsterdam), 61–75 [= id. in A. Bagordo and B. Zimmermann (eds.), *Bakchylides. 100 Jahre nach seiner Wiederentdeckung* (Munich 2000), 113–30].

Smith, L.P. 1993. "A Duke Papyrus of Euripides' Orestes 939–954." *ZPE* 98, 15–8.

Snell, B. 1931. "Sapphos Gedicht φαίνεταί μοι κῆνος." *Hermes* 66, 71–90, 368.

Solomon, J. 1977. "Orestes 344–45: colometry and music." *GRBS* 18, 71–83.

Sommerstein, A.H. 1982. *Aristophanes. Clouds* (Warminster).

Spranger, J.A. 1920. *Euripidis quae inveniuntur in codice Laurentiano pl. XXXII. 2 phototypice expressa* (Florence).

——. 1939–46. *Euripidis quae in codicibus Palatino Graeco inter Vaticanos 287 et Laurentiano Conv.Soppr. 172 (olim Abbatiae Florentinae 2664) inveniuntur phototypice expressa* (Florence).

Stanford, W.B. 1969. "The lily voice of the cicadas (Iliad 3. 152)." *Phoenix* 23, 3–8.

Stark, R. 1963. "Theocritea." *Maia* 15, 359–85.

Stinton, T.C.W. 1975. "More rare verse-forms." *BICS* 22, 84–108 [= id., *Collected Papers on Greek Tragedy* (Oxford 1990), 113–42].

——. 1977. "Pause and period in the lyrics of Greek tragedy." *CQ* 27, 27–66 [= id., *Collected Papers on Greek Tragedy* (Oxford 1990), 310–61].

Stockert, W. 1992. *Euripides. Iphigenie in Aulis*, 2 vols. (Vienna).

Svenbro, J. 1991. "La lecture à haute voix. Le témoignage des verbes grecs signifiant 'lire'." In C. Baurain, C. Bonnet and V. Krings (eds.), *PHOINIKEIA GRAMMATA. Lire et écrire en Méditerranée, Actes du Colloque de Liège, 15–18 novembre 1989* (Namur), 539–48.

Tabachovitz, D. 1946. "Ein paar Beobachtungen zum spätgriechischen Sprachge-brauch." *Eranos* 44, 296–305.

——. 1955. "ἑαυτῶι = αὐτός = 'selbst'." *Eranos* 53, 76–8.

Taillardat, J. 1962. *Les images d'Aristophane. Ètudes de language et de style* (Paris).

Tammaro, V. 1980–2. "Aristoph. Nub. 1371." *MCr* 15–17, 107–9.

Tedeschi, G. 2003. "Lo spettacolo in età ellenistica e tardo antica nella documen-tazione epigrafica e papiracea." In M. Capasso (ed.), *Dal restauro dei materiali allo studio dei testi. Aspetti della ricerca papirologica*, Papyrologica Lupiensia 11/2002 (Galatina), 87–187.

Tessier, A. 1995. *Tradizione metrica di Pindaro* (Padua).

——. 2001. "Aeschylus 'more Triclinii'." *Lexis* 19, 51–66.

Torraca, L. 1994. "La tradizione manoscritta dei Caratteri XXIV–XXVIII di Teofrasto." In *Storia, poesia e pensiero nel mondo antico. Studi in onore di Marcello Gigante* (Naples), 607–16.

Turner, E.G. 1956. "Two unrecognised Ptolemaic papyri." *JHS* 76, 95–8.

——. 1980. "Ptolemaic bookhands and Lille Stesichorus." *S&C* 4, 19–40.

Usher, S. 1985. *Dionysius of Halicarnassus. The Critical Essays*, vol. 2 (Cambridge, MA-London).

Vahlen, J. 1928². *Ennianae poesis reliquiae* (Leipzig).

Van Akkeren, A. 1983. "Muziek van Euripides." *Hermeneus* 55, 259–71.

Van Groeningen, B.A. 1966. *Theognis. Le premier livre* (Amsterdam).

Van Leeuwen, J. 1968². *Aristophanis Ranae* (Leiden).

Veleni, P.A. 2002. "Una nuova epigrafe musicale." *Kleos* 7, 211–5.

Verity, A. and Hunter, R. 2002. *Theocritus. Idylls* (Oxford).

Vetta, M. 1983. "Poesia simposiale nella Grecia arcaica e classica." In M. Vetta (ed.), *Poesia e simposio nella Grecia antica. Guida storica e critica* (Bari), xi–lx.

——. 1992. "Il simposio: la monodia e il giambo." In G. Cambiano, L. Canfora and D. Lanza (eds.), *Lo spazio letterario della Grecia antica*, I. 1 (Rome), 177–218.

——. 1995. "La voce degli attori nel teatro attico." In De Martino and Sommerstein (eds.), *Lo spettacolo delle voci* (Bari), 61–78.

Voigt, E.-M. 1971. *Sappho et Alcaeus. Fragmenta* (Amsterdam).

Wahlström, E. 1970. *Accentual Response in Greek Strophic Poetry*, Commentationes Humanarum Litterarum vol. 47 (Helsinki).

Wallace, R.B. 2003. "An early fifth-century Athenian revolution in aulos music." *HSCPh* 101, 73–92.

Waltz, P. and Soury, G. 1957. *Anthologie grecque*, vol. 7 (Paris).

Wartelle, A. 1971. *Histoire du texte d'Eschyle dans l'antiquité* (Paris).

Webster, T.B.L. 1963. "Alexandrian epigrams and the theatre." In L. Ferrero, C. Gallavotti, I. Lana, A. Maddalena, A. Momigliano and M. Pellegrino (eds.), *Miscellanea di studi alessandrini in memoria di Augusto Rostagni* (Turin), 531–43.

——. 1967. *The Tragedies of Euripides* (London).

Wecklein, N. 1899. *Euripidis fabulae*, vol. 2 (Leipzig).

Weil, H. 1868. ΕΥΡΙΠΙΔΟΥ ΤΡΑΓΩΙΔΙΑΙ ΕΠΤΑ, *Sept tragédies d'Euripide* (Paris).

Weil, H. and Reinach, T. 1900. *Plutarque, De la musique* (Paris).

Wessely, C. 1892. "Le papyrus musicale d'Euripide." *REG* 5, 265–80.

——. 1892a. "Papyrusfragment des Chorgesanges von Euripides Orest 330 ff. mit Partitur." *Mitteilungen aus der Sammlung der Papyrus Erzherzog Rainer* 5, 65–73.

West, M.L. 1966. *Hesiod. Theogony* (Oxford).

——. 1967. "A note on Theocritus' Aeolic poems." *CQ* 13, 82–4.

——. 1974. *Studies in Greek Elegy and Iambus* (Berlin-New York).

——. 1982. *Greek Metre* (Oxford).

——. 1987. *Euripides. Orestes* (Warminster).

——. 1992. "Analecta musica." *ZPE* 92, 1.

——. 1998². *Aeschylus. Tragoediae cum incerti poetae Prometheo* (Stuttgart-Leipzig).

——. 2005. "The new Sappho." *ZPE* 151, 1–9.

Westman, R. 1980. *M.T. Cicero, Orator* (Leipzig).
Wilamowitz, U. von. 1889. *Euripides Herakles I, Einleitung in die griechische Tragödie*, Berlin.
——. 1895. *Commentariolum metricum* (Göttingen).
——. 1900. *Die Textgeschichte der griechischen Lyriker*, Abhandl. der könig. Gesellschaft der Wissenschaften zu Göttingen, Phil.-hist. Klasse. N.F. Bd. IV n. 3 (Berlin).
——. 1906. *Die Textgeschichte der griechischen Bukoliker* (Berlin).
——. 1921. *Griechische Verskunst* (Berlin).
Wille, G. 1967. *Musica Romana. Die Bedeutung der Musik im Leben der Römer* (Amsterdam).
Willett, S.J. 2002. "Working memory and its constraints on colometry." *QUCC* 71, 7–19 [= id., "Working memory and its constraints on colometry." Abstract in occasion of the Annual Meeting of the American Philological Association, New Orleans January 2003: http://www.apaclassics.org/Annual Meeting/03mtg/abstracts/ Willett.html].
Willink, C.W. 1986. *Euripides. Orestes* (Oxford).
——. 1989. "The reunion duo in Euripides' Helen." *CQ* 39, 45–69.
——. 2001. "Again the Orestes 'musical papyrus'." *QUCC* 68, 125–33.
Wilson, P. 2000. *The Athenian Institution of the Khoregia: the Chorus, the City and the Stage* (Cambridge).
——. 2002. "The musicians among the actors." In P. Easterling and E. Hall (eds.), *Greek and Roman Actors. Aspects of an Ancient Profession* (Cambridge), 39–68.
——. 2004. "Athenian strings." In P. Murray and P. Wilson (eds.), *Music and the Muses. The Culture of Mousike in the Classical Athenian City* (Oxford), 269–306.
——. 2005. "Music." In J. Gregory (ed.), *A Companion to Greek Tragedy*, London, 183–93.
Wright, F.W. 1931. *Cicero and the Theatre* (Northampton, MA).
Xanthakis-Karamanos, G. 1993. "Hellenistic drama: developments in form and performance." *Platon* 45, 117–33.
Yatromanolakis, D. 1999. "Alexandrian Sappho Revisited." *HSCPh* 99, 179–95.
——. 2001. "Visualizing poetry: an early representation of Sappho." *CP* 96, 159–68.
——. 2005. "Contrapuntal inscriptions." *ZPE* 152, 16–30.
Yon, A. 1964. *Cicéron, L'orateur. Du meilleur genre d'orateurs* (Paris).
Zaminer, F. 1989. "Musik im archaischen und klassischen Griechenland." In A. Riethmüller and F. Zaminer (eds.), *Die Musik des Altertums* (Regensburg), 113–206.
Ziebarth, E. 1934. "Neue Verfluchungstafeln aus Attika, Boiotian und Euboia." *SBAW*, 1022–50.
Ziegler, K. 1937. *RE* II. 6 (1937) s.v. "Tragoedia. E, Geschichte des Tragikertextes." coll. 2067–74.
Zuntz, G. 1965. *An Inquiry into the Transmission of the Plays of Euripides* (Cambridge).
——. 1984. *Drei Kapitel zur griechischen Metrik* (Vienna).

INDEX OF ANCIENT PASSAGES CITED

AELIAN
V.H.
3. 32 — 47 n. 143
36. 1 — 56 n. 175

AESCHINES
De falsa leg.
61 — 71
In Ctes.
188 — 71
201 — 72
In Tim.
168 — 102–3
Σ to *In Tim.* 168 — 102–3
(= 50 ll. 954–5 Dilts)

AESCHYLUS
Ag.
1123–4 — 135
1134–5 — 135
1176 — 134 n. 43
PV
576 — 117 n. 372
595 — 117 n. 372
Su.
125–6 — 165 n. 147
Σ to *Choe.* 44 — 149
         378 — 149
Σ to *Eum.* 785c — 149
         839 — 149, 152 n. 104
Σ to *Se.* 106d — 149
Σ to *Su.* 166–7 — 149

ALCAEUS (Voigt)
34A — 195 n. 22
38a — 194, 201 and n. 38
39 — 195 n. 22
44 — 194, 195 n. 22, 202 n. 40
48 — 195
50 — 194, 195 n. 22, 201
61 — 195
112 — 195

113 — 195
114 — 195
120 — 195 n. 22
129 — 193
130 — 193
141 — 194 n. 21
346 — 201
347 — 91 n. 288
348 — 202 n. 40
350 — 195 n. 23

ALCMAN
37b *PMGF* — 45 n. 137
158 *PMGF* — 49 n. 152

ANECDOTA GRAECA (Bekker)
II, 751 ll. 30–2 — 53–4

ANONYMA BELLERMANNIANA (Najock)
11 — 141 n. 73
68 — 67
102 — 12

ANTHOLOGIA PALATINA
7. 213 — 91 n. 289
9. 264 — 92 n. 290

ARCHILOCHUS
190 W² — 203 n. 41

ARISTIDES QUINTILIANUS
De musica (Winnington-Ingram)
p. 6. 4ff. — 18 n. 42
p. 21. 19 — 67 n. 210
p. 23. 18ff. — 67 n. 212
p. 31. 3–6 — 64
p. 31. 8–17 — 64
p. 31. 18–20 — 65
p. 31. 20–4 — 65
pp. 31. 24–32. 4 — 63, 65–6
p. 38. 28 ff. — 12
p. 77. 30ff. — 67 n. 210

ARISTOPHANES
Ach.
494 — 117 n. 372
570 — 117 n. 372

Av.
41   89 n. 280
224   92 n. 290
1095–6   91 n. 288
Nu.
1264–5   99, 100, 101
1266   99
1353–72   **86–92**
1354–6   86 n. 272
1356–7   90
1360–1   91
1364–5   91
1365–7   90
1369–70   87
1371–2   87, 97
1371   88, 89, 92, 93,
                       95, 97, 103
1377   87 n. 276
Pax
1159–60   91 n. 288
1270–87   146 and n. 88
Ra.
366   46 n. 137
823   88 n. 278
Th.
96   179 n. 196
97–8   179 n. 196
101–29   110 n. 353,
                       179
529   203
Vesp.
562   88 n. 278
fr.
101 K-A   89 n. 280
161 K-A   87 n. 276
234 K-A   87 n. 275
Σ to *Nu.* 1264   **99–102**
         1266   100 n. 322
         1356a   86 n. 272
         1357b   92 n. 292
         1360a–b   92 n. 291
         1371a   103 n. 332
Σ to *Th.* 529   203 n. 42
Σ to *Vesp.* 1239   203 n. 42

ARISTOTLE
Poet.
1452b 22   100 n. 325
Pol.
1339b 8–10   30 n. 87
1340b 1   45 n. 137
1341 a 9–17   30 n. 87
Rhet.
1409b 8   64 n. 201

[ARISTOTLE]
De audib.
801b 9–10   37 n. 107
Probl.
918a 10–12   144 and nn.
                       84–5, **151–2**
918b   85 n. 266, 151

ARISTOXENUS
El. harm.
1. 8   18 n. 42
2. 38   31 n. 90
2. 39   30–1
El. rhythm.
2. 9   65 n. 204
2. 19   13 n. 26

ATHENAEUS
1. 3a–b   77–8
5. 214d–e   78
12. 537d   102
14. 624a 10–b 3   92 n. 290
14. 631e   37 n. 107
15. 694c ff.   203

AULUS GELLIUS
N.A.
15. 17. 1   50 n. 156
19. 9. 4   212 n. 67

BACCHYLIDES
Ep. 5. 8   42 n. 128

CALLIMACHUS
Fr. 400 Pf.   204

CASSIUS DIO
63. 10. 2   95 nn. 302, 304

CHOEROBOSCUS
in Heph.180. 4   14 n. 31
   Consbr.

CICERO
Ad Att.
4. 15. 6   62
16. 2. 3   62
16. 5. 1   62
Ad fam.
7. 1. 2   62
De off.
1. 97   62
1. 113–4   62
De orat.
2. 193   62

Orat.
183–4 **59–63**
Pro Rosc. com.
20 62
Pro Sest.
120–2 62
Tusc.
1. 106 62

DEMOSTHENES
De cor.
267 71
De fals. leg.
252 99 n. 319
In Tim.
38 72

DIO CHRYSOSTOMUS
16. 68 115 n. 369
19. 4 113 n. 362
19. 5 113 n. 362

DIOMEDES
GL I, 527. 19 Keil 204 n. 45

DIONYSIUS OF HALICARNASSUS
De compositione verborum
(Aujac-Lebel)
11. 1–5 16
11. 6–10 16
11. 8 16 n. 37, 18
n. 43, 21
n. 52, 28
n. 80
11. 10 19 n. 46
11. 13–14 16–7
11. 15 17–8 and
nn. 40–1
11. 19 10 n. 12, 45
n. 137
11. 19–21 18, **20–3**, 58,
117–8
22–3 **13–5**, **19–20**
11. 24 19 n. 45, 53
n. 166
11. 24–6 17
15. 1–10 14 n. 31
11. 15–17 21 n. 54
17. 1 19 n. 47
19. 4–8 **25–7**
19. 9 25 n. 66
22. 17 64 n. 201
26. 3–5 16 n. 36, 25
n. 67

DIONYSIUS THRAX
Ars grammatica 2 (= *GG* I.
1, 6 ll. 5–14 Uhl.) 52–3
Σᵈ in Dion. Thr. *Ars gr.* 2
(= *GG* I. 3, 16
ll. 19–21 Hilg.) 53 n. 163
Σᵈ in Dion. Thr. *Ars gr.* 2
(= *GG* I. 3, 16
ll. 27–8 Hilg.) 53 n. 164
Σᵈ in Dion. Thr. *Ars gr.* 2
(= *GG* I. 3, 17
ll. 14–5 Hilg.) 53 n. 165
Σᵈ in Dion. Thr. *Ars gr.* 2
(= *GG* I. 3, 21
ll. 12–21 Hilg.) **54–6**
Σʰ in Dion. Thr. *Ars gr.* 2
(= *GG* I. 3, 476
l. 29 ff. Hilg.) 56
Σᶿ in Dion. Thr. *Ars gr.*
Goettling 1822, 59
ll. 24–8 56–7

EPHIPPUS
16 K-A 88 n. 280,
102

ETYMOLOGICUM MAGNUM (Gaisford)
s.v. εἰδογράφος
(295. 52 ff.) 29
s.v. ἐπὶ Χαριξένης
(367. 21) 50 n. 156

EUPOLIS
39 K-A 89 n. 280
148 K-A 87 n. 275
398 K-A 31 n. 92

EURIPIDES
Aiolos
T ii *TrGF* 97 n. 307
Ba.
576–641 107 n. 342,
108
865 175 n. 180
1168–215 108–10
Cyc.
474 174 n. 179
El.
154 174 n. 178
1208 165
1315 169 n. 162,
176 n. 184
Hec.
946–7 175 n. 184

Hel.

16	176 n. 185
178	174 n. 178
195	158
232	174 n. 178
385	174 n. 178
522	176 n. 184
625–99	145–6
1245	174 n. 178
1545	174 n. 178

Hcld.

874	174 n. 179

HF

116	15 n. 33
442–3	96 n. 306
525–6	96 n. 306
620	176 n. 185
875–921	145
1010–2	96 n. 306
1032–8	96 n. 306
1061–2	174 n. 178

Hipp.

170	15 n. 33
579–95	140
683	168 n. 161
817–51	145, 146
850	117 n. 372
869	174 n. 178
1148	175 n. 184

Ion

261	176 n. 185
483	169 n. 162, 176 n. 184
496–8	174 n. 180
757	101 n. 326
1439–1509	145

IA

773–83	177
784–6	170
789–90	172–3
792–3	**167–9**, 175, 176
793	119 n. 375, **173–6**, 177, 182
1491	172 and n. 172, 177 n. 190
1501–02	165, **171–2**
1503	**171–2**
1504–05	165, 170 and n. 164
1506–08	171
1506	165 n. 147
1507	167 n. 157
1509	169

1510–31	177 n. 190, 179 n. 194
1558	176 n. 185

IT

897–8	176 n. 187
1109	174 n. 178

Med.

34	147 n. 92
423	172 n. 173
653	169 n. 162, 175 n. 184
1087	79 n. 249
1088	79 n. 249
1252	117 n. 372
1253	174 n. 178
1262	117 n. 372
1271–2	101 n. 327
1273–92	151
1277–8	101 n. 327
1284–5	101 n. 327
1288–9	101 n. 327

Or.

argum. ii ll. 40–1	118 and n. 373
l. 43	124 n. 1
140–2	24, **117–8**, 136 n. 51
153–5	24
182	150
201–2	136 n. 51
203	150
325–6	130 n. 19, 132 and n. 33, 142 n. 77, 155–6
	157 n. 118, 158
335–7	126, **156–9**
338–40	119 n. 376, 121, 142 and n. 77, 143, 144 n. 82, 145, 146
342–3	
343	125, 142 n. 79, 159–60
344–6	134–5
1307	174 n. 178
1364	174 n. 178
1383	174 n. 178

Phoen.

187	135
280	176 n. 185
796	12 n. 18
1029	174 n. 178
1295	174 n. 178
1498	12 n. 18
1529	174

1530–81	110 n. 354, 178 n. 193
1557	12 n. 18
1710–36	110 n. 354, 178 n. 193
1718	15 n. 33
1738	176 n. 185
Su.	
1037	176 n. 185
1198	165 n. 148
Tro.	
162	176 n. 184
472	101 n. 326
857	169 n. 162, 176 n. 184, 176 n. 186
1079	174 n. 178
1313	174 n. 178
[*Rh.*]	
869	176 n. 185
932	169 n. 162, 176 n. 184
fr.	
696	176 n. 185
915	174 n. 179
Σ to *Andr.*	
1036	149
1273	149, 151 n. 103
Σ to *Hec.*	
626	149
Σ to *Hipp.*	
58	100 n. 325
812	149, 152 n. 104
Σ to *Med.*	
228	147 n. 93, 148
764	148
1273	148
1371	149
Σ to *Or.*	
12	154
57	73 n. 232
140	117 n. 372
176	144 n. 83, 150 and n. 98
183	150–1
314	154
327	149, 152 n. 106
332	149
340	126, **143–54**
343	147 n. 92
434	154
1038	153, 154
1287	153
1371	154

1384	144 n. 83, 154
Σ to *Phoen.*	
550	149, 152 n. 104
1520	149
GALEN (Kühn)	
XVII. 1, 603. 7–8	75
XVII. 1, 605. 13–14	75
XVII. 1, 606. 16ff.	76
XVII. 1, 606. 12–13	76 n. 241
XVII. 1, 607. 4–14	74
XVII. 1, 608. 3ff.	76
HEPHAESTION (Consbruch)	
23, 14–6 (= Sapph. 227 V)	186, 190 n. 13
34, 11–3 (= Sapph. 229 V)	190 n. 13
36, 13ff.	194
58, 16ff.	186 n. 2
59, 7–10 (= Sappho 228 V)	190
63, 4–8 (= Sappho 228 V)	190
63, 15–24 (= Sappho 228 V)	190–1
HESIOD	
Erg.	
583–4	91 n. 288
HIPPOCRATES	
Coac.	
246 (= V, 637 Littré)	94 n. 297
HOMER	
Il.	
Γ 150–2	91 n. 288
Σ to Θ 236	149
M 113	150
N 603	150
O 365b	150
X 297	150
Ω 201a	150
Ω 255–60	150
Od.	
ρ 286–7	174 n. 179
Σ to *Od.*	
α 242	151
β 271	151 n. 102
β 272	151

LASUS
702 *PMG*   90

LONGINUS
Proleg. in Heph.
83. 14–6 Consbr.   13 n. 27

[LONGINUS]
Subl.
40. 4   12 n. 20
41. 3   57 n. 179

LUCIAN
Anach.
7   94 n. 297
9   94 n. 297
Demon.
12   94 n. 297
De salt.
5   94 n. 297
27   93–4
30   45 n. 137
Hist. conscr.
1   94 n. 296
Symp.
18   94 n. 297

MESOMEDES
Hymns
27–28   11 n. 15, 13
                       n. 21

NONNUS
Dion.
20. 305   51 n. 158

PAUSANIAS
9. 12. 5   37 n. 107
9. 12. 5–6   51 n. 158

PHILOSTRATUS
Vita Apoll.
5. 16   98

PHOTIUS
Lex.
s.v. ὑποδιδάϲκαλοϲ   46 n. 137

PHRYNICUS
TrGF I 3 F 6   204 n. 44

PINDAR
Ol.
1. 102   44 n. 130
6. 87–91   42 n. 127
9. 21–6   43 n. 129

Pyth.
2. 3–4   41 n. 124, 42
   67–8   41 n. 124, 42
   69   42 n. 128
   70   42
   71   42 n. 128
12. 19   51 n. 158
Isthm.
2. 47–8   42 and n. 127,
                       44
Nem.
3. 79   44 n. 130
5. 1–3   43 n. 129
6. 32   43 n. 129
Pae.
6   83 n. 260
fr.
75. 18   51 n. 158
140b 15–17   51 n. 158
Σ to *Ol.* 2. 48c, f   **38–40**
   Pyth. 1. 5a   103 n. 331
      2 inscr.   29 and n. 83
      2. 6b   **40–5**
      2. 36b   148 n. 96
      2. 115   148 n. 96
   Isthm. 2. 68   44
   Nem. 8. 32c   148 n. 94

PLATO
Ion
536d   87 n. 276
541e   87 n. 276
Phd.
85a   101 n. 326
Resp.
398e   45 n. 137
Theaet.
172c   71
Tim.
21b   **98–9**

PLUTARCH
Mor.
46b   45–6
193f 11–12   50 n. 156
713a   37 n. 107
790e 7–f 2   46–7
816f   180
Alex.
8. 3   43 n. 129
Crass.
33. 3–6   **108–10**, 178
Demetr.
1. 6   47 n. 143,
                       50 n. 156

Lys.
23. 6   180
Sull.
26   78

[PLUTARCH]
De musica
1132b 10–c 3   26 n. 72
1132c   104 n. 334
1138b   50 n. 156
1141b   46 n. 137
Dec. or. vit.
841f   **69–74**, 77–8

PMG
897   203
902–5   203
908   203, 204 n. 43
979 (= *SH* 1001)   205 n. 50
989   205 n. 50

PORPHIRIUS
Vita Plot.
19   72

PRATINAS
708 *PMG*   90

PRAXILLAS
749 *PMG*   203 n. 42
750 *PMG*   203 and n. 42

PSEUDO-ARCADIUS
Epitom. Hdn. ch. 20   **33–38**

SACERDOS, MARIUS PLOTIUS
GL VI, 510, 25 ff.   205 n. 50
    Keil
GL VI, 536. 23 ff.   204 n. 45
    Keil
GL VI, 539. 4 Keil   204 n. 45

SAPPHO (Voigt)
43   191 n. 17, 193,
    197 n. 27
44   **191–3**, **197–201**
44Aa   191 n. 17, 197
    n. 27
44Ab   191 n. 17
45–52   191 n. 17, 197
    n. 27
55   201
56   201
57   194 n. 20
58   194

59   194
62   194
63   194
65   195
67   197 n. 26
67a   194
81   194
82b   194
86   195
88   195
94   208
103   193 n. 19, 194
    n. 20
120   194 n. 20
150   194 n. 20
227   186, 190 n. 13,
    192
228   190
229   190 n. 13
234   192 n. 19

SELEUCUS
Seleucus, *CA*, p. 176   205

SENECA
H.F.
1053   96 n. 306

SIMIAS OF RHODES
CA fr. 16   204

SOPHOCLES
Aj.
573   168 n. 161
879–90   8 n. 6
925–36   8 n. 6
Ant.
806   169 n. 162
OT
1313–68   145
fr.
144   44 n. 133
241   51 n. 158
Σ to *Aj.* 173a   149
    340b   149
    887   148 n. 96
Σ to *Ant.* 31   149
Σ to *OC* 1211   148 n. 96
    1683   149, 152
    n. 104
Σ to *Tr.* 643   148 n. 96

[STESICHORUS]
PMG 278   205 and n. 49

STRABO
8. 3. 20   205 n. 49
13. 1. 51   78

SUDA
s.v. Ἀλκμάν (α 1289)   49–50
s.v. Ἀνακρέων (α 1916)   49 nn. 150–1
s.v. Ἀντιγενίδης
    (α 2657)   48–9
s.v. Διαγόρας (δ 523)   47 n. 144
s.v. Μεσομήδης (μ 668)   49 nn.
                           150–1
s.v. Μουσαῖος (μ 1295)   49 nn.
                           150–1
s.v. Σαπφώ (ς 107)   49 nn.
                           150–1
s.v. Τυρταῖος (τ 1205)   49 nn.
                           150–1, 50
                           n. 153

SUETONIUS
Iul.
84. 2   62
Nero
20. 2   91 n. 289
21. 1   95 n. 303
21. 3   94 n. 300
21. 4   95 n. 302,
                   96 n. 304
21. 5   93, 95
21. 6   95–6

SUPPLEMENTUM HELLENISTICUM
215   204
1001 (= PMG 979)   205 n. 50

THEOCRITUS
Idylls
8   207 n. 55,
                   212 n. 66
28   187 and nn.
                   5, 9, 188
                   n. 10, 205,
                   206–8
29   **185–213**
30   187 and nn.
                   5, 9, 188
                   n. 10, 205,
                   206–8
31   187 and
                   n. 6
Epigr.
4   212
17   212

18   212
19   212 n. 66
20   203 n. 41,
                   212
21   212
22   212 n. 66

THEOGNIS
761   51 n. 158
763   98
1047   98

THEOPHRASTUS
Char.
15. 10   89 n. 283,
                   102
27. 2   89
De hist. plant.
4. 11. 4   50 n. 156
fr.
726B Fortenbaugh   92 n. 290
T 41 Fortenbaugh   78 n. 245

TZETZES, ISAAC
De metris Pindaricis
14. 21–15. 12 Drachm.   190 n. 15

VICTORINUS, MARIUS
GL VI, 41. 28 ff. Keil   13 n. 28

XENOPHON
Symp.
6. 3   88 n. 279

PAPYRI
P.Aberd. 7   195
P.Ashm. inv. 89B/31, 33   152 n. 105
P.Berol. inv. 6870   13 n. 21,
                              162 n. 135
P.Berol. inv. 9569   195
P.Berol. inv. 17051 +   130 n. 19,
    17014   156 n. 113
P.Berol. inv. 21257   79 and
                              nn. 249–50
P.Columb. inv. 517A   153
P.Duke inv. MF 74. 18   153
P.Fouad 239   191 n. 17
P.Hibeh I 13   45 n. 137
P.Hibeh I 24   80 n. 250
P.Hibeh I 25   80 n. 250
P.Köln VI 252   24, 117–8,
                              136 n. 51,
                              153
P.Köln inv. 21351 +   80 n. 250,
    21376   195, 208

	n. 56, 212	PSI II 147	84 n. 260
	n. 67	PSI VII 768	72
P.Laur. III/908	136 n. 51, 153	PSI XIII 1300	39 n. 117
P.Leid. inv. 510	70 n. 222,	P.Stras.W.G. 306	24 n. 63, 79
	104, 110,		n. 249, 79–80
	119, 120,		n. 250, 85
	121, **160–81**,		n. 266, 110
	182–3		n. 354, 119, 120,
P.Lille 76	39 n. 117		121, 133, 153,
P.Lit.Lond. 73	164		173 n. 175,
P.Lond. Pack² 407	79 n. 249		174 n. 178,
P.Mich. inv. 2958	13, 85 n. 265,		178 n. 193
	162 n. 135	P.Vind. G 2315	9 n. 9, 40, 58,
P.Mil.Vogl. 17	39 n. 117		70 n. 222, 81
P.Osl. inv. 1413	11 n. 15, 13		n. 255, 85
	n. 21, 85 n. 265,		n. 267, 104,
	113 n. 364, 162		117, 119, 120,
	n. 135		121, **125–60**,
P.Oxy. 413	181 n. 202		182–3
P.Oxy. 841	83 n. 260	P.Vind. G 29825 c	138 n. 63, 139
P.Oxy. 1175	136	P.Vind. G 29825 a/b	141 n. 73
P.Oxy. 1178	153	P.Vind. G 29825 f	141 n. 73
P.Oxy. 1232	191–3, 199	P.Zen. 59533	162 n. 135
P.Oxy. 1233	195 and n. 22,		
	201 nn. 38, 39	**INSCRIPTIONS**	
P.Oxy. 1786	162 n. 135	*FD* III.3, 86	107 n. 343
P.Oxy. 1787	194–5	*IDidyma* 181	115 n. 369
P.Oxy. 1792	84 n. 260	*IG* II² 2320	123 n. 1
P.Oxy. 2076	191–3, 199	3779	114 n. 366
P.Oxy. 2165	193	*IKourion* 104	106 n. 339
P.Oxy. 2166	194, 195	*IMagn* 107	46 n. 141
P.Oxy. 2224	140	*ITeos* 82	46 n. 141
P.Oxy. 2294	194 n. 20	*SEG*	
P.Oxy. 2369	136	XI 52c	104, 105 n. 337,
P.Oxy. 2436	136 n. 51, 162		**111–16**, 178
	n. 135	*SIG*³	
P.Oxy 3704	162 n. 135	450	48 n. 145, 107
P.Oxy. 3716	153		n. 344
P.Oxy. 4461	136 n. 51	648A	105 n. 336
P.Oxy. 4546	181	648B	88 n. 277,
P.Ross.Georg. I 9	153		**104–10**, 178
P.Ryl. II 234	72	662	48 n. 145

GENERAL INDEX

actors: interpolations in dramatic texts, 69–70, 73 and n. 232; vocal mimicry, 110 n. 353, 179–80; multiple roles, 180; protagonist, 180

Alcaeus: Alexandrian edition of, 196 n. 24; stanzaic nature of poems in glyconics with dactylic and choriambic expansion, 189–96; enjambement across stanza end, 201–2

Alcman: Alexandrian edition of, 49–50 and nn. 152–3

Alexander the Great: reciting tragic speeches at symposia, 102–3; fondness for Euripides, Sophocles and New Music, 43 n. 129; and musical training, 47 n. 143

Alexandrian scholarship: musical competence and use of musical scores, 8–9, 28–9, 33, 38, **51–8**, 63–4, 68, 118–9, 124–5, 138; and the Lycurgan *Staatsexemplar*, **68–78**; and *Satzphonetik* 35 n. 101, 80

Antigenidas of Thebes: 48–51

Apollonius eidographos: and the classification of Pindar's odes, **28–33**

Aristides Quintilianus: on rhythm in general, 64–5; on rhythm in music, 65–6

Aristophanes of Byzantium: and accentuation system **33–6**; and punctuation system 33–4 n. 99, 34 n. 100; graphic shape of accents and analogy from music 35–6; graphic shape of breathing and analogy from music 37–8; colization of Pindaric text, 38–40; prosodic interests, 35 and n. 101; dramatic hypotheses, 118 and nn. 373–4

Aristotle: stricture on professional musicians, 30 and n. 87

Aristoxenus: and the autonomy of rhythmics, 13 n. 25; on the distinction between κίνηϲιϲ ϲυνεχήϲ/ διαϲτηματική, 18 n. 42; on παραϲημαντική, 30–1; on the constituents of rhythm, 65 n. 204

chorus: ancillary role of in performing tragic excerpts, **107–110**, 178

cicada: song of, 91–2

Cicero: rhythm in prose vs. rhythm in poetry, **59–63**; and the staging of old Roman dramas, 61–3

colometry: modern debate on 7–8, 57 n. 179, 78–83; musical papyri and manuscript tradition, 78–83, 117–21, 123–5, 125–38 (P.Vind. G 2315), 166–73 (P.Leid. inv. 510), 182–3

Diagoras of Melos: 47 n. 144

Dionysius of Halicarnassus: musical skill, 21 and nn. 51–2; distinction between spoken language and song **15–19**; speech-song tonal mismatches **20–3**; use of musical score: 20–1, 27–8

Dionysius Thrax: on delivery, 52–3; scholia on the delivery of lyric poetry, **53–8**

education in music: oral training, 45–7; school scenes on vase-paintings, 46 and n. 139; melographia and rhythmographia, 46 n. 141

eisthesis/ekthesis: denoting change of speaker and/or metre, 136 and nn. 51–2

elegy: performance of, 98–9 and n. 320

Euripides: actors' interpolations, 73 and n. 232; teaching the choreuts, 45–6; excerpts performed at symposia, 86ff., 102, **108–10**; iambic passages converted to song in the Hellenistic and post Hellenistic period: 93–4 n. 296, 107–8, **108–10**; popularity on the Hellenistic stage, 123 n. 1, 153

Galen: and the Athenian copies of Attic tragedy, **74–8**; digression on Hippocrates' χαρακτῆρεϲ, 75–6

κῶλα as instrumental pieces: 66–8, 103

λέγειν/ἀιδειν: 88–9, **97–103**
Lycurgan *Staatsexemplar* of tragic texts:
9 n. 10, 10, 40, **68–78**

metre: dochmiacs: *brevis in longo* in,
134–5; responsion with hypδ, 117
n. 372; pyrrhic fourth element, 134;
lyric lengths converted in iterated
stichic series, 186 and n. 2, 203–6,
207, 208; Stinton's 'pause' and 'period',
189, 206 n. 53; glyconics with
dactylic and choriambic expansion
outside Lesbian lyric, **202–6**
musicians: versatility, 50–1, 105 and
n. 337

Nero: 'tragic' performances of, 93, 95–7
notation, musical: emergence of, 40
n. 120, 51–2; and vase paintings, 40
n. 120; and solmization, 40 n. 120;
leimma, 11 n. 15, 12–13, *diastolé* 126
n. 9, 139, 141, 155; *stigmé*, 138 n. 63,
139 n. 64; ᒧ in P.Vind. 2315,
127, 129–30, 132–3, 137, **138–43**,
155–6, 159

Pindar: monodic and/or choral
performance of epinicians, 42 n. 127,
44–5; re-performances, 31 n. 91, 32;
decline from the end of the 5th BC
onwards, 31 and nn. 91–2, 39 and
n. 114; ὠιδὴ ἀποϲτολική and the
transmission of text and music, **40–6**;
imagery of 'shipping' and 'receiving'
a song, 41 and n. 124, 42, 43
n. 129; reification of the song, 42–3;
Aristophanes' edition, **38–40**;
classification of odes according to
musical modes by Apollonius
eidographos, **28–33**; colometrical
divergences within Pindar's tradition,
83 n. 260

recitative or chanted delivery (*parakataloge*):
88 and nn. 279–80, 89, 97 and
n. 310, 99, 101–2, 103, 113, **144–52**
re-performances of παλαιὰ δράματα:

on the Greek stage, 33 n. 96, 62
and n. 195, 70 n. 222, 123 n. 1,
124 n. 2; on the Roman stage, 61–2
re-setting, musical: 81 n. 255, 82, 85,
104 and n. 334, **111–16**, **123–4**
(see also 'conversion to song' s.v. song)
responsion: disruption of, 125, 134
n. 41, 160; free responsion in choral
and dramatic lyric and its
performative counterpart, 12
and nn. 17–8
rhythm: correspondence between musical
rhythm and verbal metrics, **10–23**

Sappho: Alexandrian edition of, 190,
192–3; fourth book, 194; book of the
Epithalamians, 192–3 n. 19; stanzaic
nature of poems in glyconics with
dactylic and choriambic expansion,
189–96; enjambement across
stanza-end, **196–202**
Satyros of Samos: **104–10**, 178
score, musical: ancient vs. modern
practice, 104 n. 334, 124 and n. 3,
181; *Orestes* papyrus, **125–160**,
182–3; *IA* papyrus, **160–81**, 182–3
Simonides: as representative of
'old-fashioned' poetry, 86 and
n. 272, 87 n. 275, 90
song: conversion to song of spoken
and/or recitative metres, 85 and
n. 265, 86, 93, 95, 102, **105–110**,
185 n. 1; astrophic and/or monodic
re-performance of choral lyric, 85 and
n. 266, 110, 114, 116, 178–9, 181
symposia: monodic performance of choral
lyric at, 31 n. 91, 81 n. 254, 86 and
n. 272, 87 and n. 275; performing
tragic passages at, **86–103**;
Socratic-sophistic stricture on reciting
and singing at symposia, 92

Themison (Gaios Ailios): **111–16**, 178
Theocritus: audience and performance
of, 188 n. 10; and the Lesbian
tradition, 186–8, **202–13**; stanzaic
patterns in, 188 n. 10, **206–13**

SUPPLEMENTS TO MNEMOSYNE

EDITED BY H. PINKSTER, H.S. VERSNEL,
I.J.F. DE JONG AND P. H. SCHRIJVERS

Recent volumes in the series

165. ALBRECHT, M. VON. *A History of Roman Literature.* From Livius Andronicus to Boethius with Special Regard to Its Influence on World Literature. 2 Vols.Revised by G.Schmeling and by the Author. Vol. 1: Translated with the Assistance of F. and K. Newman, Vol. 2: Translated with the Assitance of R.R. Caston and F.R. Schwartz. 1997.
ISBN 90 04 10709 6 (Vol. 1), ISBN 90 04 10711 8 (Vol. 2), ISBN 90 04 10712 6 (Set)
166. DIJK, J.G.M. VAN. Αἰνοί, Λόγοι, Μῦθοι. Fables in Archaic, Classical, and Hellenistic Greek Literature. With a Study of the Theory and Terminology of the Genre. 1997. ISBN 90 04 10747 9
167. MAEHLER, H. (Hrsg.). *Die Lieder des Bakchylides.* Zweiter Teil: Die Dithyramben und Fragmente. Text, Übersetzung und Kommentar. 1997. ISBN 90 04 10671 5
168. DILTS, M. & G.A. KENNEDY (eds.). *Two Greek Rhetorical Treatises from the Roman Empire.* Introduction, Text, and Translation of the Arts of Rhetoric Attributed to Anonymous Seguerianus and to Apsines of Gadara. 1997. ISBN 90 04 10728 2
169. GÜNTHER, H.-C. *Quaestiones Propertianae.* 1997. ISBN 90 04 10793 2
170. HEINZE, T. (Hrsg.). *P. Ovidius Naso. Der* XII. *Heroidenbrief: Medea an Jason.* Einleitung, Text und Kommentar. Mit einer Beilage: Die Fragmente der Tragödie *Medea.* 1997. ISBN 90 04 10800 9
171. BAKKER, E.J. (ed.). *Grammar as Interpretation.* Greek Literature in its Linguistic Contexts. 1997. ISBN 90 04 10730 4
172. GRAINGER, J.D. *A Seleukid Prosopography and Gazetteer.* 1997. ISBN 90 04 10799 1
173. GERBER, D.E. (ed.). *A Companion to the Greek Lyric Poets.* 1997. ISBN 90 04 09944 1
174. SANDY, G. *The Greek World of Apuleius.* Apuleius and the Second Sophistic. 1997. ISBN 90 04 10821 1
175. ROSSUM-STEENBEEK, M. VAN. *Greek Readers' Digests?* Studies on a Selection of Subliterary Papyri. 1998. ISBN 90 04 10953 6
176. McMAHON, J.M. *Paralysin Cave.* Impotence, Perception, and Text in the *Satyrica* of Petronius. 1998. ISBN 90 04 10825 4
177. ISAAC, B. *The Near East under Roman Rule.* Selected Papers. 1998. ISBN 90 04 10736 3
178. KEEN, A.G. *Dynastic Lycia.* A Political History of the Lycians and Their Relations with Foreign Powers, c. 545-362 B.C. 1998. ISBN 90 04 10956 0
179. GEORGIADOU, A. & D.H.J. LARMOUR. *Lucian's Science Fiction Novel* True Histories. Interpretation and Commentary. 1998. ISBN 90 04 10667 7
180. GÜNTHER, H.-C. *Ein neuer metrischer Traktat und das Studium der pindarischen Metrik in der Philologie der Paläologenzeit.* 1998. ISBN 90 04 11008 9
181. HUNT, T.J. *A Textual History of Cicero's* Academici Libri. 1998. ISBN 90 04 10970 6
182. HAMEL, D. *Athenian Generals.* Military Authority in the Classical Period. 1998. ISBN 90 04 10900 5
183. WHITBY, M. (ed.).*The Propaganda of Power.*The Role of Panegyric in Late Antiquity. 1998. ISBN 90 04 10571 9
184. SCHRIER, O.J. *The* Poetics *of Aristotle and the* Tractatus Coislinianus. A Bibliography from about 900 till 1996. 1998. ISBN 90 04 11132 8

185. SICKING, C.M.J. *Distant Companions.* Selected Papers. 1998. ISBN 90 04 11054 2
186. SCHRIJVERS, P.H. *Lucrèce et les Sciences de la Vie.* 1999. ISBN 90 04 10230 2
187. BILLERBECK M. (Hrsg.). *Seneca.* Hercules Furens. Einleitung, Text, Übersetzung und Kommentar. 1999. ISBN 90 04 11245 6
188. MACKAY, E.A. (ed.). *Signs of Orality.* The Oral Tradition and Its Influence in the Greek and Roman World. 1999. ISBN 90 04 11273 1
189. ALBRECHT, M. VON. *Roman Epic.* An Interpretative Introduction. 1999. ISBN 90 04 11292 8
190. HOUT, M.P.J. VAN DEN. *A Commentary on the Letters of M. Cornelius Fronto.* 1999. ISBN 90 04 10957 9
191. KRAUS, C. SHUTTLEWORTH. (ed.). *The Limits of Historiography.* Genre and Narrative in Ancient Historical Texts. 1999. ISBN 90 04 10670 7
192. LOMAS, K. & T. CORNELL. *Cities and Urbanisation in Ancient Italy.* ISBN 90 04 10808 4 *In preparation*
193. TSETSKHLADZE, G.R. (ed.). *History of Greek Colonization and Settlement Overseas.* 2 vols. ISBN 90 04 09843 7 *In preparation*
194. WOOD, S.E. *Imperial Women.* A Study in Public Images, 40 B.C. - A.D. 68. 1999. ISBN 90 04 11281 2
195. OPHUIJSEN, J.M. VAN & P. STORK. *Linguistics into Interpretation.* Speeches of War in Herodotus VII 5 & 8-18. 1999. ISBN 90 04 11455 6
196. TSETSKHLADZE, G.R. (ed.). *Ancient Greeks West and East.* 1999. ISBN 90 04 11190 5
197. PFEIJFFER, I.L. *Three Aeginetan Odes of Pindar.* A Commentary on *Nemean* V, *Nemean* III, & *Pythian* VIII. 1999. ISBN 90 04 11381 9
198. HORSFALL, N. *Virgil,* Aeneid 7. A Commentary. 2000. ISBN 90 04 10842 4
199. IRBY-MASSIE, G.L. *Military Religion in Roman Britain.* 1999. ISBN 90 04 10848 3
200. GRAINGER, J.D. *The League of the Aitolians.* 1999. ISBN 90 04 10911 0
201. ADRADOS, F.R. *History of the Graeco-Roman Fable.* I: Introduction and from the Origins to the Hellenistic Age. Translated by L.A. Ray. Revised and Updated by the Author and Gert-Jan van Dijk. 1999. ISBN 90 04 11454 8
202. GRAINGER, J.D. *Aitolian Prosopographical Studies.* 2000. ISBN 90 04 11350 9
203. SOLOMON, J. *Ptolemy* Harmonics. Translation and Commentary. 2000. ISBN 90 04 115919
204. WIJSMAN, H.J.W. *Valerius Flaccus,* Argonautica, *Book VI.* A Commentary. 2000. ISBN 90 04 11718 0
205. MADER, G. *Josephus and the Politics of Historiography.* Apologetic and Impression Management in the *Bellum Judaicum.* 2000. ISBN 90 04 11446 7
206. NAUTA, R.R. *Poetry for Patrons.* Literary Communication in the Age of Domitian. 2000. ISBN 90 04 10885 8
207. ADRADOS, F.R. *History of the Graeco-Roman Fable.* II: The Fable during the Roman Empire and in the Middle Ages. Translated by L.A. Ray. Revised and Updated by the Author and Gert-Jan van Dijk. 2000. ISBN 90 04 11583 8
208. JAMES, A. & K. LEE. *A Commentary on Quintus of Smyrna,* Posthomerica V. 2000. ISBN 90 04 11594 3
209. DERDERIAN, K. *Leaving Words to Remember.* Greek Mourning and the Advent of Literacy. 2001. ISBN 90 04 11750 4
210. SHORROCK, R. *The Challenge of Epic.* Allusive Engagement in the *Dionysiaca* of Nonnus. 2001. ISBN 90 04 11795 4
211. SCHEIDEL, W. (ed.). *Debating Roman Demography.* 2001. ISBN 90 04 11525 0
212. KEULEN, A.J. *L. Annaeus Seneca* Troades. Introduction, Text and Commentary. 2001. ISBN 90 04 12004 1
213. MORTON, J. *The Role of the Physical Environment in Ancient Greek Seafaring.* 2001. ISBN 90 04 11717 2

214. GRAHAM, A.J. *Collected Papers on Greek Colonization*. 2001. ISBN 90 04 11634 6
215. GROSSARDT, P. *Die Erzählung von Meleagros*. Zur literarischen Entwicklung der kalydonischen Kultlegende. 2001. ISBN 90 04 11952 3
216. ZAFIROPOULOS, C.A. *Ethics in Aesop's Fables: The* Augustana *Collection*. 2001. ISBN 90 04 11867 5
217. RENGAKOS, A. & T.D. PAPANGHELIS (eds.). *A Companion to Apollonius Rhodius*. 2001. ISBN 90 04 11752 0
218. WATSON, J. *Speaking Volumes*. Orality and Literacy in the Greek and Roman World. 2001. ISBN 90 04 12049 1
219. MACLEOD, L. *Dolos and Dike in Sophokles'* Elektra. 2001. ISBN 90 04 11898 5
220. MCKINLEY, K.L. *Reading the Ovidian Heroine*. "Metamorphoses" Commentaries 1100-1618. 2001. ISBN 90 04 11796 2
221. REESON, J. *Ovid* Heroides *11, 13 and 14*. A Commentary. 2001. ISBN 90 04 12140 4
222. FRIED, M.N. & S. UNGURU. *Apollonius of Perga's* Conica: Text, Context, Subtext. 2001. ISBN 90 04 11977 9
223. LIVINGSTONE, N. *A Commentary on Isocrates'* Busiris. 2001. ISBN 90 04 12143 9
224. LEVENE, D.S. & D.P. NELIS (eds.). *Clio and the Poets*. Augustan Poetry and the Traditions of Ancient Historiography. 2002. ISBN 90 04 11782 2
225. WOOTEN, C.W. *The Orator in Action and Theory in Greece and Rome*. 2001. ISBN 90 04 12213 3
226. GALÁN VIOQUE, G. *Martial, Book VII. A Commentary*. 2001. ISBN 90 04 12338 5
227. LEFÈVRE, E. *Die Unfähigkeit, sich zu erkennen: Sophokles' Tragödien*. 2001. ISBN 90 04 12322 9
228. SCHEIDEL, W. *Death on the Nile*. Disease and the Demography of Roman Egypt. 2001. ISBN 90 04 12323 7
229. SPANOUDAKIS, K. *Philitas of Cos*. 2002. ISBN 90 04 12428 4
230. WORTHINGTON, I. & J.M. FOLEY (eds.). *Epea and Grammata*. Oral and written Communication in Ancient Greece. 2002. ISBN 90 04 12455 1
231. McKECHNIE, P. (ed.). *Thinking Like a Lawyer*. Essays on Legal History and General History for John Crook on his Eightieth Birthday. 2002. ISBN 90 04 12474 8
232. GIBSON, R.K. & C. SHUTTLEWORTH KRAUS (eds.). *The Classical Commentary*. Histories, Practices, Theory. 2002. ISBN 90 04 12153 6
233. JONGMAN, W. & M. KLEIJWEGT (eds.). *After the Past*. Essays in Ancient History in Honour of H.W. Pleket. 2002. ISBN 90 04 12816 6
234. GORMAN, V.B. & E.W. ROBINSON (eds.). *Oikistes*. Studies in Constitutions, Colonies, and Military Power in the Ancient World. Offered in Honor of A.J. Graham. 2002. ISBN 90 04 12579 5
235. HARDER, A., R. REGTUIT, P. STORK & G. WAKKER (eds.). *Noch einmal zu....* Kleine Schriften von Stefan Radt zu seinem 75. Geburtstag. 2002. ISBN 90 04 12794 1
236. ADRADOS, F.R. *History of the Graeco-Latin Fable*. Volume Three: Inventory and Documentation of the Graeco-Latin Fable. 2002. ISBN 90 04 11891 8
237. SCHADE, G. *Stesichoros*. Papyrus Oxyrhynchus 2359, 3876, 2619, 2803. 2003. ISBN 90 04 12832 8
238. ROSEN, R.M. & I. SLUITER (eds.) *Andreia*. Studies in Manliness and Courage in Classical Antiquity. 2003. ISBN 90 04 11995 7
239. GRAINGER, J.D. *The Roman War of Antiochos the Great*. 2002. ISBN 90 04 12840 9
240. KOVACS, D. *Euripidea Tertia*. 2003. ISBN 90 04 12977 4
241. PANAYOTAKIS, S., M. ZIMMERMAN & W. KEULEN (eds.). *The Ancient Novel and Beyond*. 2003. ISBN 90 04 12999 5
242. ZACHARIA, K. *Converging Truths*. Euripides' Ion and the Athenian Quest for Self-Definition. 2003. ISBN 90 0413000 4
243. ALMEIDA, J.A. *Justice as an Aspect of the Polis Idea in Solon's Political Poems*. 2003. ISBN 90 04 13002 0

244. HORSFALL, N. *Virgil*, Aeneid *11*. A Commentary. 2003. ISBN 90 04 12934 0
245. VON ALBRECHT, M. *Cicero's Style*. A Synopsis. Followed by Selected Analytic Studies. 2003. ISBN 90 04 12961 8
246. LOMAS, K. *Greek Identity in the Western Mediterranean*. Papers in Honour of Brian Shefton. 2004. ISBN 90 04 13300 3
247. SCHENKEVELD, D.M. *A Rhetorical Grammar*. C. Iullus Romanus, Introduction to the Liber de Adverbio. 2004. ISBN 90 04 133662 2
248. MACKIE, C.J. *Oral Performance and its Context*. 2004. ISBN 90 04 13680 0
249. RADICKE, J. *Lucans Poetische Technik*. 2004. ISBN 90 04 13745 9
250. DE BLOIS, L., J. BONS, T. KESSELS & D.M. SCHENKEVELD (eds.). *The Statesman in Plutarch's Works*. Volume I: Plutarch's Statesman and his Aftermath: Political, Philosophical, and Literary Aspects. ISBN 90 04 13795 5. Volume II: The Statesman in Plutarch's Greek and Roman *Lives*. 2005. ISBN 90 04 13808 0
251. GREEN, S.J. *Ovid*, Fasti *1*. A Commentary. 2004. ISBN 90 04 13985 0
252. VON ALBRECHT, M. *Wort und Wandlung*. 2004. ISBN 90 04 13988 5
253. KORTEKAAS, G.A.A. *The Story of Apollonius, King of Tyre*. A Study of Its Greek Origin and an Edition of the Two Oldest Latin Recensions. 2004. ISBN 90 04 13923 0
254. SLUITER, I. & R.M. ROSEN (eds.). *Free Speech in Classical Antiquity*. 2004.
     ISBN 90 04 13925 7
255. STODDARD, K. *The Narrative Voice in the* Theogony *of Hesiod*. 2004.
     ISBN 90 04 14002 6
256. FITCH, J.G. *Annaeana Tragica*. Notes on the Text of Seneca's Tragedies. 2004.
     ISBN 90 04 14003 4
257. DE JONG, I.J.F., R. NÜNLIST & A. BOWIE (eds.). *Narrators, Narratees, and Narratives in Ancient Greek Literature*. Studies in Ancient Greek Narrative, Volume One. 2004.
     ISBN 90 04 13927 3
258. VAN TRESS, H. *Poetic Memory*. Allusion in the Poetry of Callimachus and the *Metamorphoses* of Ovid. 2004. ISBN 90 04 14157 X
259. RADEMAKER, A. Sophrosyne *and the Rhetoric of Self-Restraint*. Polysemy & Persuasive Use of an Ancient Greek Value Term. 2005. ISBN 90 04 14251 7
260. BUIJS, M. *Clause Combining in Ancient Greek Narrative Discourse*. The Distribution of Subclauses and Participial Clauses in Xenophon's *Hellenica* and *Anabasis*. 2005.
     ISBN 90 04 14250 9
261. ENENKEL, K.A.E. & I.L. PFEIJFFER (eds.). *The Manipulative Mode*. Political Propaganda in Antiquity: A Collection of Case Studies. 2005. ISBN 90 04 14291 6
262. KLEYWEGT, A.J. *Valerius Flaccus*, Argonautica, *Book I*. A Commentary. 2005.
     ISBN 90 04 13924 9
263. MURGATROYD, P. *Mythical and Legendary Narrative in Ovid's* Fasti. 2005.
     ISBN 90 04 14320 3
264. WALLINGA, H.T. *Xerxes' Greek Adventure*. The Naval Perspective. 2005.
     ISBN 90 04 14140 5
265. KANTZIOS, I. *The Trajectory of Archaic Greek Trimeters*. 2005. ISBN 90 04 14536 2
266. ZELNICK-ABRAMOVITZ, R. *Not Wholly Free*. The Concept of Manumission and the Status of Manumitted Slaves in the Ancient Greek World. 2005.
     ISBN 90 04 14585 0
267. SLINGS, S.R. (†). Edited by Gerard Boter and Jan van Ophuijsen. *Critical Notes on Plato's* Politeia. 2005. ISBN 90 04 14172 3
268. SCOTT, L. *Historical Commentary on Herodotus Book 6*. 2005. ISBN 90 04 14506 0
269. DE JONG, I.J.F. & A. RIJKSBARON (eds.). *Sophocles and the Greek Language*. Aspects of Diction, Syntax and Pragmatics. 2006. ISBN 90 04 14752 7
270. NAUTA, R.R., H.-J. VAN DAM & J.J.L. SMOLENAARS (eds.). *Flavian Poetry*. 2006.
     ISBN 90 04 14794 2
271. TACOMA, L.E. *Fragile Hierarchies*. The Urban Elites of Third-Century Roman Egypt. 2006. ISBN 90 04 14831 0